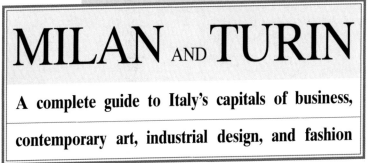

◆ THE HERITAGE GUIDE ◆

MILAN AND TURIN

A complete guide to Italy's capitals of business,

contemporary art, industrial design, and fashion

Touring Club of Italy

Touring Club of Italy

President and Chairman: *Giancarlo Lunati*

Chief Executive Officer: *Armando Peres*

Managing Directors: *Adriano Agnati* and *Radames Trotta*

Editorial Director: *Marco Ausenda*

Coordination: *Michele D'Innella*

Managing Editor: *Anna Ferrari-Bravo*

Senior Editor: *Gemma Mattei*

General Consultant: *Gianni Bagioli*

Jacket Layout: *Federica Neeff*

Map Design: *Cartographic Division - Touring Club of Italy*

Authors: *Giacomo Corna Pellegrini* (An ancient Duchy amid rivers and lakes); *Stefano Zuffi* (The artistic background); *Flavio Conti* and *Raffaella Ronzi* (How to visit Milan); *Antonio Ive* and *Palma Scrivanti* (Chapters 1, 2, 3, 4 of Milan); *Gian Michele Tortolone* (Historical and artistic aspects of Turin); *Giovanna Zanoni* (Turin: Instructions for Use); *Silvia Ghisotti* (Chapters 1 and 2 of Turin) .

Translation: *Antony Shugaar*

Copy Editor: *Andrew Ellis*

Drawings: *Giorgio Pomella* (Milan); *Antonello* and *Chiara Vincenti* (Turin)

Route maps and plans of monuments: *Graffito S.r.l.*

Layout and editing: *Studio Tragni*

Production: *Giovanni Schiona, Vittorio Sironi*

Picture credits: *Action Press*: M. Cappelli 161, 172, 196, *M. Pedone* 165, *H. Rader* 30, 33; *Archivi Alinari*: 25, 71, 169, 194; *Archivio T.C.I.*: 39, 74, 79, 100, 104, Nicolini 28, 89, 125, 144, F. Radino 16, 26, 29, 50, 68, 80, 97, 107, 121, 123, 170, 171, 173, 174, 210; *G. Cigolini*: 24; *Image Bank / G.A. Rossi* 21, 132, 134, 162, 212; *L. Ronchi: P. Liaci* 38, 90, *V. Lombardo* 41, 117, 126, *G. Lucci* 56, *G. Mairani* 93, 129, 136, 167, 185, 188, 205, 208, 214, *R. Meazza* 22, Tignonsini 55, *M. Vacca* 75; *L. Ronchi / T. Stone*: 15, 34, 43; *Saporetti*: 18, 19; *Scala*: 197, 198.

Cover: *Milan: the Cathedral* (F. Scianna/Magnum).

Pictures p. 3: *Garden of the Civico Museo Archeologico, Milan* (Archivio T.C.I. / Radino); *Porta Palatina, Turin* (L. Ronchi: G. Mairani).

Pictures pp. 4-5: *Stazione Centrale, Milan* (L. Ronchi: R. Meazza); *Via della Spiga, Milan* (L. Ronchi: V. Lombardo); *Central hall of the Palazzina di Caccia at Stupinigi, Turin* (L. Ronchi: G. Mairani); *Costume pageant at the La Mandria Regional Park, Turin* (L. Ronchi: G. Mairani).

We have taken great pains to ensure that the information provided in this guide is accurate. Some schedules, numbers, and addresses may have changed; we cannot accept responsibility for those changes, nor for any loss, injury, or inconvenience sustained by any traveller as a result of information or advice contained in the guide.

Typesetting and colour separations: *EMMEGI MULTIMEDIA - Milano*

Printed by: *G. Canale & C. - Borgaro Torinese (Torino)*

© 1999 Touring Editore s.r.l. - Milano
Code L2E
ISBN 88-365-1519-3
Printed in October 1998

Foreword

This guidebook, part of "The Heritage Guide" series, focuses on two of Italy's largest cities, Milan and Turin, which, though not exactly classifiable as "cities of art" on a par with Rome, Florence, or Venice, can undoubtedly call themselves "capital cities." Their contribution to Italy's economic development, both past and present, has ranked them as strategic hubs at European level.

Of the two, Milan's history goes further back in time, and besides its importance as one of Italy's leading powerhouses, besides also its own headlong economic growth and physical expansion, the city has managed to hold on to its past, and preserve cultural features of immense interest and value. Two of the opening chapters of this guide are in fact devoted to the history of the ancient Duchy of Milan, its urban development, and the artistic background; a third introductory chapter offers suggestions for getting the most out of the city. There follow three chapters with fourteen detailed itineraries that take the visitor around the city and its suburbs,

Garden of the Civico Museo Archeologico (Milan)

with a description of each quarter or district, pointing out streets and squares, landmarks, monuments, and other particulars that best illustrate the modern face of what was once the medieval see of Saint Ambrose, and subsequently the stronghold of the Visconti and Sforza dynasties. The tour ends with four excursions into the Milanese hinterland, through the Brianza district, and along the River Ticino and River Adda.

More modest in size and more contained in its offering of artistic and historical features, Turin is assigned a smaller chapter of its own, in which an overview of the historical and artistic background is followed by suggestions of how to make the most of one's time in Turin. The tour of

Porta Palatina (Turin)

the city is broken up into three separate itineraries, followed by a further chapter describing three excursions round the castles and parks in the surrounding plains and hillsides.

The guide to each city is complemented by a section of useful tips and addresses, with lists of the finest hotels and restaurants, leading stores and boutiques, cafés and pastry shops, and the most important art galleries and museums.

Contents

6 Milan: Excursion Key Map and Index of Route Maps
8 Turin: Excursion Key Map and Index of Route Maps
10 How to Use this Guidebook
12 Conventional Signs Used in the Maps
13 Index of Maps and Plans
14 Italy: Useful Addresses

15 MILAN AND ENVIRONS

Introductory Chapters

16 An ancient Duchy amid rivers
    and lakes
22 The artistic background
30 How to visit Milan

Itineraries and Excursions

34 1 Milan: the center
    City map of Milan pp. 44–45 (I)

35 1.1 Piazza del Duomo
42 1.2 Between the Duomo, Piazza della
    Scala, and San Babila
48 1.3 Between the Duomo, Ca' Granda,
    and Piazza Missori
52 1.4 From the Duomo to Cordusio and
    the Carrobbio

56 2 Milan: a city of canals and ramparts
    *City maps of Milan pp. 58–59 (II), pp.60–61 (III), pp. 62–63 (IV), pp. 64–65 (V), and Milan:
    subway lines pp. 66–67*

57 2.1 Corso Garibaldi and Via Brera
72 2.2 Via Manzoni and Corso Venezia
81 2.3 From Monforte to Porta Vittoria and Porta Romana
86 2.4 The Porta Ticinese Area and the Outer Canals
94 2.5 Sant'Ambrogio, Santa Maria delle Grazie, and the Monastero Maggiore
101 2.6 From the Castello Sforzesco to the Magenta District

107 3 Milan and its suburbs
    City maps of Milan pp. 110–111 (VI) and pp.112–113 (VII)

108 3.1 The West and Northwest Areas
114 3.2 The Northern Sector
118 3.3 The East and Northeast Sector
121 3.4 The Abbeys of the Southern Milanese Area (Bassa Milanese)

126 4 North Milan and Brianza

126 4.1 The Martesana and the Adda Valley
130 4.2 Monza and the central-eastern area of Brianza

137 4.3 The Seveso Valley and
     the Strada Varesina
140 4.4 The Strada del Sempione
     and the Ticino Valley

Tourist Information

146 Travel Information: Hotels,
     restaurants, places of inter-
     est. Addresses and opening
     times

161 **TURIN AND ENVIRONS**

Introductory Chapters

162 Historical and artistic aspects of Turin
171 Turin: Instructions for Use

Itineraries and Excursions

174 1 Turin
     *City maps of Turin pp. 178–179 (I),
     pp.180–181 (II), pp. 182–183 (III)*
175 1.1 The old city center
191 1.2 The 19th-century boulevards
     and the museums
200 1.3 Urban expansion toward the
     River Po

207 2 The environs of Turin
207 2.1 The Hills and the Plains
     around Turin
212 2.2 The Road to France, Venaria
     and La Mandria
215 2.3 Two residences of the House of Savoy

Tourist Information

216 Travel Information: Hotels, restaurants, places of interest. Addresses and opening
     times

Index of Places and Things

221 Milan and Turin: Index of Places and Things

Milan: Excursion Key Map and Index of Route Maps

The key map on these pages indicates the urban and surrounding areas relative to each itinerary in the city and environs. The number in the colored square corresponds to an itinerary and a route map.

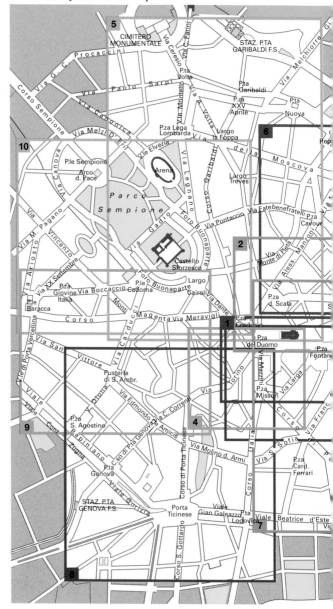

Below is a numbered list of the itineraries and their respective page number.

1 Piazza del Duomo, p. 35

2 Between the Duomo, Piazza della Scala, and San Babila, p. 42

3 Between the Duomo, Ca' Granda, and Piazza Missori, p. 48

4 From the Duomo to Cordusio and the Carrobbio, p. 52

5 Corso Garibaldi and via Brera, p. 57

6 Via Manzoni and Corso Venezia, p. 73

7 From Monforte to Porta Vittoria and Porta Romana, p. 82

8 The Porta Ticinese Area and the Outers Canals, p. 87

9 S. Ambrogio, Santa Maria delle Grazie, and the Monastero Maggiore, p. 94

10 From the Castello Sforzesco to the Magenta District, p. 102

11 The West and Northwest Areas, pp. 108-109

12 The Northern Sector, p. 115

13 The East and Northeast Sector, pp. 118-119

14 The Abbeys of the Southern Milanese Area (Bassa Milanese), pp. 122-123

15 The Martesana and the Adda Valley, p. 127

16 Monza and the central-eastern area of Brianza, p. 135

17 The Seveso Valley and the Strada Varesina, p. 137

18 The Strada del Sempione and the Ticino Valley, p. 140

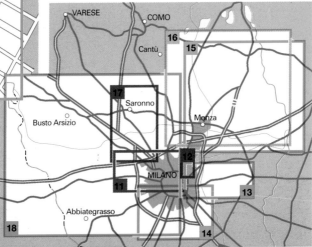

Turin: Excursion Key Map and Index of Route Maps

The key map on these pages indicates the urban and surrounding areas relative to each itinerary in the city and environs. The number in the colored square corresponds to an itinerary and a route map.
On the facing page is a numbered list of the itineraries and their respective page number.

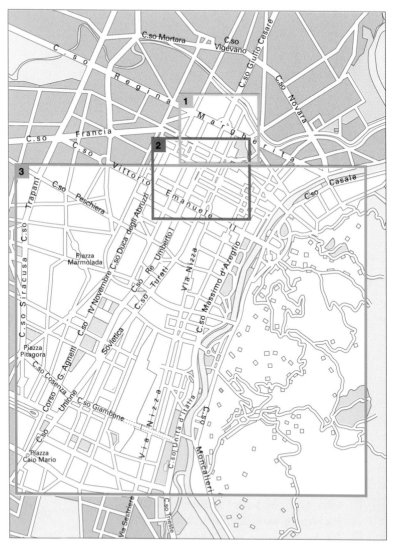

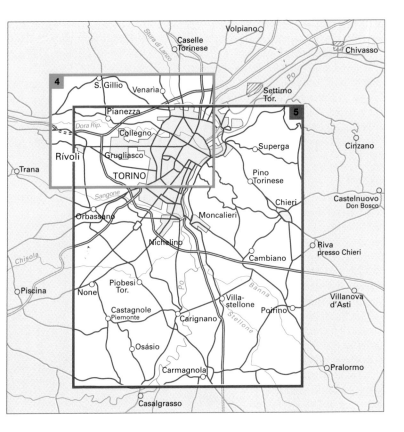

1 The old city center, pp. 176-177

2 The 19th-century boulevards and the museums, pp. 192-193

3 Urban expansion toward the River Po, p. 201

4 The Hills and the Plains around Turin, p. 207

5 The Road to France, Venaria and La Mandria, p. 213

How to Use this Guidebook

■ We have attempted to use the original Italian names of all places, monuments, buildings, and other references where possible. This is for a number of reasons: the traveller is thus made more comfortable with the names as he or she is likely to encounter them in Italy, on signs and printed matter. Note also that maps in this book for the most part carry the Italian version of all names. Thus, we refer to Castello Sforzesco and Via Meravigli rather than to Sforza Castle and Meravigli Street. On first mention, we have tried to indicate both the Italian and the English equivalent; we have renewed this dual citation when it is the first mention in a specific section of text. In Italian names, one of the most common abbreviations found is "S." for "saint" (and "SS." for "saints"). Note that "S." may actually be an abbreviation for four different forms of the word "saint" – "San", "Sant'", "Santo", and "Santa". Many other terms, while generally explained, should be familiar: "chiesa" is a church, "cappella" is a chapel, "via" is a street, "ponte" is a bridge, "museo" is a museum, "biblioteca" is a library, "torre" is a tower, "campanile" is a bell tower, "giardino" is a garden, "parco" is a park, "pinacoteca" is an art gallery, "teatro" is a theatre, "piazza" is a square, "ospedale" is a hospital, "porta" is either a door either a city gate.

Maps and Plans

Milan, Turin and all the main towns and cities described in this guide have one or more accompanying *city maps*. The principal monuments and museums together with the hotels, restaurants, and other public facilities are marked directly on the maps, and are followed by a reference to their location on the map or street plan (e.g., I, A3, meaning map I, square A3); hotels and restaurants are marked with letters in bold. The notation "off map" indicates that the monument or location mentioned lies outside the areas shown on the maps. Floor plans of monuments are marked with letters or numbers for identification, and correspondingly linked to the descriptions in the text. The walking itineraries around the city are marked on the relative street-maps in blue, with an arrow denoting the direction followed by the description in the text. The excursions in the surrounding areas are also accompanied by route-maps in which the suggested route is traced in yellow. A key to the symbols used can be found on page 12.

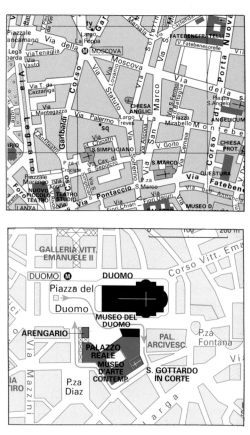

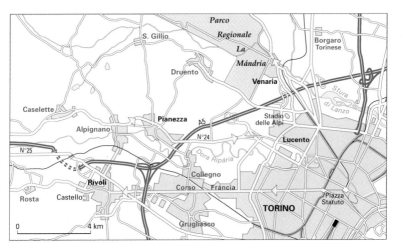

The Places to Visit

In all descriptions of monuments or landmarks differences in typography (names shown in **bold** or in *italics*) larger or smaller type size, and one or two asterisks (*) indicate the importance of each monument, museum, or other site. Written descriptions are illustrated with drawings and photos that help the reader to visualize works of art or architecture which he or she should not miss.

Information for travellers

A compendium of useful addresses, hotels and restaurants which suggests a selection of the finest hospitality facilities. Specific criteria are described on pp. 146 and pp. 216. We provide information which is up-to-date as of the writing of this book. The reader should be aware that some subsequent changes may have occurred in hours or schedules.

Notice regarding telephone numbers

As of the 18th December 1998, each location's telephone code must also be dialled for local calls and are listed next to the symbol ☎ in the section Travel information, page 146 and 216. For those calling Italy from abroad, the local code (including the 0) must be dialled after international code for Italy, followed by the subscriber's number.

The central court of the Ca' Granda, Milan

11

Conventional Signs Used in the Maps

City maps

Lines of communications

Throughfares

Main roads

Other roads

Pedestrian ramps

Pedestrian areas

Railroad lines and stations

Ⓜ S.BABILA Subway lines stations

Monuments and buildings

of exceptional interest

quite interesting

interesting

Other indications

Public offices

Churches

▫ a Hotels

• ⌐ Restaurants

✛ Hospitals

𝒊 Tourist information offices

P Principal parking areas

Gardens and parks

Cemeteries

Excursion maps

Lines of communications

Excursion, with direction followed

A1 Highway, with route number

Main roads

Other roads

Other indications

o Places to see along the excursion

○ Other places

Urban area

Parks

✈ Airports

_ _ _ _ _ Administrative borders

Index of Maps and Plans

City maps
Milan I, pp. 44-45
Milan II, pp. 58-59
Milan III, pp. 60-61
Milan IV, pp. 62-63
Milan V, pp. 64-65
Milan: subway lines, pp. 66-67
Milan VI, pp. 110-111
Milan VII, pp. 112-113
Monza, p. 131
Monza/Park, p. 133
Legnano, p. 141
Busto Arsizio, p. 142
Gallarate, p. 143
Turin I, pp. 178-179
Turin II, pp. 180-181
Turin III, pp. 182-183

Historical maps, building plans, and other sites
Milan: the Cathedral, p. 37
Milan: the Ca' Granda, p. 49
Milan: Building transformations in and around Piazza Mercanti, p. 54
Milan: Santa Maria della Passione, p. 83
Milan: San Lorenzo Maggiore, p. 92
Milan: the complex of Santa Maria delle Grazie, p. 98
Milan: the Castello Sforzesco, p. 103
Milan: the Parco Sempione, p. 105
The Certosa of Pavia, p. 124
Plan of Cassinetta di Lugagnano, p. 145
Turin: plan of the Roman colony of "Augusta Taurinorum", p. 166
Turin: the Palazzo Madama, p. 177
Turin: the church of San Lorenzo, p. 186
Turin: the Cathedral, p. 187
Turin: the Santuario della Consolata, p. 190
Turin: the Villa della Regina, p. 203
Turin: the Basilica of Superga, p. 208

Italy: Useful Addresses

Citizens of Australia, Canada, New Zealand, and the United States can enter Italy with a valid passport, and stay for a period of not more than 90 days; citizens of Great Britain and Ireland, as members of the European Union, can travel either with valid passport or with valid identification card.

Foreign Embassies in Italy

Australia:
Corso Trieste 25, Rome, tel. (06) 852721

Canada:
Via G.B. de Rossi 27, Rome, tel. (06) 445981

New Zealand:
Via Zara 28, Rome, tel. (06) 4402928

United States of America:
Via Vittorio Veneto 119/A, Palazzo Margherita, Rome, tel. (06) 46741

Great Britain:
Via XX Settembre 80/A, Rome, tel. (06) 4825441

Ireland:
Piazza Campitelli 3, Rome, tel. (06) 6979121

Foreign Consulates in Italy

Australia:
Via Borgogna 2, Milan, tel. (02) 777041

Canada:
Via Vittor Pisani 19, Milan, tel. (02) 67581

New Zealand:
Via G. D'Arezzo 6, Milan, tel. (02) 48012544

United States of America:
– Lungarno A.Vespucci 38, Florence, tel. (055) 2398276
– Via Principe Amedeo 2/10, Milan, tel. (02) 290351
– Piazza Repubblica 2, Naples, tel. (081) 5838111
– Via Re Federico 18/bis, Palermo (consular agency), tel. (091) 6110020

Great Britain:
– Via S. Paolo 7, Milan, tel. (02) 723001
– Via Crispi 132, Naples, tel. (081) 663511

Ireland:
Piazza San Pietro in Gessate 2, Milan, tel. (02) 55187569

Italian Embassies and Consulates Around the World

Australia:
12 Grey Street - Deakin, Canberra, tel. (06) 273-3333
Consulates at: Adelaide, Brisbane, Melbourne, Perth, Sydney.

Canada:
275 Slater Street, 21st floor, Ottawa (Ontario), tel. (613) 2322401/2/3
Consulates at: Montreal, Toronto, Vancouver.

New Zealand:
34 Grant Road, Wellington, tel. (4) 4735339 - 4729302

United States of America:
1601 Fuller Street, N.W., Washington D.C., tel. (202) 328-5500/1/2/3/4/5/6/7/8
Consulates at: Boston, Chicago, Philadelphia, Houston, Los Angeles, Miami, New York, New Orleans, San Francisco.

Great Britain:
14, Three Kings Yard, London W.1, tel. (0171) 3122200
Consulates at: London, Manchester, Edinburgh.

Ireland:
63/65, Northumberland Road, Dublin 4, tel. (01) 6601744

ENIT

In order to have general information and documentation concerning the best known places in Italy, you can contact the offices of the Ente Nazionale Italiano per il Turismo (ENIT), run by the Italian government; they are open Mon-Fri, from 9 to 5.

Canada:
Office National Italien du Tourisme/Italian Government, Travel Office, Montreal, Quebec H3B 3M9, 1 Place Ville Marie, Suite 1914, tel. (514) 866-7667/866-7669, fax 392-1429

United States of America:
– Italian Government Travel Office, New York, N.Y. 10111, 630 Fifth Avenue, Suite 1565, tel. (212) 2454822-2455095, fax 5869249
– Italian Government Travel Office, Chicago 1, Illinois 60611-401, North Michigan Avenue, Suite 3030, tel. (312) 644-0996, fax 644-3019
– Italian Government Travel Office, Los Angeles, CA 90025, 12400, Wilshire Blvd., Suite 550, tel. (310) 820-0098/820-1898, fax 820-6357

Great Britain:
Italian State Tourist Board, London W1R 6AY, 1 Princes Street, tel. (0171) 408-1254, fax 493-6695

Milan and environs

An ancient Duchy amid rivers and lakes

The area chosen by the Touring Club of Italy for this guide is the section of Lombardy that stretches from west to east between the River Ticino and River Adda, a domain that offers the visitor a wealth of fascinating geographical, historical and artistic treasures. Apart from a few border variations here and there, this area has a long history as a consolidated political region, with Milan at its heart, and is well known for its industriousness and spirit of renewal. The former Duchy of Milan, which more or less covered the region discussed in this guide – except for the areas south and northwest of the lakes – was officially ceded by the Holy Roman Emperor Wenceslaus to Gian Galeazzo Visconti in 1395. The Visconti dynasts had effectively held the seignory of the area for more than a century, during which time the rights and the liberty acquired by the Comuni or Communes had waned in their long struggle for freedom from the imperial and papal subjection of the late Middle Ages. One of the earli-

A picturesque stretch of the "Navigli" canal system

est extant paintings of the duchy, known then as *Mediolanensis Ducatus*, dates from much later, in 1580. The painting is among the marvelous frescoes in the Gallery of Maps in the Vatican, and offers a fascinating true-to-life depiction of both the physical and political features of the region, with schematic and symbolic representations of the cities (Milan, Pavia, Como) and main towns. Curiously, the roads are absent, perhaps because they were less important and more perilous as traffic routes than the rivers and waterways.

By this time the Spanish occupation had already replaced the dominion of the Visconti dynasty and their successors the Sforza, though a certain degree of administrative autonomy still existed in the duchy, until the Spanish were forced off the field by the Austrians in 1706. The change of rule marked the birth of a new region, coinciding with the Lombardy we know today, although it was once joined with the Veneto to form the Lombardo-Venetian kingdom, a department of the Austro-Hungarian Empire; subsequently it belonged to the Cisalpine Republic, and finally the Italian Republic.

In recent centuries, however, Milan has had close bonds with its territories to the north, to the point that they have virtually become an extension of the city. Milan's immediate hinterland and the neighboring Brianza district are essentially industrialized, becoming progressively more residential and less intensely developed as one nears the lakes.

The Waterways

The reasons for the persistence of the political division of the territory that was once the Duchy of Milan are easily seen in the morphology of the region, and above all in the distribution of its waterways. The rivers Ticino and Adda offered territorial borders that were defensible in times of war. In peacetime, moreover, they afforded key navigable waterways that led right to the Adriatic Sea, a factor that gained in importance for the city of Milan after the creation of the *navigli* or manmade canal system. The ancient Romans built the first canals (known as the *roggia Vettabia*, from the Lombard term meaning "artificial canal"). The system was improved and enlarged in the early Middle Ages by the monastic orders, and subsequently under the Duchy of Milan. But before the canals were built, the principal town in the entire Po Valley was Pavia, owing to its excellent location on the banks of the River Ticino.

The canals at the time of the duchy improved Milan's standing as a vital manufacturing center for iron and silk products, together with farming and livestock raising, which flourished on the fertile Lombard plain to the south of the river sources. Further north, toward the lakes, lay ample vineyards and mulberry farms.

One of the chief functions of the *navigli*, however, was to make possible the building of Milan's vast Duomo, or cathedral, an enormous political and religious feat. The cathedral was begun in 1386 under the Visconti, even before the duchy had been constituted, and grew as a testament to the city's greatness, to the faith of its people, and not least to the magnanimity of its ruling duke, Gian Galeazzo.

The canals provided the means for transporting the huge quantities of Candoglia marble and other materials necessary for the construction of the immense Gothic monument. Architects from outside Italy were called in to impart their knowledge of the techniques used in cathedral-building in central Europe, and over the centuries the enterprise involved generation upon generation of masons and artists. The cathedral's construction took so long that even today the Milanese refer to it when a project or venture begins to overshoot its schedule.

The first map of the area to include the road network is dated 1703 (now in the Civica Raccolta di Stampe Bertarelli, Milan). It was drawn up by Giulio Carlo Frattino for Viscount Borromeo Arese, and suggests that transport by road had meanwhile come to rival river transport. The map carries a curious *caveat*: "If you are unable to find all the small places on this map, that is because it aims to give a picture of the main towns, roads, and rivers, and will be followed by a larger map comprising everything missing from this one – and may you live happily."

Frattino's warning seems to usher in a new era in which the region came to be generally known as the "Milan area," or Greater Milan, to distinguish it from areas east of the River Adda (Bergamo and Cremona, etc.) and west of the River Ticino, in neighboring Piedmont. Even local dialects tend to change beyond these borders, becoming more aspirated to the east, and more sing-song to the west.

After the Spanish occupation and the last famines and plagues, the ancient Duchy of Milan enjoyed a period which, notwithstanding foreign rule, was efficient and dynamic, first under the Austrians and later the French, culminating finally in the Unification, at which point Italy became a single country.

A talent for entrepreneurship

The area where the northern lakes mitigate the otherwise cold climate of the subalpine valleys has always fostered thriving and advanced forms of settlement. In prehistoric times the area played host to the Golasecca culture, with its Iron Age villages and urnfield cemeteries. Later it was the setting of the rich and highly organized Roman city *Novum Comum* (modern Como), which has remained a busy center from medieval times to the present day. Como served as a gateway to central Europe, for many centuries the heart of the Holy Roman Empire. Later, during the Enlightenment in the 18th c., and especially as the industrial revolution got under way beyond the Alps, this limb of Milanese territory gained increasing importance. First of all it provided the most direct route to the growing manufacturing areas abroad. Before the arrival of coal and electricity, the fast-moving water of the alpine rivers provided the necessary mechanical power for local industry.

While the production of silk and wine dwindled (respectively because of competition from the Far East and the spread of the grape blight *phylloxera*), in the mid-19th c. modern industry began to occupy the area lying between the northern hills and the dry plain north of the city. The new activities included textiles factories, metalworks, the production of machinery, and automobile manufacturing. The region had suddenly tuned into a new work ethic, galvanizing its local industry and commerce, creating new forms of organization and new financial networks that pivoted on Milan.

Having consolidated its leading position in the area as early as the 14th c. (resuming a role it had enjoyed in the 4th c. A.D. as *Aurelia Augusta Mediolanum*, capital of the Roman Empire), Milan's prosperity depended as much on the surrounding fertile and efficiently farmed lands as it did to trade, which was fueled by the reinvestment of income from the flourishing agriculture. Typical of the Milanese tradition, all these financial forces were channeled into industry, which offered equally good returns in investment, if not better.

Milan therefore supplied both the brainpower and the financial resources for the myriad new enterprises that burgeoned throughout the so-called Milan Area, while also providing a substantial market for the consumption of the area's goods and produce. Once the supply of electric power became a reality, many of the new industries promptly relocated nearer the city: several key steel mills, for instance, moved from Lecco to the Milanese suburb of Sesto San Giovanni. In a short space of time the northern outskirts of the city were spangled with new industries of all kinds.

Urban development

This progressive concentration of industry and the consequent acceleration of urbanization in the late 19th and early 20th c. gave rise to the swelling conurbation of "Greater Milan." The master plan drafted in 1885 by Cesare Beruto was partially successful in imposing order to the urban growth, but the city expanded irregularly, like an oil slick – especially after World War II. The need for a workforce to rebuild the city after the heavy Allied bombing was compounded by rife building speculation, ongoing industrial expansion, and the rapid development of services throughout the region, attracting floods of immigrants to Milan from all over Italy.

As urbanization intensified so did its negative aspects, namely overcrowding and inadequate facilities for the growing population, chaotic traffic, and of course pollution. Lacking any official planning policy (a problem common to the whole of Italy), the city stopped growing and instead the outlying districts began to swell. One major example of defection was Alfa Romeo, which relocated its factories in Arese, 15 km north of Milan.

After a hundred years of steady "implosion," or centripetal development, the trend was reversed and the metropolis began to dilate rapidly, creating a new form of city-region, much as had happened in other countries, but in Milan's case the first in Italy.

At that time this writer was involved in establishing a definition of this new phenomenon, the "city-region." After much deliberation, the agreed formula was as follows: "An area in which, with respective consequences on the environment, the population increases with technical and cultural progress, production and consumption levels rise, accompanied by higher mobility of all social strata among the various sectors of the 'city state', with the widespread diffusion of all forms of communication" (Riv. Geogr. Ital., 1967, pp. 405–434). The said area of Greater Milan in fact addressed all these requirements. An urban lifestyle was no longer exclusive to those living in the city itself. Modern technological progress (first in industry, then in the service and professional sectors) had spread out beyond the city

An old print of the city, showing the inner ring of canals, and the outer ring of the Spanish walls, with the Castle (Castello Sforzesco), completing the city's defense

A 19th-century picture of the Foro Bonaparte

limits to the hinterland. Today the city-region of Greater Milan now embraces all the areas lying to the north of the city, and has engulfed the towns of Brianza, Como and Varese, creating a vast zone of unbroken urban sprawl.

Luigi Verme's set of maps entitled "Dinamico di sviluppo delle aree costruite del sistema urban policentrico Milanese" (published 1970) illustrate this progressive growth very clearly for the years 1936, 1950, 1967, and 1970, showing the steady urbanization of a polygonal area bounded by Milan, Busto Arsizio, Varese, Como, and Monza.

Urbanization is concentrated within the polygon (contrasting with the area south of Milan, where industrial development arrived later) and has had a dramatic effect on the environment: the landscape is an unending procession of industrial and residential development, villas, and housing projects. The result is great disorder and over-building, with the amount of undeveloped areas steadily dwindling. What little vacant land remains is used for agriculture and is seldom available for public use.

The Greater Milan area

This city-region of Milan can easily be made out from the air. Recent development in the older towns and villages is noticeable from the difference in color between the old and the new fabric. The result is a colored patchwork, in which there is conspicuously less green land than in other extra-urban areas of Italy. This fascinating pattern of human geography marks an abrupt transition from the rugged physical geography of the Alps, a difference that is especially striking when the mountains are covered in snow.

Independently of where an individual actually lives within this polygon of the city-region, all its inhabitants share the same reality. A person can work anywhere within it, and sustain a network of friends or acquaintances, even if these live dozens of kilometers away within the polygon. The region shares its shopping malls, entertainment centers, and merchandise to the point that its inhabitants lead the same urban existence. Each segment of the city-region corresponds to a "neighborhood," interrelating with the others like the quarters of a town or city.

This phenomenon, which was unknown in Milan until the last half of the 20th c., is the result of an accelerated industrial development that has brought vast improvements in living standard for the majority of the population. The dynamics of social interchange between classes has also changed, showing a departure from the typical dichotomy between rich and poor, a dichotomy that had always tended to characterize Lombardy as a whole. The new pattern of society has meanwhile allowed for a kind of social "osmosis" previously foreign to rural settings. This unprecedented *social* mobility is a direct product of the general increase in *physical* mobility within the city-region, and of the growing influence of mass communications. The Milan Area was ahead of others in developing motorized transportation. Furthermore, it boasted a good rail service to the northern provinces. The growth of mass automobile production after World War II accelerated the development of a capillary road network that served all corners of the Milanese city-region.

Improvements in communication, both private and public, made it possible to transmit information, news, and decisions independently of location. Today the region is served by a comprehensive communications network, such that in addition to access to telephones, faxes, personal computers, the term ISP or Internet service provider, is also rapidly becoming a household word.

The role of leadership that Greater Milan plays in the north of Italy and in the country as a whole is the direct outcome of the developments described above. Milan moreover boasts direct links to the center of Europe and beyond. The city's primacy is reflected in the intensive immigration to the region from all over Italy after World War II, at first to Milan itself, and later to the outlying areas of Busto Arsizio, Gallarate, Brianza, Varese, and Como north of the city.

Initially the Milanese dialect mingled with that of its neighbor, the Veneto. But this was soon colored with the accents of Apulia, Sicily, and Abruzzo. The new generations born from this mixture of diverse regional stock has given rise to a *gens nova* in which the characteristic local industriousness is blended with an easy, carefree spirit that Milan sorely lacked. Deep and abiding links with the outside world are noticeable in the heart of Milan, with its inimitable fashion enclave centered on Via Monte Napoleone – a compulsory port-of-call for cosmopolitan visitors from Los Angeles, Osaka, or Paris. Likewise, the lakes continue to be an enduring source of attraction for visitors from all over the world, whether on vacation or to attend concerts or conferences at Varenna on Lake Como, or at Stresa on Lake Maggiore. The area which, in its configuration of the Duchy of Milan under the Sforza dynasty, once played host to the fabulous inventions of Leonardo da Vinci, the architecture of Bramante, and the poetry of Petrarch, is now a hive of futuristic technology and creative innovation. Alas, as in medieval and Renaissance Milan, today's city is not without its faults. Petty and organized crime are commonplace, and the beggars of yore have their counterpart in the urban homeless of today – problems common to all modern cities. Such are the many facets of Greater Milan area, a region that is dynamic but complex, and therefore subject to a legacy of human issues.

The region's population – composed largely of white-collar workers, shopkeepers, and small businessmen – is noted for its enterprising spirit and business prowess. Many of these people soon set up their own business once they have acquired experience and expertise working for a firm. Some decide to operate from home. Others rent or buy premises, maybe taking on a handful of employees, assisted by a spouse, with a son or daughter filling in now and then, between studies at the local technical institute.

Thousands of small firms in the districts of Varese, Monza, Como, and Rho are born regularly in this way, motivated by a strong work ethic which is abetted by staunch financial support from the banks, confident in a domestic market which, though not without occasional fluctuations, has maintained a trend of steady expansion in the last few decades.

The new advanced service sector

Since the 1980s heavy industry and manufacturing have gradually been replaced by the more elaborate and complex sector that comprises electronics, telecommunications, management, marketing consultancy, and other organizational services. This growing spectrum of business requires an ever greater amount of investment capital, together with specialized experience that is acquired through training rather than on the job. The selection of candidates for this kind of work is tougher than before, but the standards of training match those required by the sector.

While a fair number of Greater Milan's advanced service activities are located in the outskirts of the city, housed in all-glass office blocks built in true postmodern style, a great many others are decentralized across the vast polygon. This pattern of decentralization also affects the universities, which now have departments based in Como, Varese, and Legnano. Similarly, public services (such as schools and hospitals) and private enterprises (publishing, advertising, communications, and tourism) are likewise subject to this new pattern of decentralization.

One of the characteristics of the Milan area and its population is its strong sense of collective effort, piloted by the local administrations, toward creating the basic infrastructure needed for the area as a whole, together with an innate local adaptability to the demands of new manufacturing technologies.

In Roman times this collective energy was invested in building sturdy defensive walls round the city, in land reclamation schemes, and in the construction of the canal system – all projects that were continued through the Middle Ages and the Renaissance until more recent times, with the addition of roads, railways, airports, hydroelectric power stations, etc. – not to mention the Milan subway network.

This ongoing program of major public projects is matched by an busy and enterprising private sector that has provided employment for the city's inhabitants, be they Milan-born or immigrants from other regions of Italy and the world. This winning combination of private and public enterprise has consistently guaranteed work for anyone willing to pull his or her weight. The ability to make good use of experience acquired abroad is another of the characteristics of the local population of this part of Italy.

Despite the steady centrifugal development of the city, Milan has nevertheless remained the primary focus of the region due to its history, its legacy of monuments, and the vast experience of its population. The city continues to attract the headquarters of major corporations and businesses, banks and finance groups, trade unions and political parties, publishing houses, press agencies, university facilities, and all sorts of cultural activities. No other city in Italy can match Milan for the variety and quality of its services, for its concentration of primary social and business focuses.

A tour of Milan therefore offers the visitor a means of understanding the city's role as the economic and social powerhouse of the country. But Milan's primacy does not merely apply to Italy – its influence spreads across Europe as well. In some ways, Milan offers a way of understanding the country as a whole, since, of all Italian cities, Milan is a kind of concentrate of all things Italian. Where other towns and cities may be superb repositories of Italy's history and art, only Milan gives a proper picture of Italy as it is today, an integral part of the economy and culture of central Europe and the world at large.

Although it exercises considerable power over a large part of Italy, the basic impression one gathers of Milan is of a hard-working but easy-going community that enjoys socializing as much as shopping.

Apart from the occasional brief interruption for a political demonstration, during which the center of town is thronged with much shouting and bell-ringing, the central piazza – the site of Milan's best-loved symbol and finest monument, the cathedral – resembles a somewhat outsize village square. At the weekend this capacious gathering place fills with people from the outskirts of the city and beyond, with tourists, with immigrants of all nations, some already fully integrated, others hopeful of a

An aerial view of the city, with the mountains in the distance

work permit. Scattered about the piazza, each group speaks its own language – Arabic, Filipino, Tamil. With such a busy center many people soon find themselves in company, and begin to feel at home.

Though not immediately apparent, Milan offers a considerable variety of artistic treasures, from the Roman remains under the sacristy of the cathedral and the superlative Romanesque basilica of Sant'Ambrogio, to the medieval cloisters, fine Renaissance churches and palazzi, and not least the imposing Castello Sforzesco, former residence of the powerful Sforza dukes. Generally speaking, Milan's visitors are more appreciative of the city's treasures than the Milanese themselves. For most Milanese, after five weekdays of hard work, the weekend is too sacred to be spent idling about the city: they flee to the countryside, to enjoy the natural surroundings or engage in sport – but mostly to forget about work.

The artistic background

Milan and its hinterland's first appearance in the annals of history and art occurs at the time of the Roman Empire, although traces of earlier settlements have been found just south of the lakes. The archaeological site of Golasecca, where the River Ticino runs out of Lake Maggiore, gave its name to a protohistorical Celtic civilization (9th to 6th c. B.C.), the main artifacts of which can be seen in the Museo Archeologico in nearby Sesto Calende, and in the Castello Sforzesco, Milan. Other remains dating from the same period have turned up

Sant'Ambrogio, seen from the atrium

on the banks of Lake Como and Lake Varese. The transfer of the imperial Roman court to Milan (A.D. 286–402) was decisive for the historical development of the city over the rest of the hinterland, and also for the development of the arts. Thenceforth Milan was the chief political and cultural focus (witness the Edict of Milan, A.D. 313, by which Emperor Constantine granted freedom of worship to Christians), and fostered the emergence of new forms of architecture that greatly influenced ensuing styles. The outcome of the merger of pre-Christian imperial forms of architecture with works commissioned by Saint Ambrose, Bishop of Milan at the end of the 4th c. A.D., was a series of masterpieces, some of which are still visible today, such as the mosaics in the side chapels of Sant'Ambrogio and San Lorenzo, the latter

basilica an exceptional example of early Christian architecture. While there are few vestiges of Roman imperial architecture in the center of Milan today, still very much in evidence are the buildings erected to sanctify the city at the behest of Bishop Ambrose, now the patron saint of Milan. The great basilicas marking the gateways into the medieval city – Sant'Ambrogio, San Nazaro, San Simpliciano and, a little later, Sant'Eustorgio – were all restored during in the Romanesque period, as were a baptistery and two other basilicas in the city center, the remains of which are visible under the sacristy of the cathedral. The production of precious votive articles wrought in gold and ivory (many conserved in Milan's museums) did not cease with the fall of the Roman Empire, but rather increased under subsequent Longobard rule, during which the balance between the city and the surrounding territories underwent a radical change. Milan suffered a period of great strife, as developing townships sought political and economic independence and ascendancy, such as Pavia, Brescia, Castelseprio, and above all Monza. Although little has survived of the buildings from the reign of Theodolinda, Queen of the Longobards (some remains are visible beneath the cathedral in Monza, which was built by the Visconti and modified in the 18th c., the little Museo Serpero vaults exhibits of exceptional historical interest that mark the transition from the Late Roman Empire (ivory diptychs in lingering classical style) to the reign of the Longobards (7th–8th c.). At Castelseprio stand the remains of the Roman *castrum* and the remarkable frescoes in the church of Santa Maria foris Portas, an important document for understanding the hardships of monastic life in the Late Middle Ages. The stout fortified tower protecting the monastery at Torba near Castelseprio is further testimony to the monks' precarious existence. Another important town whose name, urban plan, and works of art indicate its role as a halting place for pilgrims and merchants, is Chiavenna. The toponym comes from the Latin word *clavis*, in Italian *chiave*, meaning key, so named because it "opened the door" so to speak to the Splügen, September, and Julier passes over the Alps. In an article of the edict promulgated by the Longobard king, Ròtari, in A.D. 643, appears the first known mention of the "maestri comacini," a group of stonemasons and sculptors from the Como area, who worked in various Italian cities from the seventh to the 13th c. These master craftsmen continued the Roman building tradition, undeterred by the centuries of general economic unrest, and were the only builders to construct in stone. Significant examples of their craftsmanship can be seen in Como itself (Sant'Abbondio, San Fedele) and on the shores of the lake (Santa Maria del Tiglio at Gravedona; the abbey at Piona). From the 10th c. onward, the Maestri Comacini were the principal vehicles for the spread of the Romanesque style throughout Italy and Europe. The historic center of Milan boasts several imposing Romanesque basilicas built in brick, often resulting from modifications to existing, earlier constructions. The rigorous and solemn *quadrato* module on which the design of Sant'Ambrogio is based expresses a clarity of spatial rhythms derived from classical architecture. The basilica contains many fine sculptures – pulpit, ciborium, capitals, reliefs – arranged around the gilded Carolingian altar by Volvinio, a masterpiece of pre-Romanesque craftsmanship. Other important architectural complexes were being built outside Milan, however, sometimes imitating or even anticipating the Milanese Romanesque style, thereby reestablishing a stylistic continuity between the city and its territories in the 11th and 12th c. Many churches in small towns or in the country were altered or rebuilt, but the Romanesque style predominated. A popular folk festival, the "Canto della Pietra" (Song of the Stones), still held every year in various towns, is a reminder of this legacy of craftsmanship. Campaniles, crypts, baptisteries, portals, and apses in Romanesque style are typical of the area to the north of Milan, including the Ticino Canton (in Switzerland), offering a counterpart to the large Romanesque cathedrals in the Po Valley. Many of the most interesting monuments are in secluded places. San Pietro al Monte above Civate is an example of how the seclusion of the location has helped to preserve the stuccowork, frescoes, and the elaborate canopied ciborium, similar to that in Sant'Ambrogio in Milan. The basilica of San Vincenzo in Galliano, Cantù, is another example, with its beautiful fresco cycle and baptistery. Similar features can be admired in two other churches, respectively at Agliate in Brianza, and at Arsago southeast of Lake Maggiore.

From the 10th to the 13th c., therefore, an architectural tradition and style continued through many great historical events and indeed emerged stronger after the struggle against the Holy Roman Emperor, Frederick I Barbarossa, after which Milan reasserted its position as the main city of the communes that had joined forces to form the Lombard League. Meanwhile, the Maestri Comacini of the Romanesque tradition were accompanied by another breed of stoneworkers, the Maestri Campionesi. Specialized in masonry and monumental sculpture, their tradition lasted long through the Gothic period. Up until the 13th c. civic buildings were relatively rare. Exceptions include the turreted walls and Broletto, or magistrates' court, in Como; the brick town hall in Monza; and the Palazzo della Ragione in Piazza Mercanti, Milan. Guarding the small inlet on Lake Maggiore,

The Portinari Chapel in Sant'Eustorgio

23

the Rocca d'Angera, or stronghold, is the most important and ambitious of the fortified residences built before the dynasty of the Duchy of Milan. Among the interesting frescoes which decorate the main hall is a scene commemorating the Battle of Desio (1277), which marked the definitive ascendancy of Ottone Visconti over the Torriani family, and the dawn of the long history of the Visconti seignory.

This historical event is mirrored by a corresponding evolution in artistic styles, the first signs of which can be noticed in the abbeys around Milan. Of particular interest is the abbey at Chiaravalle, whose tiered tower can be seen from a considerable distance. This Cistercian abbey, founded by Saint Bernard in 1135 and named after his own abbey at Clairvaux, marks the first use of the pointed arch and groin vault – the beginnings, that is, of Gothic architecture, cleverly blended with the solid tradition of the Romanesque stonemasons.

From the Visconti to the Sforza dynasty: two centuries of ducal art

The 14th and 15th c. witnessed a period of political, economic, cultural and artistic independence in Milan and Lombardy. The Lombard style was precious, rich, and ornamental; it adopted unusual forms and materials, a miniaturistic attention to detail that was much in favor in the late Gothic courts of central and southern Europe.

The Sforza dynasty's emblem

Milan became the capital of an authoritarian seignory, under which the city reasserted its supremacy over the entire region. This notwithstanding, both the Visconti and the Sforza dynasties showed a degree of sensitivity with respect to certain towns outside Milan, helping to keep an open dialogue between city and territory. First of all, the image of Milan as the capital had to be consolidated. To this end, around 1330 Azzone Visconti began commissioning important new works. Among the prominent artists he summoned from Tuscany was the great Giotto, famous even in his own day. The frescoes he executed in Milan have long since perished, but his influence can be detected in several churches in the city and at Chiaravalle, Viboldone, and elsewhere. Visconti also summoned the Pisan sculptor Giovanni di Balduccio, who created the splendid Tomb of St. Peter Martyr (1339) in Sant'Eustorgio, together with the sculpted votive tabernacles incorporated into the ancient city gates. Within a short time the Milan of the Romanesque basilicas assumed a Gothic appearance. Work started on the cathedral in 1386 and was the natural culmination of this new chapter. The cathedral's growing structure was enhanced with works by the Maestri Campionesi (witness the Tomb of Bernabò Visconti, now in the Castello Sforzesco, sculpted by Bonino da Campione), upholding local stylistic traditions such as the gabled facade, now bristling with Gothic spires and pinnacles devised to enhance rather than hide. Meanwhile a distinctive Lombard style of painting developed, particularly for fresco work, involving a combination of a strong naturalistic slant informed with the supple rhythms of court Gothic. Fine examples are the later 14th-c. frescoes in the Visconti oratories of Solaro, Lentate, and Albizzate; others are the scenes once decorating the oratory of Mocchirolo, since detached and now on display in the Brera Art Gallery. The most important Lombardy-born painter of the 14th c. actually worked to Florence. Although he was known as Giovanni da Milano, his name testifies to the consistency of style that persisted throughout the duchy – though nominally "da Milano," Giovanni was actually a native of Como.

Some of the most significant examples of Lombard architecture belong to the second half of the 14th c., and especially to the reign of Duke Gian Galeazzo Visconti. These include the restored cathedral in Monza (1370–96), frequented by the Visconti owing to the presence of an important relic known as the Iron Crown of Lombardy; the cathedral in Como (1396); and, of course, the cathedral in Milan (1386). Owing to its compendium of international styles and craftsmanship, Milan Cathedral is something of an exception in Lombard architecture – if for no other reason than the exclusive use of the fabulous gray- and pink-veined Candoglia marble, which was transported from Lake Maggiore down the River Ticino toward Pavia and then up the Naviglio Pavese to the heart of Milan, where it was unloaded at a dock alongside the building site (now Via Laghetto). Local masters were flanked by French and German architects and stonemasons, who together achieved a daring mixture of architectural styles – witness the three enormous windows in the apse, and the use of statued niches instead of capitals on the piers inside. Signs of local tradition remain, however, in the gabled facade, and the Romanesque ratio between the length and the width of the temple's vessel.

The mass of decorative spires, gargoyles, and ornate corbels required to decorate Milan Cathedral engendered a small army of sculptors, many of whom remain anonymous, but who each contributed his distinctive personal style to the vast project. The collection of statues in the cathedral museum is a remarkable demonstration of the sheer variety of contributions. One of the sculptors at work on the cathedral, Jacopino da Tradate, was to sculpture what Michelino da Besozzo, the most refined Lombard artist of the late Gothic period, was to painting. The embellishment of architecture with statues was, after all, a longstanding Romanesque tradition, and as such perfectly in harmony with the Lombard spir-

Baptism of Christ, *by Masolino (Castiglione Olona, Battistero)*

it of the late Gothic and early Renaissance periods. The use of "humble" materials such as terracotta and, later, stucco, allowed for highly ornate decoration even for minor monuments in small towns, while marble was reserved for the more important buildings, as can be noted in the facade of Monza Cathedral, and later in the splendid ornamentation by the Rodari brothers for the cathedral at Como. For the first half of the 15th c., the evolution of painting in Lombardy followed the elegant canons of International Gothic, which corresponded stylistically to the richly embellished architecture of the day, with its subtle decorations, pointed windows, and friezes. The secular frescoes in Palazzo Borromeo, Milan, and in the Castello Mantegazza at Masnago (near Varese) are interesting examples. Meanwhile, ducal patronage also encouraged the exquisite work of miniaturists and goldsmiths, contributing to the survival of this style for some time. One outstanding exception to the prevailing trend is found in the town of Castiglione Olona, where a group of Tuscan artists were commissioned by Cardinal Castiglioni, fresh from his stay in Florence, to practically rebuild the town. Around 1430 Masolino da Panicale and his co-workers executed several frescoes in the main buildings (Collegiata, baptistery, and Palazzo Castiglioni; while the Tuscan-style church of Villa is adorned with a rich array of statuary), gracefully informing the newly discovered rules of perspective with the seduction of color and line. In blessed isolation, Castiglione Olona has remained intact for centuries, offering a unique case without parallel or sequel in the history of art in Lombardy. An eloquent comparison can be made with the frescoes of court scenes painted by the Zavattari brothers in 1444 in the chapel dedicated to Queen Theodolinda in Monza Cathedral, full of late-Gothic motifs. As for the duchy, in 1450 the Visconti were succeeded by the Sforza. Under Francesco Sforza the Duchy of Milan grew in strength, and the new architectural styles and urban planning were experimented throughout the city. Until the mid-15th c. Milan remained much as it had been in the Middle Ages, with a crown of enclosure walls, a ring of canals, and each of the city gates marked with a basilica. Assisted by his wife, Bianca Maria Visconti, the new duke began reorganizing the city. The imposing Castello Sforzesco became the residence of the court (the Visconti had lived in Palazzo Reale, next to the cathedral); though fortified on the outside, the castle interior afforded all the elegance of a nobleman's palace.

Another work of major importance was the Ca' Granda, a vast public hospital, which Francesco Sforza commissioned from the court engineer Filarete (Antonio Averlino). The complex was arranged symmetrically, with four arcaded courtyards around a central crossing housing the medical facilities. Thanks to the works commissioned by the duchy, and also to no less important private initiatives (the Banco Mediceo of Florence, designed

by Michelozzo, a portal of which can be seen in the Castello Sforzesco, and the exceptional chapel commissioned by Pigello Portinari behind the apse of Sant'Eustorgio), Milanese art and architecture developed at great speed in the last thirty years of the 15th c. The leading figure of Renaissance painting in Milan was Vincenzo Foppa, who executed the frescoes in the Cappella Portinari (1468), together with many paintings now hanging in the main museums in Milan. The collection at the Brera Gallery is fundamental for an understanding of the evolving school of Lombard art, and includes detached

Detail of Tiepolo's fresco in Palazzo Clerici

frescoes from numerous buildings. Other key collections of Lombard art are conserved in the art gallery at the Castello Sforzesco; the Museo Poldi Pezzoli; and the Pinacoteca Ambrosiana. The painter Foppa harbingered a distinct and independent Lombard style of painting that blends realism with sentiment. Other leading exponents were Antonio Bergognone, whose delicate and refined hand is visible in all the works executed in Milan and the provinces (polyptych in Arona), Bernardino Butinone, and Bernardino Zenale, who on occasion worked together.

In parallel with painting, a regional school of sculpture also flourished, distinguished by its eclectic style and varied use of media. Lombard terracotta works have long been considered classic examples of the region's art, and Lombard sculpture is considered to have reached its climax in the work of Giovanni Antonio Amadeo, Benedetto Brisco, and Bambaia (Agostino Busti). However, the appreciation of typically Lombard sculpture in wood is a recent development. A fine example is the wooden ancona or altarpiece in Como Cathedral. Also worthy of mention is the high level of craftsmanship attained by armorers in Renaissance Lombardy. The last two decades of the 15th c. were characterized by the rise to power of Ludovico Sforza (known as "il Moro"). Under his patronage, the region enjoyed a rapid succession of important artistic and cultural events. The arrival in Milan of Donato Bramante – followed shortly thereafter by Leonardo da Vinci in 1482 – brought new blood to the court and a challenge to the tradition of Foppa's school of painting, as well as to the somewhat stale tradition of late-Gothic court art. The reception these two supremely talented men received was varied. Commissioned to work on the Castello Sforzesco, to build the tribune in Santa Maria delle Grazie, and to remodel the church of Santa Maria presso San Satiro, Bramante found a team of willing collaborators with whom he devised ingenious solutions for the demanding structural problems of the drum and dome of the cathedral.

The developments in Lombard architecture at the end of the 15th c. were presages of the coming Renaissance, as testified by the apses and domes of two fine churches in Milan, Santa Maria presso San Celso, and Santa Maria della Passione. Other churches out of town such as Madonna di Campagna near Pallanza also evince the coming revolution. Together with local craftsmen, Bramante developed a distinct form of decorative, polychrome, and vibrant architecture that continued to evolve, even after the architect's departure for Rome. Leonardo da Vinci had meanwhile brought about a revolution in the regional school of painting. The tradition of Foppa and Bergognone appealed less to the new generation of artists than the fascinating continuum of man and nature, of "inward movement" and drama posited by Leonardo's work, which was developing in parallel. Although Leonardo was disinclined to set up a *bottega* as such, he was surrounded by disciples who imitated his style, sometimes to excess, catching only the exterior aspects of the master's work, the appearances, gestures, and composition, failing to grasp the essence of his intellect. The expression of that extraordinary intellect is for the most part limited to drawings, sketches, notes, reflections, and rough drafts for scientific and artistic treatises. The few actual paintings by Leonardo – fewer still of which are in Milan – describe the path of an outstanding intellectual adventure: the ill-fated *Last Supper*, the colorful frescoes in the Sala delle Asse in the Castello Sforzesco, the *Portrait of a Musician* (Pinacoteca Ambrosiana), are all that remains to mark Leonardo's two periods in Milan, before and after the arrival of the French in 1499 and the consequent fall of the Sforza duchy and the exile of Ludovico il Moro, enlightened patron to both Leonardo and Bramante. The first quarter of the 16th c. saw the French and Spanish battling for dominion of the former duchy. Despite the period of abundant strife, figurative art did not stagnate. Running parallel with the traditions of the old masters, two contrasting phenomena had begun to emerge. On the one hand was the austere experimentation of Bramantino, the author of the cartoons for the Trivulzio tapestries (Castello Sforzesco), rich in symbolic allusion and evocative perspectives; on the other was Bernardino Luini's elegant and decorative interpretation of Leonardo's style. Luini was from Lake Maggiore and executed many fine paintings and remarkable fresco cycles not only in Milan (San Maurizio) but also in other towns, notably Saronno, Como, and Lugano.

From the Borromeo family to Napoleon

The consolidation of Spanish rule in Milan coincided with the age of the Counter-Reformation and the reestablishment of the ecclesiastic hold over the diocese. The city's new archbishop, Carlo Borromeo, and his young cousin, Cardinal Federico Borromeo, notably outshone the Spanish governors as the moral and political leaders of the people of Milan. The family's native Lake Maggiore gradually became a kind of feudal realm: in Arona opposite the Rocca d'Angera stands the imposing statue of Saint Charles; further up the shore opposite Stresa lie the "Borromean Islands" with their sumptuous palaces and luxurious gardens. Because of the Borromeo family's keen interest in the figurative arts (Carlo drafted new norms for sacred art at the Council of Trent, and Federico was an indefatigable collector and patron of the arts), the Milanese school developed a new style, whose harbinger was Gaudenzio Ferrari. He moved, progressively, from his native Valduggia to the shores of Lake Maggiore and thence to Vercelli, Como, and Saronno, eventually settling in Milan to become the leading exponent of a style of painting of strong religious content expressed in an extremely accessible fashion. Gaudenzio fathered the Sacri Monti, a series of hilltop shrines, and one

The Villa Reale (Royal Villa), Monza, built by Piermarini for Ferdinand of Austria

of the most distinctive expressions of Lombard art of the 15th and 16th c. The first and most important Sacro Monte is at Varallo Sesia, where Gaudenzio merged painting and sculpture in a new and spectacular manner. The archbishop, a regular worshiper at the Santo Sepolcro in Varallo, commissioned a series of such shrines in the foothills of the Alps, serving as "bastions against heresy" – the heresy of the Protestant Reformation. The area covered in this guide includes the Sacro Monte of Varese, dedicated to the Virgin Mary,

which follows the Mysteries of the Rosary. The early 17th-c. chapels are carefully distanced to allow pilgrims time to recite a prayer between one mystery and the next.

The characteristically austere and noble style of Milanese religious art in the second half of the 16th c. was the handiwork of this devout man, Carlo Borromeo, Archbishop of Milan and later canonized. Its principal interpreters were Galeazzo Alessi and Pellegrino Tibaldi, who effected

The statue group crowning the Arco della Pace (Arch of Peace)

modifications to many old buildings, and designed many new ones. The period saw the construction of the charterhouse at Garegnano, San Vittore, San Sebastiano, Palazzo Marino, the Collegio Elvetico (now Palazzo del Senato), the Seminario in Corso Venezia. Meanwhile, the cathedral presbytery was remodeled by Tibaldi, and the large churches of Santa Maria presso San Celso and Santa Maria della Passione were completed.

There was a strong religious element in 17th-c. Lombard painting, a school comprising Cerano (G. B. Crespi), Pier Francesco Morazzone, Giulio Cesare Procaccini and other artists in the first three decades of the 17th c. Many of the major works are in Milan, and others can be seen elsewhere, such as at San Vittore in Varese. Among the many important works commissioned by Cardinal Federico Borromeo were two series of paintings celebrating the canonization of his cousin the archbishop, a collective work by Milanese artists between 1602 and 1610, displayed in the cathedral on special feast days. At Federico's behest the Biblioteca Ambrosiana (library, 1609) was opened to the public, and likewise the art gallery in 1618. The cardinal was the inspiration behind the solemn and severe Counter-Reformation style of the church of San Fedele and the Palazzo di Brera, at the time a Jesuit college. The devastating plague of 1630 brought to a close a phase of fertile artistic and cultural activity, though some villa building in the hinterland dates from this period.

Signs of an end to the stasis are visible at the beginning of the 18th c., coinciding with the development of a style known as "barochetto lombardo," a local version of rococo. Though few signs of this remain to be seen in Milan (a notable example is the fresco cycle by Tiepolo in Palazzo Clerici), many survive in the villas of Brianza. The most cogent example of Lombard painting of the 18th c. is in Monza Cathedral, by the young artist, Carlo Innocenzo Carloni. The "barochetto lombardo" style was not limited to painting alone; it emerges in woodcarving, stuccowork (principally in the Como and Ticino areas), and in the work of masters of *scagliola*, or imitation marble.

In the second half of the 18th c. Empress Maria Theresa of Austria embarked upon a sweeping program of radical social and civil reform, inspired by the principles of the Enlightenment. The buildings that symbolize this new trend were designed by a very talented architect, Giuseppe Piermarini, who perfectly interpreted the intellectual and moral clarity of the period. He built the La Scala opera house, remodeled the Palazzo Reale, and restyled the elegant neighborhood lying between Piazza Belgioioso and Via Monte Napoleone, the only quarter that retains something of the atmosphere found in the novels of the French author Stendhal, who lived in Milan from 1815 to 1821. Piermarini's most important creation was, however, the Villa Reale at Monza, and formed part of the new developments outside the city.

The Austrian empress was also responsible for transforming the Jesuit college in Palazzo di Brera into a major center of art and learning. The new library, botanical gardens, and astronomical observatory were soon complemented with an art school, the Accademia di Belle Arti, and shortly thereafter by the art gallery, which was greatly enlarged in the Napoleonic period.

The neoclassical style appeared in Milan as the direct consequence of the Enlightenment. The 1880s saw a burst of literary, scientific, and cultural activity, and much discussion in the drawing rooms of the town houses, country villas, and mansions on the lake shores: witness the experiments of the physicist Alessandro Volta (from whom comes the unit of electric potential, the volt), and the debate on law and literature in Villa Manzoni in Lecco. Significant architectural projects in Milan at the time included the construction of the Foro Buonaparte around the ruins of the Castello Sforzesco, the Arco della Pace, and the Arena. While ruler of Milan, Napoleon also commissioned the completion of the facade of the cathedral.

Mid-19th-century and 20th-century Milan

Milan was the stage of many of the momentous historical events of the Romantic period and Italian Risorgimento. Furthermore, it was the focus of the literary works of the much-loved novelist Alessandro Manzoni, author of *The Betrothed*, which has been studied by generations of Italian schoolchildren. Opera, that ultimate expression of Romanticism, also flourished in the likes of Rossini, Donizetti, and Bellini, culminating in the works of the great Giuseppe Verdi. A new school of painting also developed, centered on the new academy at Palazzo di Brera, whose director for some years was the artist Francesco Hayez. Italy's independence and unification were commemorated by many changes to the city. The transformation of the old Milan, still with its circuit of internal canals, was rapid and sometimes traumatic. While there were positive schemes (i.e., the creation of Via Dante leading from the cathedral to the castle), there were many devastating changes, brought about too quickly in the rush to build new urban districts to address the rapid industrialization process. The changes were noticeable in the relationship between the historical center and the growing,

"modern" city. Some fine churches were unjustifiably modernized, but earlier styles were revived in buildings that are now part of the region's "industrial archaeology." The turn of the century saw the creation of many new museums as a means of to preserving the local heritage. Typical examples are the collections installed in the Castello Sforzesco (daringly reworked by Luca Beltrami), the collections of Gian Giacomo Poldi Pezzoli, and those of the Bagatti Valsecchi brothers. Milan's finest museums were thus formed in this period, largely based on private collections, including those of Cardinal Federico Borromeo. On the art front, the new century began with the exuberant activities of the Futurists, who launched from Milan a movement for complete renewal in all forms of artistic expression – fine arts, music, and theater. Even after World War I Milan continued to be a key focus of cultural and social debate. In 1919 the city saw the emer-

A corner of the Monumental Cemetery

gence of the first "Fasci di Combattimento," thereby endearing itself particularly to the rising political star Benito Mussolini and his followers. The architectural repercussions were in some cases overstated and obtrusive, with ponderous gray buildings erected at historically strategic points of the city, notably the twin Arengario building overlooking Piazza del Duomo. Architecture was more promising further north, however, nearer the lakes. The town of Como and environs played host to the most important school of Rationalist architecture and painting of the 1930s. The architect Giuseppe Terragni, the sculptor Fausto Melotti, and a group of painters (Manlio Rho, Mario Radice, Atanasio Soldati, and others) all contributed to making Como the capital of the emerging school of Italian abstract art. Once again, history illustrates the important symbiosis between city and territory, as the seeds of Como's Rationalism found fertile soil in the regional capital in the activity of the Triennale, the international design exhibition, and in the works of Milan's home-grown architect Giovanni Muzio.

How to visit Milan

Milan the capital of industry, finance, and the service sector, brings together many different aspects of modern life. Its importance is not limited to the city itself but extends to the hinterland and surrounding plains, now heavily developed and industrialized. The city is the daily destination of workers, visitors, and foreign people on business, drawn by the numerous trade fairs that take place here. One of the reasons Milan has become so important is its geographical location at the center of the Po Valley, a strategic point for commercial traffic and tourist routes. The city has a long history, a wealth of remarkable cultural traditions, and many art treasures, all of which may elude the visitor. Milan's subtle charm is worth discovering, even though it is often hidden behind the frenetic rhythms of the metropolis. It is a compact city and its various districts are not easily distinguishable on a historical or chronological basis. Milan is one of the largest, richest, and

A crowded street café near the cathedral

liveliest Italian cities, despite the problems it has experienced in recent years with the transition from manufacturing to a service industry economy, despite the corruption and political scandals that have implicated an entire generation of politicians and managers, despite the huge surge of immigration from developing countries in the early 1980s. Foreign communities have thrived in Milan for decades and the city's non-Italian residents are an integral part of society. In some cases these communities have left their mark on a district of the city, such as the so-called Chinatown around Via Paolo Sarpi, and the North African community around Porta Venezia. Milan has always welcomed outsiders, an attitude that has made it distinctly unprovincial. Its role as Italy's leading industrial city and a capital of international fashion has made Milan more receptive to international trends and less set in its ways and customs.

When to visit

The best seasons to visit Milan are spring and autumn. Like most large Italian cities, Milan is deserted during the August vacation period; while this makes the city eminently more livable, most shops and many of its restaurants are closed. The city is particularly crowded during the major trade fairs, spread evenly throughout the year, and staged at the Fiera di Milano (Largo Domodossola 1, tel. 49971, fax 49977379), the largest international trade fair venue in the country. Around ninety international trade fairs are held at the Fiera each year.

How to reach Milan

By car the main toll roads and highways are connected to the Tangenziale Est (east beltway) and Tangenziale Ovest (west beltway), ring roads round the city; the Est connects the tollroad to Venice with the tollroad going south (Autostrada del Sole), the Ovest links the tollroad to Turin and the Lakes with the tollroad to Genoa (Autostrada dei Fiori) and the Cisa pass. The center of Milan (bounded by a circuit that marks the old ring of canals) is open to private traffic, but with parking charges (Blue Zone). It is nonetheless advisable to avoid using a car in the city: traffic is heavy, there are countless one-way streets and pedestrian areas, and getting parked is a nightmare (there is very little free parking and the private parking lots are expensive). The main pay parking lots (average charges 3,000–8,000 lire per hour) are in the city, near the Stazione Centrale, and near the Fiera trade fair center; but there are parking lots with custodians at the subway stations of Molino Dorino, Lampugnano, Bisceglie, Sesto Marelli (Line 1); Cologno, Gessate, Cascina Gobba, Crescenzago, Romolo, Famagosta (Line 2); Rogoredo and San Donato (Line 3).

By train the main point of arrival in Milan is the Stazione Centrale (FS Informa, tel. 147888088), which is served by all the main national and international trains. There are subway stations for Lines 2 and 3 under the station, and numerous bus and tram routes above ground outside. Line 2 of the subway also goes to Porta Garibaldi station (Centro Direzionale district, tel. 6552078), and to Lambrate station (Città Studi district). Northbound trains to Como, Varese, and Brianza run from a separate station in Piazza Cadorna (Ferrovie Nord Milano, subway lines 1 and 2; tel. 48066771).

By plane there are two international airports serving Milan and hinterland: Linate (tel. 74852200), and Malpensa (tel. 74852200). Coach services to and from the airports leave from the Stazione Centrale (to Linate every 20 minutes, and to Malpensa every 30 minutes). Buses for Malpensa only, leave from Piazza Cadorna/Largo Cairoli every hour. The regular no. 73 bus route connects Linate with Piazza San Babila in downtown Milan.

Information

The Azienda di Promozione Turistica (APT, or Tourist Office) provides visitors with information on events, monuments, and museums, with a free map of the city. Offices are in Via Marconi 1, corner of Piazza del Duomo (weekdays 8:30am–8pm; Sat. 9am–1pm and 2–6pm; Sun. 9am–1pm and 2–5pm; tel. 72524300) and at the Stazione Centrale (daily 8am–7pm; Sun. 9am–12:30 and 1:30–6pm; tel. 72524370). Detailed information about what to see and where to go in Milan is available in the magazine *Milano Mese*, free from the APT. There are also several free magazines distributed in restaurants, theaters, and night spots, including the fortnightly *Milano Magazine*, and *Hello Milano!* Tourist trips around the city are organized by the Autostradale Viaggi, Piazza Castello 1, tel. 801161.

Accommodation

The hotel booking agency, Centro Prenotazioni Hotels (tel. 167-015772) provides a comprehensive reservation service for hotels, ranging from two-star to luxury. If you require comfort and good service, prices are generally high (200,000–400,000 lire and over); there are no cheap hotels as such, and the traditional Italian classification by "stars" does not always reflect a good price-quality relationship. The APT can provide a list of hotels with prices indicated, but will not make reservations. There is a youth hostel in Milan, the Ostello Piero Rotta, Via Salmoiraghi 2 (San Siro district), tel. 39267095.

Transport

The city has a good public transport network, with three subway lines and numerous buses and trams. Tickets must be purchased before boarding, and are available at all newsstands in the subways, any above-ground newsstand marked ATM (Azienda Trasporto Milanese), tobacconists (marked by a large white T on a dark blue background), and at some bars; there are also automatic ticket machines in the subway and near some bus and tram stops. Each ticket is valid for 75 minutes on all surface transport and can be used more than once within the time limit; it can only be used once on the subway, however. Trips beyond Sesto Marelli, Cascina Gobba, and San Donato require a special out-of-town ticket "biglietto extra-urbana". Tickets can also be purchased in blocks of ten (ask for a "carnet"). A two-day touring pass is available for all public transport within the city, and can be bought at any ATM office (Cairoli, Duomo subway stations); public transport maps are available here, and at many newsstands and tobacconists. Taxis can be booked on the following numbers: 5353, 6767, 8383, 8585, and 8388. Unlike many other European cities, bicycling in Milan is not much fun and is often hazardous, what with the pollution, lack of cycle paths, and intense traffic. Biking outside the city is a safer alternative, and there is a train+bike service in the summer, organized by the railways (Ferrovie dello Stato,

Centro Compartimentale Comitive, tel. 6703514; Ferrovie Nord, tel. 8511416). For city bike trips, "Ciclobby" (Via Cesariano 11, tel. 33113664) publishes a booklet, which is available at APT tourist offices.

There are bus lines to and from Milan serving all the main regional towns and principal holiday spots in Italy. Bus companies include: Autostradale Viaggi (Piazza Castello 1, tel. 801161), Atinom (Via Novara 75, tel. 4046446), Stie (Via Paleocapa, tel. 86450614), and Sgea Lombardia (Viale Bligny 8/12, tel. 48066776, 58301618).

Parks and gardens in Milan

Local lore has it that "the only green thing you'll ever see in Milan is the traffic light." Like most such legends, its truthfulness is relative: there are several parks and gardens dotted across the city. Not far from the center, Villa Reale looks onto a charming landscaped garden at the rear, and "backs" onto the spacious Giardini Pubblici or public gardens that stretch from Via Palestro to Porta Venezia, comprising the Planetarium and the Museo di Storia Naturale. In the north of the city beyond the castle lies the vast Parco Sempione, which comprises the monumental Arco della Pace and the Palazzo dell'Arte (home of the Triennale industrial design center), the Aquarium, and the Arena Civica sports ground. Another much-frequented green area, the Parco delle Basiliche, lies between the basilicas of Sant'Eustorgio and San Lorenzo. The modest Parco Solari even boasts a swimming pool, while Parco Ravizza offers a green retreat for the busy young minds of the Bocconi University. Other small parks include the Parco Marinai d'Italia (where concerts are regularly held in the Palazzo Liberty), and the gardens in Via Guastalla, behind Milan University.

The finest parks are actually outside the city center, however. The Parco di Trenno, Boscoincittà (Via Novara 340, tel. 4522401), run by the heritage conservation group Italia Nostra, covers an area of 50 hectares and comprises woods, lawns, and a small lake. Educational programs take place in the park and volunteer work is done. The Monte Stella and the gardens of Villa Litta serve residents in the west of the city, while the Parco Lambro and the Parco Forlanini those in the east. Near Linate lies the Idroscalo, an artificial lake set in a wood, and the leisure complex Parco Azzurro (with swimming pools, tennis, golf, and restaurants). In Monza, about ten kilometers from the center of Milan, is the 18th-c. Villa Reale which is set in a vast landscaped park. Monza is also home to the world-famous Monza racetrack, and to an important golf course.

Eating out

Milan's characteristic cosmopolitan and unprovincial nature is also reflected in its eating habits. In Milan, the traditional Italian midday meal has largely been replaced by a quick snack, eaten "on the hop," and as a result fast-food outlets have mushroomed all over town. Be that as it may, for the more leisurely evening meal there is a wide selection of restaurants – in terms of quality, type of cooking, and price (although Milan tends on the whole to be expensive). There is a wide choice of regional and international cuisines: Chinese, Japanese, Mexican, Spanish, Russian, African, and Indian restaurants can be found all over the city. In addition to excellent fish restaurants, various vegetarian and macrobiotic restaurants have opened recently prompted by the growing popularity of health foods. This said, restaurants offering a home-grown Milanese cuisine are few and far between. Many offer the traditional dishes such as *risotto alla milanese*, *cotoletta alla milanese*, *cassoeula*, tripe and *ossobuco*, but authentic Milanese cooking is hard to come by. Conversely, the regional holiday cake, *panettone*, can now be found all over Italy. Bread and pastry shops often carry special sweetmeats on particular feast days such as *pane dei morti* (a cake made of dried fruit and wine, dusted with icing sugar), *pan de mej* (a sweetmeat traditionally made with millet, and now with white and saffron flour, topped with syrup), *tortelli di Carnevale* (a kind of fried doughnut covered with icing sugar, made during Carnival in February). Alongside this variety of cuisines, most restaurants offer a vast selection of wines from all over Italy and abroad.

Shopping

For many people, shopping in Milan is synonymous with the glamorous fashion enclave centered on Via Monte Napoleone, Via Borgospesso, Via della Spiga, and Via Sant'Andrea. Outlets of the world's premier fashion designers can be found here, including those paragons of Italian fashion Armani, Valentino, Ferrè, Versace, Prada, and Fendi. The high concentration of boutiques has attracted many lesser-known designers too, making this enclave a veritable showcase of international *couture*. It goes without saying that the world's most famous stores for leather goods and shoes are also found here, such as Gucci and Ferragamo, together with prestigious jewelers.

But anyone hoping for more accessible examples of Italian fashion can enjoy the busy high-street shopping meccas of Corso Buenos Aires and Corso Vercelli. In these long and lively shop-lined avenues you can find everything from chic *pasticcerie* and delicatessens, to discount bookstores and department stores, not to mention the myriad boutiques and fashion outlets for young people.

Definitely worth visiting is the La Rinascente department store next to the cathedral. There are two outlets in Milan, and the chain is considered to be the finest in Italy. That particular area of the center, Duomo to San Babila, also offers countless outlets for designer furniture and household furnishings.

Mention should also be made of Milan's numerous street markets and traditional fairs. The Fiera di Senigallia is a lively flea market held each Saturday along the Darsena at Porta Ticinese; in the same area a big Antiques Market is held along the Naviglio Grande on the last Sunday of each month; the Fiera degli "O'bej O'bej" (named after the traders' characteristic cry) runs for three or four days before the Feast Day of St. Ambrose, the patron saint of Milan (7

The opulent auditorium of the La Scala opera house

December), filling the streets around the basilica of Sant'Ambrogio.

For further information and suggestions, refer to the chapter "Information for Travelers" at the end of the guide.

Milan by Night

Although the discotheques and bars are well distributed across Milan, two districts in particular are well known for their night life, and these are the Navigli and the Brera, which offer a plethora of discotheques, night clubs, beer cellars, snack bars, live music venues, cabaret, cinemas, and theaters. There is also a wide choice of classical music; among the many concert organizations are the Società dei Concerti (Via Vittor Pisani 31, tel. 66986956), and the Serate Musicali (Galleria Buenos Aires 7, tel. 29409724). Other important musical events are held in the Salone degli Affreschi della Società Umanitaria (Via Daverio 7, tel. 55187242), and in the church of San Maurizio (Corso Magenta 15), which offers a program of early music and poetry readings (tel. 862418). There are also concerts of modern and contemporary music (Suoni e Visioni; information from Provincia di Milano, Via Guicciardini 6, tel. 77402921). For the summer, the municipal council organizes a busy season of concerts for those who remain in the city.

Suggestions for your visit

Milan is mistakenly accused of being a somewhat heartless capital of finance, fashion, and luxury shops, when in actual fact it has a wealth of art treasures, many picturesque out-of-the-way corners, secluded gardens, and other unexpected features. The city offers an extraordinary variety of architectural types and styles, testifying to a long and varied history. The most drastic changes took place in the 19th and 20th c., when Milan became the industrial capital of Italy, and soon afterward assumed the leading role in finance and the service industry. Present-day Milan has all but canceled the traces of the original city, once enclosed within its 17th-c. walls. The walls were demolished long ago, but the old city gates continue to serve as the main points of reference for navigating through the city. Milan's historic city center has changed more than those of other Italian cities. Though patently modern, Milan's history is to be sought in the churches, the palazzi with their hidden courtyards, and the occasional ruin left in the open.

1 Milan: the center

The *forma urbis* of Milan, that is, the organic shape of the city as seen in maps or aerial photographs, resembles the cross-section of a tree trunk. It is composed of a series of progressively larger concentric rings with the cathedral at the center. The most conspicuously 20th-c. of Italian cities, and one of the few that could be described as truly European, Milan's layout stems directly from the original Roman and Medieval nucleus. The city's

outward development is similar to an oil slick, particularly as the geographical location (122 m above sea level) offers an unrelentingly flat horizon for 360 degrees. On a fine day, in the distance one can make out the jagged profile of the Alps that ring the northern border of Lombardy.

One of the consequences of the city's circular plan is the lack of right angles or a recognizable symmetry. It is difficult to get one's bearings from merely looking around (though it helps to know that radial street numbers get higher away from the center). Another consequence of this form of urban growth is that Milan has only one central gathering place. In the 1960s Milan was not so different from

The octagonal crossing of the Galleria

London or Paris, but today you can see the consequences of there being no alternative focus. The area between the cathedral and Palazzo Marino (city hall) is still the hub of city life. Many major business and banks have their headquarters in the immediate vicinity. Despite the construction of an influential communications and business pole in the east periphery, this has done little to shift the balance from the historic downtown or modify the daily rhythms of life in the metropolis.

It is hard to say just what constitutes the "typical" Milanese lifestyle. The population is very mixed, to the point that the local dialect is practically extinct. The actual number of inhabitants is on the decline, falling from 1,732,000 in 1971 to 1,321,555 in 1994. But to describe how the Milanese live today is essential for an understanding of the city, once ancient *Mediolanum*. In the first place, let us debunk once and for all the notion that Milan holds no interests for tourists: the industrial and financial capital of Lombardy – once the self-styled "moral" (i.e., hardworking, honest) capital of the nation – has a great deal to offer to residents and visitors alike in terms of art, architecture, history, and culture in general.

The concentration and sheer variety of building styles, together with its considerable cultural heritage make Milan a must to visit – suffice it to consider the immense prestige of the La Scala opera house, or the enduring influence on western art of Leonardo's *Last Supper*. It is true that the ring of canals that once defined the historic nucleus of Milan disappeared some sixty years ago – for centuries this network of waterways played a vital role in daily life in the Lombard capital. It is also true that many of the fine palazzi and characteristic Milanese residential blocks that had survived until the end of the 19th c. were later either destroyed by bombing in World War II, or torn down in questionable clearance schemes. Despite such upheavals, the historical layers of which Milan is constituted have made it essential to Italy. The city's surviving monuments document the important transition from the Roman Empire to early Christianity, from the freedom of the Communes to the feudal dominion of the Visconti and Sforza duchies, from the Hapsburgs to the Risorgimento, from Fascism to the modern Italian Republic of today. The enterprising spirit of the past lives on in modern Milan, providing the country with a vital bridge to Europe. Notwithstanding the many momentous changes it has endured, the heart of this city continues to offer aesthetic stimuli of all kinds that more than justify a visit.

1.1 Piazza del Duomo

The large rectangle (map 1, pp. 44-45, C-D4-5) around the cathedral still offers a central gathering place, as it did in ancient times. The square becomes particularly crowded during public events (religious or political, trade union meetings, student demonstrations, shows or celebrations of sports victories), at weekends, and during occasions for shopping sprees, such as Christmas. People meet here on their way shopping or before going to the movies, to stop and have a chat. The square, always referred to as Piazza Duomo, is a very lived-in space that has a timeless quality. But while the piazza has been the city center for over seven hundred years, its present-day configuration is the result of a grand project by the architect Giuseppe Mengoni (1865–73), who enlarged the previous cathedral square. Opposite the cathedral stands the so-called *Palazzo Carminati*, on either side of the square run the symmetrical arcades. Set into the north flank is the lofty arched entrance of the Galleria Vittorio Emanuele and opposite this the twin towers of the Arengario (see details later for both), framing the entrance to Piazza Diaz. Opposite the cathedral, on the site where another building planned by Mengoni should have stood, rises the *Equestrian Monument to Victor Emmanuel II* (1878–96), a posthumous work

by Ercole Rosa. On the right of the cathedral is the Piazzetta Reale, bordered on three sides by the Palazzo Reale (see below); the cobbled pavement of the square was laid in 1926 to designs by Pietro Portaluppi. A large air-raid shelter was built beneath the square in 1942 and was later converted to an exhibition gallery; the gallery has been in disuse for years, but is still connected to the subway station, whose red line (built 1964) and yellow line (1990) are the mainstay of public transport in Milan.

Work on the huge Gothic temple lasted several centuries, and is the subject of a local quip when people take too long about their business. In the 14th and 15th c., while work was under way on the apse and main vessel of the cathedral, the space that is now the piazza was occupied by earlier religious buildings: an early Christian basilica dedicated to Santa Tecla, a baptistery, and the cathedral of Santa Maria Maggiore, a 9th-c. church that was progressively substituted by the cathedral. By mid-18th c. these buildings had all disappeared from the square.

The residence of the Visconti on the south side of the square, built on the site of the old Broletto (the episcopal gardens where in the 11th c. the Communes began to seek freedom from the feudal system) was remodeled by Piermarini in the late 18th c., and set a little further back from the square; the neoclassical building is now known as the Palazzo Reale.

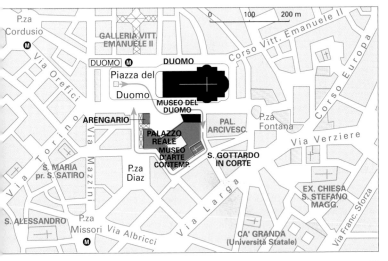

Piazza del Duomo seen from the northwest

Demolition work in and around the piazza undertaken in the last two centuries has been even more drastic. Mengoni's ambitious 19th-c. redesign of the square entailed the destruction of the Coperto dei Figini, a 15th-c. arcade erected by Guiniforte Solari on the northern foundations of Santa Tecla, together with the much earlier buildings of the so-called Rebecchino. The 20th c. witnessed the loss of the longer arm of Palazzo Reale to make way for the Arengario; the back section was replaced by a building for municipal offices in Via Larga.

Among the many restaurants, boutiques, bookstores, and record shops that surround Piazza del Duomo, one of the most successful commercial ventures is the *La Rinascente* department store, facing the north flank of the cathedral. Founded in 1890 by the Bocconi brothers (who also gave their name to Milan's university for business studies), the store's premises have had a checkered fate. The present-day building by Ferdinando Reggiori and Aldo Molteni (1945–51) was inspired by the medieval Palazzo della Ragione (see itinerary 1.4) where La Rinascente was temporarily housed when the store was bombed in World War II.

The Cathedral ** (I, C-D5). The seat of the Ambrosian diocese (whose service differs from the Roman rite) is perhaps best known by its triangular **facade** (67.9 x 56 m tall), which was finally completed 1805–13, after

centuries of indecision. Although many famous architects had tendered plans (Pellegrino Tibaldi and Martino Bassi in the 16th c.; Francesco Maria Ricchino, Carlo Buzzi, and Francesco Castelli in the 17th; Luigi Vanvitelli and Bernardo Vittone in the mid-18th) the solution that was finally adopted, after pressure from Napoleon Bonaparte, is considered hasty and out of harmony with the rest of the building. Neo-Gothic buttresses surmounted by pinnacles delimit the five main areas of the church – the nave and double aisles, the main vessel, and the portals, created in the 17th c. by Tibaldi. The most remarkable of these is the central portal (1, see plan on facing page), sculpted by Martino Solari with ornate pilaster strips decorated with plant and animal motifs. The bronze doors are of more recent date: the central one is by Ludovico Pogliaghi (1894–1908), the door on the far right (2) is by Luciano Minguzzi (1965). Ranged above the portals are five 17th-c. gabled windows, while the balcony under the central window bearing the Latin dedication "A Maria Nascente" dates from 1790. The three uppermost windows are in Neo-Gothic style and date from the 19th c. The building is clad entirely in Candoglia marble, a pinkish-white variety with gray veins quarried on Lake Maggiore, and donated by Gian Galeazzo Visconti. The weight of this huge structure is borne by the massive piers and marble-clad vessel walls.

While this brief description suggests that Milan Cathedral is an excellent example of late Gothic style (according to one French expert on 17th-c. architecture, "the finest Gothic building in the world"), it is in fact the result of a patchwork of styles added in the course of several centuries. Recent touches date from a major restoration project completed in 1994, which will not be the last. The cathedral was begun (probably in 1386, and certainly during the reign of Gian Galeazzo Visconti) in a period whose style is known as Late Gothic, as evidenced by the magnificent apse, which, as in all great European cathedrals, was the first part of the temple to be built. The bulk of subsequent construction, however, carried out from the 16th to the 19th c., corresponds more to a "posthumous" idea of Gothic. The interior (with altars, sepulchers, choir, presbytery, and transept chapels all de-signed by Pellegrino Tibaldi in the late 16th c.) tends to be styled more on the ecclesiastical concept of church form as designated by the Counter-Reformation, rather than on the northern European model of the Gothic temple.

Before entering the cathedral it is worth studying the building from the outside, starting from the south flank on Piazzetta Reale, which affords a sight that Stendhal, Milanese by adoption, considered of overwhelming beauty. Apart from the sheer size of the building (158 m long and 93 m at its widest, covering some 11,700 sq.m, the third-largest Catholic church in the world), the abundance of statuary and decorative sculpture is breathtaking – there are over 3,400 statues, not counting the figures in the splays of the windows, the 96 gigantic gargoyles, and the countless other carvings. The cathedral's construction kept genera-

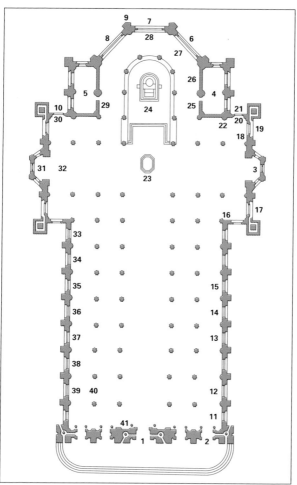

Plan of the Cathedral

tions of sculptors and stonemasons busy from the early 14th to the late 19th c. After the first few decades in which work on the apse was carried out by German, Bohemian, French, Tuscan, and Venetian craftsmen (Matteo Raverti, Dalle Masegne), complemented by the Campionese and Lombard masters (Giovanni dei Grassi, Michelino da Besozzo, Jacopino da Tradate), a new phase began in the middle of the 15th c., in which local sculptors did most of the work (Antonio Briosco, Cristoforo Solari, and Agostino Busti, called Bambaia, up to the early 16th c.; and in the following centuries Andrea Biffi, Dionigi Bussola, Giuseppe Rusnati, Elia Vincenzo Buzzi), making the cathedral an evolving gallery of the most extraordinary beauty imaginable. Though they are not easily identifiable, many figures have been replaced over the years, owing to weathering and pollution.

Turning the corner of the building one notices that the transept actually protrudes from the main vessel by a single bay. The transept ends in an absidiole (3) built in the 17th c. in place of the portal planned in the first designs. This is followed by the great polygonal **apse***, framed either side by the sacristies (4 and 5). The three *vast gothic windows* (6–8). These windows, with their exquisite marble ribbing forming rose-windows in the ogives, and the apse itself, are the work of Filippino degli Organi, the fourth of the successive engineers who held tenure on the cathedral site, coming after Simone da Orsenigo, Giovanni dei Grassi, and Marco da Carona. The large central window in the apse (7), dedicated to the incarnation of Christ, the "Sol justiciæ" of the prophecy of Malachi, includes sculptures that are fine specimens of the religious sculpture: note the *radiant sun* (insignia of Gian Galeazzo Visconti) at the center of the rose-window, the two seraphim by Pieter Monich (1408) halfway up the splays, and the pair of angels above attributed to Matteo Raverti and Nicolò da Venezia (1403). Note also the figure of the giant by Raverti (1404), and the gargoyle above the northern pillar (9). Passing beyond the elevator in the left transept (10), which leads up to the terraces (see below: the roof offers the best view of the drum and the gilded Madonnina, or little Virgin Mary, crowning it), one completes the tour of the outside and reaches the square. From here one can proceed up the steps (created in 1966) and into the church. The interior is somberly lit, as the clerestory is low owing to the small difference in height between the nave and aisles. Dominating the main interior, 52 massive clustered

piers rise from the marble pavement, bearing the bulk of the vessel's weight. The piers lining the nave (which is twice the width of each aisle), and those of the transept and apse, are crowned by *canopied niches* containing statues of saints, and surmounted by statues of prophets. The marble tracery on the ceiling is actually an elaborate trompe-l'œil; it was begun in the 16th c. and continued in the 19th c., but has not been restored since 1964. The third row of piers from the entrance marks the point where the old facade of Santa Maria Maggiore was retained from the mid-1400s to the late 1500s, as a provisional solution while the new cathedral was slowly completed.

In addition to the remarkable stained-glass **windows*** (though not all authentically Gothic), there are several features visitors should not miss. Starting from the head of the southernmost aisle: the *sarcophagus of Archbishop Ariberto d'Intimiano* (d. 1045) and window describing *scenes from the life of St. John the Evangelist** (1473–77) in the first bay (11); in the second (12) the *sarcophagus of the Archbishops Ottone and Giovanni Visconti* (d. 1295, 1354), originally in Santa Tecla; the fourth (13) contains the sarcophagus (designed by Filippino degli Organi, 1406) of *Marco Carelli*, merchant and a devout patron of the building; the fifth altar (14) the *sarcophagus of Gian Andrea Vimercati* (d. 1548) with statue by Bambaia and window inspired by Foppa with *scenes from the New Testament** (1470–75); the sixth bay (15) has a window with scenes from the life of *St. Eligius** (1480–89). Turning left into the south arm of the transept we

The high altar of the Cathedral, looking toward the south transept

ee in the right aisle the **Monument of Gian Giacomo Medici*** (16; d. 1555) known as Medeghino, an important composition showing Michelangelo's influence by Leone Leoni 1560–63). At the end of the aisle the ransept window (17) shows *scenes of St. James the Elder** (1554–64), which relates to s counterpart left of the entrance (18) to an underground passage to the Archbishop's palace commissioned by archbishop Carlo Borromeo, with (19) *scenes of the life of St. Catherine of Alexandria** (1543); next is an altar (20) with a marble altarpiece by Bambaia 1543) and in the trefoils of the next window 21), late 15th-c. *Prophets**.

After examining the gruesomely anatomical statue of St. Bartholomew flayed and carrying his skin (22) by Marco d'Agrate (1562), one ascends to the dome (23, see plan p. 37) - 68 m high – whose octagonal drum is supported by four pillars; remarkable examples of late 15th-c. statues decorate its pinnacles rounded with the Doctors of the Church) and on the corbels (60 figures of Prophets and Sibyls). The drum posed some of the most difficult problems for the stability of he cathedral. The deterioration of building materials in 1843 made the most recent structural intervention necessary (1981–86): after the piers were braced with concrete packets, they were replaced almost entirely. The problems were largely caused by the constant erosion of the water-bearing stratum on which the city lies, and secondly by the vibration from the subway which passes almost directly beneath the cathedral. The original construction of the dome inevitably affected the presbytery (24), which is separated from the apse by 10 pillars. While the presbytery was being remodeled, the 13th-c. high altar of Santa Maria Maggiore came to light, and was reconsecrated for the new church by Pope Martin V in 1418. The presbytery is framed by a pair of pulpits (1585–1602) and two gigantic organs (the right one was finished in 1577, and the left in 1590), with large paintings respectively by Giuseppe Meda (1565–81), and Giovanni Ambrogio Figino and Camillo Procaccini (1592–1602). The screen in gilded bronze (designed by Pellegrino Tibaldi, 1581–90) separates the choir from the ambulatory. There are two orders of choir stalls carved in wood (1572–1620). The raised presbytery allows for a crypt underneath. This is circular with a peribolus around the altar (accessed from the ambulatory, see below) and a communicating octagonal chapel dedicated to San Carlo designed by Francesco Maria Ricchino 1606), where a rock-crystal urn contains

the remains of St. Charles Borromeo. The neighboring **Treasury*** is composed of precious masterpieces of sacred goldsmith's art (the most antique are from the 4th and 5th c.), the ivory evangelistary cover belonging to Archbishop Aribert.

Other works of art not to be missed can be seen along the ambulatory around the presbytery; the *apse windows* were mostly replaced in the 19th c. (6–8, see above). Of particular interest: in the first bay (25) the late 14th-c. **doorway*** of the south sacristy, by Hans von Fernach, Porrino, and Giovanni dei Grassi (1393); in the second bay (26) the statue of Martin V* by Jacopino da Tradate (1424) and the *tomb of Cardinal*

One of the many colorful stained windows of the cathedral

Caracciolo, governor of Milan (d. 1538), by Bambaia; in the third bay (27) the late 16th-c. banner of the Congregation of the Rosary, embroidered and painted; in the fourth bay (28), the stone commemorating the consecration of the cathedral by St. Charles in 1577, then Archbishop of Milan, bearing lists of the relics contained in the church; in the seventh bay (29) the doorway of the north sacristy by Giacomo da Campione (1389), considered the oldest sculpture in the cathedral (traces of the original polychrome decoration are just visible).

We now move to the north arm of the transept; here you should note the lower side window with *scenes from the life of St. John Damascene* (1479); the small apse (31) with the *altar of the Madonna dell'Albero*, by Francesco Maria Ricchino, with 16th-c. reliefs inside the arch; the *Trivulzio** candelabrum (32) a late 13th–early 14th-c. seven-branched bronze candlestick standing nearly 5 m high, of French or German workmanship, donated in 1562 by a deacon of the cathedral.

The tour of the interior of the building ends with the north aisle: note *altars* by Tibaldi in the eighth (33), seventh (34) and sixth (35) bays; and late 16th-c. windows, partly by the Flemish school (34 & 35) and partly Lombard (36 and 37). The third bay contains the Monument to the Archbishops Giovanni, Guido Antonio and Giovanni Antonio Arcimboldi, by Galeazzo Alessi or Cristoforo Lombardo (1559), while the second bay (39) has two late 12th-c. pink marble reliefs (Eight Apostles) from Santa Maria Maggiore. The canopied baptistery (40) is by Tibaldi and stood in the nave until 1685. The font is an ancient Roman basin in porphyry. The first side bay is crossed by a meridian which was traced by astronomers from the observatory in Brera in 1786; it has been restored several times.

A staircase (41) leads down to the 4th-c. pavement level, about 4 m below the present level of the square. There are early Christian remains, with traces of the former octagonal baptistery, where tradition has it that Bishop Ambrose baptized, on the night of Easter Sunday in A.D. 378, the future St. Augustine; also visible are vestiges of the basilica of Santa Tecla.

Once the interior of the church has been seen, the elevator (10) in the north apse takes one up to the roof terraces, which offer a wonderful view over Milan, the Po Valley, and the distant Alps.

Weather and visibility permitting, from the rooftop toward the piazza one can see Novara straight ahead, Como to the right, Pavia to the left, and Brescia behind. From the crossing one can admire the spectacular octagonal **drum*** (see above), whose planning and construction (1490–1500), by the chief architect Giovanni Antonio Amadeo and his colleague Gian Giacomo Dolcebuono, was the crowning touch of the cathedral, and has animated Milan's skyline for five centuries. The tallest spires (108.5 m) connected to the drum by means of eight inverted arches, were not added until 1769, to designs by Francesco Croce. The statue of the Virgin, known as the Madonnina and considered one of the chief symbols of the city, is a gilded copper figure 4.16 m tall, made in 1774 by Giuseppe Bini after a model by Giuseppe Perego, and now boasts a framework of steel. There are four other spires around the drum, only one of which (northeast) was actually built when planned by Amadeo in 1507–18. The other three, and nearly all the

pinnacles for which the cathedral is famous, were added in the 19th c. The only exception is the so-called Carelli spire (built between 1397 and 1404) near the elevator, and some of the pinnacles near it four date from the 15th and 16th c., and were added over the ensuing two hundred years.

Palazzo Reale (I, D4-5), literally the "royal palace," standing next to the ecclesiastic complex of the archbishop's palace, is the traditional site of civic power, and was remodeled in rigorous neoclassical style (with a second order of Tuscan pilasters rising to include an attic) by Giuseppe Piermarini in 1772–78. The plan of the present building, which was partly based on the earlier residence of Azzone Visconti in 1330, was approved and perhaps modified by the Austrian chancellor, Anton Wenzel von Rietberg, Prince of Kaunitz, a statesman and powerful figure of the Viennese court. The building had served as the Milanese headquarters of the Holy Roman Empire (ruled at the time by Maria Theresa, who was very popular in Milan); two centuries earlier – from the definitive disappearance of the Duchy of Milan, until Austrian rule in 1757 – the palace had been home to the Spanish governors. It was enlarged in the 19th c. toward Via Larga (the back section was demolished in 1923), while the west wing of the front court was demolished in 1936 to make way for the eastern pavilion of the Arengario (Enrico Griffini, Pier Giulio Magistretti, Giovanni Muzio, and Piero Portaluppi, 1939–56). The building was severely damaged in 1943 by bombing, and has since been the subject of much controversy and endless restorations, which with scant regard for the refined interiors have made it an exhibition space, largely for temporary shows.

The first ramp of the broad steps of the Arengario leads up to the **Sala della Cariatidi***, the former ballroom that Piermarini created from a late 16th–early 17th-c. theater (the first permanent theater in Milan), which was destroyed by fire in 1776. This large hall is only open during temporary exhibitions, and it has been intentionally left in the state of disrepair caused by the bombing as a reminder of the evils of war.

The upper floor of the main palace houses the **Civico Museo di Arte Contemporanea**, the museum of contemporary art, which even in its limited size (promises to enlarge it since it was opened in 1983 have never been honored), affords an overview of 20th-c. Italian art. The various schools repesented include Futurism, Metaphysical painting, the Italian Novecento, Italian abstract painting, the Roman school, the Corrente, the Sei di Torino group, leading up to exponents of present-day styles. Most of the paintings come from private collections, and were either donated or purchased by the municipality; the artists include Boccioni (*Unique forms in the continuity of pace**), Osvaldo Licini (*Night**), Modigliani (*Portrait of Paul Guillaume*), de Chirico, Mario Sironi (*Urban landscape**), Carlo Carrà, Giorgio Morandi, Ottone Rosai, Filippo De Pisis, Lucio Fontana (*Spatial concept**),

the statues of St. Peter the Apostle (Jacobello Dalle Masegne, late 14th c.), St. Paul the Hermit (ca. 1470), and St. Agnes (attributed to Benedetto Briosco, 1491). There are also more modern exhibits including sketches and panels by Lucio Fontana, dated 1951–52.

The museum is run by the Veneranda Fabbrica del Duomo (headquartered in the building behind the cathedral's apse), the organism that has overseen the building of the cathedral since its foundation over six centuries ago. Among the many anecdotes of Milanese history concerning the Veneran-

The Palazzo Reale and forecourt

austo Melotti, Gastone Novelli (*King of Words**), and Tancredi. Note also the Jucker Collection.

Museo del Duomo* (I, D5). The best way to follow the complex history of the cathedral's construction is to visit the twenty-one rooms which make up this splendid museum in the east wing of Palazzo Reale. First opened in 1953, the collections were reorganized in the 1970s and comprise a chronological display of statues, architectural elements, and fragments of stained glass that were removed from the cathedral for conservation reasons. The museum also boasts a collection of wood models (see *Model of Duomo** by Bernardino Zenale 1519), plans for decorations, tapestries (15th-c. Flemish altarpiece featuring the Passion), hangings, liturgical vestments, furnishings, votive pieces – a total of 600 items. The statue of *Gian Galeazzo Visconti* first Duke of Milan and founder of the cathedral, by Giorgio Solari in 1404, once stood on the Carelli spire. Note the *Eternal Father** by Jacopino da Tradate (1416) and

da Fabbrica is the story of the transport of the great blocks of marble from Candoglia used in the cathedral, which traveled along Lake Maggiore, the Naviglio Grande, and then along the canals in the city to the building site. To indicate that this marble was exempt from taxes, the barges carried the initials A.U.F. ("Ad Usum Fabricæ," i.e., – for use in the cathedral yard), whence a typical local expression "a uf," meaning "free of charge."

San Gottardo in Corte (I, D5). In Via Pecorari behind the Palazzo Reale, which is reached by passing between Palazzo Reale and Palazzo Arcivescovile (see itinerary 1.3), stands the former church serving the palace of Azzone Visconti. Built in 1330–36, the church was all but swallowed up by the palace in the 18th c.: part of the facade of the church has become the wall of a stairway. You can still see the medieval apse and the graceful brick **campanile*** with its octagonal shape. It is well known in the city as the "campanile del Duomo." The *Gothic doorway* was added in 1929; in the neoclassical church interior note the stuccowork by Giocondo Albertolli and fragments of a fresco inspired by the school of Giotto, the *Crucifixion** and, on the left of the presbytery, a *monument to Azzone Visconti* by Giovanni Balducci, donated in 1930 by Alberico Trivulzio.

Piazza Diaz (I,D4). From the church of San Gottardo, after completing the circuit around the Palazzo Reale along Via Rastrelli (where one can see remains of the 14th-c. palace built by Azzone Visconti)

one comes out into a modern square created as part of the master plan of 193 Note the tall building of the *Terrazza Ma tini* (Luigi Mattioni, 1956) and the *Mon ment to the Carabiniere* (Luciano Minguzz 1980), its flame shape inspired by the em blem of the military police. Return now t Piazza del Duomo along Via Marconi, pass ing between the twin pavilions of the Are gario (see above). The eastern pavilio houses the tourist office, and at no. 3 is th entrance to the first-floor art gallery f temporary exhibitions.

1.2 Between the Duomo, Piazza della Scala, and San Babila

Through the luminous Galleria Vittorio Emanuele II (nicknamed the "drawing room" of Milan), one enters the elegant banking quarter, one of the most prestigious of the city. Although most of the buildings are no more than fifty years old, the area vaunts several buildings of signal architectural and historical importance, including the world-famous La Scala opera house, and the 16th-c. palace opposite, once the property of the Marino banking family (whence its name, Palazzo Marino) and now the seat of the city council.

After Piazza della Scala the itinerary follows two short routes, first toward San Babila and then back to the cathedral. These are among the finest shopping streets in Italy, together with the famous fashion enclave of Via Monte Napoleone. The area is a focus of

the service sector, and many banks an companies have their offices here. Few pe ple actually live in the area.

Galleria Vittorio Emanuele II* (I, C4). R ferred to locally as just "la Galleria," th monumental building with a glazed irc roof is a pedestrian mall linking Piazza d Duomo with Piazza della Scala. It is cros shaped (the longest arm is 196 m, the sho est 105 m) and its ground floor offers el gant restaurants, cafes and shops, includi several bookstores run by Italy's maj publishing houses. The Galleria wa planned as a covered street to honor t Austrian Emperor Franz Joseph in 185 construction actually began under the d rection of Giuseppe Mengoni in 1864, who so redeveloped Piazza del Duomo over th

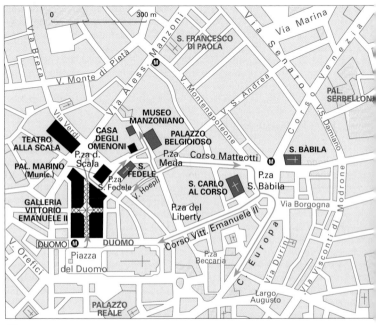

The entrance of the Galleria Vittorio Emanuele II from Piazza del Duomo

same period. Though completed posthumously in 1878 after the architect's death (Mengoni fell off scaffolding on the site), the mall was opened to the public in the year 1867. The showy new environment delighted the Milanese public and it became one of the symbols of Milan at the turn of the century. It could perhaps be paired historically and architecturally with the equally famous Stazione Centrale as an example of those large-scale buildings which, while not possessing particular architectural merits, are successful in their use of size and detail (see the dome and pavement of the central octagon in the Galleria), and fire the local imagination.

Piazza della Scala (I, C4). The square at the north end of the Galleria Vittorio Emanuele II contains a modest *monument to Leonardo da Vinci* (Pietro Magni, 1872), surrounded by four of his most famous pupils. The square was created in 1858 with the demolition of the building between the opera house and Palazzo Marino (see below). The most immediately imposing building overlooking the square is, however, the one opposite the gallery entrance, the *Palazzo della Banca Commerciale Italiana*, by Luca Beltrami (1907), built on the site of the church of San Giovanni Decollato "alle Case Rotte" (the demolished church was one of Ricchino's finest works; the street next to Palazzo Marino bears its name). The Banca Commerciale is one of the largest banks in Italy and plays a leading role in corporate finance in this country. It was founded in 1894 with German capital and is respected in the city for the independence of judgment and farsighted policies of its post-war president, Raffaele Mattioli (1895–1973).

Teatro alla Scala* (I, B-C4). On the site of a 14th-c. church commissioned by Beatrice Regina della Scala, wife of Bernabò Visconti, the Austrian government commissioned a new theater from Piermarini (the architect who remodeled Palazzo Reale) in 1776–78. The theater was technically advanced and quickly put Milan at the forefront of European culture. Although the facade is not particularly impressive (it originally gave onto a street, not a square), the theater's classic horseshoe **auditorium*** is a fabulous sight, with four tiers of boxes and two galleries (originally the ceiling concealed a huge water tank for extinguishing fires), one of the largest theater stages in Italy (780 sq.m, including backstage facilities). But its most important feature is the auditorium's extraordinary acoustics. There are plans to completely renovate the theater; performances will be transferred to the Zona Bicocca (see p. 117).
The decorations (designed by Alessandro Sanquirico, 1830), the famous central chandelier (Sanquirico, replaced in 1860), and the alterations to the foyer (1878, modernized in 1936) date from the 19th c. The building was partially destroyed in 1943, but was among the first structures to be rebuilt after the war. In a short space of time, the old theater was replaced by a perfect replica. The legendary conductor, Arturo Toscanini, who went into voluntary exile in the Fascist period, reopened the opera house with a memorable concert in 1946. La Scala has always been the most famous opera house in Italy, partly because of the glamorous premieres that take place on 7 December each year, to coincide with the feast of St. Ambrose, Milan's patron saint. In the past it saw the world premier performances of such operas as Rossini's *Turco in Italia* and *La Gazza Ladra* by Rossini, Belli-

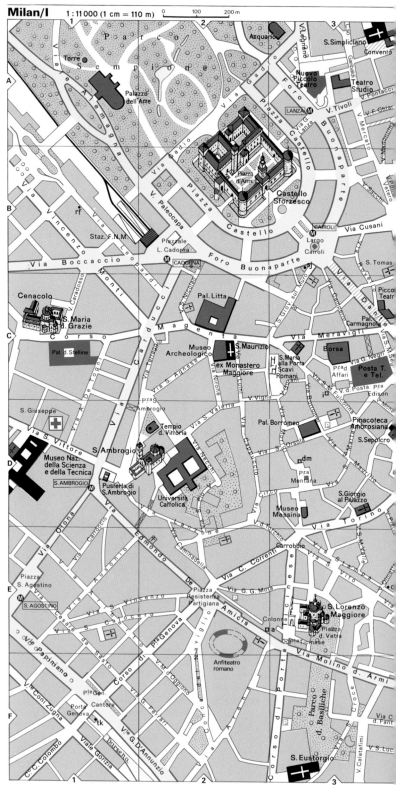

Milan/I   1:11 000 (1 cm = 110 m)   0   100   200 m

44

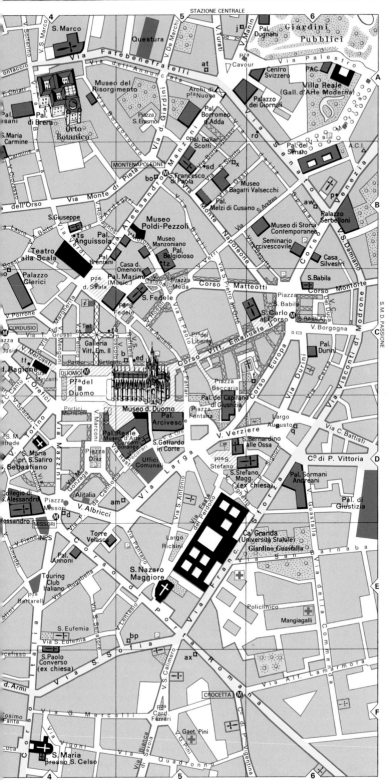

STAZIONE CENTRALE

45

The entrance to the La Scala opera house

ni's *Il Pirata* and *Norma*; Donizetti's *Lucrezia Borgia*; Verdi's *Otello* and *Falstaff*; Amilcare Ponchielli's *La Gioconda*; Arrigo Boito's *Mephistopheles*; Puccini's *Madame Butterfly* and *Turandot*; and Umberto Giordano's *Andrea Chénier*. La Scala has also helped to rid the Italian opera scene of lingering provincialism by staging operas by Wagner, Gounod, Tchaikovsky, Richard Strauss, Debussy and Alban Berg. It has also performed less traditional Italian works by such modern composers as Luigi Nono, Luciano Berio, and Sylvano Bussotti. The reaction of the audience at La Scala is often decisive for the success of a production or singer's performance, despite the endless controversies over the judgment of the fanatics up in the galleries, who are known to heckle and shout out their opinions.

Museo Teatrale alla Scala* Inaugurated in 1911, the small museum installed in the opera house carries a collection of documents and objects from Milanese and international operatic history, plus a library of over 90,000 books. The fourteen rooms, two of which are dedicated to Verdi (Raccolta Verdiana), contain portraits of musicians, musical instruments, rare relics of Greek and Roman theater, costumes, models and sketches for stage designs, writings and original manuscripts, posters and other printed matter concerning opera. After the Brera Gallery, this museum is one of the most popular with foreign visitors.

Palazzo Marino* (C4-5). Although the attractive facade that overlooks the Piazza della Scala is the result of remodeling by Luca Beltrami in 1872–92, the municipal council building is one of the finest examples of 16th-c. architecture in Milan. Tomaso Marino commissioned Galeazzo Alessi for the job in 1553, but he only managed to complete the facade overlooking Piazza San Fedele before he died, nineteen years later. In the following decades only the original facade overlooking Via Marino was completed, along with the courtyard (1588). This is accessed from Piazza della Scala, and presents an arcaded ground story of Tuscan columns bearing a loggia of pilasters set with niches bordered with herms supporting tablets. Of the building's many rooms, only the *Sala delle Feste* is open to visitors (now the Sala dell'Alessi), modified in the 19th c., the ceiling of which was destroyed in 1943. The facade abutting Piazza San Fedele, whose construction which was personally overseen by Alessi, is on three orders, with columns and pilasters framing rusticated windows with balustrade and pediment. The palace was taken over as the seat of the municipal council soon after this was formed, when Milan came under the rule of the House of Savoy (1859).

Piazza San Fedele (I, C4-5). Repaved and converted into a pedestrian promenade, conserving the *monument to Alessandro Manzoni* (Francesco Barzaghi, 1883), the small square in front of the most authentic facade of Palazzo Marino is also abutted by the church of **San Fedele** (I, C5) with its double order and large central tympanum; like the palace, the church dates from the 16th c., and was commissioned by the Jesuit Order from Pellegrino Tibaldi in 1559; work continued under the architect Martino Bassi, and Ricchino was responsible for the fine dome. The apse was built in 1723 and the facade was not added until 1835, in accordance with the original design. The church has a single nave with side altars and chapels, in keeping with the influential instructions of Cardinal Carlo Borromeo. San Fedele served as a model for many Lombard churches of the Counter-Reformation. The Mannerist influence of the period is seen in the work of Bernardino Campi (the four saints at the sides of the south altar and, in the atrium, the altarpiece with the *Transfiguration*); the *Vision of St. Ignatius* by Cerano dates from the 17th c. The atrium leads to the *sacristy* * by Ricchino (1624–28), with 17th-c. cabinets.

Casa degli Omenoni* (I, B–C5). Behind San Fedele a little street leads past the modern *tower* devised by Piero Portaluppi from the Banca Commerciale Italiana to Piazza Belgioioso. The street is named after a house in which the sculptor Leone Leoni lived and worked, dubbed the "Casa degli Omenoni" after the eight muscular telamones on the facade sculpted by Antonio Abbondio. Built in 1565, the house was frequented by illustrious personalities of the day, including Giorgio Vasari, and encapsulates the artistic personality of its inhabitant, who was well positioned at the Spanish court. The sculptor also made the central figure of the Medici monument in Milan Cathedral, and a set of bronze figures for the Escorial, Madrid. The interior of the house (privately owned) was reworked in the 1920s by Portaluppi.

Piazza Belgioioso (I, B-C5). This square is a poignant reminder of quiet, 18th-c. Milan, despite the cars that frequently tear through it today. It takes its name from the building on the northeast side, **Palazzo Belgioioso**, which was assigned to Giuseppe Piermarini in 1772 by Alberico XII di Belgioioso d'Este; this town-house one is of the largest and most typical examples of Lombard neoclassicism. The facade is divided by rusticated pilasters, with a central section framed by columns surmounted by a tympanum; inside are three courtyards, the largest with two Doric arcades.

Museo Manzoniano (I, B5). The museum devoted to the life and works of Alessandro Manzoni is lodged in a building overlooking Piazza Belgioioso, with its entrance on Via Morone. Here the much-loved Milanese writer and poet lived from 1814 until his death on 22 May 1873. Exhibited in the furnished rooms of Manzoni's home are documents, objects, pictures and writings belonging to the writer. The Centro Nazionale di Studi Manzoniani, and the Società Storica Lombarda, with its library of 40,000 books and 30,000 pamphlets, occupy the same building.

Corso Matteotti (I, C5-6). The former Corso del Littorio – as it was known when it was built (1926–34) – was made possible by knocking down a considerable number of buildings; it runs from Piazza Meda to Piazza San Babila (I, C5). In the middle of Piazza Meda is a sculpture by Arnaldo Pomodoro, entitled *The Sun* (1980); overlooking the square are several major banking headquarters, including the *Banca Popo-*

lare di Milano (Giovanni Greppi, 1928–31), while toward the rear of San Fedele is the curved glass-and-iron building, originally belonging to the *Chase Manhattan Bank* (Lodovico Belgiojoso, Enrico Peresutti, and Ernesto Nathan Rogers, 1958–69).

Via Ulrico Hoepli, a short street, starts on the corner of the former Chase Manhattan Bank; at no. 5 is the Hoepli building (Luigi Figini and Gino Pollini, 1955–57), headquarters of the publishing house founded in 1870 by the Swiss Hoepli family. Hoepli was considered the best publisher in Italy between the wars; although Hoepli still has a reputation for publishing, its main concern is the bookstore, one of the largest and best-stocked in Italy. The important cultural center of the *Jesuits of San Fedele* occupies the same building.

Corso Matteotti features examples of architecture from the 1920s and 1930s. Note the block (Emilio Lancia, 1933–36) between Via San Pietro all'Orto and Via Monte Napoleone, and the *Snia Viscosa* office tower (Alessandro Rimini, 1935–37) at no. 11.

Piazza San Babila (I, C6). In the earliest records of the city, this square was the main point of arrival in Milan from the Brianza district (see itinerary 2.2) and a vital focus of the city. In late Roman times the River Seveso entered Maximian's walls at this point. The square takes its name from the basilica of **San Babila**, before which stands a column topped by a lion, the *Colonna del Leone* (Giuseppe Robecco, 1626), the lion being the ancient emblem of the district of Porta Orientale (now Porta Venezia). The church was built in the 11th c., rebuilt in 1575, and completed in 1610 with a new facade by Aurelio Trezzi. Further work was done to it in 1853 and 1906, with the illusory hope of restoring its appearance in the year 1000; the result is another example of misconceived restoration, an all too common sight in Milan. The square is rather dominated by the tall buildings of the *Palazzo del Toro* (Emilio Lancia and Raffaele Merendi, 1935–39), which contains the Teatro Nuovo, and the arcaded building opposite (Gio Ponti, 1939–49).

The broad Corso Europa (I, C-D5-6) leads from Piazza San Babila to Via Larga (see itinerary 1.3). It was created with the master plan of 1934. There are various examples of Milanese architecture of the 1950s and 1960s (no. 22 by Vico Magistretti, 1955–57; nos. 18–20 and 10–12 by Luigi Caccia Dominioni and Agostino Agostini, 1953–59); nos. 11 and 13 also by Caccia Dominioni, 1963–66), and at no. 16 a fine example of late

16th–early 17th-c. architecture, the **Palazzo Litta Cusini**, which boasts a beautiful neoclassical hall.

Corso Vittorio Emanuele II* (I, C5-6). Piazza San Babila is now connected to Piazza del Duomo by a pedestrian promenade, today one of the most busy streets of Milan (excellent shops along the arcades and side galleries, and numerous movie theaters). On a more poetic note, the Corso offers one of the most significant views of the apse and the dome of the cathedral. The street was previously called Corso dei Servi because of the Servite monastery of Santa Maria; now standing on that site is the present-day church of *San Carlo al Corso*, a circular neoclassical temple with a tall Corinthian portico, designed by Carlo Amati and built 1839–47.

The Galleria del Corso, which leads to Piazza Beccaria (see itinerary 1.3), is of no real architectural interest, but some of the leading Italian recording companies of the postwar period had their offices here (see the large store *Messaggerie Musicali*, a reminder of the mall's history). Under the arcades opposite (which date from after the war) at no. 13 stands a *Roman statue* known as the "Omm de Preja," or "Man of stone." At no. 8 note the recomposed facade of the *former Bonomi department store* (1902–7).

Piazza Liberty (I, C5) to one side of the Corso takes its name from the decorations of the Hotel Trianon ("Liberty" is the Italian form of Art Nouveau), which were transferred to a post-war building in 1955. Before the war the hotel faced onto the Corso. At no. 10 in Via San Paolo nearby stands the fine late 16th-c. Palazzo Spinola, largely rebuilt after the war.

1.3 Between the Duomo, Ca' Granda, and Piazza Missori

The area just southeast of the cathedral was where the ring of navigable canals (replaced by roads 1928–30), arrived nearest to the cathedral and the other political and religious buildings of the city center. All that is left today of the so-called Cerchia dei Navigli, or ring of canals that circled the center of Milan and once served as a vital defensive moat, is its informal name. Now it is a busy circuit choked by town traffic and buses.

This section of that ring road is named after Francesco Sforza (1401–66), the grand duke who built the Ca' Granda (now the University of Milan), once one of Italy's finest and largest hospitals. After the Ca' Granda the

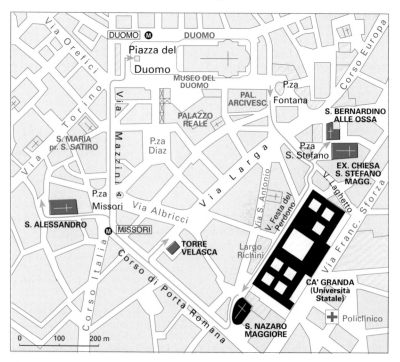

ring of canals is crossed by Corso di Porta Romana, a road that is first mentioned in a document dating from the 2nd c. as the "Via Porticata to Rome." This street, now a busy radial thoroughfare lined with shops, but also with the first residential buildings so far in this itinerary, leads more or less straight to Piazza del Duomo.

Piazza Fontana (I, D5). The large complex of the **Palazzo Arcivescovile** or Archiepiscopal Palace occupies the site next to the cathedral between the Palazzo Reale and Piazza Fontana. The square has a deep significance for Italy. A bomb exploded in the Banca dell'Agricoltura on 12 December 1969, heralding a spell of dire political unrest. Today, however, the square is a peaceful place to stop, and boasts a fountain (Giuseppe Piermarini, 1782) – something of a rarity in Milan. Abutting the square is the headquarters of the Curia, with a facade by Piermarini (1784), and a 16th-c. doorway by Pellegrino Tibaldi. The palace, where the archdiocese was governed by Saint Charles Borromeo (1560–84), and later by his cousin Federico (1595–1632), and more recently by Giovanni Battista Montini (later Pope Paul VI, 1963–78), was built in the early Middle Ages, and rebuilt in 1174 after the sack of Milan by Frederick I Barbarossa. Extensive work was carried out in the mid-14th c. and late 15th c. Most of what you see today is the work of Tibaldi who started the project in 1569; note the superb Cortile della Canonica*, visible from the entrance at no. 16, Piazza del Duomo.

The palace contains an **art gallery** begun in the 17th c. by Cardinal Monti. It is difficult to visit because the building is occupied by private offices and apartments. The collection includes paintings by Tintoretto, Morazzone, Cerano, Giulio Cesare Procaccini, Spagnoletto, and Guido Reni. It was the largest collection in Milan at the time, and is still considered of great importance, though much of the original collection went to the Pinacoteca di Brera in the 19th c., especially the examples of Renaissance art.

Piazza Beccaria (I, C5). Large flower beds separate Piazza Fontana from the *ex Palazzo del Capitano di Giustizia* (I, C-D5), begun in 1578 and now the headquarters of the Municipal Police. Next to it is *Piazza Beccaria*; at no. 8 stands the auditorium of the *Teatro Gerolamo*, now declared unsafe and closed to the public. In the center of the square is a copy of the monument (by Giuseppe Grandi, 1871) to *Cesare Beccaria*, the Milanese lawyer (1738–94) who advocated reduced punishment for less serious crimes, and also advanced the notion that capital punishment should be replaced by incarceration, with the goal of reeducating the criminal.

Santo Stefano Maggiore (I, D5-6). Beyond the traffic in **Via Larga** (widened in 1953, but once the outer perimeter of medieval *Mediolanum*), a building dating from the 1960s conceals the historical marketplace of **Piazza Santo Stefano** (I, D5). The square is dominated by the 17th-c. facade and campanile of the church of Santo Stefano. The early Christian church (5th c.) was damaged by fire in 1075, and rebuilt in 1584 by Aurelio Trezzi. No longer used for religious services, it now houses the *Historical Archives of the Diocese*. In the sacristy are paintings by Camillo Procaccini (or attributed to him). Alongside stands the late 17th–early 18th-c. church of *San Bernardino alle Ossa,* conserving an ossuary dating from 1695 containing human bones from old cemeteries in the city; there is also a *fresco* by Sebastiano Ricci. Abutting the square are several old residential buildings, but only those owned by the city have been properly restored.

Ca' Granda* (I, D-E5). Beyond the little *Via Laghetto* (so called because of a small lake

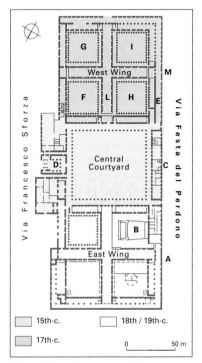

Plan of the Ca' Granda

that was once linked to the system of canals) lies Via Festa del Perdono, which passes (282 m) along the front of a building that boasts a surface area of over 43,000 sq. m – the largest structure in Milan after the Castello Sforzesco. Since 1958 it has housed the **University of Milan** (Università Statale), but for the previous five centuries it was the "Ca' Granda," the main hospital. Its origins date back to around 1456, when Francesco Sforza commissioned the court

The ornamental terracotta facade of the Ca' Granda

architect Filarete (Antonio Averlino) to build a new hospital for the poor of Milan. Although Filarete personally supervised work on the hospital until 1465 and, in his treatise on architecture, set forth detailed plans for the two cross-structures with a central courtyard (see plan page 49), work on the building actually continued until the 19th c., meaning that there were many alterations to the original plans, according to the fashions of each period. Heavy war damage has added to the general destruction of the original works, such that today's building is a palimpsest of overlapping reconstructions.

In 1939 the hospital facilities were transferred to Niguarda, on the outskirts of the city. Some parts of the Ca' Granda are still used for the administrative offices of the hospital, however, and some departments are located in the nearby Policlinico on what was the opposite side of the canal.

At Via Festa del Perdono 3 (A, in the plan) rises the facade of the section that completed the hospital in the neoclassic period (1797–1804). Now totally rebuilt, it houses the lecture halls of the department of literature and philosophy and the school of

law, as well as the main lecture hall (Aula Magna) of the University (B), recently restored after heavy use over the last thirty years for student demonstrations. Next comes the 17th-c. central block, with a Baroque *portal* (C) at no. 7, with two rows of columns and niches containing statues. Beyond the portal lies the superb arcaded **courtyard*** with first-floor loggias, built in the 17th c. by Francesco Maria Ricchino, Fabio Mangone, and Giovan Battista Pessina, integrating surviving 15th-c. decorations. Opposite the entrance is the church of the *Annunciazione* (D), with a painting by Giovanni Francesco Guercino over the altar. A doorway at the far right-hand corner (E) leads to the courtyards of the 15th-c. wing (F-I), restored and surrounded by libraries and offices belonging to the departments of the humanities. They are separated by the northern arms of the cross (L) of the ancient hospital, only recently restored, and now occupied by the university. From Largo Richini one can observe the 15th-c. wing (M) with Filarete's elegant arcaded facade, with terracotta profiles designed by Guiniforte Solari, mullioned windows and decorative terracotta cornice. The decorations of the central block, built two centuries later, were inspired by this original section of the building.

San Nazaro Maggiore* (I, E5). Next to the Ca' Granda, further on along the Largo Richini, one comes to the apse of the church of *San Nazaro Maggiore*, also known as *San Nazaro in Brolo*. This was once the Basilica Apostolorum, one of the four basilicas *extra mœnia* (without the walls) founded by Bishop Ambrose. It has a central plan, and was built in the 11th c. and later transformed by Archbishop Carlo Borromeo in 1571. It was restored in 1946 and 1963. The entrance on Corso di Porta Romana (see below) is remarkable for the square **Cappella Trivulzio ***, which was added in 1512–50. This is the only known architectural project by Bartolomeo Bramantino, and was left unfinished. The octagonal chapel was commissioned as a sepulcher for the family of Gian Giacomo Trivulzio (1441–1518). Beyond the chapel, the church itself has a single nave and apsed transepts, a large drum, and a deep main apse. The nave is decorated with frescoes by Daniele Crespi, and paintings by Procaccini (*Presentation at the Temple*) and Giuseppe Nuvolone. In the north transept, where behind the semicircular altar is a canvas by Bernardino Luini, one passes into the 16th-c. chapel of St. Catherine of Alexandria, frescoed with *Martyrdom of the Saint** (1546). From the presbytery, with an 18th-c. altar, one can observe a small archaeological collection and the little 10th-c. basilica of San Lino. In the right transept, is a *Last Supper* by Lanino, in the right exedra.

Corso di Porta Romana (I, E-F4-6). The yellow line 3 of the subway travels under one of the most ancient Milanese roads. Traces of prehistoric remains have come to light near the church of San Nazaro discussed above. The city toward which this street ran (Rome, capital of the empire from Augustus on, and of present-day Italy) has given its name to the entire quarter, and to each of the successive city gates, built progressively further out as the city expanded. Of these gateways, only the 16th-c. Porta Romana survives (see itinerary 2.3), once part of the so-called Spanish bastions. At the city end of the Corso stand several elegant old buildings, notably *Palazzo Annoni* at no. 6 (I, E4) by Francesco Maria Ricchino (1631); opposite at no. 3 is the 17th-c. *Palazzo Acerbi*.

Torre Velasca (I, E4). This odd-looking building stands higher than the nearby Madonnina crowning the cathedral. Built for apartments and offices, the tower has 28 stories, plus deep basements, and takes its name from the square at its feet, which was created in 1651 by the Spanish governor, Juan de Velasco. The tower (Lodovico Belgiojoso, Enrico Peresutti, and Ernesto Nathan Rogers, 1956–60) widens at the eighteenth floor, a feature that posed innumerable problems for the structural engineer, Arturo Danusso, in the calculation of the stresses and loads. It also makes this building one of the most interesting structures ever constructed in reinforced concrete. The Torre Velasca has become symbolic of Milanese postwar architecture and design, owing to its distinctive silhouette and the materials with which it was built. The building's merits are offset by the prohibitive costs of maintaining the upper floors, a sign of the architects' overestimation of modern technology.

Piazza Missori (I, D-E4). Corso di Porta Romana begins in a large formless square named after General Missori (1829–1911), who served under Garibaldi and is featured in the central *monument* (1916). The start of Via Albricci is divided by the *remains of the apse* of the old medieval church of San Giovanni in Conca, almost entirely demolished in the 19th c. to create Via Mazzini; the facade is now in Via Francesco Sforza, near the Ca' Granda.

A tiny road near the newspaper kiosk leads to Piazza Sant'Alessandro, which takes its name from the church of **Sant'Alessandro** (I, D4), begun in 1601 by the Order of the Barnabites. It was built on a central plan by Lorenzo Binago along the lines of the designs of Bramante and Michelangelo for the basilica of St. Peter's in Rome, but a second Greek cross has been integrated into the main plan. Francesco Maria Ricchino and his son (until 1659) supervised the project; the dome was built in 1694 and the facade in 1710. None of the works inside are particularly noteworthy except for the paintings by Procaccini (3rd chapel on the right, the chapel at the entrance to the sacristy, and the 1st chapel on left) and Daniele Crespi (3rd chapel on the right), but the church offers good examples of 17th-c. and 18th-c. Milanese art. At no. 6 *Palazzo Trivulzio* (1707–13) overlooks the square, its lush gardens partially visible behind the facade.

From Piazza Missori return to the cathedral along **Via Mazzini** (I, D4), formerly Via Carlo Alberto, built in 1878. An observant eye will note the Bramantesque chapel on the left and superb Romanesque campanile, belonging to the church of Santa Maria presso San Satiro (see itinerary 1.4).

The Torre Velasca

1.4 From the Duomo to Cordusio and the Carrobbio

In the early 13th c. the Commune, or city government, of Milan, which had recently won its freedom from the "German" Emperor at Legnano in 1176, acquired its own headquarters (a square, with a court for the magistrates) not far from the cathedral. This was the new town hall (Broletto Nuovo), now in what is Piazza Mercanti. Its precursor, the Broletto Vecchio had stood next to the cathedral on the site of the present-day Palazzo Reale. The Commune had a short life, however. In less than a century the powerful Visconti had taken over the city, and the activity of the councilors of the Broletto was restricted to legal and commercial matters.

From the square of the medieval Commune our itinerary proceeds toward a district to the south west of the center, where we find other seats of power. Here one can see the intermingling of the quarters constructed by the great Borromeo family whose two archbishops (Carlo, later Saint Charles Borromeo, and his younger cousin Federico) effectively governed Milan from the 16th c. to the 17th c. Here also is the financial core of Milan, the site of the Stock Exchange, which has made Milan the financial capital of Italy. A series of winding historical streets lead back to the cathedral, marred here and there by 19th-c. and modern buildings (often filling the gaps left by bomb damage).

Nearby, the ancient thoroughfare of Via Torino features several churches that should not be missed.

Piazza Mercanti (I, C4). Present-day *Via Mercanti* runs from Piazza del Duomo to Piazza Cordusio, passing between Palazzo della Ragione (on the left, see below) and **Palazzo dei Giureconsulti**, which has been altered several times since it was built in 1561, once in the 19th c. when it became the stock exchange, and more recently, when it was converted into the Chamber of Commerce. Although it is hard to envision now, prior to 1867 Via Mercanti was actually the north side of the little piazza, and had been one of the busiest places in Milan since the 13th c. In order to build the new street, the archway to the Peschiera Vecchia quarter was demolished (A, in plan p. 54), together with the Fustagnari gate on the opposite side (C). But these were not the only transformations to the area over the last 130 years. In 1872 the Banca Rasini (now no. 7 on the square) took over the site of the 14th-c. Portico della Ferrata, of which only the facade survives. In 1904 the Loggia degli Osii (no. 9) was rebuilt, changing the original ground plan of 1316. By 1896 all that was left of the Palazzo delle Scuole Palatine (no. 11), built in the 17th c. by Carlo Buzzi on the site of the Azzone por-

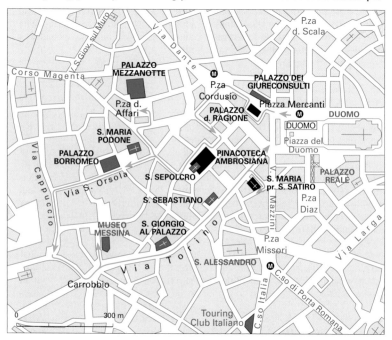

The Palazzo della Ragione in Piazza Mercanti

tico, was the facade. In 1899, Luca Beltrami started rebuilding the Casa dei Panigarola (no. 17). The modern atmosphere is completed by a restaurant that spills over into the square in the summer, and a fast-food outlet on the Piazza del Duomo side.

Palazzo della Ragione* (I, C4) is one of the finest examples of the type of town hall that was built in medieval northern Italy, known as the Broletto or magistrates' court. The building stands on an arcade of seven bays supporting a single large vessel, built for the city judiciary, whence the name Palazzo della Ragione, denoting the place where the men of law proclaimed their verdicts on controversial matters. It was built in 1233 by Oldrato da Tresseno (figured in the *equestrian monument* on the panel facing the square). As part of the general modernization drive under the Austrians, in 1771–73 the building gained another floor, designed by Francesco Croce, with large elliptical windows. The new story housed the archives of the city notaries. During World War II the main archives were housed in the new court of justice. The Palazzo della Ragione is now used for temporary exhibitions, and has been restored (Alberto Grimoldi, Marco Dezzi Bardeschi, Paolo Farina, and Lorenzo Berni, 1981–86). Memorial plaques on the pillars of the arcade (1952) commemorate Milanese soldiers who fell in the war.

Piazza Cordusio (I, C4). The name Cordusio is a popularization of the Latin *curtis ducis*, i.e., the duke's court, an expression used during the Longobard period. Today the former court is an ellipse surrounded by rather ostentatious 19th-c. and 20th-c. buildings, notably the palazzi of the *Assicurazioni Generali* (Luca Beltrami, at no. 2), the *Credito Italiano* (Luigi Broggi, between Via Tommaso Grossi and Via Broletto), and the Post Office (Broggi), all erected in 1901. The last building mentioned, now completely refurbished, was originally built as the Milan stock exchange's third site; the first was in Monte di Pietà (the street has had the same name since 1808), and the second was lodged in the Palazzo dei Giureconsulti. The buildings on this piazza were made to house financial institutions, and still do.

Pinacoteca Ambrosiana* (I, D3-4). In the middle of the financial district stands the *Palazzo dell'Ambrosiana* in Piazza Pio XI. Recently completely renovated both inside and out, the Ambrosiana was Milan's first art gallery, commissioned originally for religious purposes by Cardinal Federico Borromeo (1564–1631) from Lelio Buzzi and Francesco Maria Ricchino. The primary function of the *Biblioteca Ambrosiana* or library, whose collection was acquired by Federico's agents, sent all over Europe and the Far East, was to collect documents that might help in the correct interpretation of the Holy Scriptures, particularly with an eye to the ongoing disputations with Protestant reformers. Today the library possesses some 35,000 manuscripts and 750,000 printed works; notably, Arabic and Hebrew

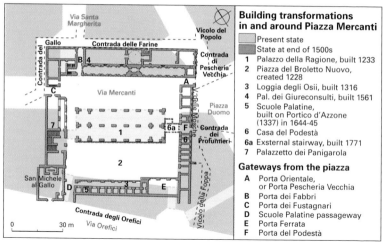

Building transformations in and around Piazza Mercanti

- Present state
- State at end of 1500s

1 Palazzo della Ragione, built 1233
2 Piazza del Broletto Nuovo, created 1228
3 Loggia degli Osii, built 1316
4 Pal. dei Giureconsulti, built 1561
5 Scuole Palatine, built on Portico d'Azzone (1337) in 1644-45
6 Casa del Podestà
6a Exsternal stairway, built 1771
7 Palazzetto dei Panigarola

Gateways from the piazza

A Porta Orientale, or Porta Pescheria Vecchia
B Porta dei Fabbri
C Porta dei Fustagnari
D Scuole Palatine passageway
E Porta Ferrata
F Porta del Podestà

0   30 m

treasures, palimpsests of Plautus and Cicero, Syriac and Gothic bibles, and codices dating as late as the 16th c. (including the renowned **Codice Atlantico** by Leonardo da Vinci, the largest collection of his notes and drawings) and hundreds of drawings by Renaissance and Baroque masters.

Some years later, its founder donated an art collection to the library, adding his personal collection in 1618. This was the original core of the gallery, which boasts works by Sandro Botticelli (*Tondo of the Madonna with Child and Angels*), Domenico Ghirlandaio (*Nativity*), Leonardo da Vinci (attrib., *Portrait of a Musician*), Bartolomeo Vivarini (*Polyptych*), Ambrogio Bergognone (*Madonna, Angels and Saints*) Bernardino Luini (*Young St. John*), Bartolomeo Bramantino (*Adoration of the Child*), Raphael (**cartoon** * for the School of Athens), Alessandro Magnasco, Giambattista Tiepolo (*Presentation in the Temple, Canonized Bishop*), Caravaggio (*Basket of Fruit* *), Federico Barocci (*Nativity*), Moretto (*St. Peter Martyr*), Pier Francesco Morazzone (*Adoration of the Magi*), Giovanni Battista Moroni (*Portrait of a Gentleman*), Titian (*Epiphany**, Ecce Homo*), Jacopo Bassano (*Adoration of the Shepherds, Annunciation to the Shepherds*), Bonifacio Veronese, Tanzio da Varallo, Daniele Crespi (*Madonna and Saints*), Cerano (*St. Ambrose*), together with a substantial group of Flemish and Dutch works (Joos van Cleve, Jan Bruegel).

The church of *San Sepolcro* (I, D3) is more or less integrated with the complex of the Ambrosiana, and dates as far back as the year 1000. The interior was altered in 1605 by Aurelio Trezzi; the facade in the 18th c., and again in 1897. In the apse of the *crypt* (the only remaining part of the original temple) is a 16th-c. *Deposition** in terracotta. The forum of imperial Roman Milan ran through Piazza San Sepolcro. Opposite the church is the 18th-c. *Palazzo Castani*, where the first meetings of the Fascist party were held in 1919.

Piazza degli Affari (I, C3). Built in 1928-40, the heart of the financial district (indeed, "affari" means "business" in Italian) has never been completed. An office block by Emilio Lancia (1939) which divides the square from Via della Posta, stands opposite the Milan Stock Exchange (Paolo Mezzanotte, 1931); it was stripped of its traditional "corbeilles" in 1991-94 when the exchange was computerized, and is now called *Palazzo Mezzanotte*, after its creator. The underground ruins behind the travertine facade hide the remains of a *Roman theater*, probably 1st c. A.D. but dismantled by the 12th c., and a cobbled way of the same period.

Palazzo Borromeo (I, D3). In the small square in Via Sant'Orsola stands the *church of Santa Maria Podone*, founded in the 10th c., restored in the 15th c. and again in 1626 by Fabio Mangone. The motto "Humilitas" on the facade marks its history, like that of the square, as property of the Borromeo family. It did not become public property until 1976. At no. 7 stands the palace of the famous Borromeo family. The palazzo was severely damaged in the war, and was completely rebuilt. The 17th-c. brick facade is noteworthy, the doorway is some two hundred years older, and original *frescoes* from the mid-15th c. decorate one of the first-floor offices on the courtyard, featuring pastimes from Milanese aristocratic life.

Via Cappuccio (I, D2). The area to the west of Palazzo Borromeo is relatively intact. Via Sant'Orsola crosses *Via Morigi* (I, D3); note the 18th-c. buildings at nos. 8 and 9, and the Roman pavement under the portico of no. 2/a; Via Sant'Orsola leads into Via Cappuccio, with patrician palazzi at nos. 21, 18, 13, and 7. After Via Cappuccio comes Via Circo (I, D2-3) so called because of the huge Roman circus (80 m x 505 m) built in the reign of Maximian (A.D. 286-305). Some of the stones are still visible in the little patch of land left after the irresponsible construction of a new building on the corner with Via del Torchio (I, D-E2-3).

Via Torino (I, D-E3-4). At the crossroads known as the **Carrobbio** (I, E3), the start of the road from Roman *Mediolanum* to the town of Pavia, begins the ever-busy Via Torino (closed to traffic in 1996). In the 19th c. stagecoaches arrived and left from here; now it's lined with shops and stores of all kinds. The street curves past the former 17th-c. church of San Sisto (now the *museum of Francesco Messina's sculptures*; I, D3); further up stands the church of **San Giorgio al Palazzo** (I, D3). Originally dating from the late Middle Ages, but now notably Baroque in appearance, the church was built in 750, rebuilt in 1129, and transformed in 1623 by Francesco Maria Ricchino; the present facade was designed in 1774 by Francesco Croce; in 1899 the transept, dome and campanile were altered by Alfonso Perrucchetti. The neoclassical interior is by Luigi Cagnola (1800-21); note the 3rd chapel on the south side, with a beautiful cycle by Bernardino Luini (*Stories of the Passion*).
Continuing along the Via Torino, after the intersection with Via della Palla, stands the cylindrical church of **San Sebastiano** (I, D4). A votive construction built to commemorate the city's salvation from the plague in 1576, the church still belongs to the municipality. It was planned by Tibaldi but left unfinished, modified by Martino Bassi and Fabio Mangone, and now contains many works of art from the 17th and 18th-c. Lombard school.

Santa Maria presso San Satiro* (I, D4). One of the best-known Renaissance churches in Milan is set back from Via Torino, and is the work of the architect Donato Bramante. On the site of a basilica founded by the archbishop Ansperto in 879, construction of the church designed by Bramante began in 1476-77. Bramante's involvement is documented from 1482. Its present-day appearance is, however, due to extensive restoration work done over the past two centuries.
It has a barrel-vaulted nave and two aisles. Because of the lack of space, on the back wall behind the altar Bramante designed an ingenious trompe-l'œil **presbytery***, which is perfectly convincing from the nave. On the main altar is a votive fresco from the 13th c., detached from the exterior wall of the chapel of Sant'Ansperto. At the end of the right transept is a marble group by Antonio Carminati, 1891 (*St. Louis Gonzaga helping a victim of the plague*). The left transept gives onto the **Cappella di Ansperto** (*Pietà*; group of fourteen terracotta figures,

Bramante's illusionistic apse in Santa Maria presso San Satiro

1482-83) by Agostino De' Fondutis. From the right aisle you can enter the sublime octagonal baptistery (or sacristy) by Bramante, comprising two orders of pilasters and a dome, but with the 19th-c. addition of a terracotta frieze by De' Fondutis. A door on the left of the main altar leads out to Via Falcone, where the rear of the church is decorated with pilasters and capitals, and a tympanum marking the false presbytery.
Via Mazzini allows a clear view of the harmonious exterior of the Cappella di Ansperto, with its Renaissance **drum*** and the thousand-year-old **campanile*** alongside.

2 Milan: a city of canals and ramparts

"The culture of Milan, or rather the great culture of Milan, was expressed in the aesthetic (and not only aesthetic) quality of useful objects, whether they were machines, clothing, furnishings, graphics, or projects of engineering. One might say that art applied to engineering was born in Milan. It is also accurate to say that the international fame of Italian Design and, later, Italian Fashion developed in the Milan Triennale."

Opinions such as this, recently expressed by a judicious connoisseur, Marco Comolli, offer a cohesive interpretation for anyone visiting the group of districts surrounding the historic city center. In reality, the area between the Cerchio dei Navigli, or former ring of canals, and the outer circuit of the Spanish walls and bastions, is where perhaps the most distinctive cultural characteristic of the city becomes fully evident – a tendency to combine manufacturing with aesthetics (utilitarianism combined with good taste, technology with quality) to which Milan owes much of its importance and influence in Italy. The financial heart

A view along Corso Venezia

of Italy's so-called "moral" capital is in fact concentrated in the oldest urban core (see Chapter 1). Although Milan's industrial drive, a strange mixture of an instinctive feel for capitalism and a strategy of eager acceptance of an immigrant work force, has on the contrary primarily affected the suburbs (especially in the north, near the Brianza district, and in the south, in the Lodigiano district), the clearest signs of that very down-to-earth Milanese creativity can be seen precisely in the intermediate urban belt. Whereas the city center continues to harbor most of the finest architecture, the quality shops, public science museums, and privately founded art collections, leading newspaper and publishing headquarters, international showrooms of Italian industrial design, and strategic nerve centers of the city's advanced service and transport networks.

In order to retrace the beginnings of these very emblematic districts, where there are also numerous ancient monuments, such as the basilica of Sant'Eustorgio, the Castello Sforzesco, the *Last Supper* by Leonardo da Vinci (who was Milanese by adoption), the reader should remember that the perimeter of the city was defined in 1545–66 with the construction of the second circle of walls during the Spanish era. The new fortified enceinte was built to protect the new areas outside the medieval walls along the great canals, which had provided a set of new urban ports serving Venice, Rome, the River Ticino and beyond. However, the new walls also encompassed many gardens and undeveloped areas, defining a vast enclosure that was gradually occupied in the course of two centuries, and was only finally saturated at the turn of the century.

Made redundant by the expanding city, the old Spanish bastions were progressively demolished, starting in 1899. Alas, today the remaining stretches of the ramparts are few and brief. All but one of the six "royal gates" that marked the major thoroughfares have vanished (though four have been rebuilt in 19th-c. style, and have retained their significance as common points of reference). The former perimeter of the bastions is now marked by an important public transport route (29/30), where the classic original trolleys with their wooden seats have been running daily for over seventy years. This trolley route is virtually all that remains to commemorate a particularly characteristic area of Milanese expansion (now distinctly multiethnic, as befits a modern metropolis). A fine black-and-white film of 1954 (*Miracolo a Milano*, by Cesare Zavattini) affectionately portrays the human aspects of this changing belt of former agricultural land surrounding the developing city.

2.1 Corso Garibaldi and Via Brera

The itineraries proposed in this second chapter do not consider the ring of the Spanish walls as an impermeable barrier. In most cases the routes follow stretches of roads between the center and the first suburbs, thereby spanning areas both within

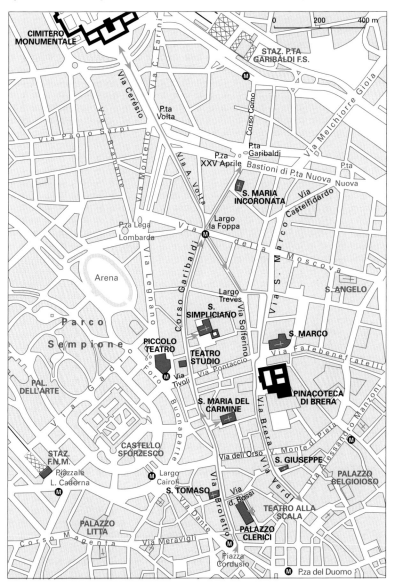

57

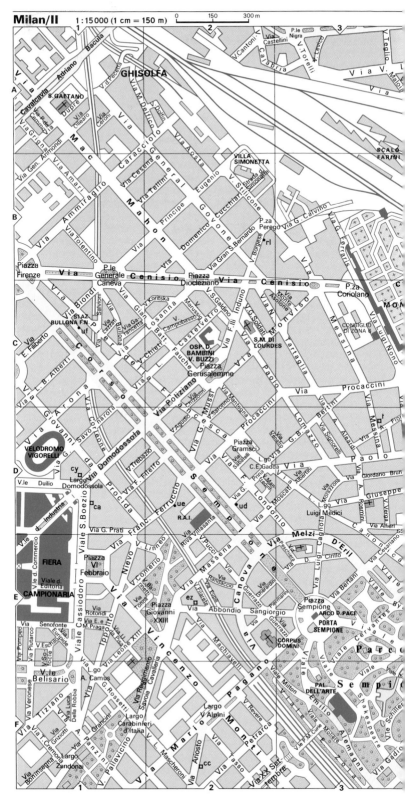

Milan/II   1:15000 (1 cm = 150 m)

0   150   300 m

58

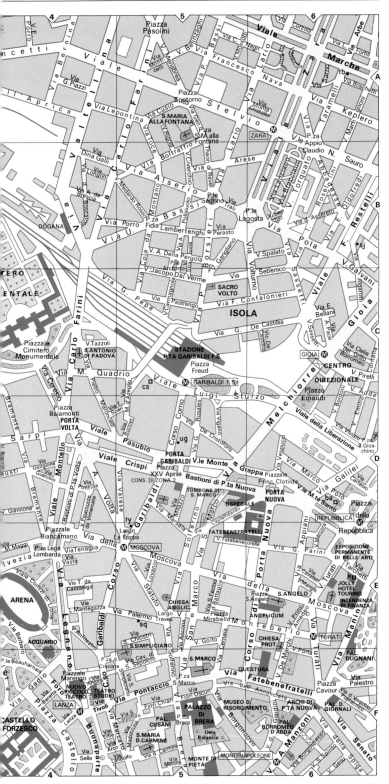

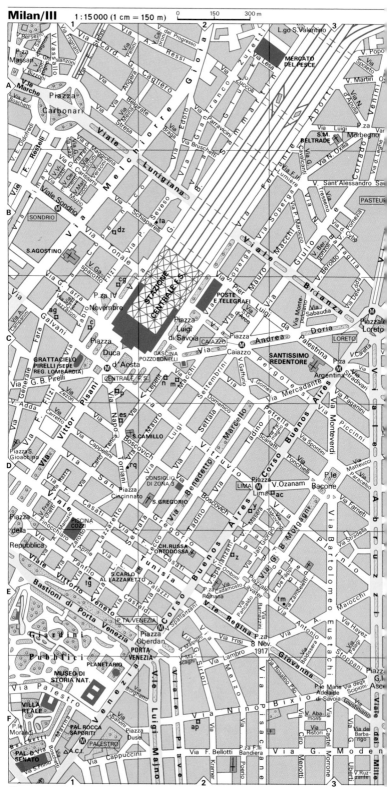

0   150   300 m

L.go S. Valentino

V. Popo

MERCATO DEL PESCE

V. Spoleto

V. Martini

V. N. d'Aquila

P.za

V.le Marche

Piazza Carbonari

S.M. BELTRADE

Via Luigi Morbegno

V. d. Leghe

PASTEUR

Viale Lunigiana

SONDRIO

S. AGOSTINO

STAZIONE CENTRALE F.S.

POSTE E TELEGRAFI

Piazza Luigi di Savoia

LORETO

Piazzale Loreto

GRATTACIELO PIRELLI (SEDE REG. LOMBARDIA)

Piazza Duca d'Aosta

CASCINA POZZOBONELLI

Piazza Caiazzo

SANTISSIMO REDENTORE

Argentina

CENTRALE F.S.

S. CAMILLO

Corso Buenos Aires

CONSIGLIO DI ZONA 3

Piazza Cincinnato

S. GREGORIO

Piazza Lima

LIMA

Bacone

Piazza S. Gioachino

PISCINA COZZI

Piazza della Repubblica

CH. RUSSA ORTODOSSA

Corso Buenos Aires

S. CARLO AL LAZZARETTO

Bastioni di Porta Venezia

V.le Regina

P.TA VENEZIA

Giardini Pubblici

Piazza Oberdan

PORTA VENEZIA

P.za 8 Nov. 1917

PLANETARIO

MUSEO DI STORIA NAT.

Via Palestro

P.le Maria Adelaide di Savoia

VILLA REALE

P.le Morandi

PAL. ROCCA SAPORITI

Piazza Duse

PALESTRO

A.C.I.

PAL. D'IV SENATO

Via Cappuccini

Via G. Modena

60

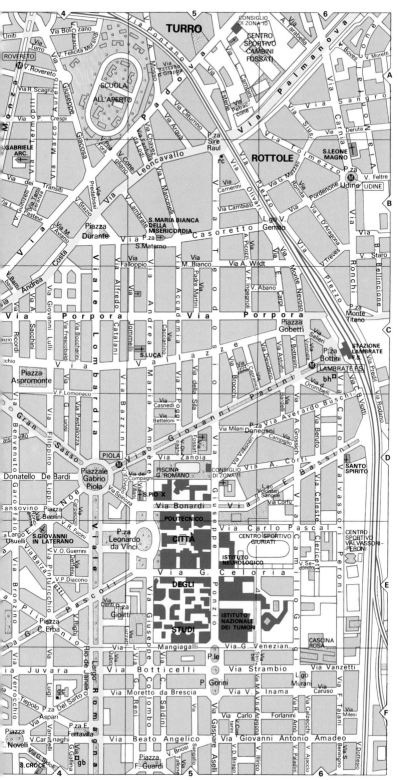

61

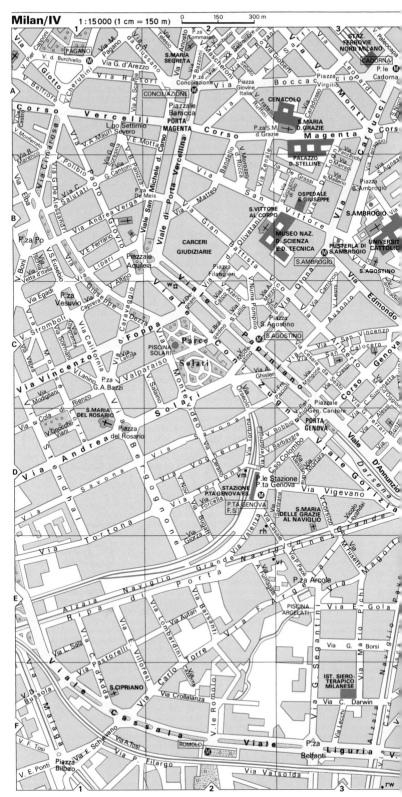

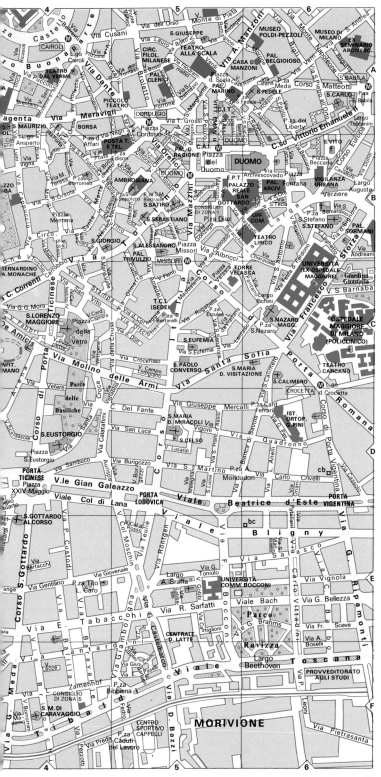

63

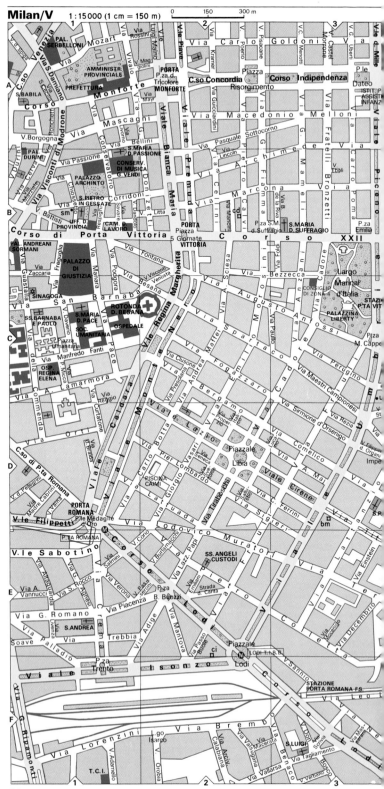

Milan/V   1:15000 (1 cm = 150 m)   0   150   300 m

A
PAL. SERBELLONI
AMMINISTR. PROVINCIALE
PREFETTURA
S.BABILA
PORTA MONFORTE
P.za d. Tricolore
C.so Concordia   Corso Indipendenza
Risorgimento
P.le Dateo
ISTIT. P ASSISTE INFANT
Corso
Monforte
Mascagni
V.Borgogna
Via Macedonio Melloni
Via Guicciardini
Sottocorno
Fratelli Bronzetti

B
PAL. DURINI
S.MARIA D.PASSIONE
CONSERV. DI MUSICA G.VERDI
PALAZZO ARCHINTO
S.PIETRO IN GESSATE
UFF. D. PROVINCIA
CAM. D. LAVORO
Corso di Porta Vittoria
PORTA VITTORIA
S.MARIA D.SUFFRAGIO
P.za S.M. d.Suffragio
P.za Emilia

C
PAL. ANDREANI SORMANI
PALAZZO DI GIUSTIZIA
SINAGOGA
SS.BARNABA E PAOLO
S.MARIA D. PACE
ROTONDA D. BESANA
SOC. UMANITARIA
OSPEDALE
San Barnaba
Via Besana
Corso di Porta Vittoria
Corso XXII
Largo Marinai d'Italia
CONSIGLIO DI ZONA 4
STAZ. P.TA VIT.
PALAZZINA LIBERTY
P.za M. Cappe
Via Maestri Campionesi
Via Sirmione d'Orsenigo
Via Rezia

D
OSP. REGINA ELENA
Via Commenda
C.so di P.ta Romana
PORTA ROMANA
PISCINA CAIMI
Via Botta
Via Lazzaretto
Via Pier Lombardo
Piazzale Libia
Viale Cirene
V.le Filippetti

E
P.TA ROMANA
V.le Sabotino
Via A. Vannucci
SS.ANGELI CUSTODI
Via Muratori
Via G. Romano
S.ANDREA
Via Piacenza
P.za B. Bonzzi
Via Adige
Via Mantova
Piazzale Lodi
LODI T.I.B.B.
P.za Trente
Viale Tibaldi
Gisonzo
STAZIONE PORTA ROMANA F.S.
Via Decembrio

F
G. Ripamonti
Via Lorenzini
l.go Isarco
Via Brembo
Via Calabria
Via Macerata
Via Valsugana
Via Tagliamento
S.LUIGI
T.C.I.
Via Adamello
Via Oroba
Via Vallarsa
Corso Lodi

64

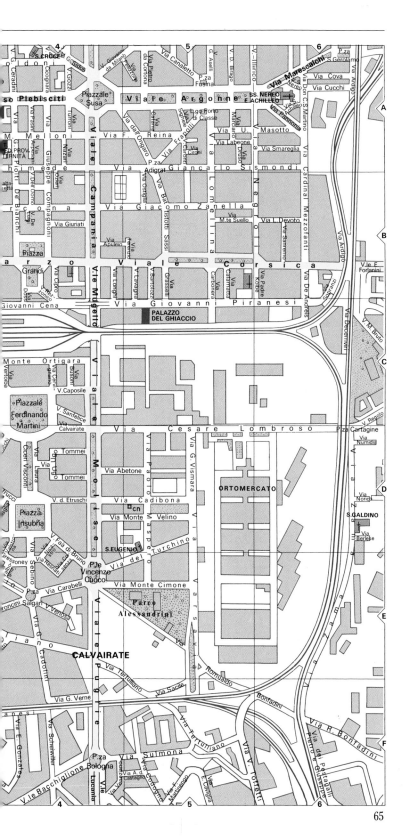

Milan: Subway lines

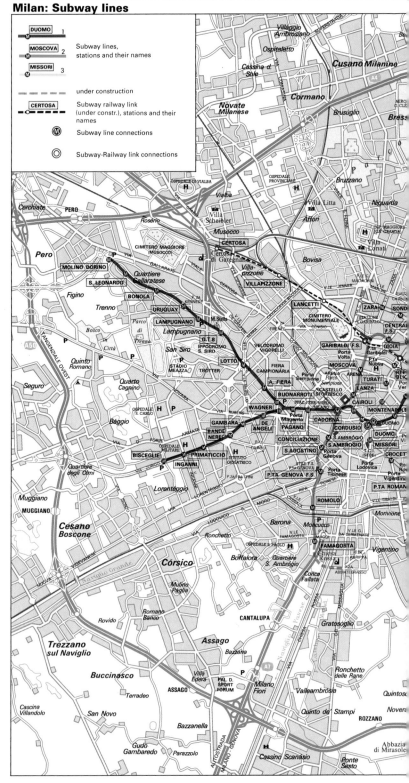

DUOMO 1

Subway lines, stations and their names

MOSCOVA 2

MISSORI 3

under construction

CERTOSA

Subway railway link (under constr.), stations and their names

Ⓜ Subway line connections

◎ Subway-Railway link connections

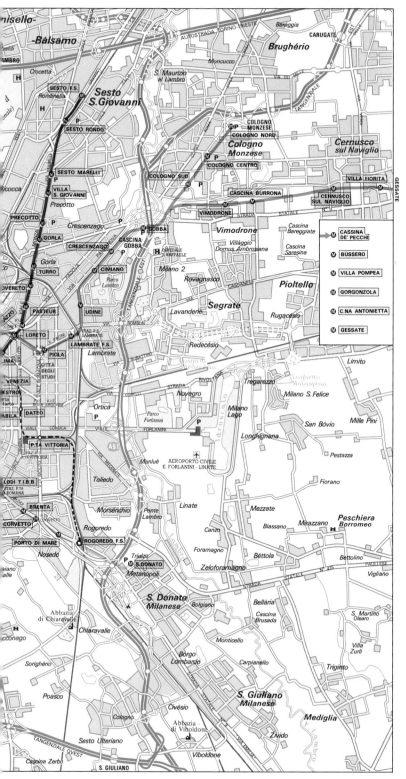

and without the circuit of walls: some quite central, such as the Brera district, Via Manzoni and Via Monte Napoleone, others just outside the ramparts, such as the Cimitero Monumentale and the Navigli. Any inconsistencies between the areas covered will be noted as they arise.

The present itinerary begins with the thoroughfare formed by Via Broletto and Corso Garibaldi, which crosses the erstwhile circuit of walls through the former Porta Comasina (now known as Porta Garibaldi) in the direction of Como. Toward the city center, Via San Marco was once a busy inner-city canal, with a port and merchant docks. This part of the city was crisscrossed with canals, like some inland Venice, connected via the Martesana canal with the River Adda and thence to the Adriatic.

The first and last portions of our route cross the once "Bohemian" area of Brera, the most lively district in Milanese cultural life in the late 1800s and early 1900s. The Scapigliatura literary movement formed here during the years of the Risorgimento (among its members were Cletto Arrighi, Emilio Praga, Ugo Tarchetti, Carlo Dossi, the brothers Camillo and Arrigo Boito, Verdi's last librettist). This group of young writers was attracted by the federalist ideas of Carlo Cattaneo and the dawn of socialism, shunning the business mentality that connoted the city. A growing crowd of avant-garde artists – from the pointillists Giovanni Segantini and Medardo Rosso, to the Futurists of Boccioni *et al.*, and the national socialist Filippo Tommaso Marinetti – together created a lively artistic climate at the turn of the century that prevailed in the

area; more recently it has been home to modern poets such as Clemente Rebora and the 1975 Nobel prizewinner Eugenio Montale (who worked at the *Corriere della Sera* offices nearby). Also frequenting the Brera were writers such as Carlo Emilio Gadda, Luciano Bianciardi, and Dino Buzzati (an editor for the *Corriere*); artists Piero Manzoni, Lucio Fontana, and Emilio Tadini; the photographer Ugo Mulas; and the cultural figure Giovanni Gandini. The dynamic atmosphere for which the Brera was once famous has completely disappeared, largely eradicated by the often ruthless speculation that hit the area, displacing its stable population.

Via Broletto (map IV, pp. 62–63, A5). Starting with Piazza Cordusio (see itinerary 1.4), this is the first stretch of the long road toward Como, a causeway that originates in distant Roman times, when the city gate was located at the intersection of Via dell'Orso and Via Cusani. Today, typical Milanese row houses alternate with modern office buildings.

Proceeding from the city, on the left is the church of *San Tomaso* (16th c., with a 19th-c. facade), marking a site that has harbored a temple since ancient times. To the right runs Via dei Bossi, which leads through the site of early Christian buildings, to the 18th-c. **Palazzo Clerici** (IV, A5) at Via dei Bossi 5; now the headquarters of the I.S.P.I., a research center for international politics. On the vault of its Galleria degli Arazzi is a *fresco** painted around 1740 by G. B. Tiepolo; the walls are hung with four 17th-c. tapestries from Brussels (access to the palazzo only by appointment).

The Circolo Filologico Milanese (1906) is located nearby. Numerous banking institutions have their headquarters in this area, including the powerful Mediobanca at Via Filodrammatici 10.

Santa Maria del Carmine (map II, pp. 58–59, F5). As you proceed along Via Broletto, Via Ponte Vetero and Via Mercato form the western boundary of the best-known areas of the Brera district (see below). The street widens as you approach the 15th-c. church dedicated to Our Lady of Mount Carmel, so as to emphasize the facade (Carlo Maciachini, 1880) inspired by Gothic-Lombard models. Inside are works by C. Procaccini and G. M. Fiammenghini including *The Resurrection of Lazarus*, and *The Coronation of the Virgin*.

Around Santa Maria del Carmine old narrow streets crisscross their way through the **Brera district**, known in medieval times as *Braida* ("pra-

The church of Santa Maria del Carmine

to" or field, from an old Germanic word), where traces of the "ligera," the small-time criminal life endemic to the city, linked to the artistic heritage of the area, could still be glimpsed as recently as the early 1960s. Today, however, exclusive buildings characterize the district's southern end (map I, pp. 44–45, B4) on Via del Carmine, Via Ciovasso, and Via Ciovassino, which connect to Via dell'Orso, Via Brera, and Via Verdi (see below). A little further north (I, A3-4), small shops, sumptuous restaurants, and night clubs, symbols of the Brera "dolce vita," punctuate Via Madonnina and Via Fiori Chiari (as well as the adjoining Via San Carpoforo, where the former church of the same name, now deconsecrated and empty, offers a lovely setting for exhibitions and multimedia events) up to the Palazzo di Brera itself, which houses the Accademia and the Pinacoteca (see below).

Corso Garibaldi (II, D-F4-5). A road in the old *borgo* of Porta Comasina which had already expanded beyond the medieval walls by the 1400s, the Corso had preserved its distinctive working-class character until a few years ago, thanks to some very prudent renovation schemes, and it may be that this was the last enclave of ordinary residents in the historic center. A little past the intersection of Via Pontaccio and Via Tivoli – which once conveyed the waters of the ring of canals to the castle moat – is the facade of the former Fossati theater (1858–59) at no. 17, now part of a group of apartment buildings belonging to the Piccolo Teatro. The complex, which includes the new site of the Piccolo Teatro at the rear on Foro Bonaparte (see itinerary 2.6), has performance areas as well as extensive archives and rehearsal studios. The former Fossati theater was remodeled by Marco Zanuso (1984–87) and became the **Teatro Studio** (II, F4), a cylindrical auditorium – interesting but somewhat uncomfortable – in which the designer used a motif typical of traditional Milanese architecture, namely, galleries with railings.

Proceeding beyond the church of San Simpliciano (see below), the road continues past Largo La Foppa (II, F5) and the Moscova subway station, to Piazza XXV Aprile (II, D5). To bypass this square, take Via Volta from Largo La Foppa and thereafter Viale Ceresio, which leads directly to the Cimitero Monumentale (see below).

On the final stretch of Corso Garibaldi (II, D5) stands the church of **Santa Maria Incoronata**, built in the second half of the 15th c. at the behest of the Augustinian Order. It consists of two buildings, which can clearly be seen even from the outside. The one on the right is the oldest and the original structure, while the one on the left was built around 1460 in honor of Saint Nicholas of Tolentino. The two buildings were joined into a single, squarish structure in 1468. Inside, 15th- and 16th-c. tombstones and funerary monuments testify to its use as a mausoleum by the Sforza court. The right apse shows traces of frescoes.

Outside in Piazza XXV Aprile stands the large neoclassical arch of Porta Garibaldi (1826). The route proceeds along Corso Como (II, D5) to the Porta Garibaldi train station (see itinerary 3.2), passing the Galleria Carla Sozzani at no. 10, a gallery for fine arts and photography.

San Simpliciano (II, E-F5). This church stands in a small square off Corso Garibaldi. Together with San Nazaro Maggiore (see itinerary 1.3), Sant'Ambrogio (see itinerary 2.5), and the former San Dionigi, San Simpliciano was one of the four churches founded by Bishop Ambrose in the 4th c., each one sited on one of the major thoroughfares leading out of ancient *Mediolanum*. Although the original church must have had a central plan, a fair portion of the vessel walls date back to the original early Christian structure. Of its numerous transformations, the most important were those of the 8th c. (a new layout with a nave and two aisles), during the Romanesque period in the 11th c. (a new apse), in the 12th c. (division of the transept into twin aisles), and finally those made in the 19th c., which included the reconstruction of the facade (Carlo Maciachini, 1870). The interior offers late 15th-c. frescoes in the first room to the right of the front wall, 17th-c. painting in the third chapel on the right, slightly earlier frescoes on the organ bases, a carved choir (1588) designed by Giuseppe Meda, the fresco of *The Coronation of the Virgin Mary** executed around 1515 by Bergognone in the cupola of the apse, fragments of other late 14th-c. frescoes in the small side chapel, and the Cappella del Rosario, a Baroque chapel added in the early 1700s.

The buildings behind the church, next to the former *San Simpliciano convent* (now the site of a theological college) at Piazza delle Crociate 6, are noteworthy and original, and include two interesting cloisters, one from the 15th c. and the other from the 16th c., perhaps by Vincenzo Seregni.

Cimitero Monumentale* (II, B-C3-4), or monumental cemetery. Carlo Maciachini built the new cemetery for the emerging Milanese middle class between 1863 and 1866, in a location that is still slightly peripheral but once lay completely outside the city, beyond the gateway through the city walls, where the toll station of Porta Volta (II, D4) was built a few years later. Originally covering some 121,000 sq.m (around 250,000 today), the cemetery was deliberately non-denominational, and offered a resting place for non-Catholics and Jews also. In the center of its wide, banded front prospect is the *Famedio* on a central plan, offering a kind of Pantheon, containing the tombs of such luminaries of Milanese history as Alessandro Manzoni and Carlo Cattaneo.

Irrespective of one's appreciation of the varying tastes of the Milanese upper class over the last one hundred and fifty years, the cemetery offers a significant overview of Italian art from the period, with works by artists such as Medardo Rosso, Mosè Bianchi, Adolfo Wildt, Paolo Troubetzkoy, Vincenzo Vela, Leonardo Bistolfi, Giannino Castiglioni, Francesco Messina, Giacomo Manzù, Arnaldo and Gio Pomodoro, Pietro Cascella and Fausto Melotti. An abstract work in bronze rod, glass and rough stone (Lodovico Belgiojoso, Enrico Peressutti, and Ernesto Nathan Rogers, 1946) commemorates those who perished in the Nazi concentration camps.

Via San Marco (II, D-F5). The thoroughfare Viale Ceresio and Via Volta, at the far end of which looms the Cimitero Monumentale (see above), terminates in Largo La Foppa and continues down Via Statuto to Largo Treves. One block from here lies Via San Marco, site of a former important merchant canal wharf (now covered over). The dock was linked via the canal system to the Martesana. The site's past is now remembered only by the name of a nearby bar which, typical of today's fashions, is very much in the style of an English pub.

At the far end of Via San Marco lies what is left of a former lock (II, D-E5) of the Martesana canal system. For centuries the Martesana afforded the easiest means of travel between Milan and the Bergamo area.
At Via Solferino 28 is the *Corriere della Sera building* (Luca Beltrami and Luigi Repossi, 1904), housing the city's leading newspaper. Founded by Eugenio Torelli-Viollier in 1876 in an office in the Galleria Vittorio Emanuele II, the newspaper has had the widest circulation in Italy for decades, with only brief interruptions; abroad many also consider it Italy's most authoritative paper.

Returning toward the city center along Via San Marco where the road crosses the former ring of canals (here, Via Fatebenefratelli), the street widens with a gentle slope into the forecourt of **San Marco** (II, F5), another of Milan's originally *extra mœnia*

churches, commissioned in 1254 by Brother Lanfranco Settala of the Augustinian Order. Vestiges of the original 13th-c. building are the ogival portal, three *statues of saints* in niches in the facade, the right head of the transept, and the *bell tower*, surmounted by late 19th-c. spires. A series of burial chapels were added in the mid-1400s along the south aisle. Inside, the *sarcophagus of the blessed Lanfranco Settala** (who died in 1264), attributed to Giovanni di Balduccio and a fresco by a Lombard master dating from the same period as the *Crucifixion* can be seen on the walls of the south transept. In the adjacent former chapel, or Cappella di San Tommaso di Villanova, are detached 13th- and 14th-c. frescoes (*Madonna and Child*) from the lower portion of the bell tower, and a 14th-c. arch with three relief panels. In the presbytery there is a painting by Cerano depicting *The Baptism of St. Augustine* (1618). Other important paintings can be seen in the north aisle: by Camillo Procaccini on the seventh arch, by Palma Giovane on the sixth arch, and by Giulio Cesare Procaccini on the fourth.

The isolated building along Via Fatebenefratelli opposite the church is the studio of the architect Gae Aulenti, author of many major projects and installations in Italy and abroad (the remodeling of Palazzo Grassi in Venice, and the Musée d'Orsay in Paris). Nearby, the *Bar Giamaica* at the corner of Via Brera seems oblivious of the decades in which it was the favorite meeting point for the Brera's population of artists and writers.

Palazzo di Brera (II, F5). The Pinacoteca di Brera (see below) contains one of the largest art collections in Italy and ranks among the world's finest art museums. It is located in the imposing complex at Via Brera 28, where the Jesuit Order was located from 1572 to 1772. The building began to take shape in 1591 through the conversion and expansion (under Martino Bassi) of a former monastery of the Humiliati Order. Much of the present layout, nevertheless, is the product of later radical reconstruction by Francesco Maria Ricchino (1651) and Giuseppe Piermarini (1774). Of particular note is *central courtyard* by Ricchino, presenting two orders of arches supported by slender twinned columns.
When the authority of the Jesuits was dissolved as a result of the reforms through which the Hapsburgs imposed their imperial rule during the last thirty years of the 18th c., the building was confiscated and used for state scientific institutes,

which included *an astronomical observatory* founded in 1772, the library, or *Biblioteca Braidense* (which later became national) established in 1773, *botanical gardens* in 1774, and in 1776 an *Accademia delle Belle Arti*, or academy of fine arts, opened to the public, the first of its kind in Milan. The collections of the academy were greatly augmented under Napoleon Bonaparte, who is immortalized as a classic deity in the *statue* at the center of the courtyard, based on a model by Antonio Canova. The various functions of the complex continue to operate, although the botanical gardens are not used to their fullest, while pollution and poor visibility have made it necessary to transfer the principal instruments of the observatory to Merate (see itinerary 4.2). The library, still the largest in the city though now somewhat cramped, is worth a visit, particularly the solemn catalogue and reading rooms.

Pinacoteca di Brera**. From the courtyard of the palazzo a broad stairway leads up to the main floor, where the collection is located. Originally based on plaster casts of the best-known classical or Renaissance sculptures used as models to train fine arts students, the collection was greatly expanded under the rule of Napoleon I, when enormous numbers of works removed from the suppressed churches and monasteries of many areas of northern Italy were added to the collection, which opened to the public in 1809. The foundation of the Pinacoteca as a separate entity took place under the House of Savoy in 1892, when preservation functions were separated from the academy's educational programs.

The recent history of the Pinacoteca di Brera, which has not always benefited from its status as a state institute dependent on Rome, in a city where many museums are directly managed by the municipal government, includes an episode involving the *Jucker Collection* (now property of the municipal council; part of the collection is on display at the Palazzo Reale museum, see itinerary 1.1) and the *Jesi Bequest*, an important collection of Futurist works, Metaphysical art, and other 20th-c. schools. The institute is renowned for a chronic lack of funding and space that thwarts its enormous potential.

At least three of the many works of the Italian Renaissance at the Pinacoteca are known worldwide: the great **Brera Altarpiece*** by Piero della Francesca (1472–74), where a devotional scene with a figure bearing the arms of the artist's patron, the Duke of Urbino, revolves around the perfect

The Marriage of the Virgin, *by Raphael (Brera Gallery)*

symbolism of an egg suspended from a half-shell; Mantegna's **Dead Christ**** (ca. 1480), a remarkable early exercise in the new laws of perspective charged with indescribable pathos; and more universally well-known, Raphael's **Marriage of the Virgin*** (1504), set against a background of Bramantesque architecture. The Pinacoteca also has a **polyptych of Saint Luke**** by Mantegna, while an exceptional example of detached 14th-c. fresco decoration is offered in the **Mocchirolo oratory series***, ascribed to the circle of Giovanni da Milano. The detached frescoes have been remounted in a setting similar to the original. The extraordinary beauty of the pieces, "is a product of their suspension between opposite sources of light, without ever receiving a direct ray" (Giulio Argan).

Only a rapid listing of the artists and works which make up this heritage of Brera is possible here, divided into homogenous groups as follows:

Venetian school of the 15th/16th c.: Jacopo Bellini (*Madonna and Child*), Antonio Vivarini, Giovanni Bellini (**Virgin*** and two different **Madonnas with Christ Child***), Gentile and Giovanni Bellini (**St. Mark's Sermon at Alexandria in Egypt****), Carlo Crivelli (*Madonna of the Candle*), Vittore Carpaccio (*Debate of St. Stephen*), Lorenzo Lotto (*Portraits of Men*), Titian (*Portrait of the Count of Porcia, St. Jerome*), Paris Bordone (*The Venetian Lovers*), Veronese (*Supper in the House of the Pharisees*), Tintoretto (**Discovery of the Body of St. Mark****), Jacopo Bassano (*St. Rocco Visits the Plague Victims*), Gerolamo Savoldo (*Virgin in Glory with Saints*), Moretto, and G. B. Moroni (*Virgin and Child with Saints*).

Lombard School of the 15th/16th c.: Vincenzo Foppa (polyptych of *Madonna and Saints**), Ambrogio Bergognone, Bramantino (*Holy Family*), Bernardino Luini (*Madonna of the Rose Garden, Crucifixion*, and a series of frescoes of Santa Maria della Pace), Andrea Solario, and Ambrogio de Predis (*Portrait of a Youth*).

Emilian School of the 15th/16th c.: Correggio (**Adoration of the Magi, Nativity**), Francesco del Cossa (*St. John the Baptist*), Lorenzo Costa (*Adoration of the Magi*), Dosso Dossi, Ercole de' Roberti (*Madonna Enthroned and Saints**), and Francesco Francia.

Central Italian Schools between the 14th/15th c.: Ambrogio Lorenzetti (**Madonna and Child***), Gentile da Fabriano (**polyptych of Valle Romita***), Bramante (**Christ at the Column***, frescoes from the destroyed Palazzo Panigarola on Via Lanzone), and Luca Signorelli (*Flagellation*).

17th-c. Italian: Ludovico Carracci (*The Canaanite Woman*), Annibale Carracci (*Samaritan at the Well*), Agostino Carracci (*The Adulteress*), Guercino (*Repudiation of Hagar*), and Caravaggio (*Dinner in Emmaus**).

European Schools: Anthony van Dyck (*Portrait of Amelia di Solms**), Pieter Paul Rubens (*Last Supper*), Rembrandt (*Portrait of Sister*), and El Greco (*St. Francis*).

Venetian School of the 18th c.: Giambattista Tiepolo (*Madonna of Mount Carmel, Temptations of St. Anthony*), G.B. Piazetta, Alessandro and Pietro Longhi, Francesco Guardi, Canaletto, and Bernardo Bellotto.

19th-c. Italian: Andrea Appiani, Francesco Hayez, Silvestro Lega, and Giovanni Fattori.

Jesi Collection: paintings by Amedeo Modigliani, Umberto Boccioni, Gino Severini, Carlo Carrà, Massimo Campigli, Giorgio Morandi, Mario Sironi, Filippo De Pisis, Scipione (Gino Bonichi), Pablo Picasso, Georges Braque, as well as sculptures by Medardo Rosso, Arturo Martini, and Marino Marini.

Via Verdi (map IV, pp. 62–63, A5). From the Palazzo di Brera, at Via Brera 15 stands the imposing *Palazzo Cusani* (Giovanni Ruggieri, 1719); at no. 16 the *Galleria Il Diaframma*, which pioneered of photography exhibits in Italy; and at nos. 12–14 the 18th-c. Rococo *Palazzo Citterio*. At the corner of the intersection where the street becomes Via Verdi, is the porticoed building of the *Cassa di Risparmio delle Provincie Lombarde* (Giovanni Greppi and Giovanni Muzio, 1934–42), one of Lombardy's largest banking groups, founded in 1823 in support of agricultural savings.

The bank is followed by the elegant church of **San Giuseppe** (IV, A5), designed by Francesco Maria Ricchino (1607–30) based on an octagonal plan inscribed in an ellipse. Opposite the flank of the opera house is the tiny bookstore noted for its publication of *Linus*, founded jointly by Umberto Eco (*The Name of the Rose*) and three writer colleagues – Oreste del Buono, Giovanni Gandini, and Elio Vittorini. The street ends in Piazza della Scala (see itinerary 1.2).

2.2 Via Manzoni and Corso Venezia

The historic area northeast of the opera house, lining the elegant thoroughfare of Via Manzoni, is particular important to modern Milan. The fashion enclave of Via Monte Napoleone, Via Borgospesso, Via della Spiga, and Via Sant'Andrea is directly accessed from here. The enclave plays host to the headquarters of most of the world's leading fashion designers. Always a lively quarter, it becomes almost hysterical when new seasonal collections are being presented (usually September and October for the following spring/summer collection, and March for the fall/winter season). Except in August, when the entire city shuts down for summer vacation, the enclave offers a year-round opportunity to admire the most famous and up-to-date fashions that Italy has to offer.

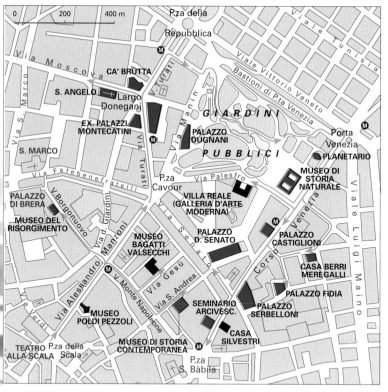

The artistic collections of two important museums nearby, the Poldi Pezzoli and Bagatti Valsecchi museums, once the residences of the founding families. The museums have something of a love-hate relationship with busy designer world around them: despite their undoubted superiority over the ephemeral world of fashion, they acknowledge their dependence on it for custom. As institutions, they could not do without the patronage of the wealthy fashion world. The contradiction is rather emblematic of Milan's mixture of unfussy utilitarianism and refined taste.

This itinerary leads us out of the ancient city gate of Porta Nuova Antica, to Piazza Cavour, past the 18th-c. public gardens, and into a quite different quarter distinguished by large 20th-c. buildings, including several key examples of Milanese architecture from the interwar period. The gate at the opposite corner of the Giardini Pubblici gives onto Corso Venezia, another important historical road which, in the days of the Lombardo-Venetian kingdom passed through the ancient Porta Orientale (now Porta Venezia) in the direction of the imperial capital, Vienna. Here, 18th-c. buildings even larger and more elegant than those on Via Manzoni are proof of the area's past prestige. Proceeding past these magnificent facades one reaches once again the former ring of canals; the street comes to an end in Piazza San Babila, not far from the cathedral.

Via Manzoni (map I, pp. 44–45, A-B4-5). Leading out of Piazza della Scala, Via Manzoni marks the course of an ancient causeway (see itinerary 1.2) which in late Roman times extended from the *cardo* of the early street system. It now runs above a stretch of the subway Line 3 (the "yellow line"). Known as Corsia del Giardino in the 1700s and 1800s, several of its neoclassical portals still allow glimpses of the large tree-filled gardens behind. At nos. 6 and 10 stand two fine neoclassical buildings designed by Luigi Canonica (1829–31), *Palazzo Brentani* (I, B4-5), which in 1848 served as the royal headquarters for the Piedmontese government, and *Palazzo Anguissola* (I, B5). The latter's gardens look onto another neoclassical building of earlier date (Carlo Felice Soave, 1778).

The *Fondazione Feltrinelli* has had its offices at the Via Romagnosi 3 (I, B4) since 1973. This foundation contains extremely important documents and bibliographies on the international history of the workers' movement and social dissent from the 18th c. to the present. The institute, whose archives may be consulted, also sponsors study projects and publishes; it takes its name from the industrialist and publisher Gian Giacomo Feltrinelli (1926–72), who was killed in Segrate (see itinerary 3.3) under circumstances which have never been fully explained, but undoubtedly linked to his revolutionary beliefs.

The publishing company of the same name, founded in 1954, is located around the corner at Via Andegari 6.

Proceeding outward beyond the Museo Poldi Pezzoli and Via Monte Napoleone (see below for both), on Via Manzoni stands the 18th-c. church and refectory of *San Francesco di Paola* (I, B5), with its 1891 facade. Nearby (at no. 30) is the Baroque *Palazzo Gallarati Scotti*, from the early 18th c. Across from the latter building is the *Palazzo Borromeo d'Adda* (at nos. 39–41), reconstructed early in the 19th c. The gallery at no. 40, which leads to the popular *Teatro Manzoni* (1950) and the Einaudi international bookstore, gives directly onto the start of the "fashion enclave."

Portrait of a Young Woman, *by Pollaiuolo (Museo Poldi Pezzoli)*

Museo Poldi Pezzoli* (I, B5). The fine building at Via Manzoni 12 on the corner of Via Morone houses one of the best-known museum-homes in the world. Its collection was started in 1846 with the growing number of antiques acquired by the well-traveled and scholarly figure Gian Giacomo Poldi Pezzoli (1822–79). The museum's collections are exceptionally rich in works of art, such as the 15th-c. **Portrait of a Young Woman***, attributed to Pollaiuolo, and basically the emblem of the museum. There are also exceptionally valuable examples of applied art: weapons and armor, carpets, textiles, jewelry, gold, enamels, ceramics, glasswork, furniture, and clocks. The building itself was remodeled by its owner, and the rooms were gradually redecorated and furnished to harmonize with their precious contents, resulting in a series of exquisitely refined setting that exemplify the tastes of the 19th-c. European collector. The home, which by the owner's behest was opened "to the public, for its permanent use and benefit" as early as 1881, has increased its collection through bequests. Badly damaged by Allied bombings in 1943, the building's new configuration (work terminated in 1951) tends to emphasize the museum over the earlier domestic setting, and the works displayed in the 23 rooms are now accompanied by explanatory captions.

On his mother's side, Gian Giacomo Poldi Pezzoli was a descendant of the venerable house of Trivulzio, and even now the museum has strong links with the aristocracy of the city, both noble and entrepreneurial. Names of important local families accompany the collections acquired over recent decades: the small bronzes donated in 1968 by the Crespi family, paintings that belonged to the Viscounts Venosta until 1973, **mechanical clocks*** from the collection of Bruno Falck (1973), and the sundials of Piero Portaluppi (1979). In the same spirit, private sponsors have financed the restoration of a portion of the extraordinary collection of **textiles*** (altar cloths from the Sforza era, rare Coptic fabrics from the 5th to 7th c., and more) and **rugs*** (for example, an exceptional Persian hunting rug, signed and dated 1542–43).

In addition to the famous female portrait mentioned above, the most valuable paintings personally acquired by Gian Giacomo include **St. Nicholas of Tolentino*** by Piero della Francesca, **The Madonna of the Book*** and a **Deposition*** by Sandro Botticelli. The founder is also responsible for the establishment of a remarkably representative group of 14th-c. Sienese, 15th-c. Tuscan, early 16th-c. Lombard (Bergognone, Giovanni Antonio Boltraffio, Cesare da Sesto, Andrea Solario, Vincenzo Foppa, and Bernardino Luini), and 18th-c. Venetian works. Later acquisitions include works such as *St. Margaret* by Lippo Memmi, a **Madonna and Child*** by Mantegna, *St. Mau-*

relio by Cosmè Tura, two paintings by Lucas Cranach the Elder, three paintings by Tiepolo, and the evocative **Gray Lagoon*** by Francesco Guardi. Other great masters – a *Devotional Cross* was recently attributed to Raphael – are present in such great numbers that it would be impossible to list them all in this guide.

Via Monte Napoleone (I, B-C5-6). At the point where Via Manzoni widens to form Largo Croce Rossa, below which is the Montenapoleone subway station, with the controversial *Monument to Sandro Pertini* (Aldo Rossi, 1990) that appears to obstruct it at street level, what is perhaps Milan's most famous street runs southeast on the other side, offering an uninterrupted series of display windows, among the most luxurious in Europe. Some of the buildings housing these glittering showcases are neoclassical, and offer clothing, furs, and luxury items along with sumptuous jewelry boutiques. The *Galleria d'Arte Philippe Daverio*, at Via Monte Napoleone 6, is well-known to dealers and collectors.

During the Sforza era, the town residence of the Marliani family was built on this street (which follows the line of the former Roman walls of Maximian). Now at Via Monte Napoleone 12, the building was transformed by Giuseppe Piermarini in 1782 into the headquarters for the "Monte di Santa Tere-

Down the side streets of Via Santo Spirito and Via del Gesù, stand the two Bagatti Valsecchi buildings, the larger of which houses the museum of the same name (see below).

From Largo Croce Rossa, heading in the opposite direction from Via Monte Napoleone, is Via Borgonuovo, with its historic area of private gardens around **Via dei Giardini** (I, A-B5), greatly reduced between 1938 and 1939 by building speculation, on the right. The small *Piazza Sant'Erasmo* (I, A5) lies on Via dei Giardini; in the background, the remains of the 15th-c. convent of Sant'Erasmo.

Via Borgonuovo (I, A-B1-5) has a distinctive, even exclusive atmosphere. The studio of the "guru" of Italian industrial design Ettore Sottsass Jr. is located here. Notable is the neoclassical facade of *Palazzo Moriggia*, at no. 23, home of the documents, mementos, paintings, sculptures, and printed materials of the **Civico Museo del Risorgimento**, documenting the movement for the liberation and political unification of Italy, complete with specialized library. Beyond the corner of Via Fiori Oscuri, which bounds the northern side of the Palazzo di Brera, the street ends on a line with the apse of the church of San Marco (see itinerary 2.1).

Museo Bagatti Valsecchi* (I, B5). With its entry at Via del Gesù 5, well worth a visit is

A high-fashion store in Via Monte Napoleone

sa" pawnshop, changing its name to "Monte Napoleone" in 1804. Of the historical buildings still standing, the most important is the *Palazzo Melzi di Cusano* (I, B5) at no. 18, built in 1830 by G. B. Bareggi in a form that echoes Palazzo Serbelloni (see below).

the larger of the two buildings reconstructed in neo-Mannerist style (1878–87) by the brothers Fausto and Giuseppe Bagatti Valsecchi, sons of a famous miniaturist. The brothers, both attorneys, were keen art collectors and members of the emerging city aristocracy of the time. This is the other important museum-home, like the Museo Poldi Pezzoli. Although it has fewer individual art masterpieces than its rival, the Museo Bagatti Valsecchi is more captivating because, spared from the bombings of the last war, physically inhabited until just a few years ago, and submitted to a meticulous conservative restoration, the mansion today has retained its authenticity – qualities lacking in the Poldi Pezzoli. As the eminent art historian Federico Zeri has noted, it possesses great "character as a historical document, and is a testimony to good taste, to a particular chapter of post-Romantic Milan between Positivism and the Scapigliatura." The location itself is crucial: no other museum-home of this type, not even the Jacquemart-André in Paris or the Ca' d'Oro in Venice, manage to be so utterly authentic. Nor should it be forgotten that this is the only antique art museum opened in Milan (in November 1994, to be exact) since Italy became a republic.

The main floor is accessed via a period staircase that offers a fine compendium of authentic pieces of 15th- and 16th-c. workmanship meticulously set in modern reconstructions (some with modern functions: a carved cupboard conceals a piano, a neo-Renaissance water trough has a hydraulic shower system, and a wrought-iron washstand receives running water through the chain that supports it), while the most exciting works of art – **St. Justine Borromeo*** by Giovanni Bellini and the paintings by Bernardino Zenale and Giampietrino – can be identified despite their crowded positions, thanks to explanatory material distributed in each room; the idea is to avoid panels and captions that would mar the impression of being a guest in one of the most sophisticated Milanese homes of the late 1800s. Numerous works of applied art have been integrated with the rich furnishings – invariably superb collectors' items, and often rare, such as the carved pine bed in the Stanza di Fausto, and the wood paneling in the Sala della Stufa, both works from 16th-c. Valtellina. There is also a 15th-c. folding chair, various wedding chests and coffers, a 15th-c. stall decorated with xylographic motifs, world maps in the library, and a profusion of stone, marble, and stucco decorations, weapons and armor, ceramics, glass, jewelry, ivory, hangings, and sumptuous tapestries.

At Via del Gesù 8, not far from the entrance to the Museo Bagatti Valsecchi, stands the new *Four Seasons Hotel*, where recent renovation work revealed 15th-c. frescoes from the former Jesuit convent, closed in 1782.

Along Via San Andrea, the next side-street in Via Monte Napoleone, is a series of elegant shops surrounding the 18th-c. *Palazzo Morando Attendolo Bolognini* (no. 6), the site of the *Civico Museo di Storia Contemporanea* (I, B6), a modern history museum containing mementos and documents relative to national affairs during the first half of the 20th c. The same building also hosts the *Civico Museo di Milano*, a collection of paintings primarily useful for reconstructing the 18th- and 19th-c. history of Milan, and the *Civico Museo Navale "Ugo Mursia."* The latter, a maritime museum with a specialized library, is named after the well-known publisher (1921–93) who founded and directed the publishing company that bore his name. The figureheads displayed come from Mursia's personal collection, as he himself was a sailing fan and a faithful translator of the novels of Joseph Conrad.

Piazza Cavour (I, A5-6). At the end of Via Manzoni, where the street once led out beyond the medieval walls and the ring of canals, stand the *arches of Porta Nuova*, a double archway rebuilt at the turn of the century, reworking the remains of the city gate built here in 1171 and fortified in the 14th c., and later enveloped by minor buildings. Roman tombstones are inserted into the inner face, while a marble tabernacle from the 14th c. can be seen on the outer face. The piazza that follows, named after the Piedmontese politician who was responsible for national unity (with a bronze *monument* by Odoardo Tabacchi, 1865), is bounded by the *Palazzo dei Giornali* on the right (1937–42), built by Giovanni Muzio. The building was originally the headquarters for the Fascist party newspaper *Il Popolo d'Italia*, while inscriptions and lighted panels indicate which newspapers or agencies occupy the building. The facade bas-relief is by Mario Sironi.

Visible from here is the westernmost corner of the Giardini Pubblici (see below), which hosts the 17th-c. Palazzo Dugnani with its entrance on Via Manin 2 (map II, pp. 58–59, E-F6), the former municipal school district headquarters and now an exhibition and conference venue. The central hall contains frescoes by G. B. Tiepolo.

The *Museo del Cinema* collection is now lodged in Palazzo Dugnani. This film museum contains documents and equipment of considerable importance to the history of Italian and international cinematography. The **Cineteca Italiana** itself does not have adequate space to show its significant wealth of *period films** to its members, and so each season it rents a hall in another area of the city.

Next to the Palazzo dei Giornali, between it and the international-style *Svizzera Turismo* building (Armin Meili, 1952), 78 m tall, is the short Via del Vecchio Politecnico, offering a fleeting glimpse of the Villa Reale gardens beyond (see below).

At Via Carlo Porta 5, not far off, the first side-street left of Via Turati, stand the headquarters of the *Fondazione Corrente*, with the museum studio of Ernesto Treccani. This Milanese painter joined the Corrente group when he was quite young, in the years immediately preceding World War II.

Via Turati begins at Piazza Cavour (see below), with Largo Donegani about midway.

Largo Donegani (II, E6). Where Via Turati and Via Principe Amedeo meet, with the latter street emerging from the greenery of Via dei Giardini (see above), is a triangular clearing of great interest for the history of 20th-c. Italian architecture. A central fountain recently returned to its place precedes the concave facade (no. 1) of the former Montecatini building (Gio Ponti and Antonio Fornaroli, 1951), a 13-story edifice that includes the American Consulate General among its occupants. Next to it (no. 2) is another former Montecatini building (Ponti, Fornaroli, and Eugenio Soncini, 1936–38) with its H-shaped form dominating the start of Via Moscova, which it looks onto with an imposing recessed facade and forecourt. The opposite corner between Via Turati and Via Moscova consists of the block of houses known as **"Ca' Bruta"** – a well-known youthful work (1919–22) of Giovanni Muzio. The facade is composed of horizontal strips (two different shades of plaster dominate the travertine facing), and is set with classic elements such as columns and pilasters, tympanums and cornices, niches and balustrades – all these are distorted and stylized in an ironic and surreal manner.

Not far from Largo Donegani, in Via Moscova, stands the *Franciscan convent of Sant'Angelo* (II, E6), established in the 16th c. Construction on its church with its double-order facade was begun in 1552, to designs by Domenico Giunti. The interior and the sacristy conserve paintings by Antonio Campi, the Fiamminghini, and the Procaccini. The original church was demolished in 1931, and the present-day monastery (Giovanni Muzio, 1939–47) includes the Angelicum auditorium. In the little tree-lined square of Piazza Sant'Angelo stands a statue group depicting *St. Francis Preaching to the Birds* (Giannino Castiglioni, 1926), a very popular market of plants and flowers is held each year on Easter Monday.

Via Turati (II, E-F6). Beyond Largo Donegani, beneath which is the Turati subway station, stands the *Palazzo della Permanente* at Via Turati 34 (II, E6), the headquarters of an association that has been promoting the visual arts since 1833. The structure consists of a small, two-story building designed by Luca Beltrami (1883–85), whose back section was enlarged to designs by Achille and Piergiacomo Castiglioni (1951–52) to create new exhibition space. A little further on, the street ends in the broad **Piazza della Repubblica** (II, D-E6), the former Piazza Fiume, built in the 1930s after the demolition of the first mainline railway station (1864) that lay transversely almost two hundred meters in length.

The two office buildings by Gio Ponti in Largo Donegani

At the end of Via Vittor Pisani looms the immense bulk of the Stazione Centrale (see itinerary 3.2). Halfway up this street rises a tower block (Eugenio Soncini, Ermenegildo Soncini, and Luigi Mattioni, 1954), the first of its kind in Milan, which was quickly dubbed "Don Quixote." The surrounding district is no more than a few decades old, and there are various buildings; those at Piazza della Repubblica 7–9, built by Giovanni Muzio in 1935–37, are architecturally interesting.

At the end of Via Turati, take an immediate right onto the short Via Tarchetti and begin the most direct route to the Giardini Pubblici (see below). After passing the *Feltrinelli house* on Via Manin 37 (Alberico and Lodovico Belgiojoso, 1934–35), we enter the gate of the public gardens and walk along the inside path parallel with the former ramparts of *Porta Venezia* (map III, pp. 60–61, E1). This section of the old Spanish walls became an elevated public walkway as a result of the late 19th-c. arrangement of the gardens, but now acts as a major thoroughfare for automobile traffic.

Giardini Pubblici (III, E-F1). One of the few municipal parks in Milan, these fairly central gardens (covering 177,000 sq.m) were the first to be opened to the public. Laid out by the architect Giuseppe Piermarini, they were begun in 1783–86 on a plot of land obtained after the closure two monasteries located approximately on the site of the Museo di Storia Naturale (see below). The park reached its present extension – stretching from the ramparts of Porta Venezia to Piazza Cavour in the east – in 1857, the year in which work was begun on landscaping the grounds; further work was carried out in 1881. Always considered fondly by the Milanese and popular even today, the Giardini Pubblici once provided an exhibition area for the trade fairs – an important part of Milan's technical and economic history – which were held in 1871, 1872, and 1881. Subsequent phases of the park's history are the construction of the science and natural history museum, and the later construction of the planetarium (see below).

Going through the gate nearest the Piazza della Repubblica, to the right are the new landscaped gardens that replace the zoo along Via Manin; some of the zoo's buildings have been reused, together with the imitation rock-pools. Near the ramparts stands the eclectic building of 1863 known as the "Padiglione del Caffè," or Coffee Pavilion, remodeled in 1920 by Giuseppe De Finetti and since transformed into a nursery

school. At the westernmost corner of the park stands one of Gio Ponti's creations, the curious Casa Rasini (1933–34), a 20-story tower that overshadows Porta Venezia.

Porta Venezia (III, E-F1-2). The wide clearing where the two neoclassical customs houses (Rodolfo Vantini, 1827–28) occupy the former *Porta Orientale*, now Porta Venezia, is one of those areas whose official name, Piazza Oberdan, is rarely used by the Milanese in everyday conversation. Indeed, the history of this place and the force of its name have caused it to be referred to always as "Porta Venezia." This was one of the principal gates in the Spanish walls, and today greets those arriving directly from Brianza or the crowded industrial area immediately north of the city. Several noteworthy Art-Nouveau buildings remain in the area, such as the *Hotel Diana* (1908), formerly the "Kursaal," at the beginning of Viale Piave, and *Casa Galimberti* (1903–04) at Via Malpighi 3, its facade enlivened by decorative polychrome tiles.

Beneath the piazza, or rather in that limited stretch of Corso Buenos Aires (see itinerary 3.3) up to the intersection of Viale Tunisia and Viale Regina Giovanna, is the *Porta Venezia subway station*, one of the largest on Line 1 (the "red line"), which came into operation in the 1960s between Sesto San Giovanni and the Trade Fair district. Like the other twenty original stations, the walls are faced (both on the mezzanine floor for passenger transfers, and at the lower level where the train tracks are located) with panels of artificial stone framed with metal, hung away from the walls enough to allow a plenum for pipes and other systems; a strip along the top carries all the signing. Not only was this type of finishing work (based on a design by Franco Albini, Franca Helg, Antonio Piva, and Bob Noorda for graphics) used subsequently throughout public underground areas, but it was a new departure in contemporary urban furnishings and communication design for public areas in Italy in general; notable also were the choice of colors and use of the Haas Helvetica uppercase font.

Corso Venezia (III, F1). Within the perimeter fence of the Giardini Pubblici (see above) stands the pseudo-classical *"Ulrico Hoepli" Planetario* (Piero Portaluppi, 1930), a planetarium donated to the city by the publishers Hoepli (see itinerary 1.2), and the neo-Romanesque building erected between 1888 and 1893 that houses the **Civico Museo di Storia Naturale**. This natural history museum – which was founded in 1838 when the collections of Giuseppe De Cristoforis and Giorgio Jan, known throughout Europe, were donated to the city – made up for its

The Villa Reale's rear prospect, overlooking the quiet gardens

losses from bomb damage by reassembling its collections, and reasserting its role as a busy research center and efficient training college. The approximately twenty rooms on two floors are occupied by the exhibition space, where displays of minerals, fossils, and examples of taxidermy are accompanied by models, new **dioramas***, and explanatory panels. Of particular historical and scientific interest are the materials remaining from the 17th-c. *Museo Naturalistico Settala**, the recomposed Allosaurus, Critosaurus, and Camptosaurus skeletons, several dinosaur eggs, a skeleton of a whale 19 m long, specimens of extinct vertebrates (*Equus quagga, Alca impennis*), a unique colorless topaz crystal (weighing 40 kg.) and a fine specimen of a *Tridacna gigantea*. The collection is copletement by a specialized library of over 30,000 volumes and by extensive study collections.

Near the intersection of Via Palestro (subway station), at Corso Venezia 40 stands the neoclassical *Palazzo Rocca Saporiti* (built to a scheme by the La Scala stage designer Giovanni Perego, 1812). Opposite, at Corso Venezia 51 rises the *Palazzo Bovara* (1787), also neoclassical in design. At no. 47, all that remains of the **Palazzo Castiglioni** (Giuseppe Sommaruga, 1903) is the Art-Nouveau facade and staircase. The rest of the building was rebuilt by the Unione Commercianti for its headquarters. At the time of the building's inauguration, a lobby of indignant citizens forced the architect Sommaruga to remove a pair of female statues from the front (now located at the Clinica Columbus, see itinerary 3.1), which had quickly earned the building the good-natured nickname of "house of buttocks." Further along the Corso stand Palazzo Serbelloni and Casa Silvestri (see below for both).

Through a tall barrel-vaulted archway (Piero Portaluppi, 1930) opposite the Museo di Storia Naturale, the short Via Salvini forms a right angle with the Corso, leading to the elegant Piazza Duse (III, F1-2), graced by a handsome residential building at no. 2 (Gigiotti Zanini, 1934).

At Via Cappuccini 8 nearby (III, F1-2) stands the **Palazzo Berri-Meregalli** (Giulio Ulisse Arata, 1914), a vivid example of eclecticism that comprises a variety of architectural styles (Romanesque, Gothic, Renaissance, and neo-Romanesque), surpassing Art Nouveau in sheer panache. The atrium is graced with a sculpture by Adolfo Wildt.

The panorama of the surrounding blocks, among the most exclusive in the city, would not be complete without mentioning the group of homes and other residential buildings located between Via Serbelloni (III, F1) and Via Mozart (map V, pp. 64–65, A1), which include **Palazzo Fidia** at Via Melegani 2 (Aldo Andreani, 1930), a brilliant synthesis of eclecticism and Futurism.

Villa Reale* (III, F1). The noble neoclassical residential complex in Corso Venezia, built in 1790 by Leopold Pollack of the powerful court family Barbiano di Belgiojoso, dominates the curving Via Palestro, which runs from Corso Venezia along the perimeter of the Giardini Pubblici. Intended to bring the comfortable isolation of the great noble villas of the countryside to the heart of Milan, this building is deliberately inward-looking. Somewhat aloof, it turns its back courtyard to the street, following the example of the Parisian "hôtel particulier," the main building set back from the street with a dividing wall and two sets of arcades. The true **facade*** of the manor, with its rusticated base, surmounted by a colossal order of pilasters with tall balustraded windows and attic, actually faces the **gardens** at the rear, which were the first gardens to be landscaped in the fashionable Romantic style.

Via Marina (formerly Via I Boschetti), an elegant sylvan boulevard which Giuseppe Piermarini had designed with Arcadian intentions three years before the villa was built, runs along the side of the manor's back gardens (map I, pp. 44–45, A-B6). Built when the French Revolution was already

cio and Francesco Hayez), to the turn of the century (the Scapigliati artists Daniele Ranzoni and Tranquillo Cremono, Giovanni Segantini, and Medardo Rosso): works from later periods have been on display at the Museo d'Arte Contemporanea at Palazzo Reale since 1984 (see itinerary 1.1). Among the works added to its initial collection are the *Vismara collection*, with works by Arturo Tosi, Amedeo Modigliani, Filippo De Pisis, and Giorgio Morandi, the *Museo Marino Marini*, through a 1973 donation by the Tuscan sculptor Marino Marini (*Horse and Rider*, Portraits* of 20th-c. personalities), and the **Grassi Collection***, which includes varied artifacts, Oriental cloths and rugs, works by great Dutch painters (Jan van Coyen and Gerard Dou), and above all paintings by

One of the halls of Palazzo Serbelloni

well under way, the manor was bought by the ensuing republican authorities and donated to Napoleon. Here resided the Viceroy of Italy, Eugene Beauharnais (whence the "royal" in Villa Reale), and later Field Marshal Radetzky, when the Hapsburgs returned.

The **Galleria d'Arte Moderna***, or Gallery of Modern Art, which has been situated here since 1921 (its curator was Piermarini, and Pollack was his pupil) was created by gathering up the more modern pieces from the civic collections, until then conserved in the Castello Sforzesco. With some emphasis on local Lombard art, the gallery's collections focus on modern Italian artistic developments from the neoclassical period (with works by Antonio Canova and Andrea Appiani) to the Romantic period (Pic-

19th- and 20th-c. French artists (Jean-Baptiste Corot, Alfred Sisley, Édouard Manet, Paul Cézanne, Paul Gauguin, Vincent van Gogh, Édouard Vuillard, Pierre Bonnard, Henri de Toulouse-Lautrec, and Maurice Utrillo), as well as Italian artists from the same period (Silvestro Lega, Daniele Ranzoni, Giovanni Boldini, Giuseppe De Nittis, Antonio Mancini, Armando Spadini, Giuseppe Pellizza da Volpedo, Giovanni Segantini, Giacomo Balla, Umberto Boccioni, and Giorgio Morandi). The single most interesting work in the gallery is perhaps the colossal **Fourth Estate*** by Pellizza da Volpedo (1901), a work of great symbolic force that has always been immensely popular. The painting was acquired in 1920 through public fund-raising.

Near the Villa Reale stands the smaller

Padiglione d'Arte Contemporanea (map I, pp. 44–45, A6), an austere work (Ignazio Gardella, 1954) considered among the best examples of Italian architecture in the mid-1900s, which was successful as the city's primary exhibition space for contemporary art. The building was destroyed by a bomb in the summer of 1993. The explosion took the lives of four firefighters and a civilian. The building has been successfully rebuilt, identical to the original plans of the architect.

Palazzo Serbelloni (I, B6). On a corner between Corso Venezia and Via S. Damiano stands the neoclassical building that perhaps best combines elegance and sobriety. Commissioned in 1793 from the architect Simone Cantoni by the noble Serbelloni family, the building's main facade presents a first-floor Ionic distyle portico *in antis* crowned by a tympanum. Despite repeated threats of eviction, the *Circolo della Stampa*, the uniquely Milanese-style journalism club, still has its headquarters here. Here in the *Salone degli Specchi* at the top of the spiral staircase and in the adjacent decorated rooms, well-attended presentations of new publications are staged.

From Palazzo Serbelloni, the old canal circuit was crossed by the so-called Ponte delle Sirenette, a little iron bridge (now in Parco Sempione, see itinerary 2.6), outside the 17th-c. *Palazzo del Senato* (I, B6); the site is now marked by a large sculpture by Joan Miró. Built between 1608 and 1630 to house the Collegio Elvetico (where the Counter-Reformation church trained its priests for the Catholic enclave in the Ticino Canton), the building has an eye-catching concave facade, the work of Francesco Maria Ricchino, and two courtyards of Tuscan and Ionic orders by Fabio Mangone. The palazzo hosted government offices during the reign of the Austro-Hun-

garian Emperor Joseph II (1787), while in the Napoleonic era, until 1814, it housed the Senate. In 1872 it received the **Archivio di Stato**, comprising the ducal archives of the Sforza dynasty and government documents from Spanish, Hapsburg, and Renaissance times; consequently, the archives are the largest source of documentation on the history of Milan and Lombardy. As its exterior shows, a large portion of the building had to be rebuilt after the air-raids of 1943.

The general headquarters of the *Garzanti publishing company*, which has been in business since 1938, were formerly located at no. 25 on Via Senato, as the circle of canals is called in this area. The company was established by taking over the Treves publishing company (founded 1861).

Casa Silvestri* (I, B6). Abutting the Corso toward the end near San Babila (see itinerary 1.2) are two important sights: the rugged portal (at no. 11) built in 1652 by Francesco Maria Ricchino, leading to the *Seminario Arcivescovile* (Vincenzo Seregni, Pellegrino Tibaldi, Aurelio Trezzi and Fabio Mangone, 1565–1608); and Casa Silvestri (no. 10), formerly Casa Fontana, one of Milan's rare examples of non-religious Renaissance architecture. Built in the style of Bramante in the late 15th c., and encompassing a residence dating from the previous century, Casa Silvestri has been modified numerous times, most recently in 1961 by Ferdinando Reggiori. The facade on Corso Venezia has an arched portal, surmounted by a 17th-c. balcony, and an irregular distribution of brick-framed windows. Some of these, partially encased in the masonry, belonged to the original 14th-c. dwelling. The frescoes on the front have all but disappeared; sources nearly coeval with the building's construction attribute the work to Bramante, or to Bramantino. The courtyard still blends harmoniously with the rest of the building.

2.3 From Monforte to Porta Vittoria and Porta Romana

At the turn of the century the southeast segment of the city stretching from Corso di Porta Vittoria to Corso di Porta Romana was still graced with gardens, cloisters, and patrician courtyards, with *botteghe* and trade outlets running the length of both streets, which led respectively to Brescia and distant Rome.

The 20th c. has seen the addition of major public administrative buildings (notably the huge Palazzo di Giustizia, or Law Courts), hospitals, theaters, and libraries, resulting in a general saturation of the area such that today there is not a sign of vacant

space. The former convent buildings were converted (the cloisters of Santa Maria della Passione now house the Conservatorio di Musica) or demolished (the monastery of San Pietro in Gessate). The great archway of Porta Romana, originally part of the Spanish walls, stands on its own, heavy traffic on all sides; the only original gardens still accessible to the public are those of the Guastalla. And yet numerous monuments from various periods have survived (even some fine buildings of more recent construction), and here and there a tranquil corner can still be found.

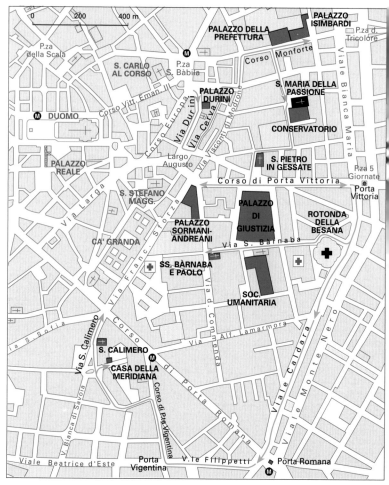

The first part of this itinerary starts within the old canal circuit, along Via Durini and Via Cerva, proceeding along Corso Monforte. On Corso di Porta Vittoria stands the hulking courthouse, built in the Fascist era. But not far away lies the unusual Rotonda di Via Besana, comprising a church (deconsecrated) set in a colonnaded rotunda, testifying to the centuries-old tradition of religious hospitals in the area. Further along the former Spanish walls along Viale Regina Margherita and Viale Caldara, we reach the roads adjacent to Corso Porta Romana and Corso Porta Vigentina. From there we take a slightly more circuitous route back to the circle of canals, passing by the church of San Calimero.

Via Durini (map V, pp. 64–65, A-B1). From Piazza San Babila, leaving Corso Europa (for both, see itinerary 1.2), enter the road running through the old quarter known as the Contrada del Durino, now bristling with high fashion outlets and stores offering famous Italian furnishing design products (including the shop of the designer Giorgio Armani, one of the greatest influences on international fashion today). Two buildings on this street are of particular historical interest: **Palazzo Durini** (no. 24), built in 1648 by Francesco Maria Ricchino, its facade is on two orders, each with an attic, with heavy cornices but a marked vertical pattern; and the church of *Santa Maria della Sanità*, or Santa Maria dei Crociferi. This church, built in 1708 at the behest of the Camilliani family, has preserved its pleasing curvaceous facade of plain unfaced brickwork.

Via Cerva (V, A-B1). Running nearly parallel to Via Durini is the narrow Via Cerva, which extends from Largo Augusto at the historical site of the **Verziere**: the 16th-c./17th-c. *Verziere column* once stood among the fruit and vegetable stands that give this area its name. The old marketplace, abandoned between the wars, extended to the former Palazzo del Capitano di Giustizia on Piazza Fontana (see itinerary 1.3), while now it is greatly reduced by the block of buildings that has been added.

Via Cerva is itself an old quarter that, despite extensive demolition and reconstruction work, still boasts a late 18th-c. appearance. A portal and a few wrought-iron balconies inserted in the modern building at no. 28 are all that remains of the Palazzo Visconti di Modrone. This secondary branch of the leading ducal family of Milan, of which the director Luchino Visconti was a member, gives its name to the adjacent stretch of the ring of canals. You can reach it by walking a short way on Via Borgogna (to the right, coming out of Via Cerva), and then following it to the left to the intersection of Corso Monforte.

Corso Monforte (V, A1-2). This first stretch of the thoroughfare leading out of town in the direction of Brescia (though now an inbound one-way street) probably owes its name to the Piedmont town of Monforte d'Alba, various inhabitants of which moved to Milan in the 13th c. In the stretch between the old canals and the former circuit of Spanish walls are the general headquarters of the province of Milan: state offices at no. 31 in the 18th-c. *Palazzo della Prefettura* (V, A1), formerly known as the Palazzo dei Somaschi, and at no. 35 the offices of the elected provincial administration in **Palazzo Isimbardi**, a large 15th-c. building which has been converted numerous times. In this latter building, the vault of the *Sala della Giunta* is decorated with a large painting by G. B. Tiepolo (**Triumph of the Doge Francesco Morosini**), originally commissioned for the Palazzo Morosini in Campo Santo Stefano in Venice.

Santa Maria della Passione* (V, A-B1). Slightly to the south of Corso Monforte, at the intersection of Via Conservatorio and Via Bellini (on the latter street, note the Art Nouveau house at no. 11 by Alfred Campanini, 1904) stands the former convent built in the Sforza era for the Lateran Canons. The church was built in 1486 on a central Greek-cross plan, and was completed in 1530 by Cristoforo Lombardo, who added the dome (49.7 m) and octagonal drum. The conversion to a Latin-cross plan by lengthening one of the arms into a nave and two aisles and six side chapels (according to the scheme in the plan shown here), was commenced in 1573 to designs by Martino Bassi. The layout of the new church,

the largest in the city after the cathedral, became definitive upon the construction of the facade (1692–1729), designed by the Barnabite priest Giuseppe Rusnati.

Inside, in the first chapel (1) in the left aisle, on the right wall, is *The Fast of St. Charles*, a painting by Daniele Crespi. The vault of the nave has extensive late-16th-c. decoration, while on the pillars of the octagon (2) below the dome hang eight paintings from the early 17th c., most of which are also by Crespi. The left transept (3) has a large *Last Supper* by Gaudenzio Ferrari (1543); to the left is a *Crucifixion* by Giulio Campi (1560). The **organ panels*** (depicting the *Washing of the Feet* on the outside and the *Crucifixion* and *Deposition* on the inside) in the left niche (4) of the presbytery are all by Crespi. The altar in the right transept (5) contains a *Deposition with Sts. Ambrose and Augustine*, attributed to Bernardino Luini.

From the right niche (6) of the presbytery, with an organ by Gian Giacomo Antegnati (1558), proceed to the **Museo della Basilica** (7–10), established in 1972 with paintings from the 17th-c. Lombard school (Crespi, Campi, Francesco del Cairo, Carlo Francesco Nuvolone, and Giuseppe Vermiglio) and other works testifying to the history of the church and the order that owned it. Note the 15th-c. atmosphere of the *Sala Capitolare* (8), designed and frescoed by Bergognone.

Except for the museum, since 1808 the convent building has been used for the

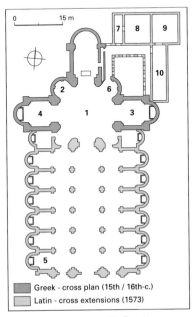

Plan of Santa Maria della Passione

"Giuseppe Verdi" Conservatorio di Musica (V, B1), the city's leading music school. The interior, reconstructed by Ferdinando Reggiori after it was damaged by bombings during World War II, contains the *Sala Grande*, which, with its 1,800 seats and excellent acoustics, is the most popular concert hall in Milan.

On the corner between Via Conservatorio and Via Passione is the *Palazzo Archinto* (V, B1), a large and noteworthy neoclassical building (1833–47). It houses the Collegio delle Fanciulle, an institute founded in 1808 by Napoleon Bonaparte.

San Pietro in Gessate (V, B1). Located between the area of Santa Maria della Passione and Corso di Porta Vittoria, and facing the latter, although it is set back from the rest of the buildings on the street, is the church of San Pietro, a gothic-Renaissance structure dating back to 1475, originally the work of either Pietro Antonio or Guiniforte Solari, though the facade was remodeled in 1912. In that year additions and decorations dating back to the 17th/18th c. perished in the course of questionable restoration work; nevertheless, a *fresco* has survived, perhaps transferred from the fifth chapel in the right aisle by Bergognone, together with other works by the 15th-c. Lombard school (left aisle). The left transept forms the **Cappella Grifi***, richly decorated with Renaissance frescoes (*Stories of St. Ambrose*) by Bernardino Butinone and Bernardino Zenale, works which were uncovered in the 19th c. and thereafter restored numerous times.

Palazzo di Giustizia (V, B-C1). The block covering the area between Corso di Porta Vittoria and Via Freguglia, Via San Barnaba, and Via Manara was built up between 1932 and 1940, along with the daunting marble-clad court house, which covers some 31,000 square meters and contains 65 courtrooms, 13 courtyards, and 1,200 office units. It was designed by Marcello Piacentini and Ernesto Rapisardi in homage to the Fascist spirit. The building has never been very popular with the city, perhaps because it is also seen as an obtrusive reminder of the hulking and inefficient bureaucracy of Rome. Such objections aside, it contains numerous decorative works, including sculptures, relief work, frescoes, and mosaics created by some of the finest Italian artists of the day (Mario Sironi, Arturo Martini, Gino Severini, Guido Cadorin, and Massimo Campigli). Italians have become quite familiar with the building's lumbering facade owing to its

regular appearance on television during the "Clean Hands" investigation into local council corruption that began in 1992. The trials that ensued saw most of the leading politicians and businessmen of the 1980s dragged before the court to answer accusations of graft.

Corso di Porta Vittoria (V, B1-2). The street that runs from the Verziere (see above) to the Spanish walls ends in a square that takes its name from the Cinque Giornate di Milano (March 18–22, 1848), a five-day battle in which the city echoed other European uprisings of the mid-19th c. The rebellion of the Milanese, led by Carlo Cattaneo and others, forced the retreat of twenty thousand men of the Austro-Hungarian garrison led by Field Marshal Josef Radetzky. At no. 43 on this road is the recessed brick facade of the *Palazzo della Camera Confederale del Lavoro*, formerly the offices of the Sindacati Fascisti dell'Industria (1932).

Toward the city end of the Corso stands **Palazzo Sormani-Andreani** (V, B1), a noble building dating to the 17th c., whose front section was added in 1736 by Francesco Croce. Since 1956 this building, almost totally reconstructed inside after the war, has housed the central municipal library, and is commonly known as the "Sormani." The *Sala del Grechetto*, almost totally covered with paintings (*Orpheus Taming the Animals*) by the 17th-c. Genoese painter and engraver Grechetto is used for exhibitions; access is from Via Francesco Sforza.

Porta Vittoria (V, B2). Corso di Porta Vittoria ends in Piazza Cinque Giornate, marked by a central obelisk (Giuseppe Grandi, 1895) in memory of the **Cinque Giornate***, the patriotic uprising noted above. The last of these famous five days is commemorated in the name of the road that continues out of town, Corso XXII Marzo (V, B2-4). A special bus service (no. 73) follows this road direct to Linate airport (see itinerary 3.3).

Rotonda della Besana* (V, C2). Just south of Porta Vittoria along the former circuit of the Spanish walls in Viale Regina Margherita, stands the elegant 18th-c. complex of San Michele, once a graveyard, established in 1725 for use by the Ca' Granda hospital (see itinerary 1.3). At the center of the arcaded enclosure, which due to its form and proximity to the Via Besana is improperly known as the Rotonda della Besana, stands the deconsecrated church of *San Michele ai Nuovi Sepolcri* with its central plan (Attilio

Arrigoni, 1713), now a city exhibition space for temporary shows.

Throughout the summer the enclosure is used for open-air movie projections.

Following Via Besana and Via San Barnaba, to the space between them in which, in the arch between Via Pace and Via Fanti, the factories of the Tecnomasio stood between 1863 and 1907 (see itinerary 3.4), one passes behind the Palazzo di Giustizia. The extensively restored church of *Santa Maria della Pace* (V, C1) dates back to the 15th c., and its original frescoes by Bernardino Luini are now in the Brera. After it was despoiled in 1805, the church remained empty for nearly a century; now it belongs to the order of the Knights of Malta.

Most of the former convent is now occupied by the *Società Umanitaria* (V, C1), an important benevolent and training center founded in 1898 through a bequest by Prospero Moisè Loria. From Via Daverio one can visit the *cloisters*, often utilized for temporary exhibitions, and the former refectory, now the *Sala degli Affreschi*, with a fresco by Marco d'Oggiono depicting the *Crucifixion*.

At the intersection of Via della Commenda (V, C1), to the right lies the *Giardino della Guastalla* (gardens which used to belong to the Guastalla boarding school), which originally bordered the canals along the Ca' Grande (see itinerary 1.3). At the same intersection with Via della Commenda stands the church of **SS. Barnaba e Paolo**, built in 1558 by the Chierici Regolari di San Paolo. Its design is attributed to Galeazzo Alessi, who introduced architectural solutions that were innovative for their time (such as elevating the presbytery and the chapels above the level of the nave). Various works from the Lombard school of the 15th c./17th c. can be seen here.

Porta Romana (V, D1). Following the traces of the old Spanish walls, at the point where they intersect with Corso Porta Romana (see itinerary 1.3), is *Piazza Medaglie d'Oro*, where heavy traffic rushes obliviously round the free-standing arch of the 16th-c. gate once guarding the road to Rome. Built in 1598 to designs by Aurelio Trezzi to celebrate the marriage of Mary Margaret of Austria and Philip III of Spain (the bride is supposed to have entered the city here, before moving to Madrid), the gate is similar to other structures of the same period done by Michele Sanmicheli for the Republic of Venice, in turn inspired by the triumphal arches of imperial Rome. The exterior bears a Doric order of coupled columns, surmounted by an attic set with a panel inscribed with a dedicatory inscription.

Alongside the arch remains of a bastion of the *Spanish walls* occupy the space between Viale Filippetti and Viale Sabotino; other fragments can be seen further up the next street, Viale Beatrice d'Este, almost the only tracts of wall left of the over 11 kilometers of ramparts that once encircled the city.

At Corso di Porta Romana 124, near the city gate, stands the *Teatro di Porta Romana*, formerly a movie theater and now managed by a company in which stage and film director Gabriele Salvatores (whose film "Mediterraneo" won an Oscar in 1992 for best foreign film of the year) has long played a leading role.

Much further up the Corso, at no. 65, is the much older and more stately *Teatro Carcano*

The deconsecrated church of San Michele in its arcaded enclosure

(map IV, pp. 62–63, C6), founded in 1803, the theater once also staged operas, including the world premiers of works by Donizetti and Bellini. Its architecture has now been modernized. A third important venue not far from Porta Romana is the modern *Teatro Franco Parenti* at Via Pier Lombardo 14 (V, D2); it takes its name from its late founder, one of the finest and most innovative dramatic actors in Milan in the postwar period.

West of Porta Romana, *Porta Vigentina* marks the site of another city gate in the Spanish walls (IV, D6), though it is only a place name today. Heading toward the center along Corso Vigentina and the subsequent side-streets of Via Quadronno and Via Gaetano Pini – the latter is also the name of the noted orthopedic center located there – one reaches the tree-lined Piazza Cardinal Ferrari and Via San Calimero beyond.

Via San Calimero (IV, C-D6). Closed at the top end to automobile traffic, the street owes its name to the old church of *San Calimero*, founded in early Christian times, re-built in the 13th c. and remodeled in 1609 by Francesco Maria Ricchino. Now, however, it has been irreparably impaired by questionable restoration work performed in the late 19th c. The facade dates from this period (1882). In the arch to the right of the entrance is a *Crucifixion* by Cerano, while the raised apse corresponds to the 16th-c. crypt, with vaults frescoed by the Fiamminghini. In the sacristy is a 15th-c. fresco.

The short dead-end street Via Marchiondi runs from Piazza Cardinal Ferrrari. At no. 3 is the **Casa della Meridiana**, an interesting home (Giuseppe De Finetti, 1927) originally conceived as a residence for five apartments, custom-built for each of the resident families. A "multiple villa," it was the first house in Milan where the common stairway was replaced by internal elevators directly serving the apartments. The *Meridiana* (sundial) is the work of the painter and architect Gigiotti Zanini.

Via San Calimero ends at the old canal circuit at the junction of Via Santa Sofia and Via Francesco Sforza (see itinerary 1.3).

2.4 The Porta Ticinese Area and the Outer Canals

Strange as it may seem today, until a few decades ago Milan still had its docks and canal wharves. In the great Darsena dockyard between Viale D'Annunzio and Viale Gorizia, water from the Ticino made its way up the Naviglio Grande, turned the corner and flowed out again down the Naviglio Pavese; barges traveling from the north, borne along by the down-current, docked here to unload their cargoes. And not so long ago passersby could still watch the cranes and the transit of the barges, similar to those that still travel the canals of continental Europe. These were the last signs of the dockyard's role as a transit point, a role that had been of utmost importance in centuries past. Greatly reduced in the 19th c. by competition from the railroads, and made definitively redundant in the 20th c. by road transport, water transport has now completely disappeared from Milan. Even the little passenger barge that cruised the canals in the early 1980s has been discontinued – an unsuccessful attempt at exploiting the merchant transport system for tourist ends.

The district takes its name "Ticinese" from the River Ticino which flows through it via the canals, and has a history as the most infamous quarter of the city, typical of many port neighborhoods. With its close-knit fabric of working-class homes, forcibly thinned out by the air-raids of 1943 (which gave us the parks at Sant'Eustorgio and San Lorenzo), the Ticinese area has retained perhaps a little of its old atmosphere, where the spirit of self-sufficiency is tinged with the radical anarchy for which it was notorious. Expensive apartments rented by foreign fashion models, photographers' studios, pricey condominiums, design studios, and dozens of shops selling "modern antiques" and other bric-à-brac have almost completely replaced

The Touring Club headquarters

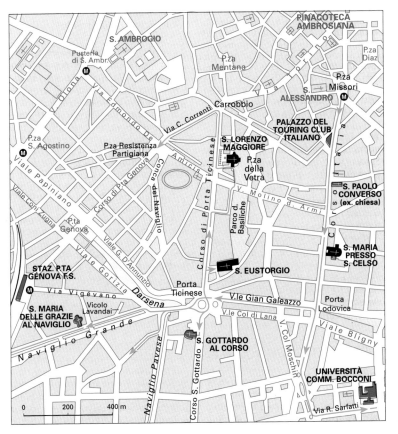

the traditional shops and former hand-to-mouth lifestyle of the original tenants. Nevertheless, there are enclaves that resist change, such as the so-called "social club" on the Via Conchetta. These days, instead of leafleting, the social clubs surf the Internet or run jazz clubs (the Tangram on Via Pezzotti, or the more classic Capolinea at the end of Via Lodovico il Moro), where live music is much preferred.

This itinerary covers several historic monuments in its course as it moves outward along Corso Italia, crossing the old Spanish walls near the Università "Luigi Bocconi," proceeding to the Darsena, and thence along the other road running almost parallel to Corso di Porta Ticinese. Other important landmarks include the 19th- and 20th-c. buildings further out, between and along the two canals (especially the former Ansaldo metal works on Via Bergognone and the former Richard Ginori ceramics factory on Via Morimondo). No longer in use and not yet converted, they are not open to the public.

Corso Italia (map IV, pp. 62–63, C-D5). A relatively modern road built in the wake of Mi-lan's first master plan (the Piano Beruto of 1889) runs from Piazza Missori in the middle of the historic center (see itinerary 1.3). The irregularity of the corners which the road forms with its side-streets is proof that the historical urban network was oriented differently as far back as Roman times.

The building standing at Corso Italia 10 is none other than the *Palazzo del Touring Club Italiano* (map I, pp. 44–45, B4). We include it here, not just as one of Milan's monuments (purpose-built for the T.C.I. in 1915 to designs by Achille Binda) but also to pay homage to the organization that publishes the famous guides. The building contains offices and a well-stocked bookstore of maps and guides in all languages. In the lobby in the main entrance a bronze by Giannino Castiglioni honors *Luigi Vittorio Bertarelli*, the man who basically fathered the T.C.I. The adjacent piazza where the road widens is named after Bertarelli.

Just beyond the Touring Club building stands an innovative shopping and office complex (Luigi Moretti, 1952–56), and at no. 24 another interesting building serving mixed purposes (Luigi Caccia Dominioni, 1957–61). Then comes the Milanese headquarters of the *Riunione Adriatica di Sicurità* (Gio Ponti, Antonio Fornarolo, Alberto Rosselli, and Pietro Portaluppi, 1959–60) dominating the crossroads. This modern building stands on the site of a convent built by order of the Countess Ludovica Torelli della Guastalla, demolished in 1804. At the preceding intersection of Via Sant'Eufemia stands the deconsecrated church of **San Paolo Converso**, occupied by an auction firm. Built no later than 1580, perhaps based on a design by Domenico Giunti, the building was completed in 1613, with its elegant tabernacle facade, the work of Cerano. The interior is divided into various areas for the faithful and the nuns, and boasts a highly coherent decorative apparatus of stucco reliefs, paintings, and frescoes, some of them illusionistic, by the Cremonese family of Antonio, Giulio, and Vincenzo Campi. Outside the church stands an early 17th-c. *column*, previously located in Piazza Bertarelli.

Santa Maria presso San Celso* (IV, D5). Corso Italia continues across the intersection of Via Santa Sofia and Via Molino delle Armi (the former drab, the latter lively), past two adjacent churches. At the back of a closed garden, stands the little church of *San Celso*, a Romanesque temple of Benedictine origins (11th- to 12th c.); its two front bays were removed after the monastery was closed (1783); the church was rebuilt by Luigi Canonica (1851–54). The central *portal* rebuilt on the new facade, and the Lombard-Romanesque bell tower from the medieval structure, can still be seen from the outside. Traces of the former bays can be seen on the wall that bounds the garden.
The larger church alongside, preceded by a graceful *atrium** by Cesare Cesariano, is rightly considered one of the finest examples of early 16th-c. architecture in the city. Dedicated to the Virgin, the church is also known as *Santa Maria dei Miracoli*. Designed in 1493 by Gian Giacomo Dolcebuono, and constructed substantially completed by 1506 by Cristoforo Solari and Giovanni Antonio Amadeo, it was expanded over the following decades through the work of Cesariano, Vincenzo Seregni, and Galeazzo Alessi. It has had the status of a basilica since 1950. Beyond the atrium, which is accessed by three doorways from the street, rises the remarkable ornate facade, which presents two main orders incorporating attics between paired pilasters; begun in

1572, the facade is the work of Martino Bassi, who worked to plans by Seregni. The lively arrangement of sculpted figures is the work of Stoldo Lorenzi (the statues in the middle niches and those above the central gate) and Annibale Fontana (on the central tympanum and in the side niches, together with the bas-reliefs depicting *Gospel stories*, and the five angels crowning the tympanum silhouetted against the sky). Inside, the nave extends to a set of piers supporting the polygonal drum and dome. Here are other statues by Stoldo Lorenzi (*Baptist*; *Elijah*) and Annibale Fontana (*St. John the Evangelist*). The statue (**Our Lady of the Assumption***, 1586) on the altar of the Madonna, based on a design by Bassi, is also by Fontana. Behind the altar frontal (which can be opened) is a wall that was once decorated by a fresco, now mostly perished, of Our Lady of Miracles, to whom the temple is dedicated. In the presbytery is the carved **choir***, begun in 1570 and based on a design by Galeazzo Alessi. Other particularly important works are *The Holy Family and St. Jerome* by Paris Bordone on the altar of the south transept, and, in the ambulatory, the *Baptism of Jesus* by Gaudenzio Ferrari in the fifth bay on the right, and the *Conversion of St. Paul* by Moretto in the ninth bay. The altar in the north transept includes a *sarcophagus* from the 5th c. Again, in the first chapel to the left is a **Virgin Adoring the Christ Child***, with an altarpiece by Bergognone. The sacristies contain remarkable specimens of religious jewelry, but the most valuable, a *processional cross* in red jasper, gold and gemstones, donated by Ottone Visconti in 1296, has been wisely stored elsewhere.

Università Commerciale "Luigi Bocconi" (IV, E5). Beyond Corso Italia, which ends in a square named after the demolished Porta Lodovica (IV, D5), and following Via Teulié and Via Castelbarco, one reaches a district that boasts an unusual quantity of green space, the site of Italy's most important university of economic studies, at Via Sarfatti, Via Gobbi, Via Toniolo and Via Bocconi (Giuseppe Pagano Pogatschnig and Gian Giacomo Predaval, 1937–41). The university was founded in 1902 by the businessman Ferdinando Bocconi (who also founded the La Rinascente department stores), in memory of his son, who had died in battle in Adua, Ethiopia six years before. It is still a private university, although its board of directors also includes representatives in public office.
Around the university's main building are

various postwar extensions, including the residence hall on Via Bocconi 12 (Giovanni Muzio, 1953). At the corner of Via Bocconi and Via Sarfatti, a double-headed hammer (placed at the suggestion of Enzo Mari) commemorates the Bocconi student Roberto Franceschi, whose death on this site in 1972 was attributed by the courts to a bullet fired by security police during a particularly tense period in the post-1968 student demonstrations.

Porta Ticinese (IV, D4). Two blocks west of Porta Lodovica, Viale Col di Lana leads into *Piazzale XXIV Maggio*, a historic market place and junction between city and countryside, still lively with business as well as traffic. The site is the location of an important gate in the old ramparts, which Luigi Cagnola replaced between 1801 and 1804 with the present-day self-standing **Atrium*** in a Vitruvian Ionic order, one of the most significant neoclassical works in Milan. The imposing Baveno granite structure, on columns and pillars surmounted by tympana – note its interior coffered vault – was originally named after the Napoleonic victory at Marengo (1800), but fifteen years later the Holy Alliance rededicated it to "the peace that frees the people." It was part of an urban redevelopment scheme for the area around the gate, but never completed. The pair of customs houses remain, characterized by their imitation ashlar masonry.

From the gate, the stretch of the Roman road toward Pavia is now known as **Corso San Gottardo** (IV, E4), a frenetic thoroughfare along which, between 1600 and 1700, the first of the great communities outside the city developed around the ramparts: the quintessential suburb. The

church of *San Gottardo al Corso* was originally located here, founded in the 13th c. by the Benedictines and converted into a parish church by Archbishop Carlo Borromeo (1565). It was rebuilt in the 19th c. Corso San Gottardo itself, historically known for the foreign trade functions it assumed in 1818, when the Pavese canal nearby (see below) was made navigable, still conserves a portion of the port-like liveliness mentioned at the beginning of this itinerary.

Darsena (IV, D3-4). The broad dock at Porta Ticinese, a municipal junction in the Lombard internal water system, was created in 1603 by the Spanish governor, the Count of Fuentes, and took on its present form (enlarged through the demolition of a stretch of ramparts) in 1920. About 20 meters across and around 750 meters long, the Darsena dockyard is a meter and a half deep. In addition to the outer canals (see below), the River Olona also flows into it from underground. The old commercial dock along Via D'Annunzio was unnecessarily paved over in the 1980s and turned into a parking lot; this was decided when the traditional Saturday market known as the "Fiera di Sinigaglia" was evicted from its location on nearby Via Calatafimi and the city decided to transfer it here.

The Darsena was connected with the ring of canals through a basin, now filled in, located at the present-day *Conca del Naviglio* (IV, C-D3-4). The proposal to reopen it as a waterway advanced in the 1980s by the local council was the most important episode in the course of repeated debates which over past decades have stressed the appropriateness of a general reopening of Milan's internal water systems. Despite proposals from several political parties, the actual likelihood of realizing such projects seems slim at present.

One of the canals during the street festival

What was historically the largest of Milanese canals originally flowed into the Darsena from the Ticino north of Turbigo (see itinerary 4.4). One of the largest civil engineering works in medieval northern Italy, the so-called **Naviglio Grande** (IV, D-E1-3) was opened in the 12thc. (probably in 1179) and was completed by 1239 on the 50 km stretch that it still follows. Rendered navigable in 1272, for centuries it played a major role in foreign trade between Milan and central Europe, through the lake, or Lake Maggiore, and, further north, by land, through the passes of Sempione (Simplon) and San Bernardino (Little St. Bernard). Here in the city you can follow the first stretch along the towpaths, where only a few of the buildings are still in the period style: the towpaths of *Ripa di Porta Ticinese* on the southern shore and *Alzaia del Naviglio Grande* on the northern side. The quaint *Vicolo Lavandai* runs from the latter, not far from Porta Ticinese (IV, D3). It owes its name to the old wash-houses, with their characteristic canopies on wooden beams. A little further on, the church of *Santa Maria delle Grazie al Naviglio* (IV, D3) has a 19th-/20th-c. neo-Gothic appearance.

Via Vigevano (IV, D8) still has a typical appearance defined by large residential buildings with courtyards built between 1800 and 1900, and several interesting shops and, at no. 41, the bookstore and visual arts gallery *Idea Books*. The street ends at the *Porta Genova station* (IV, D2), the site of the subway station of the same name on Line 2 (the "green line"), a junction for a number of city train stops. Crossing the group of tracks is an iron pedestrian bridge, originally (1865–70) an integral part of the ring of railways in operation around Milan but now and slated for demolition. Past the bridge are late 19th-c. working-class neighborhoods, which include the abandoned and empty sheds of the large machine-tool plant at *Via Bergognone 30-34* (IV, D-E1-2). Opened in 1904, it belonged from 1966 on to the Ansaldo metalworks. Under the name "Spazio Ansaldo," in recent years it has been used by the city for temporary exhibits or live performances. Further out along the Naviglio Grande towpath is the church of **San Cristoforo sul Naviglio** (IV, E1; off map). The church is comprised of two adjacent structures – the one on the left is probably from the 13th c., while the other (the Cappella Ducale) dates to the 14th/15th c. The interior, where the two buildings form a single space, is decorated by coeval or slightly later frescoes of the Lombard school.

The **Naviglio Pavese** (IV, E-F3-4) flows from the Darsena, and 33 km downstream once again issues into the River Ticino near Pavia. Excavated for irrigation purposes in the late 14th c., it did not become navigable until 1819. A 17th-c. interruption in its expansion work further out toward the outskirts is memorialized by the name of the area, *Conca Fallata*. Further still, well out of the city, is the Carthusian monastery near Pavia (see itinerary 3.4). Along the canal, permanently abandoned in 1978, remain the twelve lock basins that permitted boats

The canal-side church of San Cristoforo

to navigate the rise of more than 52 m. The two banks in this first urban stretch of the canal are somewhat different in appearance: the bank on *Via Ascanio Sforza* on the hilly left is rather characteristic and old-fashioned in appearance, while the opposite *Alzaia Naviglio Pavese* is modern and rather characterless. A few stretches of old fabric have survived on the side-street *Via Magolfa* as well (IV, E3).

Corso di Porta Ticinese (IV, C-D4). Further inward along the same road at present-day Porta Ticinese is another older city gate (see above). The straight Corso di Porta Ticinese, a road that originally protruded like a thorn from the borough outside the city walls that even in medieval times occupied the area between present-day Via Santa Croce and Conca del Naviglio, connects the gates, from the ramparts to the ring of canals. This is the heart of the Ticinese area as it has been briefly described in the introduction to the itinerary, a district with an alternative lifestyle that has attempted to survive over recent decades by turning to small trade. The main street and side-streets are lined with shops (offering alternative fashions, sophisticated leather crafts, handmade toys, and "organic" ice cream), testifying to the strong creative bent of this area's retail businesses. Nevertheless, as in Brera, the progressive displacement of the stable tenant population has proceeded rapidly, and one of the most important religious structures of the city is now located near recently-constructed condominiums lining the road.

Sant'Eustorgio* (IV, D4). Do not be misled by the neo-Romanesque appearance of this basilica, whose facade was built in 1862–65. What lies behind it is a very old church, as evidenced by the late 14th-c. chapels to the side and the late 13th-c. *bell tower*, despite the fact that it has been changed and modified countless times over the years. Perhaps founded by Bishop Eustorgio himself (ca. 315–331), later made a saint, or perhaps by a successor of the same name in the 6th c., the existence of the church is documented back as early as the 8th c., and portions of its structure still date back to its Romanesque reconstruction (starting in 1190), made necessary by Frederick Barbarossa's sack of Milan. Passed on to the Dominicans in the early 13th c., in the 14th c. the temple assumed its present layout, with new chapels added during the next century. The restructuring and restoration work that followed was not completed until 1966. Its history is bound to that of the supposed relics of the Three Magi, originally brought to the city by Bishop Eustorgio, transferred to Cologne in 1164 at the behest of Frederick Barbarossa, and returned in part in 1903.

The nave and two aisles inside, with the nave extended to form the apse, are supported and divided by slightly inclined cruciform pillars with capitals from the 11th and 14th c., for the most part rebuilt. In several chapels on the right there are tombs, and in the vault there are 14th- and 15th-c. frescoes. The first of these, dating from the late 15th c., a separated triptych (*Madonna and Saints*), is a late work by Bergognone. In the third chapel, rendered Baroque by Francesco Croce, is *the tomb of Protaso Caimi* (ca. 1360), from the Campionese School. The fourth chapel holds *the tomb of Stefano Visconti** (died 1327), the tomb of Giovanni Balduccio, with a sarcophagus that was remodeled in 1359 by

Bonino da Campione, and a 14th-c. painting of the *Crucifixion* on the left wall. In the south transept is the *Cappella dei Magi*, a chapel which contains a late Roman sarcophagus that holds the supposed relics of the Three Magi. The main altar includes an unfinished marble *dossal** built in successive stages between 1300 and 1400: the panels that can be seen may be based on designs by Giovanni dei Grassi, the central *Crucifixion* betrays Tuscan influence, and the small statues that provide the final touch are attributed to Matteo da Campione.

From the false crypt in the rear, where you can see masonry work and a portion of the early Christian structure, go to the detached **Cappella Portinari****, one of the earliest and finest Renaissance structures in the city (1462–66), commissioned by the Florentine nobleman Pigello Portinari, who was the procurator for the Banco dei Medici in Milan. Based on two rooms of different sizes (the smaller used for the altar), both with a square plan and crowned with a dome, and following a scheme formulated and applied in Florence by Filippo Brunelleschi, the architecture of this chapel was traditionally attributed to Michelozzo, but is now thought to be the work of a Lombard master in contact with Tuscan circles. The impact of its spatial design is tempered by the richness and color of its decorations, the work of local craftsmen accustomed to handling structural aspects decoratively. In the drum is a procession of stucco *angels* bearing festoons. The upper area carries **frescoes*** (*Life of St. Peter Martyr*; 1468), considered the masterpiece of Vincenzo Foppa. In the center, transferred here from the church in 1737, is the extraordinary marble **Tomb of St. Peter Martyr*** (1336–39), by Giovanni di Balduccio and assistants: the sarcophagus contains the remains of the Dominican Pietro da Verona, who persecuted the Catharist heretics and carried out his inquisitorial functions with such zeal that he was killed by the populace near Seveso in 1252.

A small annexed *museum* contains 17th-and 18th-c. paintings and religious articles and leads to the three underground rooms, the remains of the only *Roman and early Christian cemetery* in Milan. From the gate at Piazza Sant'Eustorgio 3, we enter what remains of the *cloisters* of its former Dominican convent, until 1559 the seat of the Inquisition.

Behind Sant'Eustorgio, passing by the little shops along the street, turn down the side-street Via Vetere into the **Parco delle**

Basiliche (IV, C-D4), a park constructed after the buildings in this area were bombed in World War II and never rebuilt.

Piazza della Vetra (IV, C4). The Parco delle Basiliche proceeds beyond Via Molino delle Armi until the street opens out onto a square that was once an important place in the city's history, before it was changed by development in the 1930s. In ancient times numerous watercourses met in this area and connected with the ring of canals, while from 1045 to 1840 a scaffold bore witness to the site's institutional use as a place for public torture and executions. From the square, a favorite with photographers, you can enjoy the best views of the apsidal section of San Lorenzo. You reach the front of the church by passing the period houses lining Via Pioppette.

San Lorenzo Maggiore** (IV, C4). The essentially late 16th-c. appearance of this basilica, flanked by the pair of 17th-c. avant-corps belonging to the *rectories* (whose construction began with Aurelio Trezzi and was concluded by Francesco Maria Ricchino), reinterprets the early Christian form of basilica based on a central plan which, dating back to the 5th/6th c., is exceptional for what was at that time the western Roman Empire. In reality, though not only perceived as being an "ancient Roman" temple by the city, its historical and architectural importance is comparable to the basilica of San Vitale in Ravenna or the cathedral of Aix-la-Chapelle (Aachen). Neither the Romanesque remodeling of the 13th c. nor the interior and exterior reconstruction work done by Martino Bassi when the dome was rebuilt (after it collapsed in 1573) has altered the essential original plan. Nevertheless, the facade was changed in 1894. Sixteen Roman **columns*** 8.5 m tall, dating back to imperial times, stand opposite the basilica. They come from a 2nd/3rd-c. Roman temple and were brought here and rearranged in the 5th c. as part of a former four-sided atrium. In the church square, created in the 1930s after the demolition of the houses that had filled the area of the atrium, note the 1942 copy of a statue of Em-

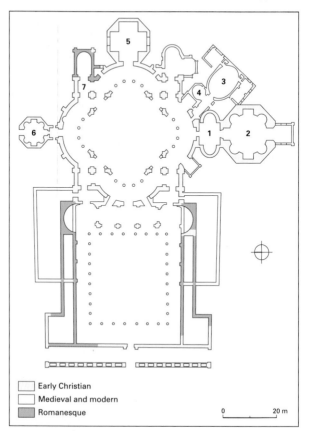

	Early Christian
	Medieval and modern
	Romanesque

0   20 m

Plan of the basilica of San Lorenzo Maggiore

The basilica of San Lorenzo Maggiore seen from the park

peror Constantine, who in 313 issued the edict (known as the Edict of Milan) permitting the practice of the Christian religion. The interior of the church, which is remarkably solemn, is composed of a majestic circular space in which four radiating exedrae with semidomes open onto the large ambulatory, and at the upper level, onto the women's galleries. Passing an atrium on the right (1, in the plan shown here), with the remains of its 5th-c. mosaics and a Roman portal which may date back to the 1st c., a doorway leads to the **Cappella di Sant'Aquilino**** (2), on a noteworthy octagonal plan, quite well preserved, dating from the 5th c., when it was created as an imperial mausoleum. There are mosaics in two niches (*Christ with the Apostles* and *The Abduction of Elijah*), also from the 5th c. To the right of the entry is a *sarcophagus* from the 4th c.; at the altar is a 16th-c. silver *urn* with the remains of Saint Aquilinus. A small stairway descends into a chamber discovered in 1911, where the foundations constructed with material possibly from an imperial-era amphitheater are still visible.

In the church, which has an adjacent *sacristy* (3) attributed to Francesco Croce (1713), and an adjoining *baptistery* (4) acknowledged to be of 18th-c. origins, is the main altar of the *Cappella di Sant'Ippolito* (5), on a central plan, dating from the 5th c. but now devoid of any decorative work. Before entering a third early-Christian chapel, the *Cappella di San Sisto* (6), with its lower portion from the 7th c. that opens at the left,

which contains 17th-c. frescoes from the Helvetic school, one comes to the tomb of *Giovanni del Conte* (7), the work of Marco d'Agrate and Vincenzo Seregni (1568).

Returning outside, note how close the sixteen columns are to the large arches of the medieval **Porta Ticinese**, at the point where Corso Porta Ticinese crosses the former ring of canals. The structure dates back to the 13th c., but was reworked in the 14th c. and finally transformed by Camillo Boito between 1861 and 1865. Its outer face contains a tabernacle with reliefs of saints, a 14th-c. work by the workshop of Giovanni di Balduccio.

In the opposite direction, toward the city center, the road ends not far from Largo Carrobbio (see itinerary 1.4). The name of the side-street Via Gian Giacomo Moro is a reminder that in 1630 Moro was unjustly accused of having spread the plague to the city and was horribly tortured. His house was demolished and on its site the "infamous column" was placed, which was later described by Alessandro Manzoni in his *Storia della colonna infame*, 1842.

Via Cesare Correnti (IV, C4). From Largo Carrobbio, Via Torino leads down to the square, now called Resistenza Partigiana after the partisan resistance movement of World War II, where the road to Genoa passed through the medieval city walls. The train station called "Porta Genova" (see above) actually lies within the old circuit of canals, and its Corso marks the start of the route to the suburbs.

2.5 Sant'Ambrogio, Santa Maria delle Grazie, and the Monastero Maggiore

Although some of the greatest works of art dating from medieval and Renaissance Milan are located here, such as the basilica dedicated to Saint Ambrose, the city's patron saint, and the refectory of Santa Maria delle Grazie, which Leonardo da Vinci decorated with his work *The Last Supper*, most of the district northwest of the center is a wealthy 19th- and 20th-c. residential district. These residential buildings become increasingly exclusive a little further north (see itinerary 2.6), along the route from Cordusio to Castello, and then along the Parco Sempione. Here, however, we will limit ourselves to the area around the first stretch of the thoroughfare heading west toward Novara and Vercelli, or as was commonly said after the decisive victory at Magenta against the Austro-Hungarians in 1859, "toward Magenta." This is a very historical area: the well-preserved stretch of ancient road allows us to glimpse, if not always the walls, at least the areas which until Napoleonic times were occupied by a dense network of monasteries constructed in the Middle Ages, although nearly all of them were renovated prior to the 1600s. Without listing all the convents that have since vanished (there are at least ten of them, to give an idea of the influence that

the church had on Milan), suffice it to note that the Università Cattolica is located on the premises of the former Cistercian monastery of Sant'Ambrogio, while the Museo della Scienza e della Tecnica is located on the site of the Olivetan Order of Saint Victor, and the Museo Archeologico stands on what remains of the great women's cenoby at San Maurizio, and it goes without saying that the *Last Supper* refectory also belonged to a convent.

As noted above, the tone of the area today is wealthy residential, dotted with expensive shops. Essentially, there are more costly pastry shops than standard bakeries, and a host of antiques shops and specialized stores, including a bookstore that deals only with the cinema and theater, Milan's exclusive classical-only music store, a good jazz record store with imports as well as Baroque music, an extremely elegant chocolate shop, a boutique that sells only Irish tweeds and wools, and the best-known artisan bookbindery in the city.

This itinerary takes up where the previous one left off at the end of the road to Genoa, where you can explore an area that still lies within the ring of canals; sites therefore include the historic Via San Vittore, which was built in the 17th c. After visiting the

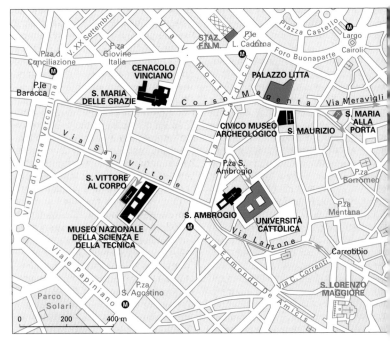

church of Sant'Ambrogio and its former convent, one comes to the route of the demolished Spanish walls along the Viale di Porta Vercellina. A short distance away is the former Porta Vercellina, now Porta Magenta. Skipping the sophisticated Magenta district for the moment (located directly to the north), we turn back toward the center of town along Corso Magenta, visit the famous church of Santa Maria delle Grazie, and, further down, the church of San Maurizio and the Monastero Maggiore. We then proceed to Piazza Cordusio, passing behind the Stock Exchange (for a description, see first chapter).

Via Lanzone (IV, B-C3-4). Between the final stretch of Via Cesare Correnti (see itinerary 2.4) and Sant'Ambrogio (see above), is a street that follows an ancient and relatively winding course. Here stands the church of *Sant'Agostino* (IV, B3), located in a building complex that was renovated around 1670. It also includes the arch at no. 30/a, once the entrance of the Sant'Ambrogio monastery. The road runs out into *Piazza Sant'Ambrogio*, which flanks the basilica near the subway station of the same name. The Pusterà di Sant'Ambrogio is located here with its exhibit of medieval torture instruments, at the beginning of Via San Vittore (see below). On December 7, the feast-day of St. Ambrose, the city's patron saint, the surrounding area fills with the stalls of the *Fiera degli O'bej! O'bej!*, an annual street fair that is said to have taken its name from the cries of vendors calling out their wares to passers-by.

Sant'Ambrogio** (IV, B3). Founded in 379 as the "Basilica Martyrum" on the burial spot of the martyrs Gervase and Protase, in 397 the basilica also became a mausoleum for the city's bishop and future patron saint. Because of this dedication – a testament to Milanese ecclesiastical independence, and its ancient traditions – the church is one of the most symbolic sites in the city. By the 11th c. the building had a new presbytery and a new apse, and then, starting in 1080, it was extensively rebuilt in the Romanesque style. By the latter half of the 13th c. both the side aisles and the atrium at the front had taken on their definitive form, but in 1196 the collapse of the third bay of the nave made it necessary to perform major reconstruction work. Other work and adaptations were almost continuous over the centuries that followed, and included a new layout (now lost) for the base of the dome, done in the late 16th-c. by Pellegrino Tibaldi. Today

the basilica is often presented in art history books as a prototype of the 13th-c. Romanesque style (see section across on following page). In reality, although it essentially follows the medieval plan and proportions, its appearance largely the result of extensive construction work and stripping between 1859 and 1890. The "restorers" were operating under the illusion that they could restore the building to its appearance prior to the 1196 collapse.

The present basilica is preceded by a vast arcaded **atrium** built between 1088 and 1099, on composite columns with decorated capitals, dating for the most part from the 17th c. The result is one of the most classical images in city iconography: the gabled form the **facade*** on two superimposed orders (a narthex, and an upper loggia of five diminishing arches) seems to be framed at the base by the arcades of the atrium itself; above it is flanked by the *bell towers* (the shorter southern tower, called the *Torre dei Monaci*, dates from the 9th c., while the other, incorporating delicate pilasters and small arches, is known as the *Torre dei Canonici* and was built 1128–44). At the left portal is a pre-Romanesque *relief** depicting St. Ambrose; the central portal has lintels, door posts, and a lunette formed by intaglio fragments with a basket-like weave and monstrous figures dated 9th–11th c.

The vessel's interior presents a nave and two aisles set with apses. The cross-vaulted nave has four bays on a square plan. The aisles, half the width of the nave, follow the same plan and are crowned by women's galleries. To the left of the nave, next to a fourth pillar, is an isolated column bearing a bronze *serpent*, an 11th-c. Byzantine work. The third bay has a **pulpit***, badly damaged when the bay collapsed in 1196 but immediately reassembled. Below is an early Christian sarcophagus, the so-called *sarcophagus of Stilicho*, from the late 5th c. In the center of the presbytery, four ancient Roman porphyry columns support the **ciborium****, crowned by a canopy with polychrome Lombard-Byzantine stucco work (11th c.) overlooking the **altar*** or *Altare d'Oro*, a creation of the master goldsmith Volvinio (835), and the principal work of art in the basilica: panels of exquisitely wrought gold leaf, and on the back gilt silver leaf, are decorated with *scenes from the life of Christ* and *Saint Ambrose*, separated by enamel and gemstone ornamentation.

Arranged in the main apse are the remaining portions of the carved wooden choir in Gothic style (1469–71). A large mosaic (*The*

Redeemer with Sts. Gervase and Protase) decorates the dome above, and in part dates back to the 5th c. and 9th c. Other portions were redone in the 18th c. and the 20th c. In the *crypt* below, visible through an aperture in the raised floor of the apse, a silver *tomb* from 1897 holds the remains of Saint Ambrose, Saint Gervase, and Saint Protase. Other important works can be seen in several chapels along the south aisle. The first contains a detached fresco (*Deposition with Saints*) by Gaudenzio Ferrari. The second contains frescoes (*The Martyrdom of St. Victor* and *the Shipwreck of St. Satiro*), originally executed by G. B. Tiepolo for the sacellum (see below). In the sixth chapel is a *Madonna and Child** and 16th-c. frescoes by Bernardino Lanino.

The seventh chapel leads into the **Sacello di San Vittore in Ciel d'Oro***, a small apsidal chapel from the 5th c., given a new layout in the 18th c. and now appearing in the form Ferdinando Reggiori gave it in 1930. The dome is decorated with 6th-c. mosaics* with figures of saints. From the north aisle, which has a fresco by Bergognone (*Christ Resurrected and Angels*) in the first chapel, one can pass into the *Portico della Canonica**, built by Donato Bramante 1492–9, and rebuilt after the war with the materials that survived the bombing.

In Bramante's arcades an entrance leads to the **Museo di Sant'Ambrogio**, containing precious relics from the history of the basilica: jewelry, cloths, tapestries, marble, stucco work, wood fragments, and paintings (Bernardino Zenale, Bergognone, and Bernardino Luini).

Università Cattolica del Sacro Cuore (IV, B3-4). In the narrow strip of greenery around the basilica stands the *Tempio della Vittoria* (designed by Giovanni Muzio, 1927-30), an octagonal tower commemorating the Fallen. Numerous fairly typical statues decorate it, while the statue of *Saint Ambrose* by Adolfo Wildt, in the niche before the entry, is outstanding for its authenticity. At Piazza Sant'Ambrogio 5, dominating the front is the imposing facade of a gigantic *barracks*, now the police department, which in 1807 took over what had been the largest Franciscan monastery in the city. Perpendicular to it at Largo Gemelli is the entrance to the Milan Catholic university, established in 1921. In accordance with an agreement reached between the Church and the Fascist government, the university was assigned the site of the ancient Sant'Ambrogio convent for its premises. Construction on the *cloisters** of this convent began in 1497 to designs by Donato Bramante. There were to have been four cloisters, but only two were completed (the northern one in Ionic style, completed in 1513, and the other in Doric style, completed in 1630). Between 1929 and 1949 general remodeling and reconstruction work took place, with the addition of service areas and the residence block on the adjacent Via Necchi, by Giovanni Muzio.

Via San Vittore (IV, B2-3). A medieval city gate once stood at the canal circuit near Sant'Ambrogio (see above). What remains are parts of an arch and a few stone blocks, now incorporated into the *Pusterla di Sant'Ambrogio* (IV, B3), the result of questionable modern remodeling (1939). A stone tabernacle from the Campionese school has also been added here (*Sts. Ambrose, Gervase, and Protase*, 1360), from a nearby Visconti hospital demolished some time ago. The street that runs toward the suburbs from here takes its name from the basilica of **San Vittore al Corpo** (IV, B2), set back from the street in a square, also abutted by the Museo della Scienza e della Tecnica. The church was originally an imperial mausoleum (5th c.), but the Olivetans had it completely reconstructed between 1560 and 1602, when the Benedictines, who had been in the area for 500 years, took over. Attributed variously to Galeazzo Alessi or Vincenzo Seregni, the interior of the building contains well-preserved period furnishings, something rather rare in Milan. The only exception is the 20th-c. floor, while the compact white and gold stucco decorations, the 17th-c. paintings and the late 16th-c. wood *choir** are all original.

Museo Nazionale della Scienza e della Tecnica "Leonardo da Vinci"* (IV, B2-3) Since 1953 the largest and best-organized technical and scientific museum in Italy has been located within the vast complex of the former San Vittore monastery (founded in the 12th c., redone in the 16th c. and frequently remodeled since). Located on an exhibition area of over 35,000 sq.m are 28 theme-based sections, progressively established through donations or bequests by numerous public bodies and private industrial groups. The endowments of the institute, which recently introduced interactive computer technology for educational purposes, also include rooms for temporary shows and conventions, as well as a specialized library with about 40,000 volumes. During visits, the material displayed is presented interspersed with works of art (*de* tached *frescoes**, by Bernardino Luini, Marco d'Oggiono, Bernardino Lanino, Bernardino Campi, and others), most of which belonged to the former monastery.

The main gallery on the second floor is dedicated to Leonardo da Vinci, the extraordinary artist and researcher after whom the museum is named. On display are numerous *reconstructed models** which explain the discoveries, inventions, and architectural projects of Leonardo da Vinci, accompanied by enlargements of the handwritten drawings on which they are based,

and *air transport*, with about twenty period steam and electric engines, along with freight cars, signals, and other railway equipment, as well as historic aircraft (Blériot 11, 1909; Macchi 215 "Veltro," the La Cierva helicopter, 1936, and the Campini-Campioni CC1, the first airplane built in Italy) and maritime models and finds. The latter include the impressive educational brig "Ebe" (1921) and the bridge of the transatlantic liner "Conte Biancamano," taken out of commission in 1960. Another section is devoted to agriculture.

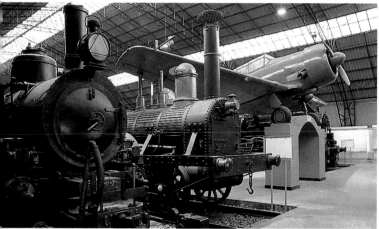

Early steam engines and airplanes in the " Leonardo da Vinci" Science Museum

many of which are from the *Codice Atlantico* in the Biblioteca Ambrosiana (see itinerary 1.4), accompanied by explanations. Other interesting and sometimes even spectacular rooms include the sections dealing with physics, computers, weights and measures, chronometry, instruments, graphic arts (*harpsichord scribe** by Giuseppe Ravizza, 1855), the string instrument workshop, astronomy (with a small interactive planetarium), electrology, and telephone systems and communications (RCA station belonging to the state broadcasting corporation, RAI, in operation between 1932 and 1971). The metallurgy and foundry section (a 17th/18th-c. workshop for casting bells, nail-making in the early 20th c., electric ovens, and rolling-mills), direct-drive engines (wind mechanisms, hydraulic turbines, steam-powered machines, and internal combustion engines), and the road transport sections (carriages, bicycles, motorcycles, and antique automobiles) are located in the basement, with extensive use of models to reproduce historical settings to illustrate methods of operation. The outside *pavilions* are devoted to *rail transport*

This former monastery also holds the **Civico Museo Navale Didattico***, constituted in 1922 by Milanese sailors on leave. Of great interest to ship enthusiasts and students of nautical history, it contains collections of models, historic boats and a vast amount of other pertinent information.

Corso Magenta (IV, A2-4). Leading west from the historic center the old thoroughfare of the Viale di Porta Vercellina changed its name in 1859, as did the relative city gate, torn down 26 years later. Piazzale Baracca (IV, A2) remains on the site of the latter, where at the corner of Corso Magenta (at no. 96) *Casa Laugier* (Angelo Tagliaferri, 1905) provides an example of the refined 19th/20th-c. buildings in the adjacent Magenta district (see itinerary 2.6). Heading out of town, the street becomes the popular shop-lined Corso Vercelli (IV, A1-2). Toward the city center, almost level with Santa Maria delle Grazie (see below), the former *Palazzo delle Stelline* can be seen at no. 59. Built by the Borromeo family in the 17th c. as a boarding school for young orphans, it has now been reconstructed as a convention center. The complex includes hotel accommodation and the separately managed *Credito Valtellinese gallery*, one of the best art galleries in the city, owned privately but actually serving public purposes. Further along this street are Palazzo Litta, the church of San Maurizio, and the Civico Museo Archeologico (see below).

Santa Maria delle Grazie** (IV, A3). Looking onto Corso Magenta stands the well-known Gothic-Renaissance church dedicated to the Virgin Mary. Founded in 1463 around an earlier chapel dedicated to the Madonna delle Grazie, most of the church was built between 1466 and 1490 under the direction of Guiniforte Solari. The fame of the complex is due not only to Leonardo da Vinci's *Last Supper*, which is located here (see below), but also to the striking domed crossing and deep tribune or **choir***, which was added starting in 1492. Ludovico il Moro had his wife Beatrice d'Este buried here when she died in 1497. The design of the crossing and tribune has long been attributed to Donato Bramante, though without any conclusive evidence. The long rectangular choir extends from the crossing and terminates in an apse. The transepts are also apsed. The sixteen-sided base of the drum and dome rises above the crossing on

decorated pendentives, and is crowned with a loggia of twinned columns. Outside, the central marble *portal** in the facade is also attributed to Bramante. The 18th-c. fresco in the lunette replaces an earlier one allegedly by Leonardo da Vinci. A major restoration program was begun in 1895 by Luca Beltrami after the adjacent Dominican monastery (the Milan headquarters of the Inquisition from 1553 until it was eliminated in 1778) had been abandoned as a barracks, and was facing demolition.

The interior of the church, its aisles set with deep side chapels, evinces Solari's Gothic style in the pointed arch bays, resting on a twin row of columns that accentuate the flow of space. The vaults are decorated with frescoes dating from the time of construction, rediscovered after having been covered up in the 17th c. Figures of Dominican saints, attributed to Bernardino Butinone, are frescoed on pillars in the side aisles. The first chapel on the right (see 1 in the plan) contains the *Della Torre tomb* (1483) on its left wall, by Francesco Cazzaniga. The fourth chapel (2) contains frescoes depicting *Scenes of the Passion* by Gaudenzio Ferrari and assistants. The dome over the crossing (3, also see above) is supported by four large arched pendentives, surmounted by a low drum divided in-

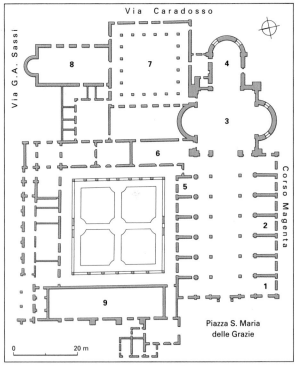

Plan of the Santa Maria delle Grazie complex

The 15th - century church of Santa Maria delle Grazie

to thirty-two sections. The hidden graffito decorations were restored in the 1980s. Notable in the deep apse (4), which is crowned by a remarkable octagonal ribbed vault lit by round windows, is the wooden choir* with inlay work (1470–1510) on two rows of stalls. Along the north aisle, the sixth chapel (5) contains an altarpiece (*Holy Family with St. Catherine of Alexandria*) by Paris Bordone (1545). Next to it, near a 17th-c. stucco composition, one enters the *Cappella della Madonna delle Grazie*, the heart of the church (6), rebuilt after the World War II. On the altar is a 15th-c. painting – the object of great veneration during the plague of 1576 – from which the complex takes its name.

From the apse one passes into the small arcaded cloister (7) which leads into the **Old Sacristy** (8), built in 1499 and restored in 1982. The walls are lined with wooden cabinets decorated with rich inlay, above which hang paintings and fragments of detached frescoes that date back to the construction of the building.

In the square outside the church a door leads to Leonardo da Vinci's **Last Supper**** (9), whose composition is ingeniously devised as an extension of the perspective of the space in which it is set (1495–97). It is one of the most famous artworks in the world, and has long been an icon of Western civilization. The scene portrays the moment in which Jesus tells his disciples that one of them is about to betray him. The conservation problems that have always plagued the painting are primarily due to the techniques used by the artist. Instead of using an appropriate fresco technique,

which prohibits pentimenti and retouching, he used a freer tempera technique – more commonly used for painting on wood or canvas – but which quickly becomes unstable on plaster. The humidity of the room, the subsidence of the wall (which has caused fractures in the painting's support), and the general aging of the painting, have further complicated the situation, requiring restoration work which will proceed for an indefinite period. On the opposite wall is a *Crucifixion* of the same period (1495) by Giovanni Donato Montorfano, a poignant testament to the lasting reliability of proper fresco technique.

Palazzo Litta (IV, A4). Abutting Corso Magenta further uptown at no. 24 is the long Rococo prospect (1763) of this residential building, begun in 1648 by Francesco Maria Ricchino for Count Bartolomeo Arese, and later inherited by the Litta family. In addition to the Teatro Litta, this building houses the district management offices for the Italian state railway (FFSS), soon due to be transferred.

Civico Museo Archeologico* (IV, A4). Almost opposite Palazzo Litta in Corso Magenta 15 stands the 15th-c. **Monastero Maggiore** building, once the largest women's convents in old Milan. Partially demolished between 1864 and 1872 and seriously damaged during the air-raids of 1943, the complex still includes the church of San Maurizio (see below), while the main corpus of the **archaeological and numismatic** collections belonging to the city has been housed here since 1965, with a smaller section at the Castello Sforzesco (see itinerary

2.6). In the area which was once the convent, two late Roman towers are still visible, one square, which may have been part of the prisons of the circus, and the other polygonal, from the walls of Maximian.

The material on display, the main corpus of which was established in 1900 with the merger of collections previously kept at the Brera and the Castello Sforzesco, consists of material excavated in various parts of the city. This is especially true of the Ro-

The interior of San Maurizio

man collections, which include sculptures (*Aphrodite-Aura*), portraits (*Maximinus the Thracian?*), mosaics, ceramics, glassware (the extraordinary *Diatreta Cup*, formerly Trivulzio Cup), bronze work and silverwork (**patera of Parabiago***, *relics of tombs** from Lovere), as well as a selection of later Ostrogoth, Alemanni, and Longobard funeral goods. The *Riquier Collection* includes Attic, Italiot (*bowl of the Painter of Parrish*) and Dauno-Messapic ceramics, while the Etruscan collection, including the *Lerici Donation* from the necropolis of Cerveteri, dates from the Villanova age (9th/8th c. B.C.) to the 2nd/1st c. B.C., with ceramics (*heads of canopic jars*), bronzes, urns, and a large clay *sarcophagus* from Tarquinia. Other collections include materials from Gandhâra (sculptures from western India from the 2nd–4th c. B.C.) and the Greek age (Corinthian, Attic, Italiot, and Gnathian ceramics, antefixes, helmets, items in pâte-de-verre, a fragment of a *vase from Euphronios* from the late 6th c. B.C., and a *bell-shaped bowl* depicting the

farce "The Gluttons," dating back to the 4th c. B.C. Other finds document various Mediterranean cultures.

San Maurizio al Monastero Maggiore* (IV, A4). Construction began on the church next to the present Museo Archeologico (see above) in the early 16th c., perhaps to designs by Gian Giacomo Dolcebuono, and its facade was completed by 1581. The front that appears today, however, and the left flank along the relatively new street Via Luini, are the result of further work carried out over 1872–96. The cloistered atmosphere of the building is evident in the clear division between the space to the front, open to the faithful, and the *nuns' choir* at the back. Both areas are covered with **frescoes***, most of which are 16th-c. Lombard works from the circle of Bernardino Luini, Calisto Piazza, and Antonio Campi. Attributed to Luini are the *Life of St. Catherine* in the third chapel to the right, and the ornamentation on the dividing wall, as well as the *Stories of the Passion* on the partition wall of the cloister choir, while the tondi with figures of *saints* in the loggia are attributed to Giovanni Antonio Boltraffio.

Not far off, at the site of the *decumanus maximus* of the Roman road network is a short street that takes its name from the church of *Santa Maria alla Porta* (IV, A4); construction was begun in 1652, to designs by Francesco Maria Ricchino. Inside are paintings and sculptures coeval with its construction.

Immediately following, Via Brisa (IV, B4) runs from the eastern end of Corso Magenta, quickly coming to an area where archaeological digs have uncovered the ruins of a late Roman construction from the age of Maximian.

Via Meravigli (IV, A4-5). This is the nearly continuation of Corso Magenta, lined with modern buildings that include the *headquarters of the Camera di Commercio, Industria Artigianato e Agricoltura* (Achille and Pier Giacomo Castiglioni, 1952). Behind this Chamber of Commerce building lies Piazza degli Affari (with the Stock Exchange), and the street ends at Piazza Cordusio (for both, see itinerary 1.4).

2.6 From the Castello Sforzesco to the Magenta District

To say that the most exclusive residential areas of the city are found "in the direction of Paris" may seem fanciful, but there is some truth in the claim.

The thoroughfare that passes the old Porta Giovia, later named Porta Sempione after the Alpine pass (Simplon), which became easier to cross after a train tunnel (radically advanced for its time) was completed in 1906, is distinguished not only by the enormous Castello Sforzesco, but also by the handsome residential areas created in the 1890s, after the quarter ceased to be used for military purposes.

During that brief period of the century, post-Unification Milan, which was reaping enormous commercial and financial benefits from the abolition of the internal customs stations throughout the peninsula, realized that the old fortress was a superb historical monument and might be used to advantage to bolster the city's image. A dual opportunity arose in the construction of expensive residential buildings in adjacent areas, involving a huge financial project while providing a more clearly identified physical location for the city's new wealthy classes. The scheme included the vast Parco Sempione, previously not much more than a flat area used for garrison exercises, thereby giving the triumphal Arch of Peace a worthy setting.

Such a scheme had been suggested as far back as Napoleonic times; even the pair of semicircular avenues ringing the north of the park (Via Canova and Via Melzi d'Eril) and Foro Buonaparte, which mirrors them this side of the castle, are really the posthumous application of an urban plan which Giovanni Antonio Antolini, a keen advocate of the French Revolution's concept of "Liberté, Fraternité, Égalité," had envisioned as early as 1801. The only difference was that Antolini had imagined a more public forum, a gathering area for the general populace, while the new master plan drafted by Cesare Beruto and the restorative zeal of Luca Beltrami envisioned a far less egalitarian city – in May 1898 the "ferocious monarch" Bava Beccaris ordered his men to fire on a crowd of Milanese demonstrators protesting against the high cost of living.

Across from Via Dante our itinerary leads to the Castello Sforzesco, exploring this castle, its museums, and the vast park behind it; then detours to the elegant and varied adjoining Magenta quarter. We then turn back to the castle, passing the Ferrovie Nord train station, which, despite remains a primary thoroughfare for communication between the city and its lively northern suburbs (see chapter 3).

Via Dante (IV, A 4-5). From Piazza Cordusio (see itinerary 1.4) a broad street leads straight toward the wide turreted profile of the Castello Sforzesco (see below). The street was opened in 1890 by demolishing a vast area of working-class homes, which were replaced with large new buildings: those at nos. 13, 15, and 16 won architectural awards. The 15th-c. *Palazzo Carmagnola* at Via Rovello 2 was spared, however. The **Piccolo Teatro della Città di Milano** (IV, A5) has been located in the adjacent building since 1947, and is considered one of the leading theaters on the European continent for the quality and prestige of its stage productions.

It was founded during the general enthusiasm after the war by a group of people who have since become icons of contemporary Italian culture: Nina Vinchi, Paolo Grassi (later director of La Scala and president of the Italian broadcasting corporation), and the Trieste-born theater director Giorgio Strehler.

Earning its reputation with avant-garde productions of works by Brecht, Shakespeare, Pirandello, and Chekhov that made history, over time the Piccolo Teatro has evolved a rigorous and wholly characteristic style that could now be defined as a genre. Other municipal venues where the Piccolo stages its productions are the larger Teatro Lirico (Via Larga), the Teatro Studio (discussed in itinerary 2.1), or its own recently completed premises (see below).

In front of the Piccolo is a barbershop which has become famous due to its exclusive clientele. Proceeding toward the castle, one passes lines of fine shops, before reaching **Largo Cairoli** (IV, A4), near the subway station of the same name. The *monument to Giuseppe Garibaldi* (Ettore Ximenes, 1895) marks it at street level.

Foro Buonaparte (IV, A3-4). A sweeping semicircular boulevard lined with imposing late 19th-c. buildings curves round the front of the Castello Sforzesco (see below). Worthy of note are the residential buildings at no. 16 (1896) along the left segment of the circle, and those at nos. 1–5 (1890) and no. 27 (1895).

Toward the northeast end of Foro Buonaparte, near Corso Garibaldi (see itinerary 2.1) and the Lanza subway station, rises

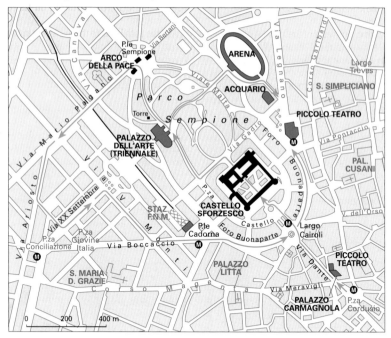

the new building of the Piccolo Teatro (designed by Marco Zanuso, 1982–95), with its entrance on Via Rivoli (II, F4), comprising a main hall that seats 1,200.

Not far from the theater, at Foro Buonaparte 50, is one of the rare privately run art venues in the city, which hosts excellent, non-commercial exhibitions. Known as the *Fondazione Antonio Mazzotta*, the gallery is situated next to the offices of the Gabriele Mazzotta publishing house (at no. 52), which owns it.

Castello Sforzesco** (plan II, pp. 58–59, F4). Though it is usually passed off as the largest Renaissance edifice in Milan, in its present form the castle is actually a brilliantly eclectic reconstruction carried out at the turn of the century, prompted by the impulse of the well-to-do Milanese to celebrate the growing economic and political importance of the city. After the armed forces left the building in 1893 and ownership was transferred from the state to the city, work began to designs by the architect Luca Beltrami, who supervised operations until 1905. The scheme that was intended to restore the castle "to its ancient glory" turned out to be an indulgent reconstruction involving considerable stylistic license. The castle is nevertheless the city's largest historical complex and most certainly deserves a visit, both for what remains of the oldest structure and for its outstanding museum col-

lection (leaving aside the fact that now, a century later, this clever reconstruction has acquired historical status itself).

The original 14th-c. Visconti nucleus must have stood immediately outside the medieval walls, on the site of what was then Porta Giovia, using that stretch of the city's canals as a moat. Destroyed or at least damaged during the Repubblica Ambrosiana (1447–50), the founder of the Sforza dynasty, Duke Francesco Sforza, undertook to enlarge the fortress, which, upon his death in 1466, became the residence of his successor Galeazzo Maria Sforza. The latter commissioned the enlargements and decorative apparatus, calling on Vincenzo Foppa, Cristoforo Moretto, and Benedetto Ferrini. Work continued under Ludovico il Moro (duke from 1494 to 1499), who summoned Donato Bramante, Filarete (Francesco Averlino), Bernardino Zenale, Bernardino Butinone, and Leonardo da Vinci to contribute. The general plan of that time was probably not much different from today's.

The Duchy of Milan fell with the advent of Spanish dominion (1535), and thereafter the castle was used for military purposes, with the construction of further defensive walls and imposing ramparts, making the castle one of the largest and best-fortified strongholds on the continent. Be that as it may, the assault of the French troops of Louis XV much later in 1733 left the castle so seriously damaged that in 1800 Napoleon ordered its demolition, to make room for a huge civic project. Luckily, only the outworks were demolished, without affecting the main walls or the Sforza fabric. Beltrami's eclectic reconstruction projects were in fact based on that work.

The majestic profile that greets visitors arriving from Via Dante is almost entirely 20th c. The relief of *Umberto I* (Luigi Secchi, 1906) placed halfway up the central entrance *tower* known as the **Torre del Filarete** (1, in the axonometric scheme below) is evidence enough that the lofty structure with its bell tower does not date from the Renaissance. The original tower, not as tall, was destroyed in an explosion in 1521, followed by a fire that swept through the munitions store. As for the massive corner towers (2-3), Beltrami rebuilt and even raised them to enable the municipal water tank inside the one on the right to supply the higher floors of the surrounding residential neighborhoods, taking advantage of the principal of communicating vessels. The gateway leads into a vast main courtyard called **Piazza d'Armi** (4), bordered at far end by the Rocchetta (5, original castle nucleus), the central *Torre di Bona di Savoia* (6, originally from 1477) and the *Palazzo di Corte Ducale* (7), which now contains the main rooms of the castle museum (see below). The perimeter section with the Torre del Filarete is home to the collections of the *Raccolta delle Stampe "Achille Bertarelli,"* (8), a collection that catalogues and makes available for consultation over 600,000 prints and documents, from popular illustrations to valuable historical graphic works; the specialized *Biblioteca d'Arte* (9), an art library with some 5,000 volumes; and the well-stocked *Biblioteca Gabinetto Numismatico*. Beyond Piazza d'Armi one passes through the central archway to the splendid **Ducal Court*** (right), with its characteristic *Portico dell'Elefante* (ca. 1473) and to the side a Renaissance loggia on two orders (from the floors below ground level one enters the *Sala Viscontea,* a room used for temporary exhibits); a passage to the left leads into the next courtyard, or Cor-

tile della Rocchetta, bordered on three sides by 15th-c. arcades, while straight ahead the path leads to the main gate in the front prospect of the castle, the *Porta del Barco* (10), which gives directly to the Parco Sempione (see below). Next to this is the entrance to the lower levels of the "Ritrovare Milano" exhibition (see below). From the austere Rocchetta courtyard one can enter the **Archivio Storico Civico**, a large and splendid resource for the reconstruction of the city's past, and the adjacent **Biblioteca Trivulziana**, a library that was originally the private property of the Trivulzio family but was acquired by the city in 1935, along with the tapestry collection (see below). The library conserves a great number of manuscripts (including the **Codice Trivulziano*** by Leonardo da Vinci), together with many incunabula and other early printed works. From the courtyard a small doorway leads down to the branch gallery of the city's archaeological and numismatic collections (see below).

The **Musei del Castello**** (Castle Museums) are the largest of their kind in the city, devoted primarily to the visual and applied arts from medieval times to the 18th c. (later periods represented in the city collections are on display at the Galleria d'Arte Moderna, see itinerary 2.2, and the Civico Museo d'Arte Contemporanea at Palazzo Reale, see itinerary 1.1). The history of the collections is exemplary of the development of collecting and patronage in Milan, and sheds light on the rapport between the city and its population. For the most part, the collections can be visited in sequence, following the setup devised in 1956 by the museum's director Costantino Baroni, and structured according to a scheme of **installation*** (Lodovico Belgiojoso, Enrico Peressutti, and Ernesto Nathan Rogers) whose validity is some-

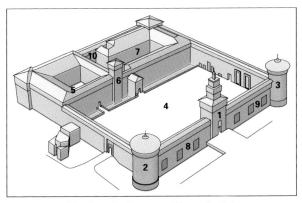

The Castello Sforzesco (Sforza Castle)

times questioned today, but is none the less still appealing, and styled on the idea of a "museum within a museum." The design for the installations of the picture gallery (by Franco Albini, Franca Helg, and Antonio Piva) is more recent, from the 1970s. The more important rooms include the *Sala del Gonfalone* (with the coats of arms of the Spanish sovereigns and their governors in Lombardy, as well as the **Milan Standard**, embroidered and painted in 1566), the *Sala delle Asse* (its vault frescoed with a complex architecture of laurel branches to designs attributed to Leonardo da Vinci, but extensively restored), as well as the *Cappella Ducale* (with 15th-c. frescoes); on the main floor of the Rocchetta is the *Sala della Balla*, where the remarkable **Arazzi dei Mesi** or *Trivulzio tapestries* are preserved, begun in 1503 by the ducal tapestry makers of Vigevano, to designs by Bramantino. By appointment one can also visit the *Sala del Tesoro*, with frescoes by the Lombard school and the Argus figure by Donato Bramante. Following is a brief summary of the works displayed:

Civiche Raccolte d'Arte Antica. Early Christian art (**marble head of the Empress Theodora**, 7th c.), Longobard (capitals of Santa Maria d'Aurona, 10th/12th c.), Romanesque (bas-relief detached from the old Porta Romana, 13th c.), Gothic (**Tomb of Bernabò Visconti**, a 14th-c. work by Bonino da Campione), sculptures and architectural features

The Rondanini Pietà, *one of Michelangelo's last works*

of the 15th and 16th c. (**St. Sigismund** by Agostino di Duccio, *Apostles* by Antonio Mantegazza, the **Portal of the Banco dei Medici**, attributed to Michelozzo, now located among the 17th- and 18th-c. **arms** collection, as well as the **Tomb of Gastone di Foix** by Bambaia (Agostino Busti), recently completed with his statues and relief work from the Arconati collection, and the **Rondanini Pietà**, a moving late work by Michelangelo, acquired by the city in 1952). The aforementioned Sala delle Asse is also host to the *Belgiojoso Collection*, consisting of 17th- and 18th-c. Flemish and Dutch paintings and portraits, while the main floor houses furniture from the 15th to the 18th c. (*Passalacqua writing desk* and the pre-

cious 15th-c. wooden chair known as the **Torrechiara private chapel**), tapestries, paintings, statues and wooden 15th- and 16th-c. bas-reliefs. Placed here in order to recreate the atmosphere of a room in the Roccabianca Castle (Parma) is that castle's cycle of 15th-c. frescoes depicting the **Story of Griselda**.

The **Pinacoteca** follows, which comprises and outstanding collection of paintings, including works by Andrea Mantegna (**Madonna and Saints**), Benedetto Bembo (**Polyptych**), Giovanni Bellini (**Madonna and Child**), Vincenzo Foppa (**St. Sebastian**, *The Trivulzio Madonna* and **Madonna of the Book**), Ambrogio Bergognone (**Virgin** and **Charity of St. Benedict**), Bramantino (*Virgin*), Cesare da Sesto (*Polyptych of St. Rocco*), Correggio (*Madonna and Portrait of Giulio Zandemaria*), Giovanni Bellini (**Poet Laureate**), Lorenzo Lotto (**Portrait of a Young Boy**), Tintoretto (**Portrait of Jacopo Soranzo**), Fra' Galgario (*Self-Portrait*), Cerano (*Miracles of St. Francis*), Alessandro Magnasco (*Market*), Tiepolo (*Communion of St. Lucy*), and Francesco Guardi (*Tempest*). Two other great paintings by Canaletto were acquired by the city in 1995.

Le Civiche Raccolte d'Arte Applicata are collections of applied art which include ceramic sections (Italian 15th- and 16th-c. incised ceramics; Italian and foreign ceramics, china and majolica from the 15th to 19th c.), Italian and foreign jewelry, enamels, ivory and small Renaissance bronzes, textiles, and vestments. The **Museo degli Strumenti Musicali** contains 640 items in five sections: period string instruments, plucked instruments, keyboard instruments, wind instruments, and exotic instruments. There is also a 18th- and 19th-c. **costume collection**. From the Rocchetta courtyard a doorway leads to the prehistoric and Egyptian sections of the city's **archaeological and numismatic collections**, a sub-section of those at the Civico Museo Archeologico (see itinerary 2.5). The former includes materials from the Paleolithic to the second Iron Age, particularly representative of Lombard culture (Lagozza di Besnate, Canegrate, Golasecca, etc.), while the latter contains burial goods and tools. The **Medagliere** (which can be visited upon advance request) with its 230,000 items from the 6th c. B.C. to the present day, with rotating exhibits displayed at the above-mentioned main archaeological center, and the **Ritrovare Milano** collection, financed by a city-owned company and containing Roman stelai, statues and medieval bas-reliefs, capitals, and Renaissance medallions, complete the collection.

Parco Sempione (II, E-F3-4). The area once known as the Barco, or ducal garden, later converted to a military parade ground, is now a large park landscaped in the English style, covering 47,200 sq.m, designed by Emilio Alemagna (1893).
Within the park, at Viale Alemagna 6 stands the **Palazzo dell'Arte** (A, in plan), designed by Giovanni Muzio (1932–33) and bequeathed to the city by Antonio Bernocchi. The building was designed to receive the **Milan Triennale** international exhibitions of industrial design which, with occasional interruptions and organizational problems, have run since 1923, playing a vital role in the international debate on modern trends of architecture and design in Italy and abroad. The exhibitions of 1933, 1940, and 1947 were particularly significant; the last of these focused on the scheme for Milan's experimental residential district, known as QT8 (see itinerary 3.1).

During the 1960s the Palazzo d'Arte hosted a dance hall. The Triennales of the 1970s and 1980s exhibited uninspired revivals of style – as promising as they were short-lived. Recently, however, the exhibition and seminar activities are regular once more, and rather than complying with the three-year formula implied by its name (which no one has ever paid much attention to anyway), the building now functions runs an ongoing program of thematic exhibitions, most of which are set up jointly with similar international organizations. This rebirth under way also includes the Triennale's comeback as one of the leading institutions of this type worldwide, on a par with the Pompidou Center in Paris, the MoMA in New York, and the MoCA in California. The most important events are staged in the **Galleria della Triennale***, a first-floor exhibition area remodeled with installations by Gae Aulenti (1994).
Also in the building are the independently run *Teatro dell'Arte*, which has been renovated numerous times during the course of the past thirty-five years and, in the semi-circular wing, the new *Museo del Design*, approximately 500 works in the first phase, illustrating italian creativity in this sector since 1945.

A walk through the park should include the *Fontana Metafisica* or *Bagni Misteriosi* (B) behind the Palazzo dell'Arte designed by Giorgio De Chirico (1973), as well as the

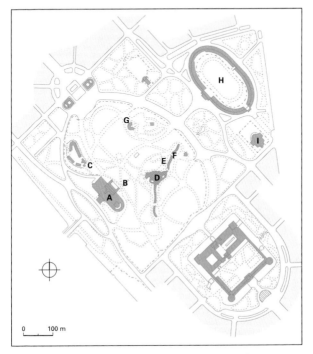

Site plan of the Parco Sempione and the castle

nearby **Torre del Parco** (C), formerly known as the Torre Littoria (109 m high), a structure in steel tubing (Cesare Chiodi, Gio Ponti, and Ettore Ferrari, 1932) with its panoramic terrace. Restoration work after its long period of abandonment (financed by the Milanese firm Fratelli Branca, producers of Fernet liqueurs), has finally led to it being open to the public once again.

Visitors should also be sure to see the center of the park, where a pond (D) is located halfway between the Castello Sforzesco and the Arco della Pace (see below). Until a faction of local administration ordered its removal a few years ago, the view from here toward the arch was framed by a sort of stage apparatus (Teatro Continuo) created by Alberto Burri in 1973. Also interesting are a nearby work (E) in cement and metal (*Musical Accumulation and Session*, 1973), the so-called *Ponte delle Sirenette* (F), which originally (1841–42) stood near the canal near Palazzo Serbelloni (see itinerary 2.2) and a small library (G) established in 1954.

At the northeast edge of the park is the *Arena*, a neoclassical structure designed by Luigi Canonica (1807), still used as an athletics field, and the fine Art-Nouveau building (Sebastiano Locati, 1906) that holds the *Civico Acquario e Stazione Idrobiologica* (I), an aquarium and marine biology station. Its 48 tanks contain freshwater and saltwater fish from temperate and tropical zones, as well as amphibians and invertebrates.

Arco della Pace* (II, E3). At the far end of the Parco Sempione stands the grandiose Arch of Peace (designed by Luigi Cagnola, 1807), built for the French in classical triumphal style on the imperial Roman model, and significantly facing the direction of Paris. Napoleon intended to symbolically pass through as he entered the Italian domains of his kingdom. Striking, outsize and solemn in appearance, with its colossal fluted Corinthian columns, crowning statue group *Sestiga della Pace* above (Abbondio Sangiorgio), complex sculpted decorative scheme and coffered barrel vaults, the arch was never completed in time for Bonaparte to admire it. Instead, it was inaugurated by the Hapsburg emperor in 1838, who had the inscriptions changed, together with some of the relief work, to match the new political climate of restoration; things were further altered with the advent of the House of

Savoy. Corso Sempione (see itinerary 3.1) continues the central axis of the park and the arch, leading out of the city.

Via XX Settembre (map IV, pages 62-63, A2). This is the street that runs through the **Magenta district**, an elegant example of the residential fabric provided for by Cesare Beruto's new master plan (1884–89), comprising Via Mario Pagano (II, E-F2-3), Via Ariosto (II, F2), Parco Sempione (see above) and Piazza Conciliazione (IV, A2), where the subway station of the same name is located. This route gives at least a brief idea of the eclectic mixture of architectural styles and interesting examples of Art-Nouveau buildings that characterize the area. Start with *Casa Agostoni* (1906) at Via Ariosto 21, then turn into Via Mascheroni (IV, A2) at the corner where the church of *Santa Maria Segreta* (1918) stands, and from here turn through the line of trees on Via XX Settembrini, proceeding to *Casa Borletti* on the opposite side at Via Roveri 2 (remodeled in 1935 by Ignazio Gardella with the addition of an avant-corps on Via Vincenzo Monti) and the neoclassical *Casa Falck* at Via Tamburini 1 (Mino Fiocchi, 1938).

Along the middle side-street consisting of Via Tasso and Via Gioberti is Casa Apostolo (1907) at Via Tasso 10–12, and Casa Donzelli (1903) at Via Gioberti 1, both by Ulisse Stacchini.

From Casa Borlotti follow Via Vincenzo Monti (IV, A3) to Via Boccaccio (IV, A2-3), which leads to Piazzale Cadorna in the direction of the city center.

Piazzale Cadorna (IV, A3). This square, on the former canal circuit not far from the Castello Sforzesco, is named after the general who led the capture of Rome (1870). Underground is the Cadorna subway station, while at street level stands the independent *Ferrovie Nord Milano* train station building, reconstructed in 1956, with a network of 218 kilometers of tracks in the directions of Varese, Como, and Erba.

This itinerary concludes by following an arm of the aforementioned Foro Buonaparte, where at no. 31 you will find the head offices of Montedison; back to Largo Cairoli near the *Teatro Dal Verme* (Giuseppe Pestagalli, 1872), currently being redeveloped as a concert hall.

3 Milan and its suburbs

Everything that has been said so far about the Lombard capital concerns the central, relatively small area (8.32 sq. km) of historical Milan, an area whose monuments and historical sites can be readily toured on foot and by public transport. Beyond the crown of the Spanish walls, however, where the historical city yields to the metropolitan area, the churches and important buildings become few and far between, giving way to low-income housing and modern condominium blocks, and the distance between the places of interest is no longer easily covered on foot. For this reason it is advisable to resort to private transport. The ideal means for getting around would of course be a bicycle or motor scooter, if it were not for the traffic fumes. General atmospheric pollution levels are high in Milan, and anyway, bicycle rental is not available.

From the territorial point of view, almost all the places covered by this itinerary have only become part of Milan in relatively recent times. Outside the ramparts the first significant expansion took place in 1873 when the "Corpi Santi," or Holy Bodies, were annexed and became

The XXV Aprile sports complex in the QT8 quarter

part of the city, followed in 1923 by eleven neighboring boroughs that had been independent until then, including several discussed in this guide: Baggio, Affori, Niguarda, Lambrate, and Ortica. Despite these accretions, Milan's administrative territory is still relatively small (181.74 sq. km), less than that of Verona (199 sq. km), and obviously much smaller than such European capitals as Prague (497 sq. km) and Rome (almost 1,308 sq. km). This figure clearly does not reflect the city's sphere of influence, nor the physical extension of its building fabric. Apart from road signs and differences in public transport fares, there is nothing that noticeably separates Milan from outlying boroughs such as Bresso, Sesto San Giovanni, Segrate, San Donato, and Rozzano, and yet there seems not to be a higher administrative body capable of resolving the complex problems that inevitably arise from this situation.

In any case the significance of the places and the features illustrated in this chapter remain unaltered: among the dwindling farmlands of the Bassa Milanese south of Milan, the superb Chiaravalle Abbey, and further afield the incomparable Certosa di Pavia, vie for attention with the glittering high-tech headquarters of industrial corporations at Assago and the ultramodern Mondadori publishing campus at Segrate. Postwar residential quarters commemorating the Resistance (the QT8 district near San Siro) can be found alongside suburban Renaissance residences (such as Villa Simonetta, Villa Litta Modignani in Affori, and Villa Litta in Rodano); elsewhere, popular if ugly landmarks (such as the hulking Stazione Centrale, its style ironically referred to as "Assyro-Milanese") contrast with spaces so magnificent they are excluded to the public (such as the Trenzanesio estate on the way to Bergamo). In other words, Milan extends its influence not just in terms of sheer building volume, but because as a metropolis it embraces a legacy of past and present (albeit in an intermittent and inconsistent way) that is well worth visiting and getting to know.

3.1 The West and Northwest Areas

Today the name Sempione, the Italian for Simplon (whose famous tunnel leading through the Alps to France, completed in 1906, opened new channels for Milanese trade) is used to refer to a large district behind the Castello Sforzesco and the adjacent park (see itinerary 2.6). The itinerary suggested here starts from Corso Sempione, once the initial section of the Napoleonic road that leads to Switzerland and thence Paris, and turns sharply west, along the highway to the town of Abbiategrasso.

The initial part of the route, as far as the stadium and sports complex of San Siro, can still be considered part of the urban fabric. Unless you have your own transportation, however, it is not easy to reach the borough of Baggio, which has been under Milan's administration since 1923. It is even more difficult to arrive at the developed suburb of Cusago (approximately 13 km).

Corso Sempione (map II, pp. 58–59, C-E1-3). A wide road inspired by the Parisian idea of the *boulevard* – though without the same charm – this road features a number of fine buildings, including the headquarters of the state broadcasting corporation (RAI) built in 1929 at no. 27; the *town residence* of the architect Piero Bottoni (built 1955–57) at no. 33; and on the other side of the road at no. 36 the interesting *Casa Rustici* built in the Rationalist style by Pietro Lingeri and Giuseppe Terragni (1934).

Approximately midway along the Corso on the left, *Via Domodossola* (II, D1) leads straight to the exhibition precinct (ca. 600 x 540 m) of the **Fiera di Milano**, or Trade Fair (II, D-E1), while on the opposite corner is the Amendola Fiera subway station ("red" line). Two pavilions in the vast grounds of the Trade Fair, which has a year-round calendar of hundreds of specialized exhibitions, national and international, are of particular interest: the *Padiglione dell'Agricoltura* (Ignazio Gardella, 1957–61) and the *Padiglione della Meccanica* (Melchiorre Bega, 1968–69). In 1994 the pressing need for enlargements prompted a formal decision for preliminary work on a new exhibition site at Pero, near the town of Rho (see itinerary 4.4).

At the head of *Via Buonarroti* (II, F1, off map) the main entrance to the Trade Fair gives onto Piazza Giulio Cesare, with the *Clinica Columbus* at no. 48 in an Art-Nouveau villa designed by Giuseppe Sommaruga (1912–13), and at no. 29 is the "*Giuseppe Verdi*" *Casa di Riposo per Musicisti*, a rest home for musicians (Camillo Boito, 1899), where the bodies of the composer and his wife, Giuseppina Strepponi, are buried.

Returning to Corso Sempione, almost at the end of the road on the right Via Principe Eugenio leads straight to **Villa Simonetta** (II, B2), a Renaissance construction that now houses the Civica Scuola di Musica. Originally the suburban residence of Gualtiero Bascapè, chancellor of Ludovico il Moro, this building was remodeled in 1547 by Domenico Giunti, and was completely rebuilt after the war, due to extensive bomb damage.

Further out in the same urban sector, in the borough of Affori, stands the fine *Villa Litta Modignani* (VI, A3). The once "suburban" villa was built in 1687 for the secretary of the chancellery, Pietro Paolo Corbella, and was subsequently renovated in the first half of the 18th c. Today it is the property of the city council. According to period records, the villa's interiors were sumptuously decorated, though there is little evidence of this now. The adjoining grounds were remodeled in the 19th c., and again in recent times.

Charterhouse of Garegnano (map VI, pp. 110–111, B1). Named after the charterhouse, Viale Certosa runs out into the out-

skirts of town, a continuation of the urban thoroughfare of Corso Sempione (see above). This is the site of a former Carthusian abbey, founded in 1349 by Archbishop Giovanni Visconti. The only surviving part of the charterhouse complex is the admirable 16th-c. church of *Santa Maria Assunta*, completed in 1608 to designs variously attributed to Vincenzo Seregni and Galeazzo Alessi. The church is decorated with splendid frescoes by Daniele Crespi depicting the history of the Carthusian Order (1629). In the presbytery are various frescoes and paintings (1578) by Simone Peterzano.

QT8 (VI,CI). The elevated highway that passes close to the Garegnano charterhouse (see above) also skirts the southern corner of the *Monte Stella*, a manmade hill 170 meters tall, now part of a public park, built with the rubble of the many buildings that were bombed in the air-raids of 1943. Near the hill lies a residential enclave covering an area of 878,000 sq.m, planned and

constructed in 1960 in the wake of the eighth Milan Triennale exhibition (see itinerary 2.6), which was held soon after the war's end in 1947. The overall plan of the housing project was designed by Piero Bottoni, Ezio Cerutti, Vittorio Gandolfi, Mario Morini, Mario Pucci, and Aldo Putelli, and the most important buildings include the constructions at 2-12 Via Sant'Elia (Cerutti, Gandolfi, and Putelli with Vittoriano Viganò, 1947), at Via Goya, no. 17 (Gabriele Mucchi, 1947–48), and at Via Pogatschnig, no. 40 (Pietro Lingeri and Luigi Zuccoli, 1950–51).

Three stops away from QT8 on the "red" subway line next to Bonola station, is the *Centro Commerciale Bonola*, a large shopping complex inaugurated in 1988, and the first of its kind in the Milan area. In nearby Via Cilea at no. 106 is the *Complesso Residenziale Monte Amiata* (Carlo and Maurizio Aymonino, Alessandro De Rossi, and Sachin Messarè, 1967–74). One of the housing complex's most interesting buildings stands at Via Falck 53, with a harmonious portico of thin pillar-walls, built by Aldo Rossi.

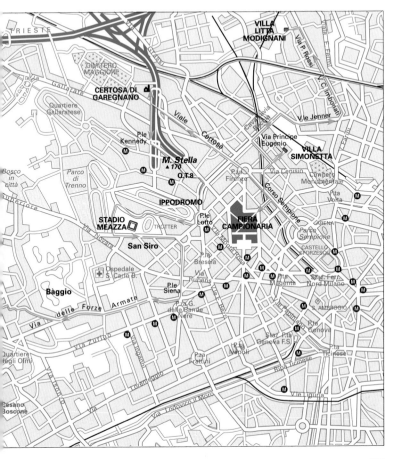

Milan / VI

1:55.000 (1 cm = 550 m)   0   500   1000 m

COMO km 45

Baranzate

Ospedale di
Vialba L. Sacco

Vialba

Staz. Affori
F.N.M.

Bovisasca

Villa Litta
Modignani

Affori

NIGUARDA

Parco Nord

Ospedale
Maggiore

Cimitero
Maggiore

Certosa di
Garegnano

Villapizzone

Staz. Bovisa
F.N.M.

gm

Dérgano

Garegnano

Staz. F.S.

P.le
Lugano

Via Jenner

fn.

P.le
Maciachini

Quartiere
Gallaratese

URUGUAY

P.za
Kennedy

Staz. F.S.

ga

P.le
Accursio

ab

Via Monte Ceneri

Certosa Firenze

Cimitero
Monumentale

Staz.
F.

Malpensa
Air Terminal

LAMPUGNANO

Monte
Stella

Lampugnano

A. De Gasperi

cp

V.

Corso

Cenisio

Via Ippodromo

Q.T.8

Q.T.8

Serra

P.le
D. Chiesa

Velodromo
Vigorelli

S.Sempione

GARIBALDI F.S.

P.za Volta

Ippodromo

Lido

V.le Scarampo

S. SIRO

Via Harar

Stadio
Meazza

Trotter

P.le
Lotto

LOTTO

P.le
Arduino Campionaria

Fiera

P.za VI
Febbraio

P.le
Lega
Lombarda

P.le
Garibaldi

MOSCOV

Arco
d'Pace

Via d. Rospigliosi

Museo di Arte
estremo oriente

bV

Via Novara

P.le
Selinunte

P.le
Brescia

A. FIERA

Casa di riposo
G. Verdi

BUONARROTI

P.le
G. Cesare

Castello

LANZA

Brera

V.le M. Pagano

Via Legnano

CAIROLI

Ospedale
S. Carlo B.

Rembrandt

Rubens

DE ANGELI

P.za
Piemonte

WAGNER

V.le Teodorico

CONCILIAZ.

Staz.
F.N.M.

S.M.d. Grazie

CADORNA

C°

Magenta

S. Ambrogio

CORDUSIO

DUOM

Via d. Forze
Armate

GAMBARA

V.le Misurata

V.le Caterina
da Forlì

P.za G. dalle
Bande Nere

BANDE NERE

V.le Brizi

Washington

P.za
Tripoli

Magenta

S. AMBROGIO

S. Ambrogio

V.le Col. di Lana

V.le Col.

MISSORI

T.C.I.

PRIMATICCIO

INGANNI

uq

V.le Gimignano

D'Alviano

P.za
Napoli

V.

Fabbia

S. AGOSTINO

P.za
Genova

Ticinese

Lorenteggio

Lorenteggio

Via

Giambellino

Staz. Porta
Genova F.S.

P.TA
GENOVA F.S.

P.za
Ludovico

Staz.
S.Cristoforo F.S.

Via

Lodovico

Naviglio

S. Cristoforo

il Moro

Ripa

V.cassala

Ticinese

Ticinese

ROMOLO

V.le Liguria

C° S.Gottardo

C° Lodi

V.le Tibaldi

Robarello

Ronchetto
sul Naviglio

Parco d. Barona

S. Rita da
Cascia

Barona

V.le Famagosta

FAMAGOSTA

bs

Via C.Sforza

V.le G.
da Cermenate

P.za
Agrippa

Córsico

Boffalora

Quartiere
S. Ambrogio

Ospedale
S. Paolo

Conca
Fallata

Chiesa
Rossa

Autostrada

A7

Parco Agricolo -
Urbano del Ticino

GENOVA km 143   PAVIA km 35

110

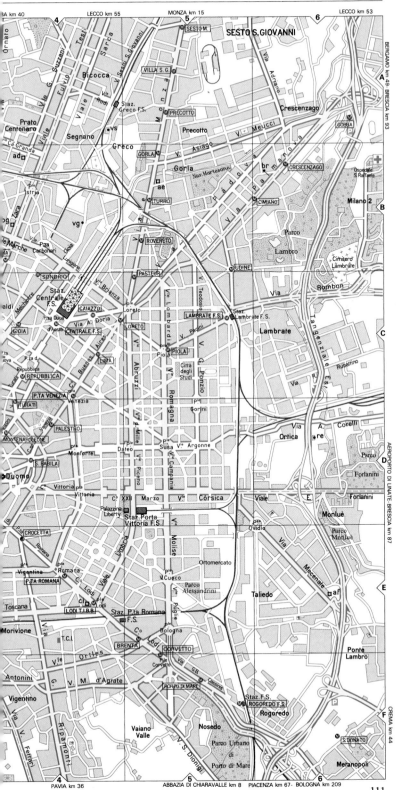

SESTO S. GIOVANNI

SESTO M.

VILLA S.G.

Bicocca

Staz. Greco F.S.

PRECOTTO

Prato Centenaro

Segnano

Precotto

Greco

GORLA

Gorla

CRESCENZAGO

Crescenzago

GOBBA

Ospedale S. Raffaele

Milano 2

TURRO

CIMIANO

Parco Lambro

ROVERETO

Cimitero Lambrate

PASTEUR

UDINE

Rombon

SONDRIO

Staz. Centrale F.S.

CAIAZZO

LAMBRATE F.S.

Staz. Lambrate F.S.

Lambrate

GIOIA

CENTRALE F.S.

LORETO

PIOLA

Città degli Studi

Rubattino

LIMA

REPUBBLICA

P.TA VENEZIA

TURATI

PALESTRO

MONTENAPOLEONE

S. BABILA

Ortica

Corelli

Parco Forlanini

Duomo

Forlanini

Vittoria

XXII Marzo

Corsica

Viale

Forlanini

Palazzina Liberty

Staz. Porta Vittoria F.S.

Monluè

CROCETTA

Parco Monluè

Vigentina

P.TA ROMANA

Ortomercato

Parco Alessandrini

Taliedo

Toscana

LODI T.I.B.B.

Staz. P.ta Romana F.S.

Morivione

T.C.I.

BRENTA

CORVETTO

Ponte Lambro

Antonini

M. d'Agrate

PORTO DI MARE

Vigentino

Staz. F.S.

ROGOREDO F.S.

Rogoredo

Vaiano Valle

Nosedo

Parco Urbano di Porto di Mare

S. DONATO

Metanopoli

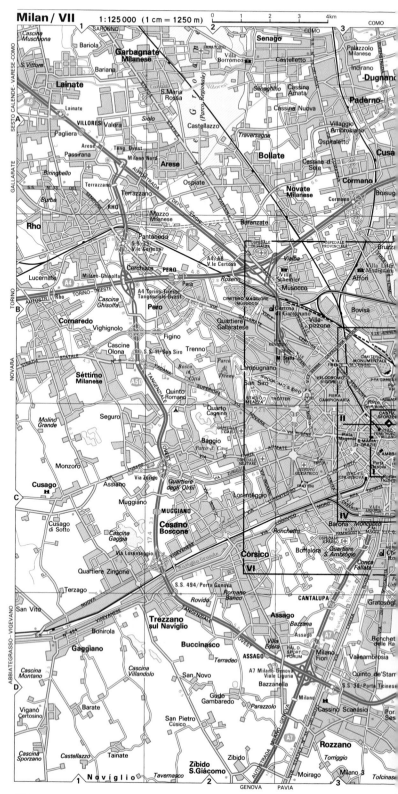

Milan / VII

1:125 000 (1 cm = 1250 m)

0 1 2 3 4km

COMO

SARONNO

COMO

Cascina
Muschiona

S. Vittore

Bariola

Garbagnate
Milanese

Bariana

Senago

Villa
Borromeo

Castelletto

Palazzolo
Milanese

Incirano

Dugnano

Lainate

S. Maria
Rossa

Senaghino

Cassina
Amata

Lainate

VILLORESI Valera

Cassina Nuova

Paderno-

Pagliera

Arese

Castellazzo

Villaggio
Ambrosiano

Passirana

Milano Nord

Traversagna

Ospitaletto

Cusa

Biringhello

Terrazzano

Arese

Ospiate

Bollate

Cassina d.
Sole

Cormano

Burba

Terrazzano

RHO

Mazzo
Milanese

Baranzate

Novate
Milanese

Cormano

Brusug

Rho

Pantanedo
V.le Certosa

OSPEDALE
DI VIALBA

OSPEDALE
PROVINCIALE

Bruzze

Lucernate

Cerchiate

Milano-Ghisolfa

Pero

A4 AB
V.le Certosa

Roserio

Vialba

Villa
Scheibler

Musocco

Villa
pizzone

Affori

Madonnin

A4 Torino-Trieste
Tangenziale Ovest

A4

TORINO

Comaredo

Cascina
Ghisolfa

Pero

CIMITERO MAGGIORE
(MUSOCCO)

Certosa
di Garegnano

Villa-
pizzone

Bovisa

Vighignolo

Figino

Quartiere
Gallaratese

CIMITERO
MONUMENTALE

Cascine
Olona

S.S. 11/ Bel Siro

Trenno

Parco
di
Trenno

Lampugnano

San Siro

Stella

VELODROMO
VIGORELLI

FIERA
CAMPIONARIA

Séttimo
Milanese

Quinto
Romano

Bosco
in
Città

IPPODROMO S. SIRO

STADIO
MEAZZA

TROTTER

Molino
Grande

Seguro

Quarto
Cagnino

OSPEDALE
S. CARLO

CASTELLO
SFORZESCO

II

Monzoro

Baggio

Parco d. Cave

OSPEDALE
MILITARE

S. MARIA
D. GRAZIE

Porta
Magenta

Cusago

Assiano

Via Zurigo

Quartiere
degli Olmi

ISTITUTO
ORTOPEDICO

Porta
Genova

AMBR

Cusago
di Sotto

Cascina
Gaggia

Muggiano

MUGGIANO

Lorenteggio

IV

Barona

Monteper

Quartiere Zingone

Cesano
Boscone

OSPEDALE
DI BAGGIO

Ronchetto

Cor

Terzago

Corsico

Boffalora

Quartiere
S. Ambrogio

Conca
Fallata

San Vito

VI

S.S. 494 / Porta Genova

Romano
Banco

Rovido

CANTALUPA

Gratosogl

Trezzano
sul Naviglio

Assago

Bazzana

Assago

Por
Urb

Bonirola

Gaggiano

Buccinasco

Villa
Edera

PAL. D.
SPORT
FORUM

Milano
Fiori

Ronchet
delle Ra

Cascina
Montano

Cascina
Villandolo

San Novo

Terradeo

ASSAGO

A7 Milano-Genova
Viale Liguria

Valleambrosia

Quinto de' Stan

Viganò
Certosino

Barate

Gudo
Gambaredo

Parazzolo

Milano

S.S. 35 / Porta Ticinese

Cassino Scanásio

Por
Ses

Cascina
Sporzano

Castellazzo

Tainate

San Pietro
Cúsico

Zibido
S. Giácomo

Zibido

Moirago

Rozzano

Torriggio

Milano 3

Tolcinase

Naviglio

Tavernasco

GENOVA   PAVIA

112

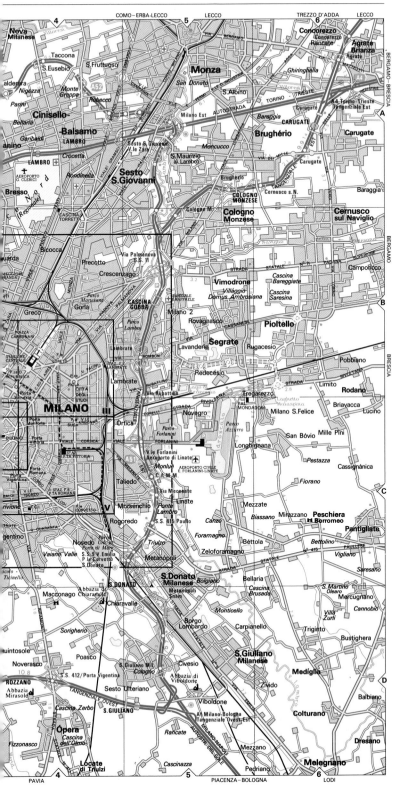

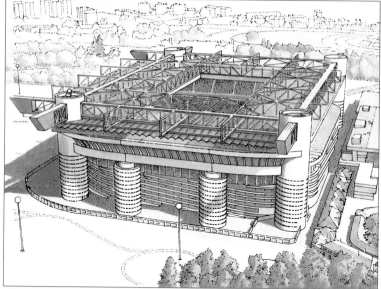

The huge Sports stadium (Stadio Meazza) at San Siro

San Siro (VI, C1). South of QT8 is Milan's largest sports district, which offers a racetrack and horse track (both built in the 1920s), the swimming pool and recreational facilities of the *Lido* (VI, C2) near Lotto subway station, and the huge **Stadio Meazza** soccer stadium, built in 1926 and drastically modified and enlarged in the 1950s; further enlargements were made in preparation for the 1990 World Soccer championships, when the stadium was enhanced with a controversial sliding roof supported on massive external pillars. The new *Palazzo dello Sport* adjacent to the soccer stadium collapsed during the winter of 1985 after a heavy snowfall, when the hyperbolic dish-shaped roof of the building gave in under the weight of the snow.

Beyond the main route of Via Novara, which leads out to Highway 11 (Padana Superiore), stands the *Ospedale San Carlo Borromeo* (VI, D1) whose *chapel* (1961–67) was built to plans by Gio Ponti, Antonio Fornaroli, and Alberto Rosselli. Beside this, between Via Cannizzaro, Via Marx, and Via Pio II, are the

1,100 apartments of the *Quarto Cagnino* quarter (supervised by Vincenzo Montaldo, 1967–73), which sprawls into the surrounding farmland; this is the most recent of the large-scale housing projects carried out by the city.

Baggio (map VII, pp. 112–113, C2). Via Forze Armate leads out of the city to Baggio, a borough that has a past of its own, and bears lingering traces of its old rural layout. At its center stands the church of *Sant'Apollinare*, rebuilt in the 19th c. but sparing the original Romanesque campanile; and nearby in Via Gianella stands *Villa Dellora,* which dates from the first half of the 18th c.

Cusago (VII, C1). The same road that passes through Baggio (see above) leads to Cusago (elev. 126 m, pop. 2,124), whose main square rather resembles a broad farmyard and is dominated by a 14th-c. *castle.* The building was originally a hunting lodge belonging to Bernabò Visconti and is now the nucleus of a residential centre.

3.2 The Northern Sector

Completed at the beginning of the 1930s in what then constituted the northern outskirts of the city, the Stazione Centrale is one of the city's most signal landmarks and an important point of reference for human movement in and around the metropolis. It is also the mainline station for trains bound

for other regions. Near the station, just beyond the site of the abortive postwar enterprise zone, runs Viale Zara, one of the most vital thoroughfares connecting Milan to the industrial hinterland that sprawls as far as Brianza.

An automobile is a must for the suggested

itinerary (map below) along Viale Zara and Viale Fulvio Testi, though the first stage to Villa Mirabello can be reached on foot. Be warned, however, that the area around the railway station is choked with traffic and pollution is high. Moreover, petty theft is more frequent in this area than in any other part of the city.

Stazione Centrale (map III, pp. 60–61, B-C1-2). The station is served by subway lines 2 and 3 (the "green" and "yellow" lines respectively) and stretches right along the north flank of Piazza Duca d'Aosta. Second only to the cathedral, the railway station is one of Milan's most memorable landmarks. The broad front prospect of the building (some 207 m long), entirely sheathed in Aurisina stone, is studded with eye-catching sculpture groups which, in the course of construction (1927–31), were discovered to be heavier than Ulisse Stacchini had envisioned in his original project of 1912, intended as a cross between Art Nouveau and Eclectic. Although popular with the general public, the sheer bulk of the building and its overstated decoration tends to escape the notice of the hurrying commuters and passengers with their luggage. Among the architecture's interesting features are the winged animals on the facade, and the "propylaeum" on Piazza Luigi di Savoia (III, C2), the sculpted medallions by Giannino Castiglioni inside the *Galleria delle Carrozze* at street level, and the portraits of Milan, Venice, Rome, Florence, Bologna, and Turin in colored tiles in the *Galleria di Testa* (at track level); the **vaults*** (designed by Alberto Fava) that overshadow the 21 tracks are also full of detail. The most interesting feature from the technical and structural point of view is the roof, composed of five huge sections of iron and glass (the central one 335 m tall, with a 72-meter span), composed of 9,200 metric tons of pig iron, 262 metric tons of steel, 91 tons of cast iron, and 150 tons of galvanized iron. At the beginning of Via Andrea Doria stand the vestiges of the late 15th-c. *Cascina Pozzobonelli* (III, C2), with its little portico and a three-apse oratory in Lombard Renaissance style. The rest of the building was demolished in 1907.

Pirelli Skyscraper* (III, C1). Dominating the skyline of Piazza Duca d'Aosta is the sleek silhouette of Milan's only true skyscraper (currently the headquarters of the Lombard Region offices), often considered the masterpiece of Gio Ponti, who designed and built it between 1955 and 1960, in col-

laboration with Antonio Fornaroli, Alberto Rosselli, Giuseppe Valtolina, and Egidio dell'Orto. The important teamwork that took place on the construction site between Arturo Danusso and Pier Luigi Nervi (the latter often mistakenly credited with all of the work), produced one of the tallest buildings ever built in reinforced concrete. The sides of the building are sleekly tapered with respect to the elegant main facade. This contrast of depth involved complex structural calculation.

Next to the "Pirellone," as the skyscraper is known locally, is the beginning of Via G.B. Pirelli, which crosses the major thoroughfare of *Via Melchiorre Gioia* (III, A-C1-2), along which the Martesana canal carried water into the heart of the city as far as the church of San Marco (see itinerary 2.1). This busy artery is straddled by a large office *complex* that houses the municipal planning department (1955–66). Nearby in Piazza Einaudi (II, C-D6) stands the large *Telecom* building, constructed by Melchiorre Bega 1960–64.

At a certain point the Martesana canal emerges from its underground channels and is visible between Via De Marchi and Via Padova, crossing

View of the Pirelli Skyscraper and the Stazione Centrale

Viale Monza (see itinerary 3.3); a long section of towpath can be explored on foot or by bike, making this one of the few inner-city waterside environments left in Milan.

The aforementioned planning department building and Telecom offices are situated in the abortive **Enterprise Zone** (Centro Direzionale, map II, pp. 58–59, C-D6), planned after the war in an attempt to concentrate public and private administrative headquarters in the area of the Stazione Centrale. Today only the name itself remains to mark the rather nebulous scheme. Not far away in *Viale della Liberazione* (II, D6) stood the Porta Nuova railway station, known locally as "Le Varesine." The station was renamed *Milano Porta Garibaldi* (II, C5) and relocated in 1963 to its present site (Garibaldi subway station on the "green" line). In the station precinct are two tall postmodern towers belonging to the railway authorities (built 1990–92), built in Manhattan style. Near the immense station complex lies Corso Como, a pleasant street that leads directly to Porta Garibaldi proper (see itinerary 2.1 for both). There are two interesting constructions on Via Galvani (III, C1), the most direct road from the Stazione Centrale to the beginning of Viale Zara (see above). The first of these stands on the corner of Via Fabio Filzi and is a school building (1890) with an interesting eclectic design by the architect and man of letters Camillo Boito, who belonged to the Scapigliatura literary movement, while the other is the *Galfa tower* by Melchiorre Bega (1959) situated at no. 41.

Viale Zara (map II, A-B6). From the roundabout of Piazzale Lagosta (II, B5-6), leaving the old quarter known in the 19th c. as the

Isola (island) because it had been cut off from the rest of the city fabric by the railway, the long and wide artery of Viale Zara heads off in a northeast direction toward the towns of Bresso, Cinisello Balsamo, and Sesto San Giovanni. The road was planned around 1910 as the backbone of an extensive industrial enclave (Quartiere Industriale Nord Milano), whose founding consortium was headed by some of the most important Milanese businessmen of the time (Piero Pirelli, Ernesto Breda, Otto Joel, and Ettore Conti).

Just before Piazzale Istria (map VI, pp. 108–109, B4) Via Ragusa leads to Via Arbe, beyond which stands the 15th-c. **Villa Mirabello** a suburban residence purchased in 1455 by Pigello Portinari, mentioned earlier in connection with the superb chapel in Sant'Eustorgio (see itinerary 2.4); the villa later passed to the Landriani family. For a couple of centuries it was used as a farm, before being restored in two phases, 1916 and 1930. On the other side toward Via Gioia lies an unusual and picturesque quarter known variously as the Maggiolina, or *Villaggio dei Giornalisti*, whose streets are named after well-known Italian writers such as Vergani, Barzini, and Torelli-Viollier. Construction began in 1912 as an offshoot of the said Quartiere Industriale Nord Milano. In addition to the group of characteristic and original houses custom-designed for this particularly category of Milanese professionals (journalists and writers), an interesting villa raised on pilotis stands at Via Perrone 8 di San Martino, designed by Luigi Figini (1934–35) for himself; the house is one of the finest examples of Rationalist architectural in the city.

Ospedale Maggiore (VI, A-B3). Viale Zara continues on toward the outskirts of the city, changing its name to **Viale Fulvio Testi** (VI, A-B4), and from this the broad *Viale Ca' Granda* leads to the gigantic hospital complex (approximately 300,000 sq.m). In 1939 the hospital precinct absorbed the functions of the former Ca' Granda in the city (see itinerary 1.3), which now houses the university. The huge medical facility, which was initially designed by Giulio Marcovigi with the consultation of Giulio Ulisse Arata for the architecture, and Enrico Ronzani for the medical aspects, has gradually evolved over the last fifty years to meet the growing needs of the metropolis. In the center of the complex stands the church of *Santa Maria Annunciata*, also designed by Arata, on a central plan, with bas-reliefs by Adolfo Wildt and others over the altar. A little further north is the original core of the former suburban town of *Niguarda*, until 1923 an independent borough, which gives the hospital its present-day name.

Bicocca degli Arcimboldi (VI, A4). Ensconced in the Pirelli industrial site along Viale Sarca (VI, A-B4), which runs almost parallel to the aforementioned Viale Fulvio Testi, stands the remarkable Bicocca, a fortified manor originally built for Antonella Arcimboldi (died 1439). After many years as a noble residence, the building was put to different uses and was thoroughly restored on two occasions (Ambrogio Annoni, 1910, and Piero Portaluppi, 1953) before being purchased by the Pirelli company. The surrounding industrial buildings belong to the company and cover an area of approximately 750,000 sq.m. Although demand for the product has declined here in the provincial capital – where the company was founded by G. B. Pirelli in 1872 – and the tower on the site of the original Pirelli workshop (see above) was handed over to public management in 1978, the company still plays a very important role in its traditional sector. The conversion to a high-tech industrial and educational pole currently taking place in the Viale Sarca area (based on a project by Vittorio Gregotti, Pierluigi Cerri, and Augusto Cagnardi, 1986), does not,

however, call for the expulsion of Pirelli from its historical factory site. Provisions are being made to transfer the La Scala opera house functions here while the theater is being renovated. Further up Viale Sarca lies the *Borgo Pirelli*, built between 1920 and 1923 to provide housing for laborers and office workers employed at the Pirelli establishment, although only 27 of the 91 houses originally planned were actually completed in the village.

Cascina Torretta (VI, A4, off map) A little further out of town along Viale Sarca stands the huge Breda factory, originally a small electromechanical works set up in 1846 and taken over by Ernesto Breda forty years later, and later established as a major company in 1903 with financial support from the Banca Commerciale Italiana. A large section of the company's establishment is situated within the territorial boundaries of Sesto San Giovanni (see also itinerary 3.3) and from here – if you follow the continuation of Viale Sarca, called Via Milanese, in the direction of the aforementioned Viale Fulvio Testi – you can find the ruins of a country residence, part of which is overlooked by a small Renaissance tower. The complex is in total disrepair and the various projects for restoring it have amounted to little or nothing, in spite of the somewhat farfetched claims that the property once belonged to Queen Theodolinda, and that there was an underground tunnel connecting it to the Bicocca degli Arcimboldi, making it a sort of fortified outpost.

The office towers at Garibaldi station

3.3 The East and Northeast Sector

Immediately outside the eastern gate (Porta Orientale, now Porta Venezia) of the old city stood the large arcaded complex called the Lazzaretto, built in Renaissance times. Its sides extending for some 390 meters, the building was sited on the area currently bounded by Via Lazzaretto, Via San Gregorio, Viale Vittorio Veneto, and Corso Buenos Aires. The complex was originally a place of quarantine for people with the plague, but when it was no longer necessary the walls were demolished around 1880 and the entire area was redeveloped without a second thought. In recent years a North African community has established itself in the area.

Slightly to the east of Corso Buenos Aires, the starting point for the itinerary, lies the district known as Città Studi, comprising the university campus, where technical colleges and university buildings are interspersed with housing projects built at the beginning of the 20th c., together with other public service facilities (the defunct slaughterhouse, the old fruit and vegetable wholesale market, and the Porta Vittoria railway station). Further east, just outside Milan's territorial jurisdiction lies the "Enrico Forlanini" airport, usually known as just Linate, surrounded by residual farming and publicly owned parkland. The area also boasts some important relics of the past, such as in Villa Litta di Rodano and the Borromean Castle in Peschiera, once residences for the gentry.

Corso Buenos Aires (map III, pp. 60–61, C-E2-3). Corso Venezia is a busy radial artery that symbolically leads in the direction of Vienna, the imperial capital during the times of the Lombardo-Venetian kingdom (see itinerary 2.2). The Corso continues beyond the circuit of the old Spanish walls, becoming Corso Buenos Aires, now a busy commercial thoroughfare that serves as a direct link between the city and the Brianza area. The building fabric along this street offers an uninterrupted series of shops and stores of all kinds. Its sales turnover is reckoned to be among the highest at both national and European level, though business has waned since the boom of the 1960s and 1970s. In Via San Gregorio, which crosses Corso Buenos Aires (III, D-E1-2), is a section of the boundary wall of the Lazzaretto (Lazzaro Palazzi, 1488–1513), the only surviving part of the complex apart from the centrally planned church of *San Carlo al*

Lazzaretto (III, E1-2), which was the work of Pellegrino Tibaldi (1585–92) and was altered in the 19th c.

The Corso began to take shape in 1782, when it connected the Porta Orientale with the site (today Piazza Argentina; III, C3) where, from the beginning of the 17th c., there stood a sort of sanctuary, dedicated to the Madonna of Loreto (no longer extant). After 1838 this name passed to the nearby huge traffic roundabout, which is now known as Piazza Loreto (III, C3), which marks the start of the important "Via Veneta" (now Via Padova; III, A-C3-5) and the "Via Militare" leading to Sesto San Giovanni, Monza, and Lecco (now Viale Monza; III, A-C3-4). Piazza Loreto is notorious as the scene of the massacre of fifteen partisans by Nazi and Fascist soldiers on 10 August 1944, and as the place where the bodies of Benito Mussolini and his lover Claretta Petacci were strung up (29 April 1945) after their capture and execution in the village of Dongo on Lake Como, while they were attempting to escape after the collapse of the last-ditch Fascist "Repubblica Sociale."

he commercial importance of Corso Buenos ires is not a recent phenomenon, as is demon- trated by some of the small courtyards (for ex- mple at no. 23, or at 3 Piazza Lima), hidden be- ind the street facades. In another inner court- ard (at no. 2) you can find the *Galleria Lorenzelli* rte, a recently opened art gallery which is linked o a Milanese family, well known in the sector of rt. The *Galleria Gio Marconi*, situated at 15 Via adino (III, D-E2), a side street running parallel s also dedicated to contemporary art, and in fact his gallery is commonly acknowledged to be the inest private exhibition space for this type of art n the city. The *Fondazione Mudima*, another xhibition and cultural center, can also be found n Via Tadino, at no. 26.

anta Maria Bianca della Misericordia III, B5). This abbey complex, which is ot far from Piazzale Loreto and can be eached along the Via Andrea Costa and ia Casoretto, was built at the turn of the 5th c. by the Canonici Lateranensi. Also nown as the "Abbazia del Casoretto," rom the name of a village which was part f the old borough of Lambrate, the hurch has pointed windows in the sides nd was partly transformed during the Baroque era before being considerably estored in the 20th c. by Ambrogio An- noni. Next to the church one can visit the *Chiostro*, or cloisters, which date back to the beginning of the 16th c.

Politecnico (III, D-E5). Connected to Santa Maria Bianca della Misericordia (see above) by Via Ampère, the area known as **Città degli Studi** (III, D-E5) – whose development was completed by 1927 in accordance with the "Pavia-Masera" town-planning scheme of 1912 – is situated around the Piola sub- way station. The *Politecnico di Milano* (1913–27), comprising departments of en- gineering and architecture, overlooks the public gardens of Piazza Leonardo da Vin- ci (III, D-E4-5), and was the first university in Milan when it was founded in 1863. The complex continues north in Via Bonardi (III, D5), where the modern buildings of the department of architecture, completed and restored between 1970 and 1986 by Vitto- riano Viganò and Fabrizio de Miranda, are situated. South of Via Celoria (III, E5-6) and east of Via Ponzio (III, D-E5), however, are both old and new departments and labora- tories belonging to the science department of the Università Statale, including the *bi- ology department* of the science division (Vico Magistretti, 1978–81), situated be- tween Via Celoria and Via Golgi.

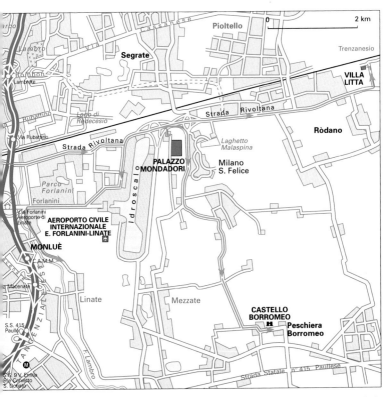

If one walks along the Viale Romagna (III, D-F4), which runs along the western side of the Piazza Leonardo da Vinci, and if one then follows the Viale Campania before turning in the direction of downtown, one reaches the *Largo Marinai d'Italia* (map V, pp. 64–65, B-C3), a park area that was built on an area that from the Fascist era (1922–43) until 1954 was the city's main fruit and vegetable wholesale market. Here stands famous **Palazzina Liberty** (1908), named after its "floral style" decorations; for years, during the 1970s, this building served as a popular if unofficial theater under the leadership of Dario Fo, the renowned Milanese actor and stage director, and his troupe "La Comune."

Palazzo Mondadori (map VI, pp. 110–111, off map). From the Città degli Studi (see above) heading in a southerly direction along Via Ponzio and Via Aselli and from there toward the outskirts of the city along Viale Argonne (V, A5), we reach the other side of the railway in the suburb of Ortica, where we join up with Via Arcangelo Corelli and then the Rivoltana highway that passes through the borough of **Segrate** (elev. 115 m, pop. 30,507). After passing the northern boundary of the *Parco Azzurro*, which surrounds the 2.5-km-long artificial lake of the **Idroscalo** (elev. 108 m) originally built in 1928 as a landing area for seaplanes, and now used for recreational and sports activities, on our left stands the vast office complex built in 1974 by Oscar Niemeyer for the famous Milanese publishing house, Mondadori, founded in 1907. Nearby is the contemporary residential quarter of *Milano San Felice* (elev. 114 m) designed by Giorgio Pedroni, Vico Magistretti, and Luigi Caccia Dominioni, while further north is the modern residential complex known as *Milano Due* (elev. 120 m), which was the first large

real-estate project undertaken by the Gruppo Fininvest (1970).

South of Milano San Felice in the borough of *Peschiera Borromeo* (pop. 18,998) is the **Borromean Castle** (elev. 103 m) built by the aristocratic Borromeo family in 1432, and owned by them uninterruptedly since. East of Milano San Felice, the Rivoltana highway runs toward *Trenzanesio* (elev. 117 m), a village in the scattered borough of **Rodano** (pop. 4,552), with a parkland estate that surrounds the 16th-c. **Villa Litta,** property of the Invernizzi family since 1955.

Linate Airport (VII, C5). Immediately south of the Idroscalo artificial lake, in the borough of Peschiera Borromeo (see above), is Linate, officially named "Forlanini" airport (elev. 107 m), after the aviation pioneer, Enrico Forlanini (1843–1930), which is easily accessible from downtown Milan via the long artery leading from Porta Vittoria (see itinerary 2.3). The original complex dates back to 1936, while the recent expansion work commissioned by the SEA, the airport authorities, was designed by Aldo Rossi, for the architecture and the facade.

Monluè (VI, D6). Back inside the territory of Milan but still close to the airport you can find the remains of an historical rural complex (today isolated by a section of the eastern ring road, or beltway), the construction of which started at the beginning of the 13th c. around an abbey in the village of *Mons Luparium.* Here the Roman church of San Lorenzo, originally built in 1267, modified in 1584, and restored at the end of the 19th c., has a 16th-c. coffered ceiling and an imposing bell tower. Monluè is also famous as the site of the first licensed outlet for selling tobacco and salt, once both state monopolies.

The characteristic Palazzina Liberty in Largo Marinai d'Italia

The Mondadori complex in Milan's east suburbs

3.4 The Abbeys of the Southern Milanese Area (Bassa Milanese)

Across the plain that extends south of Milan between the main highways to Lodi and Pavia runs a road that lies outside the urban fabric and links the abbeys of Chiaravalle, Mirasole, and Viboldone, before ending at the Certosa, or charterhouse, of Pavia. Although today the surrounding countryside appears to be mainly overrun with isolated housing estates, sections of the Milan ring road, industrial buildings, and shopping malls, the really decisive change in this area came about with the introduction of farming by the religious and monastic communities, the introduction of irrigated fields, a kind of water meadow ("marcita"), by the Cistercians of St. Bernard of Clairvaux (Chiaravalle), the profitable agricultural activities carried out by the Humiliati religious orders of Milan and Viboldone (before they were forcibly dissolved in 1571 by St. Charles Borromeo), and the work of the Carthusian monks of Pavia, though they were normally more inclined to meditation and bookish pursuits.

The first part of the itinerary that takes in the urban territory to be found along the length of Corso Lodi, corresponds to a section of Line 3 (the "yellow" line), of the subway between Porta Romana (see itinerary 2.3) and Rogoredo railroad station.

The intermediate subway station of Lodi TIBB takes its name from Piazzale Lodi (V, E-F2) where, next to Milano Porta Romana railway station, is the *Tecnomasio Italiano Brown Boveri*, a factory established in 1909. This company, which takes its blue-collar workforce mainly from the Lodigiano area, and was run by Ettore Conti from 1921 to 1957, is a pillar of the Italian electro-mechanical sector, producing among other things alternators and equipment for some of the most important power stations in Italy (including Terni, Porto d'Adda, Grosio, Piacenza, and Por-

to Tolle), as well as the engine trolleys for the trains used by the Milan subway system and various series of rolling mills for the Falck steelworks in Sesto San Giovanni. The Ligurian workshops of the Tecnomasio have in turn produced hundreds of locomotives for the national railways and generations of trains for the Ferrovie Nord Milano, a private railway line. The industrial area around Piazzale Lodi is now almost completely abandoned, waiting for new business or industrial initiatives, just like so many other similar areas in the city.

From the former suburban center of *Rogoredo*, engulfed by Milanese expansion in 1926, Via Arialdo heads in the direction (7 km) of *Chiaravalle Milanese* (elev. 102 m) where the abbey of the same name is situated. We then proceed across the territory of *San Giuliano Milanese* (elev. 98 m., pop. 32,369) until coming to the signs (11.4 km) for *Viboldone* (elev. 97 m) in the vicinity of the A1 toll road (Autostrada del Sole). The adjacent section of the eastern belt way is between the toll road exit ramps for San Giuliano and *Opera* (elev. 101 m, pop. 13,593) – where we exit from the four-lane road right beside Highway 412l, which runs from the Porta Vigentina – leading along the perimeter of the grounds of the abbey of Mirasole, visible on the left of the road coming from the direction of *Pontesesto* (elev. 99 m). This village (22.5 km) is part of the borough of *Rozzano* (elev. 103 m, pop. 36,927), where we pick up highway 35 from Giovi that runs along the side of the Pavese canal (see itinerary 2.4) and leads on in the direction of Pavia, until a fork in the road that quickly takes us (40 km) to the famous charterhouse of Pavia.

In the vicinity of this itinerary is the headquar-

121

The tiered tower of Chiaravalle Abbey

ters of *Editoriale Domus* (at Via Grandi 5-7 in Rozzano), an elegant complex designed for the publishing company by the Nizzoli partners, and completed at the beginning of the 1980s, and the parkland residential complex known as *Milano Tre* (elev. 99 m) which was built in 1979, and is situated in the far-flung borough of *Basiglio* (pop. 7,502).

Chiaravalle Abbey*

Built on land that originally belonged to the Archinto family, whose symbol can be seen the nearby small 13th-c. cemetery, this abbey (map VII, pp. 112–113, D4) was built in 1135 at the behest of St. Bernard of Clairvaux, and is one of the most important surviving Cistercian complexes in the country. Although the architecture of the *church* (1172–1221) largely follows the severe rule of the French religious order, it does show signs of the Lombard tradition in its use of brick and, inside, in the arcade of round arches resting low cylindrical pillars. The impressive *tower*, with a tiered loggias that rise to a height of 52 meters from the crossing, marked the completion of construction in approximately 1340. After a long phase of decline following the Napoleonic suppression of religious institutions, the building was renovated between the 18th and 19th c. and again after World War II. The Cistercians regained possession in 1952.

The abbey entrance dates back to 1500; the *Virgin Mary and Christ Child* fresco by Luini at the top of the right transept (A)

dates from 1512; there are 16th- and 17th-c. murals by the Campi and Fiamminghini; the choir* (B) was carved by Carlo Garavaglia in 1645. On the right of the church are the remains of the 13th-c. Gothic *cloister* (C), where the *Sala Capitolare*, or charter hall, has graffiti decorations by Bramante, as well as frescoes attributed to the Fiamminghini.

Viboldone Abbey

Founded by the Order of the Humiliati shortly after 1170, the monastery (VII, D5) saw its own *church* finished by the end of the 14th c. Following the suppression of the founding order, the abbey passed under the control of the Olivetan Order who in their turn abandoned it two centuries later. Since 1941 it has been inhabited by a community of Benedictine monks who have once again established it as a closed monastery.

Of the original building only the *church* re-

mains, and here there are fragments of frescoes from the school of Giotto (*Madonna Enthroned, The Last Judgment*) that once decorated the entire church. A large part of the building was reconstructed after World War II by Luigi Caccia Dominioni.

The former Mirasole Abbey

From the very beginning this was more a farm dedicated to raising various crops (a Benedictine "grangia") than a monastery. The badly run-down Mirasole complex (VII, D4), however, has maintained practically all the original elements of the 14th-c. structure, making it unique in this sense among the abbeys of the Bassa Milanese. The second floor of the *cloister* appears to have housed both dormitories and granary, while the two courtyards on the same side were probably used for curing wool and as sheep-pens. The other buildings were occupied by stables and lodgings for the farm

workers. The *church*, which is situated in a corner of the complex and consists of a single nave, is interesting mainly for its bell tower, and has no other particularly notable features.

When the Order of the Humiliati – who founded and expanded the monastery – was dissolved, the property was confiscated by the ecclesiastical authorities and given to the Collegio Elvetico (now the Archivio di Stato; see itinerary 2.2). The complex began to fall into disrepair at the beginning of the 19th c. when the Ospedale Maggiore, which had become its owner in 1797, rented it to an inefficient private concern. The foundation of the Associazione per l'Abbazia Mirasole has turned the abbey into a cultural center, along with the transfer of the *Biblioteca Scientifica Medica* (a library with some 22,000 volumes) and the *Quadreria dei Benefattori*, or benefactors' art gallery, of the Ca' Granda to the complex.

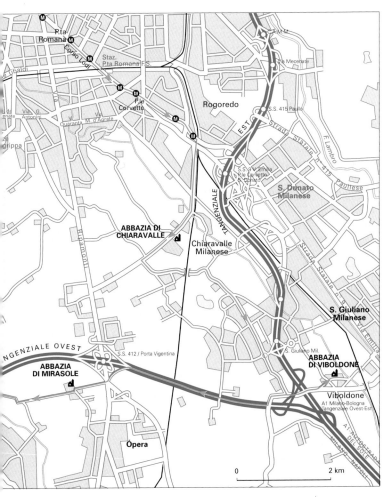

The Certosa of Pavia*

Commissioned in 1396 by Gian Galeazzo Visconti, the same duke who ordered work to start on the construction of Milan Cathedral, the charterhouse is one of the most important monuments in Lombardy (VII, D8, off map) with an eventful history as a convent, a mausoleum for the Visconti family, and a model and example of northern Italian art in the transition from Late Gothic to Renaissance. The originals scheme was designed by Bernardo da Venezia and Giacomo da Campione, and was situated on the northern borders of the vast ducal park attached to the castle of Pavia.

The unfinished church **facade**** creates an exceptional visual impact; the lower order of marble reliefs (1473–99) was designed by Antonio and Cristoforo Mantegazza and Giovanni Antonio Amadeo, with a portal depicting the *story of the Virgin Mary and of the Certosa* by Benedetto Briosco; the 16th-c. upper section was by Cristoforo Lombardo. On the right the forecourt is bounded by an elegant *foresteria** (1625), or guest house, designed by Francesco Maria Ricchino.

Works to see inside include *God the Father**, (1499) by Perugino and *Doctors of the Church* by Bergognone in the second chapel on the left, as well as a *St. Ambrose and Saints* also by Bergognone (1490) in the sixth chapel on the left. Other works by Bergognone are found above the portico of the seventh chapel on the right (two frescoes), in the fifth chapel on the right (*St. Siro and Four Saints*, 1491), in the fourth on the right (*Crucifixion**), and in the second on the right (*Evangelists*), where there is also a polyptych by Macrino d'Alba (1496). Apart from the *gates* dating back to 1660 which enclose the ends of the nave and aisles, there are other frescoes by Bergognone in the vaults of the apses in the left (*Coronation of the Virgin Mary with Francesco Sforza and Ludovico il Moro*) and right (*Gian Galeazzo Presenting a Model of the Certosa to the Virgin Mary*) transepts. In the presbytery are frescoes by Daniele Crespi (1630), carved and inlaid choir* stalls (1498), and an elabo-

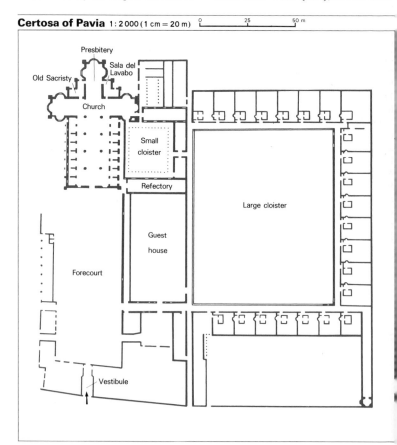

Certosa of Pavia 1 : 2 000 (1 cm = 20 m)

Presbitery

Sala del Lavabo

Old Sacristy

Church

Small cloister

Refectory

Large cloister

Guest house

Forecourt

Vestibule

Plan of the Certosa of Pavia

The extraordinary facade of the Certosa

rate 15th/16th-c. main altar. In both arms of the transept are remarkable *ducal tombs**: on the left is an empty one designed by Cristoforo Solari for Ludovico il Moro and his wife, Beatrice d'Este, while on the right the other tomb, from the same period, commemorates Gian Galeazzo with decorations by Gian Cristoforo Romano, a statue of the *Virgin Mary* by Benedetto Briosco, and allegorical representations of *Fame* and *Victory* by Bernardino da Novate. By the sides of the presbytery is respectively the *old sacristy,* with a portal by Amadeo and an ivory polyptych (*Stories from the Old and New Testaments*) from the workshops of the Embriachi (early 15th c.), and the *Sala del Lavabo,* with a *Virgin and Child,* frescoed by Bernardino Luini and a basin (1489) carved by Alberto Maffioli.

In the right transept is a door*, sculpted on the inside by Mantegazza and on the outside by Amadeo (1466), that leads to the **small cloister***, which is probably by Guiniforte Solari, with terracotta work by Rinaldo de Staulis. The cloister was designed for the community life of the Carthusians and offers a splendid view of the side and the dome of the church. Beyond this extends over 400 meters of arcades around the garden of the *large cloister,* which is possibly the most evocative part of the complex, and one of the twenty-four cells is open for viewing. Finally, do visit the monk's *refectory.*

It is possible to enjoy an excellent overall view of the Certosa from the bridge that crosses the nearby Milan-Pavia-Genoa railway track, and beside this is the station of Certosa di Pavia and the Galbani factory, famous for its cheeses.

4 North Milan and Brianza

"S'è messa un po'di Brianza in faccia," – "She's put some Brianza on her face" – was an expression used in Milan up to a few decades ago, before the so-called economic miracle of the 1950s. The Brianza in question was another word for an imitation suntan, since in the

The Martesana canal

hilly regions of Brianza, toward the higher ground north of Milan, in the direction of the lakes and the Grigne mountains, the well-to-do would go there in search of sun, to get a tan, and to pass their long summer holidays. By the end of the 20th c., however, social customs had changed and cosmetics had come a long way, so now the word "Brianza" indicates a somewhat undefined geographical area north of Milan. As Cesare Cantù wrote: "Brianza is a rather vague denomination, of which we know neither the origin, the meaning nor the limits."

To be fair, however, together with the Cremona and Mantua areas, Brianza is today one of the mainstays of the economic structure that makes Lombardy the richest region in Italy (even if the traditional efficiency of its small businesses is not immune to competition from today's more increasingly unified market). It is also a vast reservoir of skilled labor, which daily descends on Milan, either packed in the trains of the Ferrovie Nord, or stuck behind the wheel of an automobile in the heavy traffic that clogs the toll roads and highways every morning. As for the natural beauty of the countryside, the region north of the metropolis is seen by the Milanese urbanite as a residential haven: a place where children grow up without Milan's characteristic dirt and dust, free to roam without the dangers of traffic; where adults can rest their eyes after a day glued to the computer screen, and stare at the television screen instead, or better, admire the greenery of the countryside outside their homes.

Leaving aside Cesare Cantù's doubts about Brianza's existence, we need to define the geographical limits of the sub-region in question. Basically it stretches west to east between the River Ticino and River Adda, and is bordered to the north by the alpine foothills and lakes. If there were any doubt as to the area's links with the old Duchy of Milan, it is dotted with many Visconti and Borromeo family manors and castles, together with villas that once belonged to the Milanese nobility, and villas built by Milan's business classes.

4.1 The Martesana and the Adda Valley

The Martesana waterway, which Duke Francesco Sforza had diverted from the River Adda between 1457 and 1465, follows a historical route east of Milan which from the Middle Ages thrived on the trade of nearby Gorgonzola and Melzo. The canal conveyed goods and materials made in the Bergamo area; later, iron excavated from the mines of the upper regions of Lake Como also made its way to Milan via the canal. As the map shows, this highly developed area is crossed by the six-lane Turin-Venice toll road.

The Adda bears witness to the area's industrial history in the form of important examples of what is now dubbed "industrial archaeology." These sites document the technology and architecture of the first period of industrialization, which took place in the Milan area from the mid-19th c., and includes old power stations for the production of electricity (the waters of the River Adda drove the first power station in Lombardy) and textile factories, like the one at Cassano and the company towns in and around Trezzo. To these we must also add the hydraulic works of the 15th/16th-c. Paderno canal, of considerable interest from a technical point of view.

The first section of the suggested route starts from Piazzale Loreto (see itinerary 3.3), and between Cimiano and Cassina de' Pecchi follows the tracks of the "Linee Celeri dell'Adda," or Adda rapid transit line, a surface subway that began operating at the beginning of the 1960s and which more recently, thanks to the Cascina Gobba extension, has become part of Line 2 (the "green" line) of the Milanese subway system. As for the route itself, the itinerary at first follows Via Andrea Costa, Via Leoncavallo, and Via Palmanova until it reaches the suburb of Crescenzago where it then follows Highway 11 (Padana Superiore), in the direction (10.2 km) of Cernusco sul Naviglio. After passing through Cassina de' Pecchi and Gorgonzola, the road skirts Inzago (24.1 km) before encountering the River Adda (27.8 km) at Cassano d'Adda. Here the itinerary leaves Highway 11 and follows the course of the river, following signs (34.2 km) for Vaprio d'Adda (38.2 km) Trezzo sull'Adda, 2.3 km northeast of which stands the company town of Crespi d'Adda. A further section, which is only practicable for the first ten kilometers or so up to Porto d'Adda, leads to Brivio by following the right bank of the river for another 22.4 km.

From Cernusco to Inzago

Today's town of *Cernusco sul Naviglio* (elev. 134 m, pop. 27,016), which is situated slightly north of Highway 11 and was once the most important vacation resort for the Milanese aristocracy, takes its character from the new large-scale building consortiums peppering the Milanese hinterland. Among the erstwhile "luxury houses," one that stands out is the *Villa Alari Visconti*, built at the beginning of the 18th c. to designs by Giovanni Ruggeri.

Beyond Cernusco the highway goes around *Gorgonzola* (elev. 133 m, pop. 16,596) – the cheese of the same name is not made here by the way – where it is worth noting the neoclassical *parish church* (Simon Cantoni,

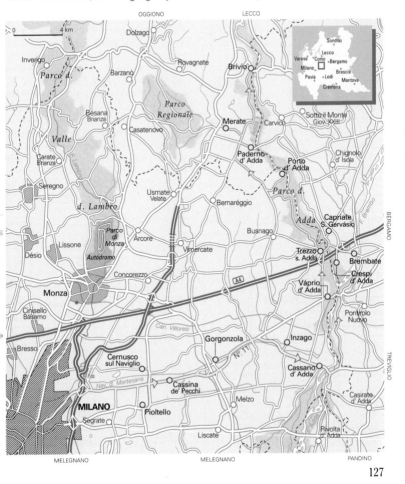

1806–20); the *Villa Sola Busca*, the oldest part of which dates back to 1571; and the hospital which is housed in the 19th-c. *Palazzo Serbelloni*.

Other country residences of the old nobility, dating back to the 17th c., are found in *Inzago* (elev. 137 m, pop. 8,746), the next town along the route. Among those that stand out is *Villa Facheris*, with its facade renovated in the 19th c., *Villa Gnecchi*, which belonged to the Franchetti di Ponte family, who operated the Lombard and Veneto postal services in the 18th c., and in front of this the town hall, housed in what used to be *Palazzo Piola*.

Cassano d'Adda

The town's history as part of the defensive frontier of the duchy explains the fortification of the historical center of Cassano (elev. 133 m, pop. 16,595), on the right bank of the river; the town grew up around the castle, or **Castello Borromeo d'Adda**, which itself dates back to the 11th c. The stronghold was enlarged in the 13th and 14th c., taking on its impressive present-day appearance, under the guidance of Francesco Sforza (Duke of Milan from 1450 to 1466), and possibly thanks to the work of his military engineer Bartolomeo Gadio. Here too are historical residences of the Lombard nobility, the most important being **Villa Borromeo**, originally called Villa d'Adda, whose neoclassical design, completed after 1781, is the work of the architect of Milan's opera house, Giuseppe Piermarini. It is worth noting that Cassano was also the birthplace of the captain of the Regio Esercito, or Royal Army, Giuseppe Perrucchetti, who in 1872 founded the mountain infantry corps known as the "Alpini."

Close to the developed area, and branching off from the River Adda, is the **Canale della Muzza**, a canal that was dug between 1220 and 1230 in order to irrigate the Lodigiano area, further south, with an interesting hydroelectric power station (designed by Pietro Rusca, 1927) built upon it. The complex was commissioned in order to provide energy for a nearby textile establishment, which is made up of three factories built in 1842 and bought by the Linificio Canapificio Nazionale company in 1873. At the end of the 19th c. the factory was equipped with British machinery (at that time the managers were also British), and employed a thousand workers, making it one of the most important establishments in the country. Behind the complex on higher ground is the company town, which dates back to 1907.

Vaprio d'Adda

Vaprio (elev. 161 m, pop. 6,281) plays a key role in Renaissance history. Here Leonardo da Vinci lived between 1506 and 1512, and here for many years were conserved his notes, sketches, and final drafts which were then bound together to form the *Codice Atlantico* (see Biblioteca Ambrosiana, itinerary 1.4). Both of these events were linked to the *Palazzo Melzi d'Eril*, which was built in 1483 (but subsequently renovated) on the initiative of the intellectual and disciple of Leonardo, Francesco Melzi. He is in fact credited with the fresco, based on a design by Leonardo himself, featuring the so-called *Madonnone*. The church of *San Colombano*, a Romanesque building of the 11th/12th c. situated in the town, is also of interest.

North of Vaprio in the town of *Monasterolo* (elev. 163 m) on the banks of the river is *Villa Castelbarco Albani*, today used for exhibitions.

Trezzo sull'Adda

This historical town (elev. 187 m, pop. 11,169) – situated on the right bank after a double bend, where today the Turin–Trieste A4 toll road straddles the river – is a well-known symbol of the Brianza area and is dominated by the ruins of a small but important fortress of the Visconti family.

A park area surrounds what remains of the **castle**, or more precisely the new castle, which was the most important defensive outpost on the eastern borders of the Duchy of Milan. The castle was constructed for Bernabò Visconti in 1365 who, after being imprisoned by his nephew Gian Galeazzo, died there, and it is also interesting for the size of the square donjon, which stands 42 meters tall.

At the beginning of the road for Vimercate in Piazza Nazionale, is the contemporary *Prepositurale dei SS. Gervasio e Protasio* (1922), which still contains a 15th/16th-c. polygonal apse from a previous building. Here there are frescoes of the school of Giotto and others by Bernardino Campi, a wooden *Saint Benedict* that may date back to the 13th c., and a *Virgin and Child* by Bonino da Campione's workshop. A little further uphill there is a fork in the river crossed by the apparatus for supplying water to the **"Taccani"* Hydroelectric Plant**, commissioned in 1906 from Gaetano Moretti and, for the hydraulic planning, Adolfo Covi of Cristoforo Benigno Crespi. This is considered to be the most interesting hydroelectric power station in Lombardy, both in terms of the architecture (it is a spectacular Modernist design that also blends in well and respects the surrounding countryside), and from the technical point of view (the tur-

The blue-collar workers' *houses* (1889–94) are built for two families with separate entrances and their respective orchards and gardens, while the houses for the white-

The power station at Trezzo sull'Adda, with the castle alongside

bine room coincides with the intake room, thereby eliminating the need for a diversion conduit). A further section 400 meters long ending in a basin 8 meters deep makes navigation possible.

Crespi d'Adda

A short distance from Trezzo, on the Bergamo side of the Adda where it converges with the River Brembo, is the well-conserved and very important **Villaggio Operaio***, or workers' village (elev. 160 m) which was constructed in 1878 by Angelo Colla, Ernesto Pirovano, and Gaetano Moretti for the textile factories of Cristoforo Benigno and Silvio Crespi. The village, which is listed among the worldwide heritage protected by UNESCO, is part of the borough of *Capriate San Gervasio* (elev. 190 m, pop. 6,838), which is in turn well known to Milanese families as the home of the very popular *Minitalia*, with its models of over 200 of the most famous landmarks and monuments in Italy on a scale of 1:500.

In the village of Crespi, styled on the criteria of 19th-c. utopian cities, is a tree-lined avenue that divides the manufacturing area along the banks of the Adda (which includes the *owners' house*, an eclectic "castle" designed by Pirovano in 1897), from the housing area, organized along a checkerboard network of roads, where the socially important constructions (such as the *church*, copied in 1893 by Luigi Cavenaghi from the Bramantesque church in Busto Arsizio, surrounded by service structures of various sorts), are spectacularly arranged.

collar workers and management (1922–25) are nearer the outskirts of the town; they are also identifiable because they are better maintained. In the "*cotonificio*" (Colla, 1875), or cotton mill, with a clock on the smokestack that rings out the hours of the lives of those in the district, the factory is divided into four shed structures that house the spinning, weaving, dye-works, and mechanical workshops, while the wrought-iron and brick Art Nouveau decorations are also interesting. The avenue comes to an end at the cemetery, where the *Crespi Mausoleo* is located (Moretti, 1907).

From Trezzo to Brivio

The concluding section of this itinerary, which is only partly accessible by car since in the final part the condition of the road and the series of no-entry areas makes the use of two-wheeled transport imperative, once more follows the course of the Adda, north of Trezzo. By car, however, it is possible to reach the inhabited areas along the terraces overhanging the river, which in some cases extend almost to the water's edge; on foot it is possible to walk along the path of the Paderno canal, or along the Paderno bridge and the weir at Robbiate.

Leaving Trezzo by either Via Adda or Via Rocca, we proceed toward *Cornate d'Adda* (elev. 236 m, pop. 8,445), as far as the picturesque village of **Porto d'Adda** (elev. 240 m), close to a ford that has been in use since Roman times. Following the road uphill we soon come onto a cobbled road that quickly goes downhill until it arrives at the neoclassical structure (Paolo Milani, 1898) of the *"Bertini" hydroelectric power station.* When this facility first came into service, and also for some years afterward, it was the most powerful in Europe with many innovative features, and – by means of a 32-km overground supply line – it carried electricity to the Edison company in Milan at Porta Volta. In the next village of Resega, in parallel with the Bertini station, the *"Esterle" hydroelectric power station* came into service in 1914, and its eclectic architecture (Alessandro Comolli) brings to mind the style adopted by Beltrami for the renovation of the Castello Sforzesco in Milan.

Returning to the Bertini power plant, we again follow the **Paderno canal** which, before it was superseded in efficiency by other means of transport, completed the navigability between Lake Como and Milan by means of a section of the Adda which is rather steep and comprises many torrents. Designed in the 16th c., the canal was not actually built until the last quarter of the 18th c. under Maria Theresa of Austria. From the towpath there are views of interesting rock formations, and it is possible to identify the six basins, now no longer in use, situated at different levels up to a height of 27.5 m. A flight of steps leads up to *Rocchetta,* once home to a community of Augustinian friars and where there are still small buildings dating back to the 14th c. belonging to the order.

A short distance after the mouth of the canal, the **Ponte di Paderno*** (1887–89) hangs, suspended 266 meters above the Adda. This iron bridge is used by both trains and cars, and its parabolic arch of approximately 150 meters rises high above the precipice formed by the river. Passing under the bridge we approach the village of Calusco, where the Robbiate weir is on the left bank of the *"Semenza"* hydroelectric power stations (1920), which, like the other power stations, was commissioned by the Edison company. Further on, inside the boundaries of *Imbersago* (elev. 249 m, pop. 1,747) we arrive at the famous *traghetto a cavo* (cable ferry), which is supposed to derive from a design by Leonardo da Vinci, though there is no proof that Leonardo did not simply sketch an already existing mechanism.

After Paderno d'Adda (see itinerary 4.2), where we pass into the district of Lecco, the next town is **Brivio** (elev. 208 m, pop. 3,820), a name of Celtic origin ("briva" = crossing) that denotes an old river ford there. This was an important religious center in the 6th c., and shortly before the year 1000 it was ranked a *castrum.* Today the town features the ruins of a *castle* that once belonged to the bishops of Bergamo and to the famous soldier Bartolomeo Colleoni, and was rebuilt in the 15th c. by the Serenissima (the Most Serene Republic of Venice). Also noteworthy is the 16th-c. parish church of *SS. Sisinio e Alessandro,* while the bridge erected to replace the ford was rebuilt in 1917.

4.2 Monza and the central-eastern area of Brianza

Situated not much more than a dozen kilometers north of Milan, Monza is both part of the city's hinterland and of the Brianza district. The town of Monza (map on facing page) is the starting point for an itinerary that follows a varied circular route across the very densely populated central section of the Brianza area (153 towns and villages in only 972 sq. km), including the glacial basin on which the town of Merate sprang up and the Valle del Lambro with the hill of Inverigo, which is separated by the charming terraced land of Montevecchia. Further down the valley, after the delightful ancient Christian basilica of Agliate, are the three towns of Seregno, Desio, and Lissone that are close together and are important components in the manufacturing basin north of Milan.

The suggested itinerary (p. 135) starts from the northeast of Monza, where we follow the signs for Villasanta before arriving (6.6 km) at Arcore. From here we follow the road in the direction of Oreno (9.6 km), and when we arrive at Vimercate we take Highway 36 that crosses into the region of Lecco and we climb to Osnago (19.1 km) to the fork in the road before Merate (3.2 km west of Paderno d'Adda). A secondary road continues climbing (23.1 km) to Montevecchia, and north of here we come across other minor roads that lead to Highway 342, which we then must take in a westerly direction. After crossing the Milano–Lecco or Nuova Valassina highway, we continue (41.1 km) to Inverigo. From here we once again head south and return to the province of Milano, passing close to Giussano, passing through Agliate (53.6 km), Seregno, Desio (57.6 km), and nearby Lissone, before completing the itinerary (65.6 km) by returning to the historical center of Monza.

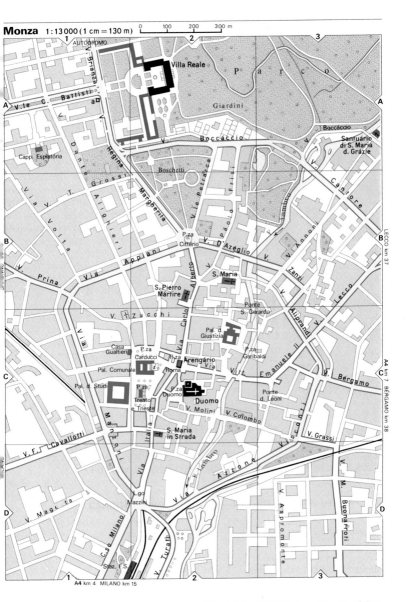

Monza 1:13000 (1 cm = 130 m)

Monza

Although always compromised by its vicinity to Milan (even its hopes of becoming the capital of Lombardy were thwarted), Monza, the "capital" of Brianza, demonstrates its outstanding originality in various ways, starting with its character as an "enclave" following the Roman religious service at the heart of the Milanese diocese. The town (elev. 162 m, pop. 120,054) affords the visitor a great many historically interesting features, including the iron crown that tradition claims belonged to the Longobard Queen, Theodolinda (died ca. 628), the Villa Reale with its sumptuous park, the anar-

chist attack of 1900 that cost the life of King Humbert I, and the world-famous Monza race track. Although the town center is not uniformly well-preserved in the areas round the River Lambro, it boasts individual and collective works that, without exaggeration, are utterly unique.

Piazza Roma (C2). Situated where many old roads converge, this square is the center of the town that is characterized by the large structure of the **Arengario** (tribune) or Palazzo Comunale (which was redesigned by Ottorino Jotta, 1905). The design is not dissimilar to that of the me-

131

dieval Palazzo della Ragione in Milan, on which its "renovation" was based; it is composed of arcades and tower with parapets, originally built at the end of the 13th c., although the work carried out in 1847 changed its characteristics. Since the demolition in the 19th c. of the adjacent Palazzo Pretorio, to which was connected

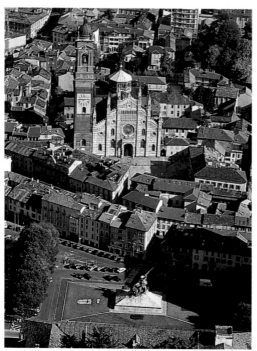

Aerial view of Monza, with the cathedral at the center

by a walkway, the Palazzo Communale seems rather isolated. From Via Napoleone, built in 1825, one quickly arrives in Piazza del Duomo.

Cathedral* (C2). Behind the famous green and white facade, originally designed by Matteo da Campione (1370–96) and renovated by Luca Beltrami between 1889 and 1908, lies the basilica dedicated to St. John the Baptist, a Gothic building which for more than a thousand years was the seat of the ecclesiastical chapter of Monza. The remarkable bold *portico* is by Matteo da Campione. Next to the church is the brick *campanile*, which was designed and constructed by Pellegrino Tibaldi in 1606.
Inside the church, in the nave, beneath the vaults which in 1557 replaced the original roof trusses, is the *evangelicatorium**, also the work of Matteo da Campione, which was made into a choir loft in the 18th c. A cycle of frescoes attributed to Lattanzio Gam-

bara (1570) can be seen in the vault of the transept on the right, while other frescoes are found on the entrance pillars to the presbytery: the frescoes on the right are from the 15th c., the ones on the left are the 16th-c. work of Bernardino Luini or his circle. The altar frontal (1357) is decorated with thin sheets of silver gilt embossed with enamel, while the choir behind it is the result of work carried out in the 16th c. when the apse was demolished.
On the left of the presbytery is the **Cappella di Teodolinda***, after Queen Theodolinda of Lombardy, ca. 595, with frescoes* by the Zavattari on the walls (44 scenes from the life of Queen Theodolinda, dating to 1444). On the altar (by Luca Beltrami) is the **Iron Crown of Lombardy***, which, according to tradition was so named because it was fashioned out of a nail from the cross of Jesus Christ. Apart from its remarkable symbolic significance, from the Middle Ages up to the time of Napoleon the crown was used for the coronation of the kings of Italy; it is also interesting for its outstanding value as an example of the early-medieval jewelers' art, dating back to between the 6th c. and 8th c., and for the gold, precious stones, diamonds, and enamel that decorate the crown.
Going out of the north aisle of the basilica one passes through a small courtyard and a *small cemetery*, which was renovated at the beginning of the 18th c., entering a building that houses the *Museo Serpero,* which contains a **Treasury*** that is among the most important in the world for its documentary and artistic value. One of the most outstanding items is in the central display case, where a group representing a **hen with seven chicks*** is an outstandingly delicate example in silver gilt of the goldsmiths' art (6th/7th c.). Other items of inestimable value are the *Cross of Adaloaldo* (6th c.), the ivory *Diptych of Stilicho* (5th c.), and a *cover of a Gospel book* from the 6th c. as well as furnishings, parchments, incunabula, and prints from the medieval and Renaissance periods.

Leaving Piazza Roma in the opposite direction to the Duomo, we take Via Carlo Alberto where approximately halfway along on the left lies a cobbled square with a *monument* to the Monza-born artist Mosè Bianchi, and the church of *San Pietro Martire* (B2), which belonged to the Dominican order and dates back to the 14th c., even though the outer part is from the 19th c. Continuing along the street you find on the right another larger square with the 13th-c. church of *Santa Maria* (B2), the only remaining example of the numerous churches that the Humiliati Order had in Monza. The bell tower dates back to 1339, while the facade is from the beginning of the 18th c.

From Piazza Roma it is easy to arrive in the nearby *Piazza Trento e Trieste* (C2) which is now dominated by the Town Hall building. During the Fascist era this building was superimposed on the historical *pratum magnum*, which once functioned as a market, also canceling the Teatro Arciducale designed by Giuseppe Piermarini.

The park covers an area of 7,325 sq. meters on the northern boundary of the town, and is one of the largest of its type in Europe. Created between 1805 and 1810 by Luigi Canonica and Luigi Villoresi on the orders of the Napoleonic Viceroy, Eugene de Beauharnais, and then arranged in 1819 by Giuseppe Tazzini, it was enlarged in 1840 and subsequently modified over the years with the introduction of various sports facilities (see below). Today it is a favorite destination for Sunday excursions for the people of Milan and its suburbs, and it even has a summer campsite that without a doubt is the best situated in the neighborhood of the metropolis.

The park took shape behind the already existing **Villa Reale*** (C1), a series of neoclassical buildings built by Giuseppe Piermarini between 1777 and 1780 for the archducal residence of the Hapsburg d'Este family, extinct since the death of Humbert I. During this century the Villa Reale has housed many important exhibitions of interior decoration and lighting (a sector in which Brianza is still famous), although currently it does not have a definite role. The *Pinacoteca*, or art gallery, which housed hundreds of 19th- and 20th-c. paintings from Lombardy, including approximately forty works by Mosè Bianchi, is now closed, but it is possible on request to visit the *Chapel*, the *Court Theater*, (possibly designed by Luigi Canonica, 1802–07), and the *Rotonda*, a circular pavilion, built after the main building, that is decorated with frescoes (*Stories of Amor and Psyche*, 1789) by Andrea Appiani.

Apart from an equestrian school (the former Ippodromo of Mirabello), polo fields, a nine-hole and an 18-hole golf course, tennis courts, and a swimming pool, the park also includes the **Autodromo di Monza** (A-B1-2), a motor-racing track (laid out by Alfredo Rosselli, 1922) that is among the most famous in the world, and which when it was opened was the most revolutionary of its type. The original track (5.7 km) was combined with the need for a *high-speed track* with wide, symmetrical, banked curves (which today no longer exist), to covering a total distance of 10 km. A large number of alterations (such as the chicanes for slowing down the cars, and the new designs of the Lesmo and Vialone curves), have been made as a result of new technical developments in motor racing, since the original track had become too fast and dangerous for modern racing regulations. Despite its uniqueness (it is impossible here to summarize the track's history, which is inextricably tied to that of the Italian automobile

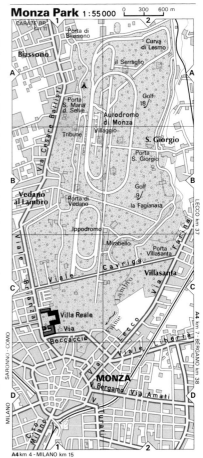

Monza Park 1 : 55 000

The sumptuous Villa Reale in Monza, which gives onto the vast park

industry), the race track has always posed environmental problems, and conservation groups periodically demand its closure, an eventuality that would entail transferring the Italian Gran Prix (Formula 1), staged on the second Sunday of September, to another race track.

Arcore, Vimercate, and Osnago

Arcore (elev. 193 m, pop. 16,342), situated on the first outcrop of the Brianza hills, has some fine examples of historical aristocratic residences, including the 17th-c. *Villa d'Adda* and *Villa Vittadini*, which is a 19th-c. reworking of the original 17th-c. hunting lodge. In **Oreno** (elev. 194 m), a village close to Vimercate, the properties belonging to the Borromeo family include the 6th/7th-c. *Villa Borromeo* (in Viale Piave) and a *hunting lodge* that is approximately three centuries older. On the second floor of this lodge are some excellent 15th-c. frescoes* (*hunting scenes*), which are also interesting because they give a reliable picture of the Lombard countryside during the Renaissance.

Vimercate (elev. 194 m, pop. 25,868), once ancient *Vicus Mercati*, has fulfilled the promise of its evidently commercial toponym, becoming a lively manufacturing center (originally specializing in textiles, but today also involved in electronics), that has not lost the original character of its historical nucleus. Since 1862 the council headquarters have been housed in the *Palazzo Trotti*, in Piazza Unità d'Italia, which boasts a cycle of 18th-c. frescoes* (*Stories of Cleopatra, Semiramis, and Hercules*, as well as other mythological subjects) distributed

in eleven rooms. From the adjacent Piazza Roma we take Via Leonardo da Vinci and arrive at the basilica of *Santo Stefano*, built in two phases between the 10th c. and 11th c. on the ruins of a building that is mentioned in records as far back as A.D. 745. The *bell tower* (1261; renovated in the 15th c.) was built using materials plundered from ruined Roman constructions. The church itself, which was used as a fort in the late medieval period, has a 16th-c. facade, an architraved portico, and, inside, frescoes by the Campi brothers (in the apse) and Antonio Busca, and paintings by Agostino Santagostino, while the *crypt* dates back to the original phase of construction.

Via Cavour also begins in Piazza Roma, and along this street stand 15th-c. buildings and the Romanesque *Oratorio di Sant'Antonio*, with a facade that was added in the 14th c. and frescoes from 1450. At the end of the street you arrive at the bridge known as *Ponte di San Rocco** or *Ponte di Ezzelino*, an interesting medieval fortification that was constructed with materials recouped from a similar Roman building. The tower that looks out over the countryside, and the upper part of the building that faces the town, date from the 14th c., while the rest of the construction is two hundred years older.

In **Osnago** (elev. 249 m, pop. 3,124), a short distance from Merate, on the right side of the central Via Roma stands the magnificent **Villa Arese Lucini**, built in 1559 on the site of an existing residence, and renovated in the later 17th c. by Francesco Maria Ricchino and his son, Gian Domenico. However, part of the external walls are from the 19th c.

From Merate to Montevecchia

Merate (elev. 292 m, pop. 14,024) commands a delightful position in the hills close to the River Adda, and today it is mainly famous for the *Osservatorio Astronomico*, a department of the Brera observatory (see itinerary 2.1), built in 1924 a few kilometers outside the town. Near Piazza Italia is the *Collegio Manzoni* that belonged to the Order of the Somaschi, where the future author of *The Betrothed*, Alessandro Manzoni, and the brothers Pietro and Alessandro Verri (also authors) received their education. From the nearby Piazza Prinetti (with an unfinished building of the same name that dates back to the 18th c., built where the local castle stood), you cross Piazza Vittoria and go along Via Roma in the direction of **Villa Belgioioso**, which is separated from the street by an atrium. The villa was possibly founded on the site of a settlement of the Order of the Humiliati, which subsequently passed into the possession of the Novati family in the middle of the 15th c. The house took shape, along with its gardens, under the direction of Giuseppe Muttoni, but it was substantially transformed after 1749 when it

passed to the Belgioioso family. Continuing on past the villa we arrive at a piazza dominated by the parish church of *Sant'Ambrogio*, which was enlarged in 1640 and conserves a series of memorial stones from the original construction, situated on the left side of the building.

Nearby, along Via Fornaci just outside **Paderno d'Adda** (elev. 266 m, pop. 2,692), whose iron bridge over the river has already been mentioned in the description of the route along the Adda (see itinerary 4.1), is the important **Cascina Assunta** (1882), one of the finest examples in Lombardy of agricultural residences of this era.

West of Merate, on the other side of the Lecco highway, the charming village of **Montevecchia** (elev. 479 m, pop. 2,356) is surrounded by 2,200 hectares of chestnut, oak, and birch trees that form the *Regional Park of Montevecchia and the Valle del Curone*. The mixed sandstone and limestone mount on which the village is situated is a traditional devotional destination, thanks to the 16th-c. *Santuario della Beata Vergine del Carmelo* and its "Via Crucis" crowning on the summit. Because of the

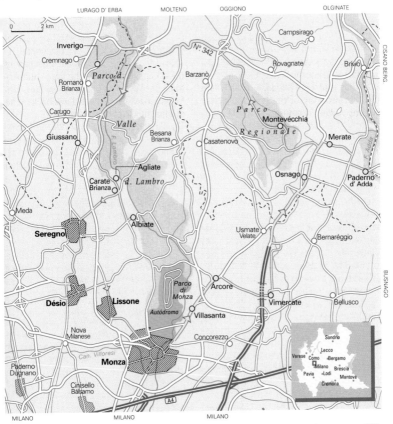

135

well-marked paths, 18th-c. houses, and lively restaurants, it is also popular for weekend excursions.

Along the Erba–Asso section of the Ferrovie Nord Milano, which in itself offers a pleasant experience, the town of Inverigo (elev. 346 m, pop. 7,873) is built on sloping hills above the valley of the River Lambro. Near to the 16th–20th-c. *parish church* (inside of which is a *Virgin and Child with Saints*, signed by Bernardino Campi) is a cobbled street that climbs the hill to the *Villa Crivelli*, an old ruined residence of one of the most important families of the Milanese nobility. After arriving at the Dominican

Interior of the basilica of SS. Pietro e Paolo, Agliate

complex it is best to walk round the outside of it in order to get a good view from high up of the **Cypress Avenue*** (Viale dei Cipressi), which is almost 2 km long and represents one of the most famous and symbolic natural sights in Brianza. The view also looks over the surrounding countryside, and next to the avenue in the direction of the village of *Santa Maria alla Noce*, which up to the end of the 19th c. was the main regional marketplace for silk-worm cocoons, it overlooks a 16th-c. church (*San Carlo)* that contains an altar frontal by Morazzone. The village, which can be reached by car from the above-mentioned parish church, has examples of stores and warehouses once used in the silk trade. Another hill, which can be reached by returning to Inverigo and following Via Filippo Meda, is immersed in the trees encircling the **Rotonda**, a neoclassical villa (today the property of the Pro Juventute Don Gnocchi foundation), built in 1813 by Luigi Cagnola as his personal residence. The villa displays a mixture of styles (Greek, Roman, Renaissance, Egyptian) that are easily recog-

nizable; in the chapel stands Cagnola's *cenotaph*, the work of Francesco Somaini.

Close to Inverigo are the villages of *Cremnago* (elev. 335 m), with the 18th-c. **Palazzo Perego**, which has a chapel containing frescoes by Bergognone (*Crucifixion and Saints*, 1495) that were taken from the suppressed convent of Sant'Erasmo in Milan (see itinerary 2.2), and *Romanò Brianza-Villa Romanò* (elev. 312 m.), where Francesco Maria Ricchino is said to have contributed in 1646 to the designs for *Villa Gallarati Mezzanotte*.

Further south of Inverigo, beyond *Giussano* (elev. 260 m, pop. 20,236), traditionally the birthplace of the famous Alberto da Giussano of the Battle of Legnano (see itinerary 4.4), cradled in the green countryside by the banks of the River Lambro is the small village of **Agliate** (elev. 217 m), close to Carate Brianza (see below). The village is famous for the basilica of **SS. Pietro e Paolo***, with its walls of rubble infill and "herring-bone" masonry, which dates back to either the 10th c. or the beginning of the 11th c., and it was boldly renovated by Luca Beltrami between 1893 and 1895. The building has a bell tower with two-light windows (1899), and the three-aisle interior has a row of pillars (some of which date from the 4th and 5th c.) supporting a beam roof. In the nave, on the last two arches on the left, it is possible to recognize the remains of a cycle of 10th-c. frescoes that were partially repainted in the 19th c., while access to the crypt is through the side apses. On the right side of the church is the **baptistery***, probably more recent, which also has some rather faded frescoes (11th to 15th c.).

In *Carate Brianza* (elev. 250 m, pop. 15,887) there is a Biblioteca Civica, or public library, housed in the 15th/16th-c. *Villa Cusani Confalonieri*, which was originally converted from a medieval fortress; there remains a donjon with fake battlements. Next to the villa is an English-style park, and in the parish church, which was renovated by Simone Cantoni between 1803 and 1807, are paintings by Daniele Crespi, Francesco Hayez, and Malosso.

Along the old Valassina road, a little to the west of the main highway, is the town of

Seregno (elev. 222 m, pop. 38,401), a modern industrial and service-sector center whose traditions as a manufacturing area go back at least to the 16th c. The early church of San Vittore, which was the fulcrum of the medieval town, bequeathed the 11th-c. bell tower, known as the *Tower of Barbarossa*, that is now found in Via Cavour. In the same street is the *Oratorio di San Rocco*, built in the late-15th c. and renovated in the 18th c. The inside of this church is completely decorated with frescoes by artists from the circle of Bernardino Luini and Gaudenzio Ferrari. In Piazza Libertà is an interesting 18th-c. building that houses the *Collegiata di San Rocco*, while in the western part of the town one can visit the Neo-Gothic *Sanctuary of Santa Valeria*, a very popular place of devotion that has a rich collection of 17th- to 20th-c. votive panels.

Between Desio and Lissone

Even though Seregno has for many centuries been the most important center in the area, it is the nearby **Desio** (elev. 196 m, pop. 34,397) which was nominated area capital by the administrative authorities. It

was also a place of retreat in the 16th and 17th c., as testified to by *Villa Cusani* (subsequently *Villa Traversi*) in Via Lampugnani, a neoclassical building designed by Giuseppe Piermarini and subsequently remodeled in the middle of the 19th c. by Pelagio Palagi. The villa was built on the site of a medieval castle belonging to the Visconti family, and in fact it was here that, in 1277, Bernabò Visconti defeated the Torriani family, clearing the way to his rule of Milan.

On the other side of the highway (the Nuova Valassina) is **Lissone** (elev. 191 m, pop. 32,817), famous since the 18th c. as a furniture manufacturing center. In the central Piazza della Libertà, *Palazzo Terragni* (the former Fascist headquarters, designed, as the name suggests, by Giuseppe Terragni, 1938) houses the *Civica Galleria d'Arte Contemporanea*, a town gallery of contemporary art (visits by appointment), containing works of art that were awarded prizes between 1946 and 1967 in the local art competition.

At this point we are once again very close to Monza, where the itinerary comes to an end.

4.3 The Seveso Valley and the Strada Varesina

One of the busiest lines of the independent railroad company Ferrovie Nord is the one that follows the course of the River Seveso to the town of Meda, along the route of an ancient Roman road; after the town of Meda, whose name derives from the *Media Via* meaning "midway," the road continued along the river toward *Comum*, namely, ancient Como. Today this road is known as the Vecchia Comasina (part of Highway 35, Giovi), and it follows the route chosen at the end of the 19th c. by the state railway, for the international service from Chiasso to Zurich.

Almost parallel to the Valle del Seveso (where in the past the community mixed its business with the proceeds from the ecclesiastical landholdings of Dugnano, Varedo, Lentate, etc.), a little further west, between Milan and Varese, is another Roman road that today is known as Highway 233, Varesina. The itinerary recommends taking this road on the way back from Meda to the metropolis, thereby crossing a section of the Milanese plain that, just before the villas and the Alfa Romeo plant of Arese, includes the town of Saronno and the Parco delle Groane.

As far as traveling by car is concerned, on

the way out the itinerary follows the Seveso–Meda highway, or the Nuova Comasina (which starts in Milan near the Ospedale Maggiore di Niguarda, see itinerary

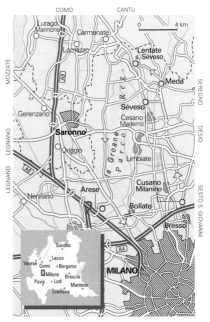

The sanctuary of the Madonna dei Miracoli, Saronno

3.2), although for the first section, as far as Cusano Milanino, this highway is not used. It is better to take the first part of the old Valassina highway in the direction of Niguarda and Bresso (north of the hospital, following the tram lines that link Milan to Milanino), or the old Comasina state highway (from Piazza Maciachini, along Via Imbonati). After Cusano both the new Seveso–Meda highway and the old state road run past Cesano Maderno (14 km), Seveso (15.8 km), and, 23 kilometers northeast of the latter, Meda, while at Lentate sul Seveso (20 km) the Seveso–Meda highway comes to an end and joins up with the state road. When returning to Milan, we pass first through Lazzate, and then pick up Highway 133 that goes past the Parco delle Groane. Near Saronno, the major road junction of which is 6 km west of Highway 133, we take Highway 233, at Arese, which is 58 kilometers from Milan.

Cusano Milanino

This town (elev. 152 m, pop. 20,810), which is now more or less uninterruptedly built up all the way to the neighboring towns of *Cormano* (elev. 149 m, pop. 18,349), *Bresso* (elev. 142 m, pop. 28,791), and *Paderno Dugnano* (elev. 163 m, pop. 44,498), is the only town of this group that is of any historical interest. At the beginning of the 20th c. an experimental garden-city was built, with the name of Mi-

lanino, by the Unione Cooperativa, the idea of which was to create – by the year 1914 or 1915 – a hundred or so villas served by public facilities. Even today the avenues of Milanino are peaceful and pleasant, dotted here and there with unusual buildings.

Toward Como

In **Cesano Maderno** (elev. 198 m, pop. 31,768) – the site of many furniture factories and chemical plants – is **Palazzo Arese**, subsequently called *Borromeo Arese* (now owned by the local council), an example of Lombard Baroque that was begun in 1618 and finished between 1640 and 1670 by the then president of the Senato di Milano, Count Bartolomeo Arese. Inside the building the *salone d'onore*, or great hall, is decorated with frescoes of the Lombard school (Giulio Cesare Procaccini, Giuseppe Nuvolone, the Montalto), which have been here since the church was built. The building's garden is also interesting, although it is in a very bad state of repair. The town of **Seveso** (elev. 211 m, pop. 18,053), which takes its name from the river whose course this itinerary follows, has a number of examples of historical buildings, one of which is the *Prepositurale*, or provostal, built in the 16th c.

In the countryside around Seveso every trace has been removed of the Icmesa chemical plant, which was owned by the Swiss Hoffman-La Roche group; the complex stood near the highway. On 10 July 1976 an accidental leak of an undisclosed quantity of deadly chlorinated organic composites (dioxin), together with other poisonous gases, seriously affected the health of the local population (many were hospitalized) and caused great alarm to the general public. It has been suggested on more than one occasion that the end product of the Icmesa plant were chemicals for use in chemical warfare, in violation of Italian law.

Nearby, on the opposite side of the highway from Seveso in the direction of Seregno (see itinerary 4.2), lies the town of **Meda** (elev. 221 m, pop. 21,182), which has also been famous for hundreds of years for furniture manufacturing. The town's history is closely linked to the old nunnery of San Vittore, which existed for a thousand years or so before being suppressed in Napoleonic times. In another part of the town the **Oratorio di San Vittore**, dating back to the beginning of the 16th c., has coeval frescoes of the Lombard school (attributed to the circle of Bernardino Luini) inside the building, as well as an altar frontal by Cerano, while the facade dates back to 1730. Next to the church stands **Villa Antona Traversi**, a neoclassical conversion of the convent buildings that may have been done by Leopold Pollack and Pelagio Palagi, comprising the *Sala del Coro* with frescoes by Giovan Mauro Fiamminghini.

The part of the itinerary furthest from Milan is the town of **Lentate sul Seveso** (elev. 250 m, pop. 14,353), where the *Oratorio di Santo Stefano* (1369) with frescoes by the Lombard masters of the 14th c. is well worth a visit.

Saronno and the Groane Regional Park

The religious traditions of **Saronno** (elev. 212 m, pop. 37,870), today an important manufacturing center in the province of Varese, can be seen in the northeast area of the town in the sanctuary of the **Madonna dei Miracoli***, built between 1498 and 1510 by Giovanni Antonio Amadeo. The church – which has a fine Mannerist facade (Pellegrino Tibaldi, 1596–1612) and a bell tower (Paolo della Porta, 1511–16) that was probably used as a model for many other such towers – houses many important works of art, including the *Concert of Angels* (1534), a fresco by Gaudenzio Ferrari in the vault* of the dome, frescoes by Bernardino Luini, and a 16th-c. polychrome group featuring *The Last Supper* in the chapel of the Cenacolo, and other frescoes* by Luini (*The Wedding of Mary, Jesus Among the Doctors, Adoration of the Magi, Presentation in the Temple*, 1521–31) in the Chapel of the Virgin Mary.

In the center of the town is the church of *San Francesco* (15th c.) with a baroque facade and a Renaissance dome in brick on the left side (inside is a *Madonna of the Rosary* by Aurelio Luini). A local specialty is the celebrated "Amaretto di Saronno," a liqueur that is also very popular in northern Europe, where for marketing reasons it is exported under the name of "Disaronno."

East of the town are approximately 3,200 hectares of land spread out over 15 kilometers along the north–south axis of the Seveso and Guisa rivers, which since 1976 are protected areas, and form the **Groane Regional Park**. The area, which lies entirely within the boundaries of the province of Milan, is characterized by the presence of a thick surface-layer of moraine, or glacial sediment, and it is also important for the woods of oak, beach, chestnut, hornbeam, and Scotch pine trees; the landscape is rugged and areas of scrub are punctuated with expanses of yellow broom.

Arese

Near to the boundary of Milan along the A8 Laghi toll road lies the town of Arese (elev. 160 m, pop. 18,785), which owes much of its current fame to the presence of the most recent of the *Alfa Romeo car factories* (now part of the Fiat group), transferred here in 1963 after the closure of the Milanese factory in Portello, near the Fiera di Milano (Milan Trade Fair), and the company *office block* (1970–75), designed by Ignazio Gardella. The manufacturing history of the company can be seen in the hundreds of vintage vehicles that are exhibited in the 4,800 sq. m of the **Museo Storico "Alfa Romeo."**

A short distance from Arese is the town of *Bollate* (elev. 156 m, pop. 43,685), site of the *Castellazzo* estate (elev. 164 m), which includes the old Dominican residence of **Villa Arconati***, now the property of the Radice Fossati family. The villa is historically and architecturally of utmost interest, having been constructed in the later 17th c. over an existing medieval structure, and subsequently remodeled and equipped with a garden around 1730. The *Salone delle Feste*, where grand parties were held, has decorations dating from the 1770s.

We re-enter Milan at Viale Certosa and Corso Sempione (see itinerary 3.1).

The old Dominican residence of Villa Arconati, Bollate

4.4 The Strada del Sempione and the Ticino Valley

In the section of Lombardy situated between Milan, Varese, and the Piedmontese border, there are three fundamental elements that form a rough triangle: the virtually uninterrupted conurbation along the route of Highway 33 from Sempione, formed by Legnano, Castellanza, Busto Arsizio, and Gallarate; the broad and twisting course of the River Ticino which flows down to Pavia; the Naviglio Grande, the canal which in the north deviates slightly from the river before striking out on its own in the area of Abbiategrasso. The route suggested here is, therefore, exceptionally long and varied, passing through manufacturing, naturalistic, and historically and architecturally interesting areas.

The itinerary sets off from Milan along Highway 33, from Sempione, which starts in Via Gallarate on a route that branches off from Viale Certosa (see itinerary 3.1) in Piazzale Accursio. Once in Rho (14 km) the itinerary skirts Nerviano and Parabiago on the left, reaching Legnano (25.5 km), after which near Castellanza we switch to the Varese

Highway. Crossing Busto Arsizio (32 km) and Gallarate (39 km), 6 kilometers from Malpensa airport, we head toward Somma Lombardo (46.5 km), where we take the provincial highway that more or less runs parallel with the River Ticino and the initial section of the Naviglio Grande. Returning to the province of Milan shortly before Turbigo (65 km), we head toward Guggiono (82.9 km) and Magenta, which are reached via Highway 11 (Padana Superiore). We then continue south of Magenta in the direction of Robecco sul Naviglio, with the nearby Cassinetta di Lugagnano, arriving (91.2 km) in Abbiategrasso (6.1 km from Morimondo Abbey). Finally, following the ample curve of the Naviglio Grande as it enters Milan, we take Highway 494 (Vigevanese), that traverses Trezzano sul Naviglio and the suburb of Corsico, before entering Milan proper (114.7 km).

The land of the Carroccio

The town of **Rho** (elev. 158 m, pop. 52,302), today an important manufacturing center

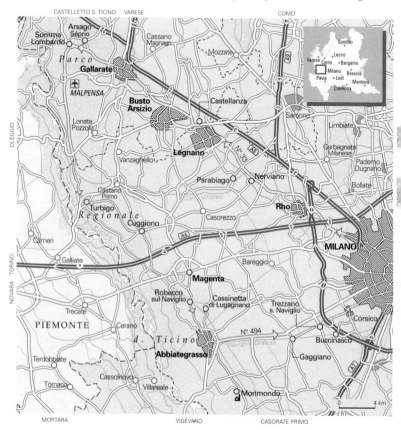

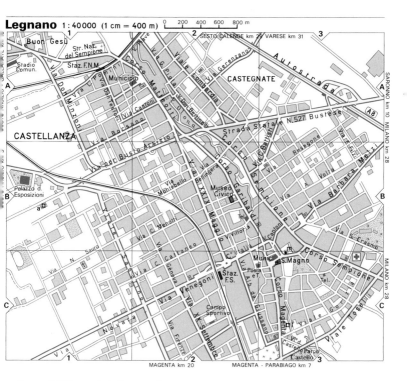

in the north-Milanese belt, has very few remaining signs of ancient *Rhaudium*, which was probably of Longobard or Frankish origin. However, the remains of a Roman burial ground were discovered in the area and are now on view in the *Saletta Archeologica Rhodense*, situated in *Villa Cornaggia Medici* (or "Villa Burba") at Corso Europa 291, while a more recent historical site can be found at the end of Via De Amicis in the **Santuario della Madonna dei Miracoli**, which was commenced in 1584 to designs by Pellegrino Tibaldi, and completed with the addition of an 18th-c. dome and a neoclassical facade (Leopold Pollack, 1821).

In the next town of *Nerviano* (elev. 175 m, pop. 16,314) the banks of the River Olona host the 18th-c. *Palazzo* and *Villa Lampugnani*. Also in this area is the **Canale Villoresi**, a canal designed by Eugenio Villoresi and constructed between 1884 and 1888 to join the Adda and Ticino to improve the irrigation and the agriculture along its 86-kilometer course.

On the other side of Nerviano a short deviation takes us to **Parabiago** (elev. 184 m, pop. 23,686), traditionally famous for its many shoe factories. Here stands the interesting 17th-c. *Collegio Marchiondi* complex, as well as the parish church of *SS. Gervasio e Protasio* built a century later, possibly to designs by Pellegrino Tibaldi.

Highway 33 then approaches the urban agglomeration that comprises Legnano, Castellanza, Busto Arsizio, and Gallarate, cradled between the provinces of Milan and Varese. The most southerly of these towns, **Legnano** (elev. 199 m, pop. 52,164), is tied to the great battle that took place in 1176 between the Guelph forces of the Lombard League, which won with the support of the Carroccio (a large cart that was taken onto the battlefield to lend encouragement), and the Ghibelline forces led by the Emperor Frederick I, nicknamed Barbarossa by the Italians.

Today, although Legnano is a manufacturing center going through a period of transition from the traditional textile industries to the more recent mechanical industries (the turbines made by the Franco Tosi Company), and the service industries, it still has many traces of a much older culture. The basilica of **San Magno** (C3), a centrally planned church in Bramantesque style (1504–13) boasts a polyptych* by Luini and a chapel with fresco decorations by Bernardino Lanino. The **Museo Civico Guido Sutermeister** (B2) has an archaeological section devoted to the Bronze and Iron Ages, as well as examples of Roman and late imperial urns and headstones, Longobard burial artifacts, 15th- to 17th-c. frescoes and architectural elements, and several paintings by Gaetano

141

Previati. The museum's coin collection is also of interest.

Castellanza (elev. 216 m, pop. 15,247), virtually a continuation of Legnano, has a *Museo d'Arte Moderna della Fondazione Pagani* with examples of Italian and foreign contemporary art arranged in one of its pavilions and in the park.

Busto Arsizio (elev. 226 m, pop. 77,567), an ancient town which since medieval times has manufactured leather and linen goods, has a recent history similar to Legnano. In the center of the town is the basilica of *San Giovanni Battista* (B2), which is originally Romanesque with the addition of a 15th c. bell tower and a Baroque exterior designed by Francesco Maria Richchino (1615–35), and the sanctuary of **Santa Maria di Piazza*** (B2), which is a Renaissance building of the Bramante style (1517–27) with a bell tower by Carlo Maciachini (1873–77) that is a renovation of an already existing tower. Inside the sanctuary the 32 niches that support the dome contain 32 wooden *statues* (1602), while the vault and the walls are decorated with frescoes from the 16th c. On the left side is a polyptych (*Virgin and Child with Saints*, 1539) by Gaudenzio Ferrari, and in the adjacent niches are frescoes with *pictures of saints* by Bernardino Luini that were transferred here from a demolished Milanese church.

Gallarate (elev. 238 m, pop. 45,086) definitely had pre-Roman and maybe even Insubre origins (an ancient Celtic people who lived in Lombardy), the evidence for which can be seen in the Celtic suffixes of the names and in the early Iron Age objects found in nearby Golasecca. Today, like Castellanza and Busto, the town is an important manufacturing center in the province of Varese. Worth visiting here is the church of **San Pietro** (B1), built in the Romanesque style in the 11th c., its apse remodeled in 1907; and the 19th-c. basilica of *Santa Maria Assunta* (B1), which has a campanile four hundred years older, and the attached *Museo d'Arte Sacra* with paintings by Daniele Crespi, Morazzone, and Carlo Francesco Nuvolone. The *Museo della Società Gallaratese di Studi Patrii* (A1) in Via Borgo Antico, offers an exhibition of prehistoric objects from Golasecca (9th to 5th c. B.C.) and has Celtic and Roman sections, as well as a collection of antiquities, works by local artists, and works from the Renaissance. The *Civica Galleria d'Arte Moderna* in Viale Milano (B2) houses hundreds of works of contemporary Italian art (Afro, Renato Birolli, Carlo Carrà, Bruno Cassinari, Giuseppe Migneco, Ennio Morlotti, Mario Radice, Atanasio Soldati, Vittorio Tavernari, Emilio Vedova, Renzo Vespignani). The *Museo della Tecnica e del Lavoro "MV Agusta"* (B2) chronicles the history of the famous motorcycle manufacturing company, between the years 1945 and 1977.

The **Aeroporto Intercontinentale Malpensa**, established in 1949, comes under the jurisdiction of Somma Lombardo (see below), the next town on the route. The airport will probably take on all the international traffic currently channeled to Linate. The major airline companies use Linate airport (see itinerary 3.3).

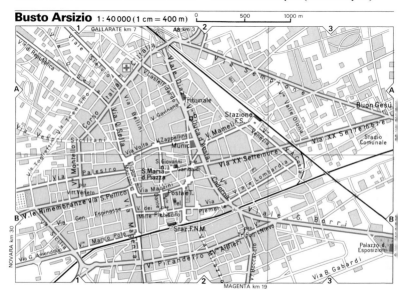

Busto Arsizio 1 : 40 000 (1 cm = 400 m)

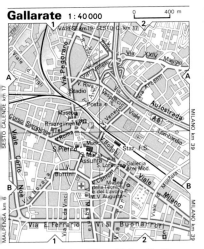

Gallarate 1 : 40 000

teal, mallard). Even though fallow-deer, wild boar, foxes and otters are found in only a very small area, the ground and water fauna (trout, grayling, sturgeon) are fairly abundant.

Across the park, the road south of Somma Lombardo leads to **Turbigo** (elev. 146 m, pop. 7,212), with a 13th-c. *Castle* standing guard on the eastern boundary of the Visconti Duchy. Close to the river are many winding service roads that come under the jurisdiction of the Genio Civile and the Consorzio Regionale di Tutela, and are accessible only by non-motorized transport.

Parco del Ticino (River Ticino Park)

Somma Lombardo (elev. 282 m, pop. 16,518) is situated in the middle of rough terrain planted with pines and robinia. During the 11th/12th c. it was the site of the Milanese monastery of San Simpliciano, though today it is more noted as a wool-manufacturing center (Somma blankets). It is also the site of the 13th-c. church of *San Vito*, which has a campanile dating back to the beginning of the 17th c. and, inside, a 16th-c. triptych by Giovanni Ambrogio Bevilacqua. The **Castello Visconteo** is a large building which originally dates back to the 12th c., although it was renovated in 1448 and again in the 19th c.

In a radius of less than three kilometers from Somma is the village of *Mezzana Superiore* and the town of Arsago Seprio (elev. 290 m, pop. 4,306). In Mezzana the parish church of *Santo Stefano* has tempera decorations by Bramantino and a triptych by Marco d'Oggiono, while the *Santuario della Madonna della Ghianza* is a late-16th-c. building by Pellegrino Tibaldi. In Arsago is the basilica of **San Vittore***, a Romanesque building variously attributed to the 9th and 12th c. with Roman capitals taken from demolished buildings, and the adjacent octagonal **baptistery** is from the 12th c.

The parkland lining the River Ticino from Sesto Calende right down to Pavia is a conservation area covering over 90,000 hectares, which forms the **Parco del Ticino**. The area was made a natural reserve (1974, 1980) to stem the urbanization that threatens to engulf the river itself. The park offers sheltered woods, the last of the hardwood forests that once extended over the Po Valley; the area south of Turbigo (see below) offers a humid-zone environment, with a large population of birds of all sorts (herons,

Magenta and the neighboring villas

Inside the Ticino Park near *Tornavento* the artificial course of the **Naviglio Grande** (see also itinerary 2.4) branches out from the river. This major engineering project was originally built for agriculture and then subsequently used for transportation purposes. Owing to the natural beauty of its setting and the easy access it provided, country residences of the aristocracy soon sprouted in and around the villages of Robecco and Cassinetta.

Leaving the river we head toward *Cuggiono* (elev. 157 m, pop. 7,296), where the facade of the late 17th-c. *Collegiata di San Giorgio* is in the graceful neoclassical style of Leopold Pollack. The next stop is **Magenta** (elev. 138 m, pop. 23,442), an ancient settlement that has become a lively manufacturing center. It is particularly famous as the site of a furious battle (1859) in which the French and Italian troops crushed the Austrians. Interesting historical buildings can be found in the central *Piazza della Liberazione* and along Via Garibaldi, which boasts three important palazzi: the 18th-c. *Palazzo Morandi*; *Palazzo Crivelli* at no. 76, which dates from the 15th c.; and *Villa Crivelli* at no. 84. Near the public gardens the facade of the late 18th-c. *Casa Giacobbe* has bullet-holes from the Risorgimento period; the bronze *monument* (Luigi Secchi, 1895) is in honor of the French general Patrice MacMahon who won the famous battle, and the obelisk-ossuary dates from 1872.

South of Magenta on the Naviglio Grande lies **Robecco sul Naviglio** (elev. 129 m, pop. 5,489), an interesting little town with many historical residences of the Milanese nobility. On the left bank of the canal stands **Villa Gandini***, originally dating from the second half of the 14th c. and later transformed into Villa Gaia by Ludovico il Moro; also facing the water is what remains of *Palazzo Archinto*, an incomplete construction from the 17th/18th c. On the other side

Villa Visconti Maineri, at Cassinetta di Lugagnano

of the canal is the 19th-c. Casa Sironi Marelli, also left unfinished, and the 17th-c. *Villa Dugnani*, built on a pre-existing building of the 15th c. Approximately 1 km further north, ensconced in a more recent complex, is "La Peralza" or *Villa Arrigoni*, dating from 1692; further back from the canal stands *Villa Gromo di Ternengo*, which was rebuilt in 1679 possibly on the site of a fortress; the 19th-c. *Villa Scotti*, now the town hall; and, almost outside town, the badly conserved *Villa Terzaghi*, once one of the finest examples of 18th-c. late-Baroque Lombard architecture.

It is possible to take a slight deviation by following the left bank of the canal to Cassinetta, but the route is closed to automobile traffic.

The first attraction in **Cassinetta di Lugagnano** (elev. 125 m, pop. 1,262) is the *Antica Osteria del Ponte*, an expensive restaurant acknowledged as one of the finest in Italy. Here historical interest is also provided by the residences of the nobility, on the left bank of the canal, with the 18th c. *Villa Nai* (no. 1 on the plan p. 145), *Villa Krentzlin* (2), and the more important 18th-c. **Villa Visconti Maineri** (3), which was completed in the second half of the on the site of an older building. Further away is the *Cascina Bardena* (4), which includes a 19th-c. Dominican residence and a fascinating garden shaped like an amphitheater. Along Via Roma on the right bank the first building of note is the neoclassical *Villa Morlin Visconti* (5), 1825, and the 18th-c. *Villa Eusebio* (6). Also in Via Roma is the L-shaped *Villa Trivulzio* from the 18th/19th c., with an English-style park behind it, while at the beginning of the adjacent Via Diaz is *Villa Clari Monzini** (8), which has been renovated many times since it was first built in the 18th c.

Abbiategrasso

Abbiategrasso (elev. 120 m, pop. 27,357), once an important fortified town under the Visconti and Sforza families, is today an important industrial and agricultural center. The most significant historical building is the basilica of **Santa Maria Nuova**, which was renamed in this manner in 1388 to commemorate the birth in the town of the son of Gian Galeazzo Visconti, Gian Maria. Preceding the church is an ample Renaissance *quadriporticus** with a large *pronaos** (1497), left incomplete by Donato Bramante before he left for Rome to work on St. Peter's. Inside the church, which was renovated in the 18th c. by Francesco Croce, are traces of 15th-c. graffito decoration in the first chapel on the north aisle. Back in the square, little of the original **Castle** remains today, although it was once a sturdy 13th-c. fortress built in line with the canal and road to Milan. Filippo Maria Visconti had the castle renovated in 1438, but it was reduced to ruins by the Spanish during in 17th c.

Morimondo

Close to Abbiategrasso, the village of Morimondo (elev. 109 m, pop. 1,128) is really a cluster of assorted houses around **Morimondo Abbey**, which was founded in 1136 by the Cistercian Order from Morimond, north of Dijon in France. Like other monasteries south of Milan (see itinerary 3.4), after the first twenty years of its existence the abbey became the focus of the developing agrarian region south of the city.

Two archways lead into the charming piazza, which is dominated on one side by the *church*, dedicated to Santa Maria, a large brick construction originally built between 1182 and 1292. Inside the church the overall spatial effect of the unadorned nave and aisles with their groin vaults

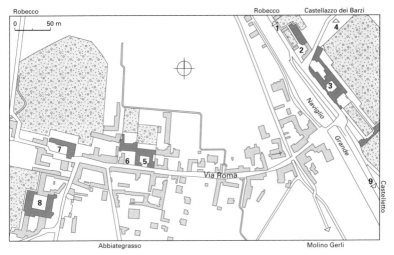

Robecco

Robecco   Castellazzo dei Barzi

Via Roma

Naviglio Grande

Castelletto

Abbiategrasso

Molino Gerli

Plan of Cassinetta di Lugagnano: 1 Villa Nai; 2 Villa Krentzlin; 3 Villa Visconti Maineri; 4 Cascina Bardena; 5 Villa Mörlin Visconti; 6 Villa Eusebio; 7 Villa Trivulzio; 8 Villa Clari Monzini; 9 Villa Negri.

is arresting. Also of interest are the 14th-c. font on the right; the fresco by Bernardino Luini; and the wooden stalls of the choir (1522). Three sides of the *cloister* have been rebuilt, while next to it the *Sala Capitolare* has two naves. At

The nave of Morimondo Abbey

the entrance to the village itself, worth visiting is the church of *San Bernardo*, recently renovated and now an art center and research laboratory.

The Naviglio Grande in the direction of Milan

From Abbiategrasso we proceed in the direction of Milan along the final section of the Naviglio Grande. Shortly before the little canal-side town of *Gaggiano* (elev. 117 m, pop. 8,056) we turn off the busy "Nuova Vigevanese" highway, and keep following the canal until open land yields progressively to the suburbs of the metropolis.

After passing through *Trezzano sul Naviglio* (elev. 116 m, pop. 18,997), we come to the glittering business towers of Corsico (elev. 115 m, pop. 35,954), whose population has quadrupled in the last fifty years. After briefly crossing *Buccinasco* (elev. 113 m, pop. 22,642) we cross the city limits of Milan, passing by several industrial complexes (notably the former Richard Ginori factory on the corner of Via Morimondo), and the large 19th-c. apartment blocks that line the canal all the way up to Porto Ticinese (see itinerary 2.4), where the canal ends in the Darsena dockyard.

Travel information:
Hotels, restaurants, places of interest

The following is a list of information on Milan divided into five sections: 1) old city center; 2) Magenta, Fiera, Sempione; 3) Centro Direzionale, Stazione Centrale, Buenos Aires; 4) northwest and northeast of the center; 5) south of the center.
Information on Milan's environs, including Brianza, starts on p. 156.
Recommended hotels, camp sites, and holiday villages are assigned "stars" according to the official classification established under Italian law (1983). The restaurants are assigned "forks" in compliance with the TCI's own classification, which is based on price, comfort, service, and atmosphere. Price ranges are indicated as follows: ⟨ up to 45,000 lire; ⟨⟨ 46,000–65,000 lire; ⟨⟨⟨ 66,000–85,000 lire; ⟨⟨⟨⟨ 86,000–105,000 lire; ⟨⟨⟨⟨⟨ over 106,000 lire.
As of 18th December 1998 the code must also be dialled for local calls, indicated in the following list next to the symbol ☎. For those calling Italy from abroad, the local code (including the 0) must be dialled after the international code for Italy, followed by the subscriber's number. The information has been carefully checked before going to print. We would, however, advise readers to confirm certain data which is susceptible to change, before departure. All observations and suggestions are gratefully accepted.

Milan   ✉ 20100 ☎ 02

ℹ️ *Tourist information offices, page 31*

Old city center

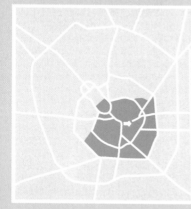

Historical monuments, museums, places of cultural interest, cinemas, theaters, and elegant shops are all concentrated in the area within the former ring of navigable canals (Cerchia dei Navigli), which encircles the historic city center. This innermost area is largely closed to traffic, and the pedestrian areas (extended in 1996) now include Piazza del Duomo, the Galleria, and Corso Vittorio Emanuele, Piazza San Fedele, Via Dante, Via Mercante, Via Rovello (partial), Via Giulini (partial), Via della Spiga and the network of narrow streets in the Brera distrcit.
Recent alterations have made Piazza San Babila partially pedestrian, also. The Galleria Vittorio Emanuele, Milan's so-called "drawing room,"

with its 19th-c. atmosphere and smart shops, runs from Piazza del Duomo to Piazza della Scala and thence to Via Manzoni, which is lined with fine palazzi with magnificent (though generally inaccessible) gardens behind their elegant facades. Leading off from Via Manzoni is Via Montenapoleone, the main artery of the fashion enclave that comprises Via Sant'Andrea, Via Gesù, Via Borgospesso, Via Santo Spirito.
As for the Brera district (Via Brera lies to the right of the opera house), although its "Bohemian" atmosphere has somewhat paled in recent years, the old houses and patrician residences have been carefully restored, and the quarter offers some excellent restaurants and other nightlife venues.
There is also a concentration of antiques shops and fine-art galleries. Another itinerary that will appeal to some visitors leads from Piazza Cordusio through the banking and finance area, past the Stock Exchange (Borsa); the street names recall the quarter's previous concentration of crafts workshops (Orefici, Spadari, Armorari, Cappellari, Speronari); traces of Roman and medieval fabric are still visible in Via Brisa, Via Circo, and Via Morigi. Slightly further south, the basilica of Sant'Ambrogio (dedicated to the patron saint of Milan), stands on the site of an imperial palace, and is one of the most significant and interesting monuments in the city; the narrow streets around it are dotted with delightful antiques shops.

Hotels and restaurants

☆☆ **Carlton Baglioni.** Via Senato 5, tel. 76015535, fax 783300. 63 rooms. Access for disabled. Air conditioning, elevator; garage (I, B6, **aw**).

☆☆☆ **Grand Hotel Duomo.** Via S. Raffaele 1, tel. 8833, fax 86462027. 153 rooms. Access for disabled. Air conditioning, elevator; garage (I, C5, **b**).

☆☆☆ **Grand Hôtel et de Milan.** Via Manzoni 29, tel. 723141, fax 86460861. 95 rooms. Air conditioning, elevator; garage (I, B5, **bo**).

☆☆☆ **Brunelleschi.** Via Baracchini 12, tel. 8843, fax 804924. 128 rooms. Access for disabled. Air conditioning, elevator; garage (I, D5, **am**).

☆☆☆ **Cavour.** Via Fatebenefratelli 21, tel. 6572051, fax 6592263. Rooms 113. Access for disabled. Air conditioning, elevator; garage (I, A5, **at**).

☆☆☆ **Crivi's.** Corso di Porta Vigentina 46, tel. 582891, fax 58318182. 86 rooms. No restaurant. Air conditioning, elevator; garage (IV, D6, **cb**).

☆☆☆ **Dei Cavalieri.** Piazza Missori 1, tel. 8857, fax 72021683. 179 rooms. Access for disabled. Air conditioning, elevator; garage (I, D4, **d**).

☆☆☆ **Galileo.** Corso Europa 9, tel. 7743, fax 76020584. Rooms 89. Air conditioning, elevator; garage (I, C6, **f**).

☆☆☆ **Jolly President.** Largo Augusto 10, tel. 77461, fax 783449. 220 rooms. Air conditioning, elevator; garage (I, D6, **q**).

☆☆☆ **Mentana.** Via Morigi 2 (corner of P.za Mentana), tel. 86454255, fax 865382. 33 rooms . No restaurant. Air conditioning, elevator; garage (I, D3, **dm**).

☆☆☆ **Pierre Milano.** Via De Amicis 32, tel. 72000581, fax 8052157. 49 rooms. Access for disabled. Air conditioning, elevator; garage (I, E2-3, **a**).

★★★ **Biscione.** Via S. Maria Fulcorina 15, tel. 8693656, fax 8056825. 25 rooms; 23 with bath/shower. No restaurant. Air conditioning, elevator; garage, garden, pool (I, C3, **i**).

★★★ **Canada.** Via Santa Sofia 16, tel. 58304844, fax 58300282. 35 rooms. No restaurant. Access for disabled. Air conditioning, elevator; garage (I, E5, **bp**).

★★★ **Imperial.** Corso di Porta Romana 68, tel. 58318200, fax 58318027. 36 rooms. No restaurant. Air conditioning; parking (I, F5, **ax**).

★★★ **Manzoni.** Via Santo Spirito 20, tel. 76005700, fax 784212. 52 rooms. No restaurant. Air conditioning, elevator; garage (I, B5, **x**).

★★★ **Star.** Via dei Bossi 5, tel. 801501, fax 861787. 30 rooms. No restaurant. Air conditioning, elevator (I, B-C4, **so**).

🍴🍴🍴 **Savini.** Galleria Vittorio Emanuele II, tel. 72003433, fax 86461060. Closed Sat lunch and Sun, Christmas-Epiphany and August. Air conditioning, garden. Lombard and classic cuisine (I, C4-5, **ra**).

🍴🍴🍴 **Alfio Cavour.** Via Senato 31, tel. 780731, fax 783446. Closed Sat and lunch on Sun, August and Christmas-Epiphany. Air conditioning, garden. Traditional cooking – fish (I, A6, **ro**).

🍴🍴🍴 **Boeucc.** Piazza Belgioioso 2, tel. 76020224, fax 796173. Close Sat and Sun lunch, August, Christmas, New Years Day and Easter. Air conditioning. Traditional and Lombard cuisine (I, B5, **tz**).

🍴🍴🍴 **Suntory.** Via Verdi 6, tel. 8693022, fax 72023282. Closed Sun, part of August. Air conditioning. Japanese cuisine (I, B4, **ts**).

🍴🍴🍴 **Ulmet.** Via Olmetto 21, tel. 86452718, fax 72002486. Closed Sun and Mon lunch, August and Christmas-Epiphany. Air conditioning. Avant-garde cuisine (I, E3, **c**).

🍴🍴🍴 **Bice.** Via Borgospesso 12, tel. 76002572. Closed Mon and Tues lunch, Easter, August, Christmas-Epiphany. Air conditioning. Tuscan and classic cuisine (I, B5, **sd**).

🍴🍴🍴 **Bistrot di Gualtiero Marchesi.** Via S. Raffaele 2, tel. 877120, fax 877035. Closed Sun and Mon lunch, part of August. Air conditioning. Lombard cuisine. (I, C5, **ed**).

🍴🍴🍴 **Porto.** Piazza Cantore, tel. 89407425, fax 8321481. Closed Sun and Mon lunch, August. Air conditioning. Traditional cooking; sea food(I, F1, **tk**).

🍴🍴 **Al Mercante.** Piazza Mercanti 17, tel. 8052198. Closed Sun, part of August and in January. Air conditioning, garden. Traditional cooking. (I, C4, **tt**).

🍴🍴 **Girarrosto-da Cesarina.** Corso Venezia 31, tel. 76000481. Closed Sat and Sun lunch, August and Christmas-Epiphany. Air conditioning. Tuscan cuisine (I, B6, **p**).

🍴🍴 **Prospero.** Via Chiossetto 20, tel. 55187646. Closed Sun, part of August and New Year. Air conditioning. Lombard cuisine (V, B1, **sm**).

🍴🍴 **Quattro Mori.** Largo M. Callas 1, tel. 878483. Closed Saturday lunch and Sunday, August. Garden. Traditional and Tuscan cuisine. (I, B3, **sj**).

Cafés and pastry shops

Cova. Via Montenapoleone 8, tel. 76000578. Very traditional and one of Milan's most frequented cafés and pastry shops in the fashionable part of the old city center.

Donini Gin Rosa. Galleria San Babila 4/B, tel. 76000461. Named after one of its famous aperitifs; equally well known is its selection of rare whiskies and other spirits.

Galli. Via Victor Hugo 2, tel. 86464833; corso di Porta Romana 2, tel. 86453112. Marrons-glacés, pralines, fondant; wrapped chocolates which can be sent anywhere.

Marchesi. Via S. Maria alla Porta 11/A, tel. 876730. In an ancient palazzo with a decorated facade, the city's oldest candy shop has treats and sweets of the highest quality.

Pasticceria Ambrosiana. Via Rugabella 1, tel. 86454811. Traditional cake and pastry shop, famous for its *panettone* (Milanese cake of sponge and dried fruit), *veneziana* (Venetian sponge cake) and numerous other delights.

Sant'Ambroeus. Corso Matteotti 7, tel. 76000540. Elegant pastry shop famous for its *panettone*, cakes, and pastries and exquisitely arranged chocolates in pretty boxes.

Taveggia. Via Visconti di Modrone 2, tel. 798687-76021257. 1930s-style café with fine interiors of briar, marble, and ornate mirrors. Delicious cakes and pastries.

Zucca. Piazza Duomo, Galleria Vittorio Emanuele, tel. 86464435. Art Nouveau aperitifs bar with a long tradition and an elegant atmosphere, old-style counter, ceiling mosaic, elaborate decorative metalwork.

Museums and places of cultural interest

Archivio di Stato. Via Senato 10, tel. 76000369. *Open: Mon 8:15–5, Tues–Thurs 8:15–5:30, Fri 8:30–2, Sat 8:15–1:30.*

Biblioteca Comunale. Palazzo Sormani, Corso di Porta Vittoria 6, tel. 76012911.

Biblioteca d'Arte. Castello Sforzesco, tel. 877004. *Open: Mon–Fri 9:15–12:15; 1:30–4:30.*

Biblioteca del Conservatorio "Giuseppe Verdi." Via Conservatorio 12, tel. 76003097. *Open: Mon-Sat 9–12.*

Biblioteca dell'Istituto Lombardo Accademia di Scienze e Lettere. Via Borgonuovo 25, tel. 86461388. *Open: 9:30–3.*

Biblioteca Nazionale Braidense. Via Brera 28, tel. 86460907. *Open: Mon–Fri 9–5; Sat 9–1:30.*

Biblioteca Trivulziana. Castello Sforzesco, tel. 86454638. *Open: Mon–Fri 9–12, 1:30–4:30.*

Casa della Cultura. Via Borgogna 3, tel. 795567. Hosts cultural debates and conferences.

Centro San Fedele. Piazza San Fedele 4, tel. 86461014. Hosts exhibitions, films, and cultural debates.

Circolo della Stampa. Corso Venezia 16, tel. 76022671.

Civica Galleria d'Arte Moderna. Via Palestro 16, tel. 76002819. Closed Mon. *Open: 9:30–5:30.*

Civici Musei d'Arte and Pinacoteca del Castello Sforzesco. Piazza Castello, tel. 62083940. Closed Mon. *Open: 9:30–5:30.*

Civico Museo Archeologico. Corso Magenta 15, tel. 8053972. Closed Mon. *Open: 9:30–5:30.*

Civico Museo d'Arte Contemporanea. Palazzo Reale, Piazza Duomo, tel. 62083943. Closed Mon. *Open: 9:30–5:30.*

Civico Museo del Risorgimento. Via Borgonuovo 23, tel. 8693549. *Open: 9:30–5:30.*

Civico Museo di Milano. Via Sant'Andrea 6, tel. 76006245. *Open: 9:30–12, 2–6:30.*

Civico Museo Navale "Ugo Mursia." Via Sant'Andrea 6, tel. 76004143. Closed Mon. *Open: 9:30–5.*

Civico Museo di Storia Contemporanea. Via Sant'Andrea 6, tel. 76006245-783797. Closed for renovation.

Conservatorio di Musica "Giuseppe Verdi." Via Conservatorio 12, tel. 7621101.

Fondazione Feltrinelli. Via Romagnosi 3, tel.

8693911. *Visit on request: Tues–Thurs 10:30–5:30, Fri 9–1.*

Fondazione "Antonio Mazzotta." Foro Bonaparte 50, tel. 878197. *Open: 10–7:30.*

Museo Bagatti Valsecchi. Via Gesù 5, tel. 76006132. Closed Mon. *Open: 1–5.*

Museo del Cinema. Via Manin 2/b, tel. 6554977. Closed Sat, Sun & Mon. *Open: 3–6:30.*

Museo del Duomo. Palazzo Reale, Piazza Duomo, tel. 860358. Closed Mon. *Open: 9:30–12:30, 3–6.*

Museo di Sant'Ambrogio. Piazza Sant'Ambrogio 15, tel. 86450895. Closed Tues. *Open: 10–12, 3–5; Sat, Sun 3–5.*

Museo Manzoniano (Alessandro Manzoni's house). Via Morone 1, tel. 86460403. Closed Sat, Mon & public hols. *Open: 9–12, 2–4.*

Museo Poldi Pezzoli. Via Manzoni 12, tel. 794889. Closed Mon, public hols & April–Sept, Sun pm. *Open: 9:30–12:30, 2:30–6; Sat 9:30–12:30, 2:30–7:30.*

Museo Francesco Messina. Via San Sisto 10, tel. 86453005. Closed Mon. *Open: 9:30–5.*

Museo Teatrale alla Scala. Piazza della Scala, tel. 8053418. Closed Sun, Nov–April. *Open: 9–12:30, 2–5:30.*

Padiglione d'Arte Contemporanea (PAC). Via Palestro 14, tel. 783330. *Open only for exhibitions.*

Palazzo Arcivescovile. Piazza Fontana 2, tel. 85561.

Palazzo Clerici. Via Clerici 5, tel. 72001705. *Visits on written request.*

Palazzo Isimbardi. Corso Monforte 35, tel. 77401. *Viewing of the "Sala della Giunta" on request.*

Palazzo Litta. Corso Magenta 24, tel. 86455471. *Open: Mon–Fri 3–5, only on request addressed to Direzione Compartimentale delle Ferrovie dello Stato (Milan office of the national railway).*

Pinacoteca di Brera. Via Brera 28, tel. 72263229. Closed Mon. *Open: 9-6. In certain periods of the year, the hours are extended to 10pm.*

Pinacoteca and Biblioteca Ambrosiana. Piazza Pio XI 2, tel. 806921. Closed Mon. *Open 10–5:30.*

Università Cattolica del Sacro Cuore. Largo A. Gemelli 1, tel. 72341.

Università degli Studi di Milano. Via Festa del Perdono 3/7, tel. 58351.

Churches

Churches generally observe the following opening times: 8–12, 3–6; variations are indicated.

Cathedral (Duomo). Piazza del Duomo, tel. 72022656; Early Christian archaeological excavations. Closed Mon. *Open: 10–12, 3–5.* You can walk (166 steps) or take the elevator to the roof and tower from small door in corner of north transept, near the Medici tomb (*Open: 9–5:45*).

S. Alessandro. Piazza S. Alessandro, tel. 86453065.

S. Ambrogio. Piazza Sant'Ambrogio 25, tel. 8057310.

S. Babila. Piazza San Babila, tel. 76002877.

S. Carlo al Corso. Corso Vittorio Emanuele, tel. 76001188.

S. Eustorgio. Piazza Sant'Eustorgio 1, tel. 58101583. *Visits to the Portinari Chapel on request.*

S. Gottardo in Corte. Via Pecorari 2, tel. 86464500.

S. Lorenzo Maggiore. Corso di Porta Ticinese 35, tel. 8322940.

S. Maria alla Porta. Via S. Maria alla Porta 10, tel. 866660.

S. Maria del Carmine. Piazza del Carmine 2, tel. 86463365.

S. Maria della Passione. Via Conservatorio, tel. 76021370.

S. Maria presso S. Celso. Corso Italia 37, tel. 58313187.

S. Maria presso S. Satiro. Via Speronari 3, tel. 874683.

S. Maurizio al Monastero Maggiore. Corso Magenta 15, tel. 866660. Closed Sat, Sun, July & August.

S. Nazaro Maggiore. Piazza S. Nazaro 5, tel. 58307719.

S. Pietro in Gessate. Piazza S. Pietro in Gessate, tel. 5450145.

S. Sebastiano. Via Torino 28, tel. 874263.

S. Stefano Maggiore. Piazza S. Stefano, tel. 76023735.

Entertainment

Conservatorio "Giuseppe Verdi." Via Conservatorio, tel. 76001755.

Corteo dei Re Magi. 6 January. Parade of the Three Kings and other characters in costume, with the Banda Civica, majorettes, and exotic animals. Proceeds from S. Ambrogio to S. Eustorgio.

Fiera degli O'bej O'bej. Runs 7–8 Dec in the streets around Sant'Ambrogio.

Mercatino dell'antiquariato di Brera. Third Saturday of month, between Via Fiori Chiari and Via Madonnina.

Piccolo Teatro. Via Angioli 3, tel. 878942.

Pittori in Via Bagutta. Outdoor painting exhibition (April).

Teatro alla Scala. Piazza della Scala (tel. 72003744).

Teatro Arsenale. Via Correnti 11, tel. 8375896.

Teatro Carcano. Corso di Porta Romana 65, tel. 55181377.

Teatro delle Erbe. Via Mercato 3, tel. 86464986.

Teatro Filodrammatici. Via Filodrammatici 1, tel. 8693659.

Teatro Lirico. Via Larga 14, tel. 861954.

Teatro Litta. Corso Magenta 24, tel. 86454545.

Teatro Manzoni. Via Manzoni 42, tel. 76020543.

Teatro Nuovo. Piazza S. Babila, tel. 76000086.

Teatro S. Babila. Piazza S. Babila 2, tel. 76002985, 795469.

Teatro Studio. Via Rivoli 6, tel. 861897.

Shops, crafts, and fine art

Newspapers and magazines from overseas are available at most large newsstands in the city center, particularly around Piazza del Duomo and the Galleria. A good selection of foreign books (English, French, German, Spanish) can be found in several of the main bookstores downtown: Rizzoli (in the Galleria), Hoepli (Via Hoepli 5), Messaggerie Musicali (Galleria del Corso 2), and Mondadori (Corso V. Emanuele 28).

English-speaking readers may want to visit the Milan branch of the British Council (Via Manzoni 38), which carries an extensive collection of British dailies and magazines, together with a large library of reference books.

Algani. Piazza della Scala. Vast selection of design magazines from all over the world and foreign press.

Armani. Via Sant'Andrea 9, tel. 76003234. Haute couture for men and women.

Artemide. Corso Monforte 19, tel. 76006930. Beautifully designed lighting.

British Council. Via Manzoni 38, tel. 772221. The definitive learning center for English, plus a library and excellent assortment of British dailies and periodicals.

Buccellati. Via Montenapoleone 4, tel. 76002153. Jewelry in Buccellati's unmistakable style.

Cartier. Via Montenapoleone 16, tel. 76002557. Jewels and precious objects in the inimitable style of Cartier.

Cassina. Via Durini 18, tel. 76020745. Furniture by famous Italian and international designers.

Chanel. Via Sant'Andrea 10/a, tel. 782514. Haute couture.

Cotti. Via Solferino 42, tel. 29001096. This wine store is practically an institution; every kind of wine, all of the best quality.

De Padova. Corso Venezia 14, tel. 76008413. Furniture and objects of essential design.

Dolce & Gabbana. Via Spiga 2, tel. 76001155. Haute couture.

Emporio Armani. Via Durini 24, tel. 76003030. Clothes for men and women.

Ercolessi. Corso Vittorio Emanuele 15, tel. 76000607. Everything to make writing a pleasure.

Etro. Via Montenapoleone 5, tel. 76005049. Clothes in silk and cashmere, textiles and scents.

Faraone. Via Montenapoleone 7/A, tel. 76013656. High-class jewelry.

Fenoli. Via Sant'Andrea 16, tel. 76021617. Haute couture.

Ferré Gianfranco. Via Spiga 11/13, tel. 794864–76000385. Haute couture.

Fiorucci. Galleria Passarella 2, tel. 76003276. There's a bit of everything in this big basement store; fun ideas for presents, clothes, furniture, household items.

Gucci. Via Montenapoleone 5, tel. 76013050. Leather goods, clothes, accessories.

Hoepli Bookstore. Via Hoepli 5, tel. 864871. Large well-stocked bookstore with excellent foreign books, art, scientific, computer, and travel sections.

Kenzo. Via Sant'Andrea 11, tel. 76020929. Haute couture.

Krizia. Via Spiga 23, tel. 76008429. Haute couture.

La Città del Sole. Via Orefici 13, tel. 86461683. Store specializing in educational toys, especially in wood.

La Rinascente. Piazza Duomo, tel. 8852501. Milan's most famous department store.

Laura Biagiotti. Via Borgospesso 19, tel. 799659. Haute couture.

Libreria del Mare. Via Broletto 28, tel. 86464426. Lovers of the sea and sailing will find everything they need here.

Libreria del Touring Club Italiano. Corso Italia 10, tel. 8526304. Books, maps (tourist and not); a trove of information for travelers.

Libreria dell'Automobile. Corso Venezia 43, tel.

76006624. Next door to the Automobile Club, offers a wide range of maps and guides.

Libreria delle Donne. Via Dogana 2, tel. 874213. Specialized in books by and for women.

Libreria La Sherlockiana. Piazza S. Nazaro 3, tel. 58307802. Specialized in thrillers, spy stories, and fantasy.

Libreria Milanese. Via Meravigli 18, tel. 86453154. A living bibliography of Milan: history, guides, unusual books.

Lorenzi. Via Montenapoleone 9, tel. 76020593. Knives, smokers' items, luxury goods.

Messaggerie Musicali. Galleria del Corso 2, tel. 76055404 (foreign section). Vast selection of books and periodicals in various languages.

Mila Schön. Via Montenapoleone 2, tel. 781190–76001333. Haute couture.

Missoni. Via Sant'Andrea 2, tel. 76003555. Haute couture.

Mondadori Bookstore. Corso Vittorio Emanuele 28, tel. 76000740. Vast selection of books and periodicals in various languages.

Moschino. Via Sant'Andrea 12, tel. 76000832. Haute couture; Via Durini 14, tel. 76004320. Prêt-à-porter and casual clothes.

Pineider. Corso Europa 13, tel. 76022353. Letter paper, visiting cards, diaries.

Prada. Galleria Vittorio Emanuele 63, tel. 876979. Leather goods, accessories, clothes.

Ricordi. Galleria Vittorio Emanuele, tel. 86460272. Records, CDs, videos, books, posters, musical instruments, and sheet music.

Romeo Gigli. Corso Venezia 11, tel. 76000271. Haute couture.

Sharra Pagano. Via Spiga 7, tel. 76003101. Jewelry and costume jewelry.

Ungaro. Via Montenapoleone 27, tel. 76023997. Haute couture.

Valentino. Via S. Spirito 3, tel. 76006478. Haute couture.

Versace Gianni. Via Montenapoleone 2, tel. 76008528. Haute couture for men; Via Montenapoleone 2, haute couture for women.

Versus. Via San Pietro all'Orto 10, tel. 76014722. Prêt-à-porter for men and women.

Vinovino. Via Speronari 4, tel. 86464055. Wines and spirits from Italy and abroad.

Virgin Megastore. Piazza Duomo, on corner of Via Marconi, tel. 72003354. Records, CDs, videos, books, videogames.

Yves Saint Laurent. Via Verri 8, tel. 76000573. Haute couture.

Magenta, Fiera, Sempione

This is one of the most sought-after residential areas of Milan with its elegant streets, beautiful stores and houses of noble architecture. It is bordered by Parco Sempione, the Fiera (trade fair precinct), and to the south by the area of Corso Vercelli, which until the 1920s was the dividing line between the city and the country. From here until 1957 the "Gamba de legn" train left for Magenta. Today Corso Vercelli is one of Milan's busiest shopping areas, and leads into Corso Magenta toward the city center (see the church of Santa Maria delle Grazie); the Magenta district is one of the city's oldest. The other main shopping street is Via Paolo Sarpi, noted for its Chinese restaurants and workshops and known locally as "Chinatown." The Sempione area was developed in the early 19th c., and its four- and five-story residential buildings have a rather Parisian air. The area around the Fiera, of more recent date, is considered one of the most up-market residential districts.

★★ **Grand Hotel Fieramilano.** Viale Boezio 20, tel. 336221, fax 314119. 238 rooms. Access for disabled. Air conditioning, elevator; garage, garden (II, D1, **ca**).

★★ **Hermitage.** Via Messina 10, tel. 33107700, fax 33107399. 131 rooms. Air conditioning, elevator; garage, garden (II, D3, **t**).

★★★ **Admiral.** Via Domodossola 16, tel. 3492151, fax 33106660. 60 rooms. No restaurant. Air conditioning, elevator; parking, garage (II, D1, **cy**).

★★★ **Ariosto.** Via Ariosto 22, tel. 4817844, fax 4980516. 53 rooms. No restaurant. Air conditioning, elevator; garage (II, F2, **cc**).

★★★ **Astoria.** Viale Murillo 9, tel. 40090095, fax 40074642. 75 rooms. No restaurant. Air conditioning, elevator; garage (VI, D2, **bv**).

★★★ **Lancaster.** Via Sangiorgio 16, tel. 344705, fax 344649. 30 rooms. No restaurant. Air conditioning, elevator (II, E2, **ez**).

★★★ **Sant'Ambroeus.** Viale Papiniano 14, tel. 48008989, fax 48008687. 52 rooms. No restaurant. Air conditioning, elevator; garage (IV, C2, **w**).

¶¶ **Infinito.** Via Leopardi 25, tel. 4692276. Closed Sat lunch & Sun, part of August & Christmas-Epiphany. Air conditioning. Traditional cooking (I, B1, **rf**).

¶¶ **Montecristo.** Via Prina 17, tel. 312760. Closed Tues & Sat lunch, part of August & New Year. Air conditioning. Sea food (II, D2, **ud**).

¶¶ **Taverna della Trisa.** Via F. Ferruccio 1, tel. 341304. Closed Mon & August. Garden. Trentino cuisine (II, D2, **ue**).

¶ **Vöttantott.** Corso Sempione 88, tel. 33603114. Closed Sun, August. Air conditioning. Milanese cuisine (II, C1, **uf**).

Cafés and pastry shops

Biffi. Corso Magenta 87, tel. 48006702. Elegant atmosphere of old Europe; top quality cakes and pastries.

Gelateria Marghera. Via Marghera 33, tel. 468641. Huge selection of ice cream and sorbets, frozen cakes.

Neuhaus. Via S. Vittore 6, tel. 72000096. Chocolate from the famous Belgian factory.

Pasticceria Grecchi. Via Piero della Francesca 7, tel. 3315172. Pralines and chocolates, cakes and pastries.

Pasticceria S. Carlo. Via Bandello 1, tel. 4812227. Cakes and pastries, candies, excellent ice cream and cold sweets.

Museums and places of cultural interest

Cenacolo Vinciano. Piazza S. Maria delle Grazie 2, tel. 4987588. Closed Mon. *Open: 8–2, 7–11pm; Sun 5–8.*

Civico Acquario & Stazione Idrobiologica. Via Gadio 2, tel. 86462051. Closed Mon. *Open: 9:30–7:30.*

Civico Museo Navale Didattico. Via S. Vittore 21, tel. 485551. Closed Mon; open Sun & public hols. *Open: 9:30–5.*

Museo della Criminologia & Armi Antiche. Piazza S. Ambrogio, Pusterla, tel. 8053505. *Open: 10–7:30.*

Museo del Design. Palazzo dell'Arte, Viale Alemagna 6, tel. 724341. Closed Mon. *Open: 10–8.*

Museo Nazionale della Scienza & della Tecnica "Leonardo da Vinci". Via S. Vittore 21, tel. 485551. Closed Mon. *Open: 9:30–5; Sat, Sun & public hols 9:30–6:30.*

Palazzo dell'Arte (Triennale) and Torre del Parco. Viale Alemagna 6, tel. 724341.

Palazzo delle Stelline. Corso Magenta 61, tel. 4818431. Hosts conferences and debates.

Villa Simonetta. Via Stilicone 36, tel. 313334. Now houses the Civica Scuola di Musica.

Churches

S. Maria delle Grazie. Piazza S. Maria delle Grazie 2, tel. 48014248.

S. Vittore al Corpo. Via S. Vittore 25, tel. 48005351.

Entertainment

Fiera di Milano. Largo Domodossola 1, free phone 167820029.

Teatro delle Marionette. Via degli Olivetani 3, tel. 4694440.

Teatro Nazionale. Piazza Piemonte 12, tel. 48007700.

Sport

Arena Civica. Viale Byron 2, tel. 341924. Athletics, soccer, gymnastics, rugby.

Shops, crafts, and fine art

American Bookstore. Via Camperio 16 (at castle end of Via Dante), tel. 878920, 72020030. Small but well-stocked bookstore.

Bardelli. Corso Magenta 13, tel. 86450734. Top quality clothes for men and women.

Bottega Discantica. Via Nirone 5, tel. 862966. A classical music-lover's haven, has literally everything.

Buscemi Dischi. Corso Magenta 31, tel. 804103, 72021907.

China Food Store. Via Rosmini 11, tel. 33105368. Exotic specialities from China, Japan, Africa and Latin America.

Coin. Corso Vercelli 30, tel. 43990001. Department store.

Gemelli. Corso Vercelli 16, tel. 48000057, 433404. Top quality clothes for men and women. In the same street Gemelli Country and Gemellino for children.

Libreria della Natura. Corso Magenta 48, tel. 48003159. Botany, gardening, agritourism.

Libreria dello Spettacolo. Via Terraggio 11, tel. 86451730. Books on cinema, theater, and drama.

Libreria dello Sport. Via Carducci 9, tel. 8055355. Books, manuals, videos on sports.

Meazza. Via Circo 1, tel. 8052407. One of the best-stocked hardware (and not only hardware) stores in town.

Pupi Solari. Piazza Tommaseo 2, tel. 463325. Top quality clothes for women and children.

Stivaleria Savoia. Via Petrarca 7, tel. 463424. Began as royal boot makers; now stocks everything for horse and rider.

Teresa Kong. Via Scarpa 5, tel. 48007157. Quality handicrafts from South America, Mexico, and Thailand.

Centro Direzionale, Stazione Centrale, Buenos Aires

Lying just outside the old city center, this mixed area comprises an elegant quarter (around Corso Venezia); a very busy commercial and shopping area with heavy traffic in Corso Buenos Aires and Stazione Centrale; private and public offices in the Centro Direzionale (or Enterprise Zone), built in the course of the 1950s and 1960s; the old "Isola" quarter; and lastly the top end of the Brera-Garibaldi district. In the 19th c. this was a poor and somewhat ill-reputed district, and up to WWII was still full of little workshops. Today the old buildings have been renovated and the sheds and factories converted into trendy lofts for architects, photographers, and the like. The same speculative displacement of the working-class population also affected the picturesque Garibaldi quarter, now a highly fashionable area.

✯✯ Palace. Piazza della Repubblica 20, tel. 63361, fax 654485. 216 rooms. Access for disabled. Air conditioning, elevator; garage (III, D-E1, **dg**).

✯✯ Duca di Milano. Piazza della Repubblica 13, tel. 62841, fax 6555966. 99 rooms. Air conditioning, elevator (II, D6, **ba**).

✯✯ Berna. Via Napo Torriani 18, tel. 6691441, fax 6693892. 115 rooms. No restaurant. Air conditioning, elevator; parking, garage (III, D1, **es**).

✯✯ Excelsior Gallia. Piazza Duca d'Aosta 9, tel. 67851, fax 66713239. 252 rooms. Air conditioning, elevator; garage (III, C1, **c**).

✯✯ Executive. Via Sturzo 45, tel. 6294, fax 29010238. 420 rooms. Access for disabled. Air conditioning, elevator; garage (II, C5, **cs**).

✯✯ Galles. Via Ozanam 1, on corner of Corso Buenos Aires, tel. 204841, fax 2048422. 105 rooms. Access for disabled. Air conditioning, elevator; garage, garden (III, D2-3, **ac**).

✯✯ Hilton. Via Galvani 12, tel. 69831, fax 66710810. 323 rooms. Air conditioning, elevator; parking, garage, garden (III, C1, **ag**).

✯✯ Jolly Touring. Via Tarchetti 2, tel. 6335, fax 6592209. 305 rooms. Access for disabled. Air conditioning, elevator; garage (II, E6, **k**).

✯✯ Manin. Via Manin 7, tel. 6596511, fax 6552160. 118 rooms. Air conditioning, elevator; garage, garden (I, A5, **j**).

✯✯ Michelangelo. Via Scarlatti 33 (corner Piazza Luigi di Savoia), tel. 6755, fax 6694232. 300 rooms. Air conditioning, elevator; parking (III, C2, **m**).

✯✯ Starhotel Ritz. Via Spallanzani 40, tel. 2055, fax 29518679. 207 rooms. Air conditioning, elevator; garage (III, E2, **z**).

★★★ Berlino. Via Plana 33, tel. 324141, fax 39210611. 47 rooms. No restaurant. Air conditioning, elevator; garage (VI, C2, **cp**).

★★★ City. Corso Buenos Aires 42/5, tel. 29523382, fax 2046957. 55 rooms. No restaurant. Air conditioning, elevator; garage (III, D2, **y**).

★★★ Club. Via Copernico 18, tel. 67072221, fax 67072050. 53 rooms. No restaurant. Air conditioning, elevator (III, B1, **dz**).

★★★ Florida. Via Lepetit 33, tel. 6705921, fax 6692867. 53 rooms. No restaurant. Air conditioning, elevator; garage (III, C2, **n**).

★★★ Nuovo Monopole. Via F. Filzi 43, tel. 66984972, fax 67073297. 80 rooms . No restaurant. Air conditioning, elevator; garage (III, C1, **cg**).

★★★ San Carlo. Via Napo Torriani 28, tel. 6693236, fax 6703116. 75 rooms. No restaurant. Air conditioning, elevator; garage (III, C1, **p**).

¶¶¶ Calajunco. Via Stoppani 5, tel. 2046003. Closed Sun, Easter, part of August, Christ-

mas to New Year; open evenings only. Air conditioning. Cooking from the Aeolian Islands (III, E3, **tm**).

¶¶¶ Hong Kong. Via Schiapparelli 5, tel. 67071790. Closed Mon. Air conditioning. Chinese cuisine (III, B2, **ta**).

¶¶¶ Alfredo-Gran San Bernardo. Via Borgese 14, tel. 3319000, fax 29006859. Closed Sun (closed Sat & Sun in June-July); closed August. Air conditioning. Milanese cuisine (II, B2, **rl**).

¶¶¶ Joia. Via Panfilo Castaldi 18, tel. 29522124. Closed Sat lunch, Sun, August & Christmas to New Year. Air conditioning. Vegetarian cuisine and fish (III, E1, **tg**).

¶¶¶ Riccione. Via Taramelli 70, tel. 6686807, fax 66803616. Closed Sat and Mon lunch, August. Air conditioning. Cuisine of Emilia Romagna, sea food (II, A6, **tb**).

¶¶ Bandiere. Via Palermo 15, tel. 86461646. Closed Sat lunch, Sun, part of August & Christmas to New Year. Air conditioning. Cuisine of Veneto, Trentino, Friuli (II, E5, **sq**).

¶¶ Berti. Via Algarotti 20, tel. 6694627, fax 6884158. Closed Sun, part of August, Christmas to Epiphany. Garden. Lombard cuisine (II, B6, **sy**).

¶¶ Cavallini. Via M. Macchi 2, tel. 6693771. Closed Sat & Sun, August & Christmas to Epiphany. Air conditioning, garden. Traditional cooking (III, D1, **rq**).

¶¶ Langhe. Corso Como 6, tel. 6554279. Closed Sun, August. Air conditioning. Piemontese cuisine; specialty mushrooms and truffles (II, D5, **ug**).

¶ Colline Pisane. Largo La Foppa 5, tel. 6599136. Closed Sun, part of August & Christmas to New Year. Air conditioning. Traditional cooking (II, D-E5, **ty**).

Caffè Radetzky. Corso Garibaldi 105, tel. 6572645. Big breakfasts, aperitifs, sweet and savory pies.

Gelateria Chiosco di Sartori. Piazza Luigi di Savoia (on corner of station underpass). This kiosk is famous for its delicious ice cream and *granita* (water-ice).

Pasticceria Ranieri. Via Moscova 7, tel. 6595308. Delicious cakes and pastries, *panettone* with pineapple.

Viel. Corso Buenos Aires 15, tel. 29516123. Ice creams including some made with exotic fruit, fruit salads, milk shakes.

Civico Museo di Storia Naturale. Corso Venezia 55, tel. 62085405. *Open: 9:30–6:30.*

Fondazione Corrente – Studio Treccani. Via Porta 5, tel. 6572627. Closed Sat & public hols. *Open: 4–7.*

Museo delle Cere (Waxworks). Stazione Centrale, tel. 6690495. *Open: 8am–11pm.*

Palazzo della Permanente. Via Turati 34, tel.

6551445. Closed Mon. *Open: 10–1, 2:30–6:30; Sat & public hols 10–6:30.*

Planetario Ulrico Hoepli. Corso Venezia 55, tel. 29531181. For details of shows and conferences contact the Ufficio Informazioni del Comune, tel. 870545.

Churches and monuments

San Marco. Piazza San Marco 2, tel. 29002598.
Santa Maria Incoronata. Corso Garibaldi 116, tel. 654855.
San Simpliciano. Piazza San Simpliciano 7, tel. 862274.
Grattacielo Pirelli. Piazza Duca d'Aosta. For permission to go up the skyscraper, apply to the Regione Lombardia, tel. 67651.

Entertainment

Teatro Out Off. Via Dupré 4, tel. 39262282.
Teatro Smeraldo. Piazza XXV Aprile 10, tel. 29006767.
Teatro Verdi. Via Pastrengo 16, tel. 6880038.

Sport

Piscina Cozzi. Viale Tunisia 35, tel. 6599703. Swimming and scuba diving.

Shops, crafts, and fine art

10 Corso Como. Corso Como 10, tel. 29002674. In a beautifully converted factory, clothes, modern and antique jewelry, furniture, and small bookstore.
Arform. Via Moscova 22, tel. 29000423. Things for the house, clothes, designer objects.
Avant de dormir. Via Turati 3, tel. 6599990. T-shirts, fun ideas for presents.
Desart. Corso Buenos Aires 61, tel. 29405004.

Jewelry made with an unusual combination of materials.
Foot Locker. Corso Buenos Aires 64, tel. 29524646. Shoes and clothes for leisure time.
High Tech. Piazza XXV Aprile 12, tel. 6590515. A fashionable shop in a converted factory, household goods, furniture, gadgets from America.
Il Libro. Via Ozanam 11, tel. 2049022. Bookstore specialized in foreign literature and books for language studies.
Ingegnoli. Corso Buenos Aires 54, tel. 29400403. Opened in 1817, famous Milanese garden shop; garden tools, flowers, plants, books and manuals.
L'Archivolto. Via Marsala 2, tel. 6590842. Specialized in books on architecture and design; rare editions, antique books.
La Borsa del Fumetto. Via Lecco 16, tel. 29513883. Old and new magazines and comics, science fiction.
Libreria Tadino. Via Tadino 18, tel. 29513268. Specializes in African and Arab literature, books on religion and philosophy. Also a cultural center.
Mariatti. Via Marsala 13, tel. 6571767. Fitted out in Art Nouveau style, this shop sells everything you need for your desk and good things for presents.
Mart Sub. Corso Buenos Aires 8, tel. 29405295. Scuba diving equipment.
N'ombra de vin. Via S. Marco 2, tel. 6552746. A famous Milanese wine store with high vaulted ceilings which was the refectory of the Augustinian monks.
Swatch Store. Corso Buenos Aires 64, tel. 29524210. Sells the famous plastic watches.
Tincati. Piazza Oberdan 2, tel. 29404326. Clothes for men and women (shop in Via Malpighi 2); many well-known designer labels.

North east and northwest of the center

The areas to the north west of the city center are densely built-up and contain many of the city's largest facilities such as the sports amenities in San Siro (the soccer stadium, hippodrome, lido) and the biggest Milanese hospital, San Carlo. The area includes the QT8 district (Quartiere Triennale 8), modern and residential, designed by Piero Bottoni and Pietro Lingeri for the 8th Esposizione Triennale of Milan in 1946 and built in

1947–53. Città Studi, to the north east, is where all the university buildings of the scientific faculties are, as well as the Politecnico di Milano, which has the faculties of architecture and engineering. Just to the north of the city center is the area where the names of the streets and squares evoke the Milanese five-day revolt against the Austrians in 1848: Porta Vittoria, Piazza Cinque Giornate and Corso XXII Marzo. This area includes some Art Nouveau residential buildings and local municipal housing.

Hotels, restaurants, campsites and holiday villages

★★★ **Antares Hotel Accademia.** Viale Certosa 68, tel. 39211122, fax 33103878. 67 rooms. No restaurant. Air conditioning, elevator; garage (VI, B2, **ab**).

★★★ **Antares Hotel Concorde.** Via Petrocchi 1, tel. 26112020, fax 26147879. 120 rooms. No restaurant. Air conditioning, elevator; garage (VI, B5, **ae**).

★★★ **Leonardo da Vinci.** Via Senigallia 6, tel. 64071, fax 64074839. 779 rooms. Access for disabled. Air conditioning, elevator; parking, garage, garden, indoor pool (VI, A3, *off map*).

★☆★ **Novotel Milano Nord.** Via Suzzani 13, tel. 66101861, fax 66101961. 172 rooms. Access for disabled. Air conditioning, elevator; parking, garage, pool (VI, B4, **ad**).

★☆★ **Raffaello.** Viale Certosa 108, tel. 3270146, fax 3270440. 147 rooms. No restaurant. Air conditioning, elevator; garage, garden (VI, B1-2, **ga**).

★☆★ **Starhotel Tourist.** Viale F. Testi 300, tel. 6437777, fax 6472516. 140 rooms. Access for disabled. Air conditioning, elevator; parking, garage (VI, A4, *off map*).

★★★ **Gala.** Viale Zara 89, tel. 66800891, fax 66800463. 23 rooms. No restaurant. Air conditioning, elevator; parking, garden (VI, B4, **bg**).

★★★ **Gamma.** Via Valvassori Peroni 85, tel. 26413152, fax 2640255. 55 rooms. No restaurant. Air conditioning, elevator; garage (III, C6, **bh**).

★★★ **Roxy.** Via Bixio 4/A, tel. 29525151, fax 29517627. 34 rooms. No restaurant. Air conditioning, elevator (III, F2, **ap**).

★★★ **Vittoria.** Via Calvi 32, tel. 5456520, fax 55190246. 18 rooms. No restaurant. Air conditioning, elevator; parking, garage, garden (V, B2, **cd**).

★★★ **Zefiro.** Via Gallina 12, tel. 7384253, fax 713811. 57 rooms. No restaurant. Air conditioning, elevator (III, F4, **gb**).

🍴🍴🍴 **Amì Berton.** Via Nullo 14, tel. 713669. Closed Sat lunch & Sun, August & Christmas to Epiphany. Air conditioning. Creative cuisine; sea food (V, A3-4, **rb**).

🍴🍴🍴 **Antica Osteria di Greco.** Via Breda 29, tel. 2551398, fax 27001670. Closed Sat lunch & Sun. Garden. Lombard cuisine & seafood (VI, A4, **vs**).

🍴🍴🍴 **Nino Arnaldo.** Via Poerio 3, tel. 76005981. Closed Sat & Sun lunch, holiday closure varies. Air conditioning. Traditional cooking (V, A2, **sn**).

🍴🍴🍴 **Valtellina.** Via Taverna 34, tel. 7561139, fax 7560436. Closed Mon, New Year to Epiphany & part of August. Parking, garden. Valtellina cuisin, pizzoccheri, game (VI, D6, **re**).

🍴🍴 **Fumino.** Via Bernina 43, tel. 606872. Closed Sat lunch & Sun, August. Air conditioning, garden. Tuscan cuisine (VI, B3, **tn**).

🍴🍴 **Piero e Pia.** Piazza Aspari 2, tel. 718541. Closed Sun, August & Christmas to New Year. Air conditioning, garden. Cuisine of Piacenza (III, F4, **gc**).

🍴🍴 **Renzo.** Piazza Sire Raul 4, tel. 2846261. Closed Mon evening & Tues, August. Air conditioning, garden. Traditional cooking, game and mushrooms (III, B5, **rc**).

🍴 **Ostarìa Vècju Friûl.** Via E. De Marchi 5 corner of Via di Giustizia, tel. 6704295. Closed Sun, August. Friuli cuisine (VI, B4, **vg**).

🛏 **Ostello Pietro Rotta.** Via M. Bassi 2, tel. 39267095. Open all year except 23 Dec. to 13 Jan.; 350 beds.

Cafés and pastry shops

La Colonna. Viale Monza 6, tel. 2846605. Homemade ice cream, and ice cream made with soya milk.
Pasticceria Piave. Viale Premuda 42, tel. 76005590. Wide selection of cakes and pastries, good ice cream.

Museums and places of cultural interest

Associazione Biblioteca Tremelloni Sistema Moda. Viale Sarca 223, tel. 66106107. *Visits by appointment.*
Galleria d'Arte Sacra dei Contemporanei. Villa Clerici, Via G. Terruggia 14, tel. 6470066. Closed for renovation.
Museo del Giocattolo e del Bambino. Palazzo dei Martinitt, via Pitteri 56, tel. 26411585. Closed Mon. *Open 9:30–12:30, 3–6.*
Politecnico. Facoltà di Ingegneria e Architettura, Piazza Leonardo da Vinci 32, tel. 23991.

Churches

Certosa di Garegnano. Via Garegnano 28 (off Viale Certosa), tel. 38006301. *Open: 9:30–12, 3–5:30; Sun 3:30–5.*

Entertainment

Centro Culturale Rosetum. Via Pisanello 1, tel. 48707203.
PalaVobis. Via S. Elia, tel. 33400551. Concerts and musical events.
Parco Esposizioni di Novegro. Via Novegro 2, Segrate (MI), tel. 70200022. Hosts trade fairs and other large events.
Teatridithalia Elfo. Via Menotti 11, tel. 716791.
Teatro Ciak. Via Sangallo 33, tel. 76110093.
Teatro Franco Parenti. Via Pierlombardo 14, tel. 5457174.
Zelig. Viale Monza 140, tel. 2551774. Has rapidly become the premier venue for the new brand of Milanese satire, and a favorite haunt of the new generation of cabaret artists.

Sport

Ippodromo di S. Siro & Trottatoio. Piazzale dello Sport, tel. 482161.
Palalido. Piazzale Lotto 15, tel. 39266100. Ice skating, tennis, swimming.
Stadio S. Siro "Giuseppe Meazza." Via Piccolomini 5, tel. 40092175, 48707123.
Tiro a Segno Nazionale. Via Papa 22/B, tel. 33002418, 33002598. Target shooting and wing shooting; firearms can be hired.
XXV Aprile. Via Cimabue 22/24, tel. 39210769. Athletics, bowls, tennis.

Shops, crafts, and fine art

Antica Cartoleria Novecento. Piazza Risorgimento 3, tel. 76006123. Greetings cards, gift paper and ribbons, letter paper in unusual colors.
Chiosco Monforte. Piazza Tricolore (corner Cor-

o Concordia), tel. 799737. Specialty mushrooms, ruffles, and exotic fruit.
Luoghi & Libri. Via Mameli 8 (corner Via Sottocorno), tel. 7388370. Bookstore specialized in travel literature, guides, maps.

Solci. Via Morosini 19, tel. 55195725. Famous wine store, Italian and foreign wines, special olive oil and vinegars.
U.A.D.G. Viale Monza 22, tel. 2847504. Objects and decorations in plaster.

South of the center

With its canal-side charm and great variety of small stores and bistros, the Navigli-Ticinese district is the unchallenged center of this sector of the city, and boasts the last of Milan's extensive network of canals (*navigli*). The area is characteristic for its humble tenements built round a yard surrounded by little workshops; access to the apartments above was along a narrow landing whose railing gave the name to this particular type of building (*casa a ringhiera*); the shared toilet facilities were outside on the landing. Sometimes there are several linked yards leading to the next street behind, where artisans often had their workshops. These houses have now all been renovated and the area has become very fashionable. There is plenty of nightlife in the Navigli-Ticinese district: bars, beer cellars, sandwich bars, and a wide variety of clubs, usually with live music.

Hotels and restaurants

★★ **Antares Hotel Rubens.** Via Rubens 21, tel. 40302, fax 48193114. 87 rooms. Air conditioning, elevator; parking, garage (VI, D2, **ch**).

★★ **D'Este.** Viale Bligny 23, tel. 58321001, fax 58321136. 79 rooms. No restaurant. Access for disabled. Air conditioning, elevator; garage (IV, E6, **bc**).

★★ **Grand Hotel Brun.** Via Caldera 21, tel. 452711, fax 48204746. 330 rooms. Access for disabled. Air conditioning, elevator; parking, garage, garden (VI, D1, *off map*).

★★ **Holiday Inn.** Via Lorenteggio 278, tel. 410014, fax 48304729. 119 rooms. Access for disabled. Air conditioning, elevator; parking, garage, pool (VI, E1, *off map*).

★★ **Novotel Milano Est Aeroporto.** Via Mecenate 121, tel. 58011085, fax 58011086. 206 rooms. Access for disabled. Air conditioning, elevator; parking, garden, pool (VI, E6, **af**).

★★★ **Major.** Viale Isonzo 2, tel. 55188335, fax 55183140. 64 rooms. No restaurant. Air conditioning, elevator; garage (V, E2, **ci**).

★★★ **Mec.** Via Tito Livio 4, tel. 5456715, fax 5456718. 40 rooms . No restaurant. Air conditioning, elevator; parking, garage (V, D3, **bm**).

★★★ **Molise.** Via Cadibona 2/A, tel. 55181852, fax 55184348. 32 rooms. No restaurant. Air conditioning, elevator; parking (V, D5, **cn**).

🍴 **Aimo e Nadia.** Via Montecuccoli 6, tel. 416886, fax 48302005. Closed Sat lunch & Sun, August & New Year to Epiphany. Air conditioning. Traditional and avant-garde cuisine (VI, D1, **uq**).

🍴 **Sadler.** Via Conchetta corner Via Troilo 14, tel. 58104451, fax 58112343. Closed Sun, part of January & August; open evenings only. Air conditioning. Avant-garde cuisine (IV, D2-3, **vt**).

🍴 **Grand Hotel Pub.** Via A. Sforza 75, tel. 89511586. Closed Mon, part of August. Garden. Padanian cuisine (IV, F3, **rw**).

🍴 **Masuelli San Marco.** Viale Umbria 80, tel. 55184138. Closed Sun & Mon lunch, mid August-mid Sept & Christmas to Epiphany. Air conditioning. Lombard and Piedmontese cuisine (V, C3, **uk**).

🍴 **Osteria del Binari.** Via Tortona 1, tel. 89406753. Closed Sun (except Fairs); open evenings only. Air conditioning, garden. Lombard, Piedmontese and traditional cooking (IV, D2, **vm**).

🍴 **Osteria Via Prè.** Via Casale 4, tel. 8373869. Closed Mon, part of August. Air conditioning. Ligurian cuisine (IV, D-E2, **rh**).

Cafés and pastry shops
Gattullo. Piazzale di Porta Lodovica 2, tel. 58310497. Cakes, pastries, and savories: sandwiches, rolls, quiches.
Gelateria Ecologica. Corso di Porta Ticinese 40, tel. 58101872. Only natural ingredients for the many flavors of ice cream.
Pasticceria Cucchi. Corso Genova 1, tel. 89409793. Top quality products: *panettone*, pralines and chocolates, ice cream.

Museums and places of cultural interest
Istituto universitario di lingue moderne (IULM). Via Filippo da Liscate 3, tel. 582181.
Palazzina Liberty. Largo Marinai d'Italia, tel. 55195967. Venue of the Civica Banda Musicale; interesting calendar of concerts.
Università Commerciale Luigi Bocconi. Via Sarfatti 25, tel. 58361.

Churches

Chiaravalle Abbey. Via Sant'Arialdo 102, tel. 57403404. Closed Mon. *Open: 9–11:30, 2:30–5:30; guided tours on Sun 11, 3, 4:30.*

Mirasole Abbey. 10 km on Vigentina road, tel. 55031. Closed Tues. *Open: 9–6.*

Morimondo Abbey. 6 km on road to Pavia, tel. 945206. *Open: 8:30–12, 2:30–6:30; public hols 8:30–12, 2:30–7.*

Viboldone Abbey. Via dell'Abbazia near Viboldone, 12 km on road to Lodi, tel. 9841203. *Open: 8–12:30, 2:30–6:30.*

S. Cristoforo sul Naviglio. Via San Cristoforo 3, tel. 48951413. *Open: 8–6:30.*

Entertainment

Atelier. Viale Montegani 35/1, tel. 89531301. Carlo Colla and sons put on puppet shows.

Ca' Bianca Club. Via Ludovico il Moro 117, tel. 89125777. Cabaret shows and jazz. Food served until late.

Capolinea. Via Ludovico il Moro 119, tel. 89122024. Legendary Milanese jazz club, live concerts. Restaurant with home-style cooking.

CRT Centro di Ricerche per il Teatro. Via Dini 7, tel. 89512220.

Festa dei Navigli. In June; stalls selling just about everything, antiques.

Fiera di Senigallia. Along the Darsena, every Sat: bric-à-brac, new and second-hand clothes, records.

Forum di Assago. Via Di Vittorio, Assago (MI), tel. 488571. Sports and musical events, concerts.

Mercatone del Naviglio Grande. Along the Naviglio Grande. Last Sun of month, from Sept. to June; antiques and bric-à-brac.

Pittori del Naviglio. In March; vast assortment of paintings arranged along the canals.

Sagra del Tartufo. Last Sun of October, in Via Ripamonti. Truffle-lover's paradise; pageant and costumes.

Scimmie. Via Ascanio Sforza 49, tel. 89402874. Restaurant-bar with jazz, fusion, and blues concerts. In summer you can also have drinks on their barge on the canal.

Tangram. Via Pezzotti 52, tel. 89501007. Live music: jazz, rock, fusion, blues. Drinks and rolls served at tables shaped like pieces of the Chinese puzzle, Tangram.

Teatridithalia Porta Romana. Corso di Porta Romana 124, tel. 58315896.

Teatro della Quattordicesima. Via Oglio 18, tel. 55211300.

Sports

Agorà. Via dei Ciclamini 23, tel. 48300946. Ice skating.

Bonacossa. Via Mecenate 74, tel. 5061277. Sports center: indoor soccer, gymnastics, hand ball, tennis.

Bowling Corvetto. Via Marco d'Agrate 23, tel. 57404495.

Bowling dei Fiori. Via Renzo e Lucia 4, tel. 8435728.

Idroscalo. Between Milan and Segrate and Peschiera Borromeo, tel. 7560190, 77403590. Includes the Parco Azzurro complex with pools, tennis courts, play grounds, restaurant; canoeing, kayak, windsurfing.

Palazzo del ghiaccio. Via Piranesi 14, tel. 73981. Milan's premier ice-skating venue.

Ice skating Saini. Via Corelli 136, tel. 7561280. Sports center: swimming, athletics, weight lifting, fencing, volley ball.

Shops, crafts, and fine art

Biffi. Corso Genova 6, tel. 58111182. Designer labels for men and women.

Idea Books. Via Vigevano 41, tel. 8373949. Exhibition space with bookstore.

Pedano. Viale Umbria 120, tel. 7383735. All-wood furniture store.

Pronti, via! Via Ascanio Sforza 17, tel. 8376452. Sauces and preserves, pies and cakes.

Environs of Milan and Brianza

Abbiategrasso

Page 144   ✉ 20081 ☎ 02

Hotels, restaurants, camp sites and holiday villages

★★★ **Italia.** Piazza Castello 31, tel. 9462871, fax 9462851. 41 rooms. No restaurant. Air conditioning, elevator.

¶¶ **Giada Verde.** Via Cassolnovo 49, tel. 94968294. Closed Mon, part of August. Air conditioning, garden. Lombard cuisine.

Àrcore

Page 134   ✉ 20043 ☎ 039

ℹ *Ufficio cultura.* C/o Municipio (Town Hall), Largo Vela 1, tel. 6013263.

Hotels, restaurants, camp sites and holiday villages

¶¶¶ **Sant'Eustorgio.** Via Gilera 1, tel. 6013718, fax 617531. Closed Fri, Sun evening; August. Parking, garden. Classic cuisine.

Museums and places of cultural interest

Villa d'Adda. Largo Vela 1, tel. 6013263. *Visits: only to outside and park.* Information from the town hall.

Arese

Page 139   ✉ 20020 ☎ 02

Hotels, restaurants, camp sites and holiday villages

★★★ **Park Hotel Giada.** Via dei Platani 6, tel. 9385441, fax 9384955. 37 rooms. No restaurant. Air conditioning, elevator; parking, garage.

¶¶ **Castanei.** Viale Alfa Romeo 10, tel. 93800053. Closed Sun and Wed evening, part of August and Christmas. Air conditioning, parking, garden. Classic cuisine.

Museums and places of cultural interest
Museo storico "Alfa Romeo." Viale Alfa Romeo, tel. 93928111. *Visits: Mon–Fri 9–12:30, 2–4:30.*

Busto Arsizio

Page 142   ✉ 21052 ☎ 0331

Hotels, restaurants, camp sites and holiday villages

⁺ **La Pineta.** Via Sempione 150, tel. 381220, fax 381220. 58 rooms. Access for disabled. Air conditioning, elevator; parking, garden (A1, *off map*).

*** **Astoria.** Viale Duca d'Aosta 14, tel. 636422, fax 679610. 47 rooms. No dining facilities. Access for disabled. Air conditioning, elevator; garage (A2, **b**).

Shops, crafts, and fine art

Buzzi. Via Cavour 1, tel. 632660. Hi-fi, records, CDs.
City Garments. Via per Fagnano Olona, tel. 626430. Large clothes store.
Enoteca Qualevino. Via Vespri Siciliani 69, tel. 681312. Wines galore.
Il Leggio. Via Ponchielli 12, tel. 620957. Books and writing instruments.

Cassano d'Adda

Page 128   ✉ 20062 ☎ 0363

Museums and places of cultural interest
Villa Borromeo. Via V. Veneto 58, tel. 60904. Visits on request.

Cassinetta di Lugagnano

Page 144   ✉ 20080 ☎ 02

Hotels, restaurants, campsites, and holiday villages

¶¶¶ **Antica Osteria del Ponte.** Piazza Negri 9, tel. 9420034, fax 9420610. Closed Sun & Mon, Christmas to mid-January, and August. Air conditioning, garden. Specialized cuisine.

Museums and places of cultural interest
Villa Trivulzio. tel. 9420196. Closed.
Villa Visconti Maineri. Via Cavour 4. *Research visits only, in the company of the owner.*

Castellanza

Page 142   ✉ 21053 ☎ 0331

Museums and places of cultural interest
Museo d'Arte Moderna della Fondazione Pagani. Via Gerenzano 70, tel. 503113. Closed Mon. *Open: 9:30–12:30, 3–one hour before sunset.*

Certosa di Pavia

Page 124   ✉ 27012 ☎ 0382
ℹ️ *APT*, at Pavia, tel. 22156.
IAT, seasonal in loco.

Museums and places of cultural interest
Charterhouse. Tel. 925613. Closed Mon. *Open: April 9–11:30, 2:30–5:30; May–September 9–11:30, 2:30–6; October–March 9–11:30, 2:30–4:30.*

Cesano Maderno

Page 138   ✉ 20031 ☎ 0362

Museums and places of cultural interest
Palazzo Borromeo Arese. Tel. 524280. *Visits on request.*

Cuggiono

Page 143   ✉ 20012 ☎ 02

Museums and places of cultural interest
Museo Storico Civico di Arti e Professioni cuggionesi. C/o Villa Annoni, Piazza XV Aprile. Tel. 9746681. *Visits on request.*

Gallarate

Page 142   ✉ 21013 ☎ 0331
ℹ️ *Pro Loco* c/o Municipio, via Verdi 2, tel. 754433, fax 781869.

Hotels, restaurants, campsites, and holiday villages

⁺ **Jet Hotel.** Via Tiro a Segno 22, tel. 772100, fax 772686. 40 rooms. No restaurant. Access for disabled. Air conditioning, elevator; parking, garage, garden, swimming pool (B2, **c**).

*** **Astoria.** Piazza Risorgimento 9/A, tel. 791043, fax 772671. 50 rooms. (Separate restaurant, see below). Access for disabled. Air conditioning, elevator; garage (A1, **a**).

¶¶ **Astoria.** Piazza Risorgimento 9/A, tel. 786777. Closed Friday. Air conditioning, parking. Lombard cuisine (A1, **a**).

Museums and places of cultural interest

Civica Galleria d'Arte Moderna. Viale Milano 21, tel. 791266. Closed Monday. *Open: 10–12, 3–6.*
Museo d'Arte Sacra. Basilica di S. M. Assunta, tel. 773836. *Open: Sept–May, Sun 3–6; other days and months on request.*
Museo della Società Gallaratese di Studi Patri. Via Borgo Antico 4, tel. 795092. Closed Monday. *Open: Tues–Fri 10–12, Sat 10–12, 3–5, Sun 10–12.*
Museo della Tecnica & del Lavoro "MV Agusta." Via Matteotti 3. Closed for renovation.

Sport

Bowling Gallarate. Via Madonna in Campagna 10, tel. 797924.

Shops, crafts, and fine art

Al Bottone. Via Mazzini 18/b, tel. 794720. Haberdashers, buttons, embroidery.
Carù. Piazza Garibaldi 6, tel. 792508. Books, CDs, videos.

Inverigo

Page 136   ✉ 22044 ☎ 031

Museums and places of cultural interest

La Rotonda. Via privata d'Adda 1, tel. 607154. *Visits on request to outside, grounds, and staircase.*

at Cremnago, km 1

Palazzo Perego. Tel. 607022. *Visits on request.*

Legnano

Page 141   ✉ 20025 ☎ 0331

Hotels, restaurants, campsites, and holiday villages

★★★   **Pagoda.** Via Edison 11, tel. 548131, fax 541112. 85 rooms. No restaurant. Access for disabled. Air conditioning, elevator; parking, garden (B1, **a**).

★★   **Al Corso.** Corso Magenta 137, tel. 597538, fax 545478. 20 rooms. No restaurant. Access for the disabled. Parking (C3, **f**).

🍴   **Barbarossa.** Corso Matteotti 3, tel. 540504. Closed Sun evening & Mon; closed August, New Year's Eve to Epiphany. Air conditiong, parking, garden. Classic cuisine (B-C3, **m**).

Museums and places of cultural interest

Museo civico "Guido Sutermeister." Corso Garibaldi 225, tel. 543005. Closed Mon. *Open: 9–12:30, 2:30–5, Sun 9:30–12.*

Entertainments

Sagra del Carroccio (last Sunday of May). Pageant of the *contrade*, ending with a *palio* contest for the Cross of Ariberto d'Intimiano; tel. 592424.

Shops, crafts, and fine art

Cristalceramica. Via Cavallotti 8, tel. 544328. Gifts, porcelain, glassware.
Erboristeria Natura Sempre. Via Palestro 35, tel. 45456. Herbs, teas, dried flowers, gifts.
Pellicceria Albertalli. Via Cavallotti 8 and piazza S. Magno 28, tel. 544513.

Lissone

Page 137   ✉ 20035 ☎ 039

Museums and places of cultural interest

Civica Galleria d'Arte Contemporanea. Palazzo Terragni, tel. 73977. *Visits on request.*

Magenta

Page 143   ✉ 20013 ☎ 02

🛈   *Pro Loco.* Via IV Giugno 80, tel. 97291515. *Consorzio Parco Lombardo della Valle del Ticino.* Via Isonzo 1, tel. 97950151.

Hotels, restaurants, campsites, and holiday villages

★★★   **Excelsior Magenta.** Via Cattaneo 67, tel. 97298651, fax 97291617. 67 rooms. Access for disabled. Air conditioning, elevator; parking, garage.

🍴   **Trattoria alla Fontana.** Via del Roccolo 5, tel. 9760826. Closed Sat midday, Sunday, part of August, Christmas, New Year's Eve. Parking, garden. Classic and Lombard cuisine (risottos, etc.).

Museums and places of cultural interest

Villa Castiglioni. Pontevecchio di Magenta, tel. 972101. *Open: Tues–Thurs 10–12, 3–5.*

at Robecco sul Naviglio, km 3.5

Villa Gandini. Via G. Matteotti 26, tel. 9470512. *Visits on request.*

Meda

Page 138   ✉ 20036 ☎ 0362

Museums and places of cultural interest

Villa Antona Traversi. Piazza V. Veneto, tel. 341557. *Visits on request.* The church of S. Vittore can be visited on the last Sunday of the month.

Merate

Page 135   ✉ 22055 ☎ 039

Museums and places of cultural interest

Osservatorio Astronomico. Via Bianchi 46, tel. 999111. *Visits first non-holiday Friday of month. 9–12:30, 2–7:30.*

Montevecchia

Page 135   ✉ 22055 ☎ 039

Agriturismo (farmhouse vacations)
Azienda agricola vitivinicola Valcurone. Cascina Casarigo, tel. 9930065. Production and sale of local wines. On request: dinner, tasting sessions, guided tour through the Montevecchia park and company vineyards.

Monza

Page 131   ✉ 20052 ☎ 039

i *Pro Monza (IAT).* Palazzo Comunale, Piazza Carducci, tel. 323222.

Hotels, restaurants, campsites, and holiday villages

★★ **De La Ville.** Viale Regina Margherita 15, tel. 382581, fax 367647. 55 rooms. Access for disabled. Air conditioning, elevator; parking, garage (A1, **a**).

★★★ **Della Regione.** Via Elvezia 4, tel. 387205, fax 380254. 90 rooms. Access for disabled. Air conditioning, elevator; parking, garage (A1, *off map*).

⊪ **Alle Grazie.** Via Lecco 84, tel. 387903. Closed Wed, and part of August. Air conditioning, parking, garden. Classic and specialized cuisine (B3, *off map*).

⊪ **Riserva.** Via Borgazzi 12, tel. 386612. Closed Fri & Sat midday, part of July. Parking, garden. Piedmontese cuisine (D1, *off map*).

Å★★ **Autodromo.** Nel Parco della Villa Reale, tel. 387771, fax 2102145. Seasonal.

Cafés and pastry shops
Pasticceria Moderno. Piazza Roma 2, tel. 322167.

Museums and places of cultural interest
Cathedral and Museo Serpero. Piazza Duomo. Tel. 323404. Closed Mon. *Open: 9–11:30, 3–5:30.*
Villa Reale. Viale Regina Margherita 2. *Visits to the Teatrino* ("ufficio musei," Comune di Monza, tel. 322086), *to the Cappella di Corte* (tel. 387389) *and to the Serrone* (open only for exhibitions).

Entertainments
Concorso internazionale della rosa (end of May).
Festa del Santo Chiodo (September). Procession of the Iron Crown.
Gran Premio d'Italia di Formula Uno (September).
Mercato dell'Antiquariato (2nd Sun of month). Via Bergamo.
Sagra di S. Giovanni (June). Music and firework displays in the gardens of the Villa Reale.

Shops, crafts, and fine art
Bergamaschi. Via Passerini 9, tel. 323142. Antiquies, bric-à-brac, ivories.
Casa del Formaggio. Via Italia 19, tel. 324437. Vast selection of regional cheeses and oils from the Lombard lakes.
Meregalli. Via Italia 24, tel. 324940. Wines.

Paderno d'Adda

Page 135   ✉ 22050 ☎ 039

Hotels, restaurants, campsites, and holiday villages

★★ **Adda.** Via Edison 27, tel. 514015, fax 510796. Camere 35. Elevator; parking, garage, garden, swimming pool, tennis courts.

Peschiera Borromeo

Page 120   ✉ 20068 ☎ 02

Hotels, restaurants, campsites, and holiday villages

★★ **Country Hotel Borromeo.** On the Idroscalo Est ringroad, Via Buozzi 4, tel. 5475121, fax 55300708. 73 rooms. Access for disabled. Air conditioning, elevator; parking, garden.

★★★ **Montini.** On the Idroscalo Est ringroad, Via G. Di Vittorio 39, tel. 5475031, fax 55300610. 51 rooms. No restaurant. Access for disabled. Air conditioning, elevator; parking.

Rho

Page 140   ✉ 20017 ☎ 02

Hotels, restaurants, campsites, and holiday villages

⊪ **Locanda dell'Angelo.** Via Matteotti 7, tel. 9303897. Closed Wed, Sat lunch and part of August. Air conditioning. Milanese cuisine.

Museums and places of cultural interest
Villa Cornaggia Medici. Corso Europa 291, tel. 93332238. *Open: Mon–Thurs 9:30–12:30, 2:30–6, Fri–Sat 9–12.*

Saronno

Page 139   ✉ 21047 ☎ 02

Hotels, restaurants, campsites, and holiday villages

★★ **Albergo della Rotonda.** Via Novara 53, tel. 96703232, fax 96702770. 92 rooms. Access for disabled. Air conditioning, elevator; parking, garage, tennis courts.

★★★ **Mercurio.** Via Hermada 2, tel. 9602795, fax 9609330. 24 rooms, 23 with bathroom or shower. No restaurant. Parking.

⊪ **Mezzaluna.** Viale Lazzaroni 25, tel. 96703593. Closed Sat & Sun, part of August and Christmas. Air conditioning, parking. Classic cuisine.

La Rotonda. "Laghi" motorway exit, tel. 96704768. Pastry shop, cakes and cookies, famous *amaretti* candies.

Museo del Biscotto. C/o Lazzaroni, via Novara 55, tel. 96424401. *Visits on request.*

Segrate

Page 120 ✉ 20090 ☎ 02

*** Air Hotel.** A Novegro, Via Baracca 2, tel. 70200009, fax 7561294. 60 rooms. Air conditioning, elevator; parking, garage, garden.

*** Jolly Hotel Milano 2.** At Milano 2, Via F.lli Cervi, tel. 2175, fax 26410115. 149 rooms. Air conditioning, elevator, parking.

Seregno

Page 137 ✉ 20038 ☎ 0362

|| **Osteria del Pomiroeu.** Via Garibaldi 37, tel. 237973. Closed Mon, midday Tues, and part of August. Garden. Classic cuisine.

Somma Lombardo

Page 143 ✉ 21019 ☎ 0331

|| **Pio.** At Coarezza, Via Alzaia 22, tel. 256667.

Closed Wed, part of January, and in August. Air conditioning, parking. Classic cuisine.

Trezzo sull'Adda

Page 128 ✉ 20056 ☎ 02

ℹ️ *Pro Loco,* via Carlo Biffi 4, tel. 9092569.

*** Longobardo.** Viale Lombardia 70, tel. 90962600, fax 90939911. 50 rooms. No restaurant. Air conditioning, elevator; parking, garden, tennis courts.

|| **San Martino.** Via Brasca 47, tel. 9090218, fax 9091978. Closed Mon. Air conditioning, parking, garden. Classic fish cuisine, mushrooms, truffles.

Castle. Tel. 9092569. *Visits: Tues–Sat on request; Sun & public hols 2:30–6, night visits on request.*

Sagra della Madonna del Rosario (first Sun of October).

Vimercate

Page 134 ✉ 20059 ☎ 039

Palazzo Trotti. Piazza Unità d'Italia 1, tel. 6084865. *Visits on request.*

at Oreno, km 1
Villa Borromeo. Via Piave 12, tel. 669004. *Visits on request.*

Potato Pageant. Lively town festival held in mid-September every odd year, tel. 66591212.

Turin and environs

Historical and artistic aspects of Turin

An ancient city open to the future. This is how Turin greets its visitors, the past alternating with the present, exciting scenes of the modern world. Since the mid-1970s Turin has seen the contraction and redistribution of the population and workforce. In the last ten years the population has dropped from 1,117,154 to 961,918. The conversion of disused industrial space and the development of alternatives to heavy industry have involved the redevelopment of certain areas and an innovative use of old industrial sites. Fiat's great Lingotto factory is a case in point. The entire plant has been converted into a modern exhibition and congress center by the architect Renzo Piano. Likewise, there are many projects for amenities along the river banks and for new parks, together with the redevelopment of areas in the city's periphery. Renovation works carried out in the historic city center have restored much of its former splendor (Porta Susa, Porta Palazzo, Via Po). Turin today is a city of many

Aerial view of Turin from the opposite hillside

dimensions, where business, industry, and international trade have in no way impaired its civic qualities as an enjoyable place to live, with a pleasant and peaceful atmosphere.

The city's markedly rational geometry of orthogonal streets and boulevards is very noticeable from any of the panoramic sites in the vicinity: from the basilica of Superga, the Monte dei Cappuccini, or the Faro della Vittoria. It is remarkably easy city to find one's way in a city like Turin. The avenues and arcaded streets are inviting and pleasant to walk down. The alignment of the wide tree-lined avenues and arcades is one of the dominant characteristics of the city, in which monuments, squares, and palaces are all geometrically interwoven. We start at the imposing Mole Antonelliana, and then proceed down Via Po, which links Piazza Vittorio Veneto to Piazza Castello, moving away from the river and the austere Gran Madre di Dio on the opposite bank. There are many traditional 18th- and 19th-c. cafés under the arcades along which our walk takes us. Also on Via Po is the old university building, with its classical courtyard and imposing staircase. This is immediately followed by Piazza Castello, which is dominated by Palazzo Madama at its center, with Palazzo Reale, the cathedral, the chapel of the Holy Shroud, and San Lorenzo all closely situated nearby. The elegant Via Garibaldi leads off from the square, its many shops set in buildings that typify the wide range of styles Turin has to offer – from Baroque to Rococo, from neoclassical to Art Nouveau and Liberty.

Not far away in the opposite direction we pass the lively Baroque facade of Palazzo Carignano. Here, between the former seat of the Subalpine Parliament and the famous Cambio restaurant,

Turin's past and present meet once again. Similarly, elegant shop-lined arcades of the last century and modern traffic can be seen coexisting harmoniously in nearby Piazza San Carlo, together with the monument to Emmanuel Philibert (nicknamed the "Caval d'Brôns" by the locals). Also abutting the square is another important link between today's modern Turin and the past, namely, the Museo Egizio e Galleria Sabauda, one of Italy's foremost museum and gallery complexes. Other squares and monuments tell us about the solid and dependable Turin bourgeoisie of the 19th c., its penchant for the essential, its rigorous style. Such is Piazza Maria Teresa, which gives onto Via Giolitti, leading to the river. Other monuments to Turin's past, however, can be found outside the city, in Moncalieri, Rivoli, and Stupinigi, where three of the many Savoyard residences lie within easy reach of the city.

Much of the local patrimony has been restored and opened to the public, such as Rivoli Castle and other residences of the Savoy, enabling a full exploration of their interiors, furnishings and fine art collections. These, together with the city's many monuments, palazzi, and charming streets are evocative reminders of the royal Turin of the past, a patrimony that in no way belies its status as a modern city, firmly rooted in the present.

From ancient times to the Middle Ages

The city is named after a people known as the *Taurini*, whose precise origin is unknown. They appear to have mingled with the people of Liguria, of Iberian origin, and it is thought that their main settlement was at the confluence of the rivers Po and Dora Riparia. The first traces of the settlers appear around 500–400 B.C. From the time of the first conflicts with the Gauls of the north, they allied themselves with the Romans. In the year 218 B.C. the Taurini were overrun by Hannibal, who laid the town to waste. Over the next two hundred years Turin's dependence as a military colony of Rome increased, so that during the rule of Julius Caesar the city took the name of *Colonia Giulia*. As part of his reorganization and control of the Piedmont to facilitate links with Gaul, in 28 B.C. Augustus founded the new *Augusta Taurinorum*. Although strategically situated at an important crossroads between the Po Valley and the Alps, as a town it remained relatively small. Its importance grew toward the end of imperial rule. In A.D. 568 the region was invaded by the Longobards, from nearby Lombardy. The new duchy they established here was to last for three centuries. The importance of Turin under the duchy is amply testified by the fact that three of its dukes became Longobard kings. In A.D. 773 the Franks invaded the area, and Turin passed to the Marquisate of Ivrea, which in turn answered to the great Carolingian Empire. The end of Frankish rule in A.D. 888 heralded a period up instability and upheaval, as the town regularly changed hands. Subsequently, Turin was made an independent marquisate, and in the year 1002 it passed under the rule of Manfred II, who governed until 1035. He was succeeded by his daughter, who ruled the marquisate until 1091. On her death the area was divided and the era of the Communes, or independent city governments, began. The church, represented by its bishops, was the first to take over the feudal holdings. In 1159 an imperial decree ceded Turin and the surrounding area to Bishop Claudius. The bishop's authority was later replaced by that of the Commune. In 1193 the Commune was granted access to the castles in the bishopric in the event of war. In 1204 authority passed into the hands of the town's populace. However, the era of the Communes, which reached its peak in 1224, was short-lived. The counts of the French dynasty of Savoie, or Savoy, made their reappearance, intent on creating a principality in Piedmont. With the support of Frederick II, the Holy Roman Emperor, a seignory in Turin was secured for the first time in 1248, but its new ruler Tommaso III had to fight to keep it (1252). Three years later, the Turinese allied with the Republic of Asti and rid themselves of Tommaso, but were forced to accept the seignory of the House of Anjou, and subsequently the rule of Guglielmo VII of Monferrato in 1272. Two years later Tommaso III of Savoy overthrew Guglielmo and took back Turin. From then on the city remained under the House of Savoy. Tommaso III, who dissolved the administrative bodies of the Commune, was succeeded by his brother Amadeus, and then his son Filippo, Prince of Acaia. The Acaia branch of the Savoy family ruled until 1418 from its base in Pinerolo, leaving the old oligarchy to control Turin; this state of affairs endured until the Moriana branch of the Savoy family emerged victorious in the power struggles within the dynasty, heralding the reign of Amadeus VIII.

From the 15th to the 17th century

Notwithstanding the decimation of the population in the plague of 1348, the city steadily grew in size and importance, becoming the principal focus of the Savoy territories in Piedmont. The year 1404 saw the founding of the university, and the start of large building projects for castles and palaces. In 1424, under Amadeus VIII, the marquisate was made a duchy.

From the very outset Turin struggled against the rival town of Moncalieri for the title of capital of the duchy. Although Amadeus's successor in Turin assumed the title of Prince of Piedmont, Turin itself developed slowly during the 15th c. At the end of the century, however, owing to the city's strategic position, the European armies that crossed the Alps into the peninsula were compelled to pass through it. During the long conflict between France and the Hapsburgs, Charles VIII of France invaded Italy, passing through Turin (1494). The Italian Wars were resumed by Francis I of France, who likewise passed through Turin. Welcomed at first as allies, the French soon assumed an increasingly dominant role, and eventually occupied Piedmont in 1533. The reigning duke of Piedmont, Charles III, abandoned Turin in 1536, and the duchy was promptly seized by France. The French governor strengthened the city walls, built bastions, and eliminated the villages outside the walls. The physical transformation of the city was accompanied by sweeping changes in social organization, which the citizens gladly accepted. It has to be said that the people of Turin were not enthusiastic about the prospect of a return of the House of Savoy after Emmanuel Philibert had signed the treaty of Cateau-Cambrésis in 1559. Yet it was the same Emmanuel Philibert who chose Turin as the capital of his territory in 1563. He identified potential areas of economic and political development on the Po basin, re-organized the city's administration, and opened up new perspectives for the city. A symbol of this new energy was the construction of the Cittadella (1564–66), an excellent point of defense that preluded the general reorganization and expansion of the city.

The 18th century

The 17th c. witnessed another serious outbreak of the plague and several dynastic conflicts, in which French and Spanish forces prevailed. Victor Amadeus chose to ally himself with the Austrian forces, but they were routed during the invasion of the French troops under General Catinat. Despite this, after the Treaty of Riswick in 1697, the duke regained all his territories. The onset of the War of the Spanish Succession in 1701 shook Piedmont. In 1704 the duke allied once more with Austria, and the French troops besieged Turin. The siege was broken in September 1706 when the Piedmontese solider Pietro Micca saved the city by blowing up the tunnel by which the French were trying to penetrate the citadel, and lost his life in the process. The heroic act signaled the defeat of the French. The Peace of Utrecht (1713) that ended the War of the Spanish Succession also accorded Victor Amadeus possession of Sicily and other territories, together with the title of king. Only ten years later, however, Sicily itself was taken from him by the Spanish, who ceded him Sardinia (1720) by way of compensation. The royal territory expanded in the course of the century, that is, until the French Revolution, when King Victor Amadeus III (as king of Sardinia) sided with the Royalists, and was subsequently obliged to relinquish Nice and Savoie; later he had to defend Piedmont too. In the wake of the sweeping victories of Napoleon, in 1796 Victor Amadeus's successor Charles Emmanuel IV fled to Sardinia, and in 1802 Turin became the capital of a French Département.

The last two hundred years

In 1814 Turin was restored to the House of Savoy. However, Victor Emmanuel's reactionary rule was unpopular, and the uprisings of 1821 forced him to abdicate in favor of his brother, Charles Felix. In 1831 Charles Albert of the cadet line of Savoy-Carignan be-

Piazza San Carlo, and the "twin" churches of Santa Cristina and San Carlo

came king and initiated sweeping reforms, during which he created the Consiglio di Stato, revised the civil code, founded the Pinacoteca and the Technical Schools, and reformed the Accademia. In 1847 he carried out administrative reforms and in 1848 gave the city a new statute. While there was dissent in Milan and the first national Parliament held session in Turin, the king declared war against Austria. He was defeated at the gates of Milan in 1848 and again at Novara the following year; he then abdicated in favor of his son, Vittorio Emanuele II, and went into exile in Oporto, Portugal. In 1859 the new king began a second war of independence that led to the declaration of the Kingdom of Italy on March 7, 1861. Turin became the capital of the unified nation and thereby reached the zenith of its political prestige. The civil administration, which was already well developed in Turin, was fueled by the city's new role as the capital of national government. The decision in 1864, backed by strong pressure from the French, and effected the year after, to transfer the capital to Florence had dramatic consequences on the social and economic structure of the city (almost one-seventh of the population worked for the court and government, including

The Medioeval Village in the Parco del Valentino

hoteliers, craftsmen, and all the bureaucrats and officials). After a negative backlash in reaction to the change, including a revolt that was violently repressed, the city's sense of loss of identity was quickly transformed into an awareness of its economic potential. By 1884 Turin was in a position to host an international industrial exhibition, which was a huge success. The "Medieval Village" in the Parco del Valentino was built for the occasion. At the same time it was the first city to experiment with electrical street lights in Piazza Carlo Felice and the Parco del Valentino. Cultural life in Turin included such luminaries as Edmondo De Amicis, Vittorio Bersezio, and Davide Calandra. In 1898 the industrial exhibition was successfully repeated. The next year saw the completion of the extraordinary Mole Antonelliana tower (begun in 1863). Reaching a height of 167 meters, it was the tallest building in Europe.

In 1895 the first automobiles were already in circulation in Europe. And in 1899 at the Caffè Burello, Giovanni Agnelli Sr. and friends founded the world-renowned automobile manufacturer, Fiat. The company started out with a capital of 800,000 lire and 50 workers. In 1900 the first Motor Show was held in Turin and another famous Turin car manufacturer, Lancia, was founded in 1909. Another major event of the period took place in 1904, namely, the opening of the first Italian film studio; among the first productions of Itala Film produced was the colossal *Cabiria*, directed by Giovanni Pastrone, with subtitles by none other than Gabriele D'Annunzio. In 1911 Turin staged a World Expo. Then came the Great War with the demonstrations of 1917 and the occupation. Between the wars, Turin was relatively uninvolved in the rise of Fascism, and the city harbored many dissidents to the growing movement. At the outbreak of World War II half the population deserted the city, which was heavily bombed. The liberation of Turin by the fighters of the Resistance movement took place over April 25–28, 1945. A vast program of reconstruction began almost immediately, and by 1953 Turin was primed and ready for the coming economic boom, or "miracle," as it is often referred to in Italy. The city had a winning card in the form of the first genuinely utilitarian car aimed at the general public, produced by Fiat. The first model, the tiny "Seicento," was followed not long after by the ever-popular "Cinquecento," which has now become a kind of collectors' item, many examples of which can still be seen on the Italian roads. From 1950 to 1960 Turin was undeniably the most industrialized and advanced city in Italy. As a consequence, floods of people hopeful for a job migrated to Turin, which seemed to become one huge factory, and urban expansion went out of control, swallowing up the little peripheral towns. The 1970s saw a sudden change of trend and the first signs of recession. As the first large corporations began to feel the pinch in 1976, the negative effects of rapid industrial growth started to show throughout the city: housing and transport problems were rife, and the old city center was found to be lacking modern facilities. The period witnessed a surge of social movements and popular political activity, led by such groups as Sermig and Gruppo Abele. Turin was not immune to terrorism, either. Now these problems are a thing of the past, the city seems to have reclaimed its traditional role of a workshop or test-lab for new experiences in the economic, social, and cultural spheres.

Urban development: from the Roman urbs to the 16th century

The fortified Roman camp denominated *Julia Augusta Taurinorum* after Augustus was a rectangular *castrum* measuring 760 meters by 670. The streets were straight and divided the camp into *insulae*, or blocks, of about 75 meters per side. The old *decumanus* (the principal east–west causeway) lies under what is now Via Garibaldi. Though it is difficult to establish the layout of the camp with precision, the Roman *forum* probably stood where the Palazzo di Città stands today. No ruins of temples have been found, and the city does not seem to have had a triumphal arch. However, the remains of a theater can be seen in Via XX Settembre, and an amphitheater may have stood on the site of today's Piazza San Carlo. The roads were paved in gneiss, a stone quarried from the Susa area. The *castrum* boasted a system of sewers, rediscovered at the beginning of this century. The city walls, the ruins of which can best be seen near Porta Palazzo, stood 6–7 meters tall and 2 across, and were made of stone, brick, and mortar. They were fortified with towers, and four gates were positioned at the furthest points of the two main roads almost bisecting the camp perpendicular to one another (the *decumanus* and the *cardo*). This structure determined the city perimeter until the Middle Ages. In the 14th c. the city was still contained within the Roman walls, but developments began to spread outside toward San Donato, the River Dora, the Humiliati hospital, and the River Po. A castle was built near Porta Prae-

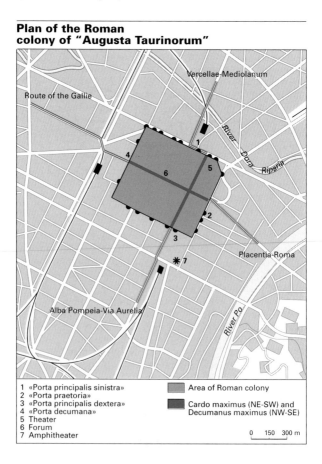

Plan of the Roman colony of "Augusta Taurinorum"

1 «Porta principalis sinistra»
2 «Porta praetoria»
3 «Porta principalis dextera»
4 «Porta decumana»
5 Theater
6 Forum
7 Amphitheater

Area of Roman colony

Cardo maximus (NE-SW) and Decumanus maximus (NW-SE)

0   150   300 m

still provided open land for cultivation, and was divided among the noble houses (*magna hospicia*) and the poorer areas (*carignoni*), with stables and vegetable gardens. This layout began to change toward the close of the 15th c., when there was a sharp increase in the construction of churches, monasteries, and houses in the Lombard style. The nobility used terracotta, with decorations, porches, and towers. The less elaborate type of housing was built largely in wood, and the simplest were structured around a central courtyard, although from 1464 this type of house was banned. At the beginning of the 16th c. the roads were nearly all paved.

Urban transformation in the 17th century

After the construction of the citadel (1566) the first major reworking of the city began with the arrival of the architect Ascanio Vitozzi (1584), and was organized along the lines of the new models of rational town planning. The program included the rebuilding of Palazzo Ducale (not completed), modifications to Piazza Castello, a new main road, a new borough (Contrada Nuova), and a new gate to the city opposite the facade of Palazzo Ducale. The present-day Via Roma developed in the area built from 1612–17 on. Another new road was to link Piazza Castello with Palazzo del Comune (now Via Palazzo di Città). New urban planning concentrated on the squares, and there were great displays of power in the ensuing architectural creations. The construction of individual buildings was very much subordinated to the overall architecture of each street. In 1619 the urban area was extended and the defensive enceinte improved. The plan, begun by Ercole Negro di Sanfront and continued by Carlo di Castellamonte, included an extension of the walls to the south, east, and west. Work began immediately but was staggered in two phases (1619, and 1630–37). It was then suspended and the curtain of wall continued to the north beyond Porta Nuova. Completion of the other parts of the plan took place much later (1673 and 1702 respectively). It was a long time before the construction of the "new town" actually took place. Though officially begun in 1620, by 1640 very little had actually been achieved. Notwithstanding these delays,

The rear of Palazzo Madama, in the middle of Piazza Castello

the city was eventually remodeled and the old and new towns were conflated to form a larger structure. Later on, the new road toward the River Po was built, as was Piazza Carlina, modeled on the French "places royales," but was subsequently modified to accommodate commercial ventures. Finally, the western ramparts were completed in time for the French invasion.

Urban expansion and planning 1700–1800

By the beginning of the 18th c. the city's fortifications were complete. It was now necessary to make Turin a city that could rival other European capitals. The brilliant Messina-born draftsman and architect Filippo Juvarra was entrusted with this ambitious urban and architectural transformation in 1714. Juvarra strove to establish harmony between the new buildings and the city's architectural heritage. He designed the new Military Quarters to the west and Porta Vittoria (Porta Palazzo) to the north. He then worked on a program of urban planning that included Santa Cristina, Palazzo Madama, San Filippo, the Carmine, and the buildings at Porta Susina. His aim was to represent the power of the sovereigns while providing a rational plan of the city. Successive architects continued his work and during the last part of the century further building and renovation schemes were carried out. The suburbs were also developed. In 1773 work began on Borgo Po and Borgo Dora, which grew as the area inside the walls began to get overcrowded. Further radical changes in city planning came with the French Revolution and the myriad new ideas it brought in its wake. Projects for the use of land were submitted and judged on the principle of public utility. Though never implemented, the various urban projects presented in 1802 were typical of a new attitude. In the Napoleonic era the city walls were demolished, and new wide avenues encircling the city were created; new bridges were built (although not always completed, and further expansion was planned. At the time of the Congress of Vienna, while Europe attempted to create a balance of power to maintain the peace after the upheavals of the Napoleonic Wars, the city turned its efforts to the creation of a series of imposing neo-classical squares, which served to link the various parts of the city. Piazza Vittorio Veneto was an ingenious solution, linking Via Po with the Napoleonic bridge, Piazza della Repubblica, and part of Piazza Carlo Felice. The new town, Borgo Nuovo, was also built in the neoclassical style. From the second half of the 19th c., work to extend the city to the south-west recommenced. The area around Porta Nuova (the railway station for trains to Genoa) was modernized and plans were made for the station at Porta Susa (this was the railway station for Novara). Large public buildings were constructed during the last half of the century in the west of the city: the prison (Nuove Carceri, 1862–70), the slaughter-house (1870–71), shortly afterward the military barracks of Lamarmora and Pugnani, and finally the railway building (1884). All these buildings were erected in the area around Corso Vittorio, in compliance with an overall urban plan. The 19th-c. buildings embody the aspirations and needs of the city's new upper class. However, after the 1880s there was a marked distinction between the wealthy areas of the city and the suburbs, or the "barriere," as they were called.

The metamorphosis of the city in the 20th century

The layout of the city in the late 19th and early 20th c. was determined by two planning schemes. The 1887 plan concerned the expansion of the urban area beyond the city boundaries, established in 1853. The second plan (1908) focused on residential and industrial buildings. At the end of the 19th c. each area in the city expanded, with little attention to the proper alignment of new buildings. Renovations were undertaken throughout the historic city, where many banks and commercial offices relocated (Via XX Settembre is an example). This pattern was consolidated in the 1930s with the reconstruction of Via Roma and the surrounding area. New developments sprang up in the city, along the old straight roads. Roads opened up the new marketplaces (Corso Svizzera and Corso Racconigi), and a star-shaped street plan was introduced which offered new and innovative solutions. The 1908 master plan incorporated several specific area plans and was geared to the new process of industrialization. In 1912 new city boundaries were sanctioned, and in 1913 a scheme for the redevelopment of the hillside area ("collina") was introduced. Low-income housing areas were developed, and with the abolition of the city boundary in 1930 a sort of ring road was created. The next planning scheme (1959) recognized the need for industrial complexes within the city. The last master plan, introduced in 1994, reflects the post-industrial situation of a city that is no longer expanding but where previous industrial space is being converted for the service industries.

Art in Turin

From ancient times to the Renaissance. As in many cities in Italy, urban development in Turin over the centuries resulted in the loss of many testaments of the city's past, including Roman monuments, the three early churches that preceded the present-day cathedral, and the important monasteries of San Solutore and Sant'Andrea. In the course of excavation work early this century, varied remains dating from the 7th c., and others from the 8th to 12th c. were discovered by archaeologists. A floor mosaic from the ancient presbytery (12th c.) and part of a frieze, now at the Museo Civico d'Arte Antica, were also unearthed. Remarkable examples of Roman art have been found near Turin at the Sacra di San Michele and at Vezzolano Abbey, where there are also wonderful examples of Gothic sculpture. The Arcivescovado has a *Virgin and Child* (1310–20), a fine example of Gothic court art. The progressive influence of Giotto's art is evident (Cappella delle Grazie at San Domenico, 1350–60); Giacomo Jaquerio (frescoes of Sant'Antonio, Ranverso) of the late Gothic period heralded the styles of the 15th c.

The coming of the Renaissance in Turin can be seen in the structure of the cathedral, which was constructed and decorated by a series of French, Florentine, and Lombard artists. After Antoine de Lonhy, the French Catalonian artist, figurative art in Turin was especially influenced by Giovanni Martino Spanzotti. His place was taken by Defendente Ferrari who dominated the artistic scene of the early 16th c.

Court art and the arrival of Baroque. From 1563, when Turin became the capital of the dominions of Savoy, its importance as a cultural center naturally increased. Literati, goldsmiths, architects, and painters, especially from Milan and Rome, came to seek patronage in the city. Portraiture at the royal court and paintings to commemorate dynastic events was much in request. Construction began on the Palazzo Ducale and on the decorations of the gallery connecting it with the castle (now Palazzo Madama), later destroyed by fire. Among the artists who worked in Turin in the late 16th and early 17th c. were Giacomo Rossignolo, Federico Zuccari, the Moncalvo, Ambrogio Figino, Cesare Arbasia, Antonio Parentani. An inventory of the Palazzo Ducale in 1631 lists statues and antique bronzes, numerous modern sculptures, together with a well-stocked library and some 800 paintings. Among the latter are paintings by Caravaggio and the Lombard school; the Bolognese school is represented by Guido Reni, Domenichino, and Guercino, who was greatly admired by Cardinal Maurizio, son of Charles Emmanuel I. Many of these paintings were acquired in Rome, Venice, and elsewhere by emissaries of the House of Savoy, which was eager to adorn the royal palace and other residences with fine works of art. Within a few decades Turin was not only the capital of the duchy but could compete in magnificence with other European capitals, and the plan of the city was modified accordingly. The work of famous architects gave the city the shape it has today. The royal architect Carlo di Castellamonte opened Piazza San Carlo, his son, Amedeo designed the facade of Palazzo Reale (1646–58). The highly versatile architect Guarino Guarini, a Theatine father, was commissioned for a spate of new building projects, imparting his unmistakable style to Baroque Turin. His masterpieces include the church of San Lorenzo and the chapel of the Holy Shroud, a truly audacious construction; plus the Collegio dei Nobili (now the Accademia delle Scienze) and Palazzo Carignano, both in brickwork, a style that was soon copied all over Piedmont. Guarini was succeeded by Filippo Juvarra, a Sicilian who worked in Turin at the beginning of the 1800s, but whose influence was felt for the rest of the century. His light and airy style anticipated the architecture of the Enlightenment and the neoclassical schools in both the palaces and the churches he designed. His style is epitomized in the great church at Superga, the Stupinigi hunting lodge, and his fabulous staircases, the most famous being the "Scala delle Forbici" in Palazzo Reale.

Cain and Abel, *by Guido Reni (Galleria Sabauda)*

The 19th century: palaces, new developments, monuments. Juvarra's successor, the lawyer-turned-architect Benedetto Alfieri, was one of several creative minds who fostered the shift into the neoclassical style. Building continued intensely throughout the ensuing century, and some of Turin's best-known monuments and many of its beautiful streets belong to this period, which saw the creation of the Parco del Valentino (1830), and Bonsignore's church of the Gran Madre di Dio, completed in 1831. Other signal works of the period include the soaring tower, designed by Alessandro Antonelli, which was begun in 1862 as a synagogue. There were many privately sponsored undertakings in the art world during this period. In 1842 the Società Promotrice di Belle Arti was founded, the first of its kind in Italy. Its role was to provide a link between artists and private collectors, as an alternative to official collections. There was no lack, however, of the latter: the Savoyard monarch Charles Felix (who purchased from Bernardino Drovetti the collection of Egyptian antiquities that formed the core of the collection now in the Egyptian Museum) commissioned a series of battles painted by Giuseppe Pietro Bagetti (1820, now in Palazzo Reale) who, along with César van Loo, was a dominant influence among Piedmontese landscape artists. King Charles Albert meanwhile commissioned the renovation of Palazzo Reale and the residences at Racconigi and Pollenzo by Pelagio Palagi; he opened the Reale Pinacoteca (1832), later the Galleria Sabauda, and financed and added to the collection of the Accademia Albertina. When the break was made from the academic world and the court, the artistic spheres underwent an important changes. The first reaction was the emergence of the School of Rivara, to which Avondo, D'Andrade, and Pastoris belonged, and these artists later created the "Medioeval

Village" in the Parco del Valentino (1884). Both they and Antonio Fontanesi received sponsorship in exhibiting their paintings from the said Società Promotrice. Sculptors at the time were involved with the large monuments that were being commissioned for the squares; Carlo Marocchetti's equestrian monument to Emmanuel Philibert (1838) in Piazza San Carlo stands out among these, as it ventures well beyond the limits of the academic tradition.

Casa La Fleur, in florid Liberty style

From Art Nouveau (Liberty) to the international avant-garde. Art Nouveau proved enormously successful at the Modern Art Exhibition in 1902 and, although short-lived, influenced much of the new privately commissioned architecture, leaving several good examples of this style in the city. It was here that same year at the Quadriennale exhibition organized by the Società Promotrice di Belle Arti, that Pellizza da Volpedo exhibited his famous *Fourth Estate*, a powerful admixture of realism and social comment. Giacomo Grosso, famous for his fashionable portraits and his voluptuous nudes, provided a welcome counterpoint with his more sensuous brand of realism. Tending more toward experimentation, while maintaining formal rigor, the work of Felice Carena, Evangelina Alciati, and Felice Casorati influenced a generation of artists. Carlo Levi and Francesco Menzio pursued a slight European tendency, and, along with Jessie Bosswell, Gigi Chessa, Nicola Galante, and Enrico Paolucci, in 1929 founded the group known as the "Turin Six," all exponents of a formal freedom in style, derived from Impressionism. Expressionism also had its advocates (Spazzapan) as did Futurism. The poet and publicist Filippo Marinetti had recently made public his first "Manifesto" in 1911 at the Teatro Chiarelli, and Luigi Fillia was the leader of the Futurist movement in Turin. An offshoot of Futurism might be considered more fertile with Nikolai Dyulgerov, Pippo Oriani, Ugo Pozzo, and Mino Rosso. The Turin art scene only really opened up to the avant-garde movements in Europe after World War II. The Turin Prize was promoted, among others by Umberto Mastroianni in 1947, under the banner of post-Cubism. In 1959 the Civica Galleria d'Arte Moderna e Contemporanea reopened, becoming an arena for new artistic and cultural ideas and a vital meeting point for the Turin art crowd. Supported by active private art galleries, the gallery housed a special section of experimental art that welcomed Dada and Pop Art, and fostered the development of Conceptual Art and what came to known as Arte Povera (Mario Merz, Giulio Paolini, Giuseppe Penone, Michelangelo Pistoletto, and others), now well represented in the galleries of Rivoli Castle.

In 1961 Turin celebrated the centennial of national unification with a large exhibition which saw the construction of the huge Palazzo del Lavoro, designed by Pier Luigi Nervi (who had already designed the pavilion at the Turin Exhibition in 1948) and the Palazzo delle Mostre in the shape of a sail, by Annibale and Giorgio Rigotti.

Turin: Instructions for Use

This ancient city developed into the modern capital of the Duchy of Savoy, then as the cradle of the Italian Risorgimento, finally becoming the first capital of the newly united Italy in 1861. Together with Milan and Genoa it forms a triangle that contains most of the heavy industry in Italy, and is famous for its automotive industry and other manufacturing. Although somewhat "off center" with respect to other Italian cities, Turin has always had great strategic importance because of its position at the foot of great Alpine passes. Turin also has an enviable geographical position at the confluence of three rivers – the Po, the Dora, and the Stura – and for that reason many attribute magical qualities to Turin, as they do to Lyon and Prague. It is surrounded by the majestic ring of the Alps and to the east are the Turin hills, the residential area of the city. The center has an interesting geometric plan, elegant Baroque and neoclassical buildings, beautiful squares, and 18 kilometers of arcaded streets. Looking down on it from a panoramic spot such as Superga or from the terraces of one of its famous monuments, the Mole Antonelliana, the city appears ordered and harmonious. Turin has a vast artistic heritage and numerous museums, some of which are unique, such as the Egyptian Museum, the Automobile Museum, or the Cinema Museum. There are also many Savoy palaces situated in the city and in its surrounding areas. There have been various waves of immigration to Turin: in the 19th c., politicians and intellectuals from other Italian states and bearers of new cultures, Istrians who arrived after the World War II. In the 1960s, 600,000 people emigrated to Turin from the south of Italy, increasing the population to over a million, and profoundly transforming the customs of the city. Since the middle of the 1980s, many immigrants have arrived from developing countries.

When to go

Like other northern Italian cities, Turin has a continental climate. The best periods to visit are therefore late spring and early fall. Fiat, and many other factories, close in August, which means that many restaurants and shops also close in this period. Hotels are crowded during the week but offer special weekend rates. Many trade fairs and congresses take place at the new Centro Lingotto (Via Nizza 262, tel. 6644111) The Lingotto was the first Fiat factory with an assembly line; it was built in the 1920s and has recently been transformed into a multifunctional center by the architect Renzo Piano. When the fairs are on you need to book a hotel well in advance.

How to get there

By car: the city is at the center of an efficient highway and tollroad system, connected to a city ring road, or beltway. The mountain passes of Frejus, Mont Blanc, and St. Bernard complete the system, and make international connections easier. The old city center,

The superb dining room of the Del Cambio restaurant, Piazza Carignano

which corresponds to the old Roman camp is closed to traffic from Monday to Friday from 7:30 to 10:30 except for residents or those from other regions of Italy. As the city has such a geometric layout, it is easy to drive around. It is fairly easy to park in the Blue Zone, in Piazza San Carlo, Piazzale Fusi, Corso Re Umberto and Corso G. Ferraris (3,000 lire per hour) and in the underground parking lots which you find in Via Roma (tel. 5613281), in Piazza Bodoni (tel. 8125048) and in Piazza E. Filiberto (tel. 4362941) (from 1,500 to 2,000 lire per hour).

By train: all national and international trains get in to the Porta Nuova train station. It

is in the middle of city (Piazza Carlo Felice, tel. 5613333) and many trams and buses stop there. Many trains from the Valle di Lanzo and the Valle d'Aosta arrive at the Porta Susa station (Piazza XXVIII Dicembre, tel. 538513) and the Milan–Venice train stops here. The Lingotto station (Via Pannunzio 1, tel. 65493757) is an alternative stop for trains going to Cuneo, Genoa, and the Val Pellice.

By plane: the airport of Torino Caselle is 15 km from the center and has daily flights to all the major Italian cities, the islands and many European cities (tel. 5676431/2/3/4). A

One of the barges along the River Po

bus service goes into the city every 30-45 minutes, arriving at Porta Susa station. Turin is also connected to Malpensa, Milan's intercontinental airport. Two coaches leave from the Stazione Autobus every day.

By bus: there is a very efficient bus service which connects the city to all the other towns in the region and many Italian and European cities (Stazione Autobus Corso Inghilterra 1, tel. 4332525).

Information

The Tourist Office (Azienda di Promozione Turistica - APT, Piazza C.L.N. 222, tel. 535901/535181, fax 530070, 9–7:30 Mon–Sat) has information on hotels, museums, shows and fairs. APT gives out a free map of Turin and various brochures. The Information Office run by the municipal council provides a similar service at the Vetrina per Torino, in Piazza San Carlo 161, free phone 167015475. The supplement with the newspaper *La Stampa*, on Friday is useful for information on what's going on in Turin, as are magazines given to tourists by hotels such as "A Guest in Turin," often available at the hotel desk. In summer there are boat trips on the River Po (Imbarco Murazzi, tel. 888010) and you can reserve the Tram Ristorante, a trolley-restaurant which takes you round the city as you eat (ATM, tel. 576422).

Accommodation

The Easy Nite agency, Via Sacchi 22, tel. 543953, fax 542944, will make reservations at any hotel or guest house. Good hotels are expensive (430,000 to 150,000 lire for a double room) and special rates are available at weekends only. The Week-End promotion, which offers prices inclusive of guided tours and reductions in shops and restaurants, is excellent (APT, tel. 535901/535181). The Ostello della Gioventù (Youth Hostel), in Via Alby 1, tel. 6602939, is at the bottom of the hill, two kilometers from the station of Porta Nuova.

Transport

There is no subway, but there is a good tram and bus service which operates from 5 am to 1 am. You must buy tickets before boarding, available from tobacconists, bars, and shops with the ATM/TT sign, and machines at the bus stops. When you're on the bus you must stamp them in a special machine. Tickets are valid for 70 minutes and you can stamp the ticket a second time before the 70 minutes are up and continue to the terminus. It is cheaper to buy a block of 10 tickets, or a shopping ticket that lasts for four hours, or various daily passes, or group passes (info on the free phone tel. 167019152). Taxis can be booked by phone: Central Taxi tel. 3399, Pronto Taxi tel. 5737, Radio-Taxi tel. 5730. There are also many taxi stands at major intersections and at the stations. The city has 11 bicycle tracks which run along the wide avenues. The best one goes from Val del Parco delle Vallere to San Mauro, along the River Po (13.5 km).

Green Turin

There are about 50 parks, some large some small. The municipal council looks after 16 million sq. m of parks and gardens; 16 sq. m per inhabitant. The Parco del Valentino is famous, even to Italians from cities other than Turin, because of a famous song from the past. It covers an area of 550,000 sq. m, and contains the Castello Valentino, the Botanical Gardens, a Medieval Village, a Fencing Club, and the Palazzina della Promotrice di Belle Arti. Palazzo Reale, the treasury, Parco Rignon and many others have lovely gardens. Crowning the city are the large green spaces, such as the Bosco di Superga, Parco della Maddalena, Parco delle Rimembranze, Parco di Stupinigi, and Parco della Mandria.

Gourmet time

The city has welcomed and developed various dishes from Piedmont, France, Italian regions and more far-flung countries. There are restaurants catering to all tastes, but prices are quite high. Hors d'oeuvres and first courses are refined and often made even richer by the addition of truffles, in season (autumn). People tend to have a quick snack at midday and many restaurants, even good ones, offer a very reasonably priced set menu. The snack bars, such as Break, are also quite good. There are many Chinese restaurants (more than 70), which are inexpensive. Turin has a reputation for its candies and chocolate.

Turin by night

There are lots of ways to spend the evening in Turin, both in and out of the center. You can get the latest information on discotheques, pubs, bars, beer cellars, piano-bars, and night clubs from *The News*, a free weekly magazine available in hotels and shops. If you want to know about classical music, concerts, or opera and ballet, telephone: Unione Musicale, Piazza Castello 29, tel. 544523; Auditorium RAI, Via Rossini 15, tel. 8104653; Auditorium Lingotto, Via Nizza 280, tel. 5611363; Teatro Regio, Piazza Castello 25, tel. 8815241; Conservatorio G. Verdi, Piazza Bodoni 6, tel. 888470; Settembre Musica tel. 4424777. For theater: Teatro Carignano, Piazza Carignano 6, tel. 5176246; Teatro Alfieri, Piazza Solferino 2, tel. 5623800; Colosseo, Via M. Cristina 73, tel. 6698034. Information on all these theaters is available in *Torino Sette* and *Vetrina Torino*, as mentioned above.

Shopping

The shops in Via Roma, the roads crossing it, and in the Via Pietro Micca have anything that even the most demanding customer might desire. The famous Italian and foreign fashion houses all have shops here. The big names for leather goods and furs, linen, porcelain, jewels, and books are all here too. In nearby streets are two excellent department stores: La Rinascente and Coin. Anyone looking for good quality at reasonable prices can shop in Via Garibaldi and streets crossing it. It is a pedestrian area and shopping is relaxed. It is also fun to visit the Mercato della Crocetta (Largo Cassini) where you can buy designer clothes at very low prices.

The four streets, Via Maria Vittoria, Via Bogino, Via Principe Amedeo, and Via San Francesco da Paola are traditionally the area with the best antique shops. At Via Cavour 17 there is a whole building of different antique shops, called Gallerie Principe Eugenio. Bric-à-brac enthusiasts shouldn't miss the Mercato del Batôn, held every Saturday, and the Gran Batôn, the second Sunday of the month, at Porta Palazzo. Turin also boasts a tradition of antique book shops and shops selling antique prints, usually in the center. You can get the addresses from the Yellow Pages.

The characteristic "Balôn" flea market

1 Turin

An obvious starting point for any tour of Turin is Piazza Castello, the heart of the city, with Palazzo Madama in the center, built on the site of the Porta Praetoria, from the enclosure wall of the Roman colony *Iulia Augusta Taurinorum*. The Roman *castrum* or encampment was crossed by a main causeway running approximately north to south (the *cardo*), now the Via Porta Palatina, almost bisected by another running at right-angles (the *decumanus*), later becoming the Dora Grossa and now called Via Garibaldi, which was straightened in 1736. On the northern side of Piazza Castello is the so-called "command zone," representing the supreme focus of the rule of the Savoy, a rule consolidated by Duke Emmanuel Philibert, who in 1563 transferred the capital of his duchy from Chambéry, in France, to Turin. Pre-

The equestrian monument to Emmanuel Philibert in Piazza San Carlo

ceded by Piazzetta Reale, the Palazzo Reale is connected by the Galleria Beaumont (housing the Armeria Reale) to the Segreteria di Stato (secretariat of state) and the Archivio di Stato (state archives), with the Teatro Regio opera house on one side, forming a complex that is the visible emblem of the power of the former duchy and of the later Savoyard royalty. The cathedral (dedicated to Saint John the Baptist), the only Renaissance building in this enclave of power, is linked to Palazzo Reale by the extraordinary chapel containing the Holy Shroud, built by Guarino Guarini, who also designed the neighboring church of San Lorenzo. Medieval remains are few – some can be seen in Via IV Marzo and Via Milano, site of the Gothic church of San Domenico, and other around Palazzo di Città, the symbol of municipal power.

Piazza Castello was the original nucleus around which the town began to grow. The area to the south was built by Carlo di Castellamonte in 1620, around the "new quarter," now Via Roma, with Piazza San Carlo, and the churches of Santa Cristina and San Carlo. The area to the east, toward the river, was planned in 1673 by Castellamonte's son Amedeo along the course of the River Po, while Guarini built the palace for the Collegio dei Nobili, then housing the Accademia delle Scienze, and today the two most prestigious museums in the city, the Galleria Sabauda and the Museo Egizio, or Egyptian museum. Guarini also built the palace of the princes of the cadet branch of Savoy-Carignano, which now houses the Museo Nazionale del Risorgimento Italiano. These buildings, together with the church of San Filippo, complete Piazza Carignano. The third phase of urban expansion occurred in 1714 under the auspices of Victor Amadeus II, at that time king of Sicily, who commissioned the architect Filippo Juvarra to undertake the project. The assigned area lay to the west, and included Via del Carmine, the church of the Carmine and the Quartieri Militari (military quarters). Elaborate noble palaces were erected in the area, such as Palazzo Falletti di Barolo, with its characteristic workshops and laboratories on the ground floor, the homes of the aristocrats on the *piano nobile*, and rented rooms on the upper floors. The rebuilding of the city thus initiated under Savoy rule continued throughout the 17th and 18th c., canceling the traces of earlier epochs, and bestowing on Turin the distinct Baroque flavor it conserves to this day.

The diagonal road, Via Pietro Micca, which was built in 1885 from the Piazza Castello, is an exception to the rigorous perpendicular grid of the city streets. Via Cernaia, which emerges in Piazza Solferino, is the main route to the southwest quarter known as the Cittadella, commissioned by Emmanuel Philibert and demolished in the middle of the 19th c., except for the keep of the old citadel. The dismantling in Napoleon's time of the fortified walls made way for the wide tree-lined avenues, a fine example of which is the rather eclectic Corso Vittorio Emanuele II, which leads to the Galleria di Arte Moderna and to the station at Porta Nuova. The surge in building in the 19th c. can be seen in the eastern quarters, where Antonelli's tower stands and where the vast Piazza Vittorio Emanuele I (now called Piazza Vittorio Veneto) was built in 1825. The Napoleonic bridge, or Ponte Vittorio Emanuele I is the link between the Baroque city and the new quarter along the Po, the fulcrum of which is the Gran Madre di Dio, a church built during the Italian Restoration (1815–30). In the area between the River Po and the Porta Nuova, the construction of the residential Borgo Nuovo began in 1825; here we find the Balbo garden and Piazza Cavour and Piazza Maria Teresa. A line of hills starts from Piazza Gran Madre and runs up toward the wooded Monte dei Cappuccini, once dotted with "vigne," or "vineyards," a name applied to the 17th- and 18th-c. summer residences, such as the Villa della Regina. The basilica by Juvarra surveys the city from its high position on the hill of Superga. In mid-19th c. a new park was created along the left bank of the Po, the Parco del Valentino, where a 17th-c. castle shares the grounds with a reconstruction (1884) of a medieval town, and the modern Torino Esposizioni complex. The construction of the buildings for the 1961 Expo south of the city dates back to the centenary celebrations for the Unification, when Italy was made a single country. Building in the area has been rather hasty and not very well planned, however. The Fiat factories at Lingotto and Mirafiori are emblematic of industrial development in the city, a development that began at the end of the 19th c.

The Art Nouveau architecture visible around Corso Francia, the long road that starts in Piazza Statuto (1864) and runs all the way out to the Castello Reale at Rivoli, dates from the beginning of the century. Out in the suburbs, meanwhile, together with Venaria Reale, the Stupinigi palace, and the castle of Moncalieri, Rivoli Castle is one of the great treasures of the House of Savoy. Originally far outside the city limits, these three residences have been virtually swallowed up by the increasingly urbanized periphery, creating one vast area of urban fabric without interruption.

1.1 The old city center

The first itinerary suggested here (map, pp. 176–177) effectively retraces the entire history of Turin, from its days as a Roman *campus*, represented by Porta Palatina, through the Middle Ages with the Gothic church of San Domenico, to the Renaissance of the cathedral, and beyond to the glorious era of Baroque. At the heart of Turin lies the predominantly Baroque Piazza Castello, which hosts an extraordinary concentration of historical buildings. Dominating the center of the square is Palazzo Madama, whose history goes back to Roman times; along its flank runs the wing of the royal palace containing the armory and library buildings; behind the main palace building one can see the conical domes of the chapel of the Turin Shroud and San Lorenzo, both masterpieces of Guarini. Other glories of the Baroque era can be

seen along Via Garibaldi and the adjacent streets, such as the church of the Carmine, Palazzo Falletti di Barolo, the Jesuit church of the Santissimi Martiri, the Cappella dei Banchieri e Mercanti, Palazzo di Città, and the churches of Corpus Domini and the Santissima Trinità. In the course of this itinerary we see other religious buildings and houses of prayer: the sanctuary of the Consolata, the huge 19th-c. charitable institutions of the Cottolengo (1828) and the Istituto Salesiano (1846), together with the basilica of Maria Santissima Ausiliatrice.

Piazza Castello (map I, pp. 178–179, A-B4). This large square plaza has always been the political fulcrum of the city, witnessing the city's evolving history, and providing the starting point for its physical development, which began along the main causeways,

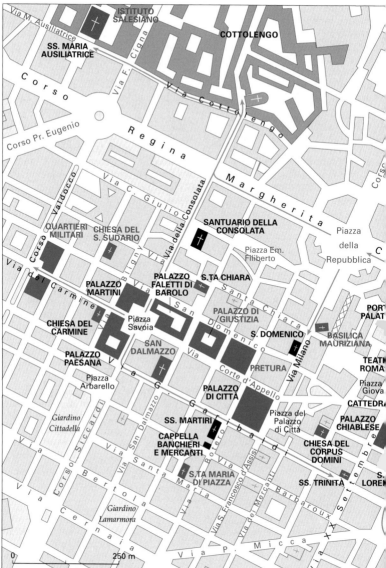

Via Roma, Via Po, and Via Micca (see itineraries 2 and 3), each one leading off in a different direction. The present aspect of Piazza Castello is the combined result of the work of three architects – Ascanio Vitozzi (1587), who developed the western side with arcaded buildings; Amedeo di Castellamonte; and Filippo Juvarra. Commanding the center is Palazzo Madama, once the ancient castle from which the square takes its name. This is surrounded by three monuments: the one in front commemorates the army of the Kingdom of Sardinia (Vincenzo Vela, 1857–59), the one to the south the Italian cavalry (Pietro Canonica, 1923),

and the one to the east Emmanuel Philibert, Duke of Aosta (Eugenio Baroni, 1937).

Palazzo Madama** (I, A-B4). The building's long history goes back to Roman times. The two anterior towers which are now enclosed in the Baroque facade of the building are the remains of the ancient Porta Praetoria from Roman times. In the 13th c. Guglielmo VII, Marquis of Monferrato, transformed the fortified gate into a castle. Later in the century the city passed definitively into the hands of the Savoy, and under the nobleman Ludovico d'Acaia in the 15th c. the castle was enlarged, with the ad-

The two ramps of the wide **staircase** sweep up from the entrance to an upper hall, one of Juvarra's many inspired creations.
In 1799 Palazzo Madama was temporarily occupied by a revolutionary government, and in 1801 the gallery linking it to the neighboring Palazzo Reale was destroyed. From 1832 to 1865 the palace housed the Regia Pinacoteca (royal picture gallery), and an astronomical observatory (demolished in 1920). The building subsequently played host to Subalpine Senate and then the Italian Senate (1848–64). After the tenancy of Supreme Court, in 1924 the first floor was donated to the city council; the city's collection of antiquities were transferred here in 1934.

Museo Civico di Arte Antica*. This museum comprises the city's collection of antiquities, and was founded in 1863 as the Museum dell'Arte Applicata all'Industria. It has been closed since 1988 for restoration on the building and the reorganization of the collections. Among its sculptures is an exceptional series from the Valle d'Aosta: the Courmayeur altar frontal (**Christ with the Virgin and Saints**, 13th c.), a *Pietà** and a *Virgin Mary* thought to be by Hans Klocker. Also of great beauty are the *Lament* from Val Vigezzo; the two *alabaster reliefs* from Novalesa and Aosta; the sculpted *stallwork** from the abbey at Staffarda, the **Virgin and Child** by Tino da Camaino (1313–15), and the six high reliefs from the *Tomb of Gastone di Foix**, by Bambaia. The collection of paintings includes some outstanding works from Piedmont, including two rare canvases by Giacomo Jaquerio relating the *Life of St. Peter** (1410–1515). There are paintings by Giovanni Martino

dition of the south section. No longer necessary for defensive purposes, the building was transformed into a ducal palace, which is named after the two figures who influenced the palace's transformation: Christine of France, wife of Victor Amadeus I, and regent for her son beginning in 1637; and Maria Giovanna Battista of Savoie-Nemours, second wife of Charles Emmanuel II, regent from 1675. Of the ambitious project presented by Filippo Juvarra only the new *facade** (1718–21) was actually executed. Giovanni Baratta was responsible for the relief of military trophies, the vases and statues on the balustrade.

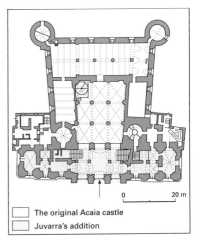

0   20 m

☐ The original Acaia castle
☐ Juvarra's addition

Plan of Palazzo Madama

177

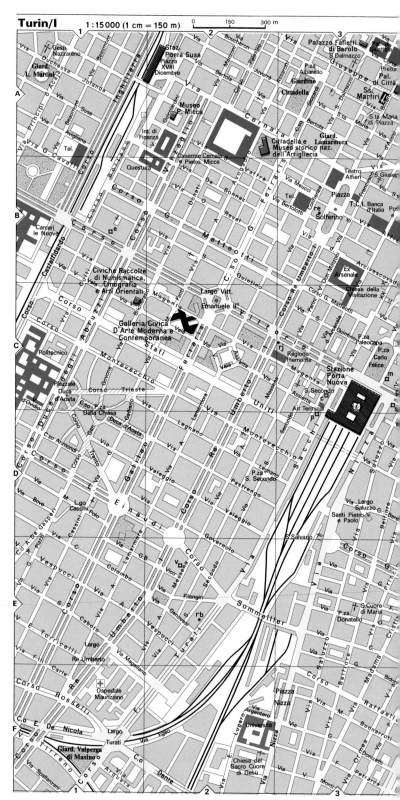

Turin/I 1:15000 (1 cm = 150 m)

0 · 150 · 300 m

Gesù
Nazzareno

Giard.
L. Martini

Staz.
Porta Susa

Piazza
XVIII
Dicembre

Palazzo Falletti
di Barolo

Pal.
di Giustizia

Pretur

Pal.
di Città

S.S.
Martiri

S.ta Maria
di Piazza

Museo
P. Micca

Int. di
Finanza

Caserme Cernaia
e Pietro Micca

Questura

Cittadella e
Museo storico naz.
dell'Artiglieria

Giardino
Cittadella

Giard.
Lamarmora

Teatro
Alfieri

S.S. Giuse

Piazza

T.C.I. Banca
d'Italia

Carceri
le Nuove

Civiche Raccolte
di Numismatica,
Etnografia
e Arti Orientali

Largo Vitt.

Emanuele IIº

Ex
Arsenale

Chiesa della
Visitazione

Galleria Civica
D'Arte Moderna e
Contemporanea

Politecnico

Piazzale
Duca
d'Aosta

Cso
Dalla Chiesa

Montevecchio

Corso Trieste

P.za
Paleocapa

P.za
Carlo
Felice

Regione
Piemonte

Stazione
Porta
Nuova

Aif Terminal

P.za
S. Secondo

Largo
Cassini Polo

Via Largo
Saluzzo

Santi Pietro
e Paolo

S.Salvario

Sommeiller

Filangini

P.za
Donatello

S.Cuore
di Maria

Largo
Re Umberto

Ospedale
Mauriziano

Piazza
Nizza

De Nicola

Giard. Valperga
di Masino

Largo
Turati

Università

Chiesa del
Sacro Cuore
di Gesù

178

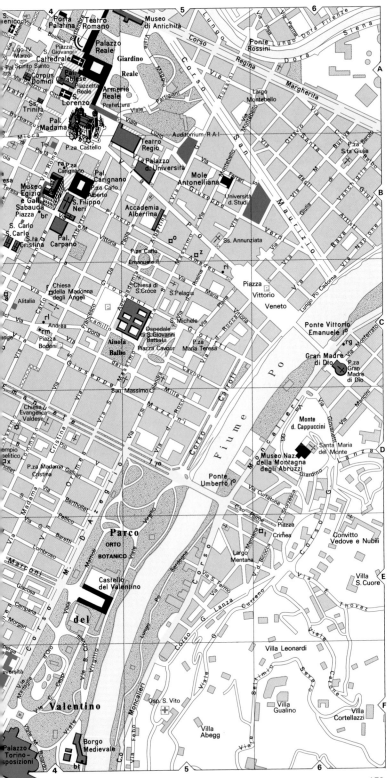

Porta Palatina
Teatro Romano
Museo di Antichità
Corso Regina Margherita
Ponte Rossini
Lungo Dora Siena

Piazza Giovanni
Basilica
Cattedrale
Palazzo Reale
Giardino Reale
Pal. Spirito Santo
Corpus Domini
Piazzetta Reale
Armeria Reale
Largo Montebello
P.za Baldi
S.ta Giulia

Ss. Trinita
Pal. Madama
S. Lorenzo
Prefettura
Auditorium R.A.I
P.za Castello
Teatro Regio

Pal. Carignano
Palazzo d. Università
Mole Antonelliana
Università d. Studi

Museo Egizio e Gall. Sabauda
S. Filippo Neri
P.za Carlo Alberto
Accademia Albertina
Ss. Annunziata

S. Carlo
S.ta Cristina
Pal. Carpano
P.za Carlo Emanuele II

Chiesa della Madonna degli Angeli
Chiesa di S.Croce
S.Pelagia
Piazza Vittorio
Veneto
Ponte Vittorio Emanuele

Alitalia
Piazza Bodoni
Aiuola Balbo
Ospedale di S.Giovanni Battista
S. Michele
Piazza Cavour
Maria Teresa

Gran Madre di Dio
P.za Gran Madre di Dio

Chiesa Evangelica Valdese
San Massimo
Monte d. Cappuccini
Santa Maria del Monte

Tempio elitico
P.za Madama Cristina
Museo Naz. della Montagna degli Abruzzi
Ponte Umberto

Parco
ORTO BOTANICO
Piazza Crimea
Convitto Vedove e Nubili

Castello del Valentino
Largo Mentana
Villa S. Cuore

Valentino
Villa Leonardi

Palazzo Torino-Esposizioni
Borgo Medievale
Osp. S. Vito
Villa Abegg
Villa Gualino
Villa Cortellazzi

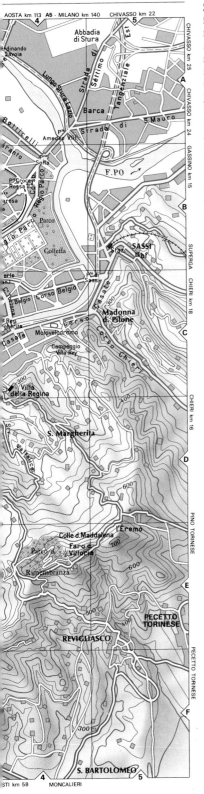

Spanzotti (**Tucker Madonna*** 1470–75), Defendente Ferrari, Macrino d'Alba, Gandolfino da Roreto, Antoine de Lonhy (*Holy Trinity**), Jan Miel (*Hunting scenes*); some landscapes by Victor Amadeus Cignaroli, and scenes of Turin life by Giovanni Michele Graneri and Pietro Domenico Olivero. The jewel of the museum is the **Portrait of a Man**** by Antonello da Messina (1476). Other paintings of note include *St. Michael and the Demon** by Jacopo Pontormo, plus works by Giulio Campi, Giacomo Ceruti, Giulio Cesare Procaccini, Tanzio da Varallo, and Orazio Gentileschi (*Our Lady of the Assumption**). Finest among the extensively *decoration* throughout the museum, are the rooms by Domenico Guidobono (early 18th c.) devoted to Spring, the Four Seasons, the Chinese study, and the northwest veranda.

The *ceramic collection*, one of the largest in Italy, has exceptional examples of foreign and Italian majolica, most from Piedmont (the Regio Parco factory in Turin, and the Rossetti factory at Borgo Po). The main European porcelain factories are also represented here (Meissen; Vienna) as are the leading Italian manufacturers, with the finest of Piedmont production (Rossetti, Vische, Regia Fabbrica, Vinovo). The *glass collection* of Murano blown glass (15th to 18th c.) is remarkable, as is that "after the Venetian tradition." Note two *lunettes* by Giovanni Martino Spanzotti and the **King's Window*** (12th c.) from the abbey of Saint Denis, Paris. The collection of *carved and stained glass* is unique in terms of quantity (about 200 pieces) and quality (early-Christian medallion, 3rd c. bearing a portrait of **Marcia Otacilia Severa***; and the triptych by Jacopino Cietario, 1460).

There is also a collection of *enamel* work from Limoges (several examples of raised-ground technique) of the 13th c.; objects in translucent and painted enamel from the 15th and 16th c.; snuff boxes; compact cases; and 18th-c. timepieces. The *ivory* collection includes French gothic objects, a large *altar* by the Embriachi (16th c.), two *sculpted groups* in ivory and wood by the Tyrolean artist Simon Troger (1741), and various miniature sculptures. Among the *furniture* of note is the inlaid furniture by Pietro Piffetti and Luigi Prinotto, and Giuseppe Maria Bonzanigo's carved furniture. A curious item is the "peota," a boat built in Venice in 1730 for Charles Emmanuel III.

The famous *Desana Horde* includes 47 ancient Ostrogothic items in gold and silver, including a set of fine **fibulae***. There is a re-

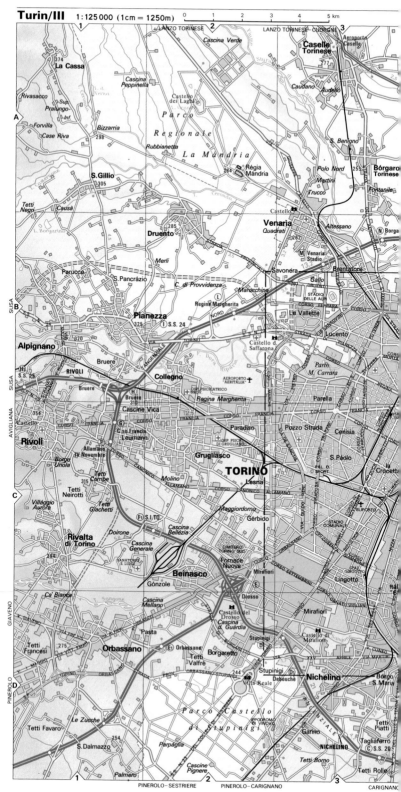

Turin/III

1:125 000 (1cm = 1250m)

0   1   2   3   4   5 km

La Cassa

Rivasacco
Pralungo Sup.
Forvilla   Inf.
Case Riva   Bizzarria
298

S.Gillio
374
305

Tetti
Negro   Causa

Druento
285

Merli

Parucca
S.Pancrázio   C. di Provvidenza

Pianezza
325   S.S. 24

Alpignano

Bruere
RIVOLI
S.S. 25   Collegno

Bruere
Brusa
310

Rivoli   Cascine Vica
354
Castello

C.sa Francia
Leumann
Allamana   Regina Margherita
IV Novembre
Borgo   315   Grugliasco
Uriola
Tetti
Combe
Tetti   Molino
Neirotti   ALLAMANO
Villaggio
Aurora   Tetti
294   Giachetti

Rivalta
di Torino   Doirone
Cascina
Generale
Ca' Bianca   SANATORIO
L. LUIGI
Cascina
Mellano   Fornace
Nuova
Gônzole   Drosso

Pasta

Orbassano   Orbassano
275   Tetti
Valfrè   Borgaretto
Tetti
Francesi

Le Zucche

Tetti Favaro
254
S.Dalmazzo
Palmero   Parpaglia

Cascina Verde

Caselle
Torinese
271

Castello
dei Laghi
Parco
Regionale
La Mandria
Rubbianetta
264   Régia
Mandria

Cascina
Peppinella

Caudano   Audello

Polo Nord   Borgaro
Torinese

Martini
Trucco   Fontanile

Castello

Venaria
Quadrati   262   Borga
Venaria
Stádio
Savonéra   Gallo
Maracchina   STADIO
DELLE ALPI
Regina Margherita
NORD   La Vallette
Lucento
Castello d.
Saffarona
Parco
M. Carrara
AEROPORTO   Parella
AERITALIA
OSP.PSICHIATRICO
PROV.   Pozzo Strada   Cenisia
Paradiso
OSP.PSICHI.
DI GRUGLIASCO   S.Páolo   la
Crocetta
TORINO
Lesna
Maggiordomo
Gérbido   STADIO
COMUNALE
S.I.TO
Cascina
Bellézia
CIMITERO
TORINO SUD
Mirafiori   Lingotto
Beinasco   Mirafiori
Castello di
Drosso   Mirafiori
Cascina
G. Guárdia
Stupinigi
Stupinigi   Nichelino
Villa Reale   Débouché   Borgo
S.Maria

Parco Castello
di Stupinigi
IPPODROMO
DI VINOVO   Garino   Tetti
Piatti
Tagliaferro
NICHELINO
S.S. 20
Cascine
Pignere   Tetti Borno   Tetti Rolle

SUSA
SUSA
AVIGLIANA
GIAVENO
PINEROLO

PINEROLO-SESTRIERE   PINEROLO-CARIGNANO   CARIGNANO
LANZO TORINESE   LANZO TORINESE-CUORGNÈ

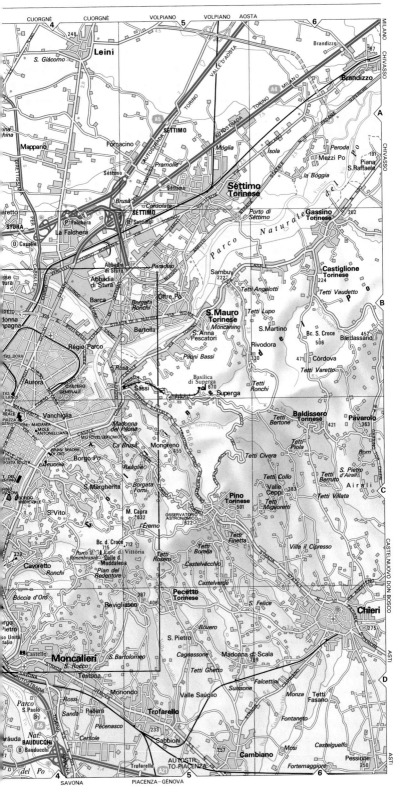

183

markable collection of Piedmont Baroque silver (*chalices** by G. B. Boucheron, dated 1789).

The museum also boasts 5,000 prints, 4,000 drawings, numerous examples of book bindings, textiles, and illuminated texts; in this last category the masterpieces are the *Bible** from c. 1270, the *Book of Hours** by Simon Marmion (ca. 1470), a *missal** by Domenico Cardinal Della Rovere (1490–92) and the famous **Heures de Milan****, the illustrations of which were begun in Paris in 1380 and finished in Flanders by Jan van Eyck and his school (1425–50).

Teatro Regio (I, A-B4-5), or royal theater. Under the arcade of Piazza Castello facing the Po (no. 215) stands the glass and metal facade of the new theater, designed by Carlo Mollino and Marcello Zavelani Rossi (with the collaboration of Carlo Graffi and Aldo Zavellani Rossi) and inaugurated in 1973; the front gate is by Umberto Mastroianni (1994). The remains of the old Teatro Regio – besides the facade, built by Benedetto Alfieri (1738–40) and destroyed in a fire in 1936 – have been annexed to the building housing the **State Archives**. This building was created by Filippo Juvarra (1731–34) for the conservation of documents, and has recently been beautifully restored.

Biblioteca Reale (I, A4. *Open Mon & Wed 8:30–5:45; Tues, Thurs, Fri, Sat 8:30–1:30*), or royal library. Passing under the arcade on the south side of Piazza Castello, finishing with the wing of the so-called *Segreterie di Stato* (Benedetto Alfieri 1737–57), we come to the entrance of the Royal Library and Armory, which occupies the west wing of the palace.

Begun by Charles Albert in 1831, the library occupies the ground floor, with a large rectangular hall with a barrel vault, designed by Pelagio Palagi.

The library boasts some 185,000 volumes, 4,300 manuscripts, rare incunabula, incisions, miniatures, bookbindings, and 2,000 drawings, including the Leonardo da Vinci collection, with his famous **Self-portrait*** in red crayon.

Armeria Reale* (I, A4. *Open Tues & Thurs 2:30–7:30; Wed, Fri, Sat & Sun 9–2; groups on Sun 9:45, 10, 10:45, 11:30, 12:45, 1pm; closed Mon*). One of the most important collections in Europe, the royal armory was opened to the public in 1837 by Charles Albert of Savoy, who had asked Vittorio Seyssel d'Aix to gather up and catalogue the material from the various arsenals of

Turin and Genoa. Additions were made to the collection through acquisition in the 19th c. It now occupies three halls on the first floor, which is reached via the *grand staircase* by Benedetto Alfieri (1740). These are the Sala della Rotonda, the Galleria del Beaumont, and the Medagliere. The Sala della Rotonda, previously a theater and later a ballroom, was refurbished by Pelagio Palagi (1841–45). The ceiling was decorated by Carlo Bellosio and Francesco Gonin. The Galleria, originally designed by Juvarra and finished by Benedetto Alfieri, takes its name from Claudio Francesco Beaumont, who painted the vaults with the *Stories of Aeneas* (1738–43,1764). The stuccowork is by Giuseppe Muttoni (1737–41), the sculptures at the side of the ovals by G. B. Bernero (1787,1790) and Giacomo Spalla (1832). The four allegorical statues were sculpted by Ignazio and Filippo Collino in 1760–63. Together with Simone Martinez, they also added the cupids under the consoles. The Medagliere room was designed by Palagi (1835–39) for the collection of medals and coins. There are paintings by Pietro Ayres and reliefs by Diego Marielloni. The collections include weapons from the prehistoric, classical, and medieval periods (*Sword of St. Maurice*), and from the 15th c. Most of the arms are from the Italian and German schools of the 16th c., however, the latter being particularly well represented. Noteworthy exhibits include the *processional apparatus* series from the Milanese school, and the work of the Lombard armorer Pompeo della Cesa; the *suit of armor of Don Diego Felipe Guzman,* standing over two meters tall. The *hunting accouterments* given to Charles Emmanuel II by Maximilian I of Bavaria in 1650 is an important part of the collections of weapons belonging to the House of Savoy. There are many firearms, swords, stilettos, poniards, daggers, knives, and spears. Dating from the 19th c. are several Napoleonic trophies (Napoleon's sword) and arms belonging to three kings of the House of Savoy: Charles Albert, Victor Emmanuel II, and Humbert I. The Oriental collection includes arms from Turkey, the Caucasus, Georgia, Japan, Indonesia, and the Indo-Persian area. Other curious exhibits include the 19th-c. *wooden horses* covered with horse hide; the one called "Favorito" belonged to Charles Albert, who took it with him into exile in Oporto.

Piazzetta Reale (I, A4). Honored guests entered Palazzo Reale via the Piazzetta Reale, with its *cast-iron gate* by Pelagio Palagi

One of the halls of the Palazzo Reale

Oporto.

Piazzetta Reale (I, A4). Honored guests entered Palazzo Reale via the Piazzetta Reale, with its *cast-iron gate* by Pelagio Palagi (1835), and the *Dioscuri* statues by Abbondio Sangiorgio (1846).

Palazzo Reale* (I, A4. *Open daily 9–7, except Mon; guided tours only; last entrance 5:40*). The building of the royal palace was begun in 1646 by Christine of France to replace the old bishop's palace. The facade by Carlo Morello (1658) has remained intact. The building has a square plan with an internal courtyard and was the residence of the monarch of the Kingdom of Sardinia until 1859, and subsequently of the king of Italy, Victor Emmanuel II, until 1865. The decorations and furnishings are evidence of the

numerous artists who worked here between the 17th and 19th c. On climbing the monumental staircase by Domenico Ferri (1864–65), embellished with statues and painting all dating from the 19th c. with the exception of the *Monument to Victor Amadeus I* (Andrea Rivalta, 1619), one reaches the first floor, where the visit begins. The spacious *Salone degli Svizzeri**, with a frieze by the brothers Antonio and Gian Francesco Fea (1658–1661) portraying the *Glories of the Saxon Race of Wittekind*, ancestors of the House of Savoy, a painting by Carlo Bellosio (1842) and another by Palma Giovane, the great **Emmanuel Philibert at the Battle of San Quintino** (1557), leads to the *Galleria della Sacra Sindone*, with access to the chapel, the *Galleria delle Battaglie,* and the ingenious **Scala delle Forbici*** by Juvarra (1720), followed by a series of reception rooms. The first of these is the *Sala dei Corazzieri* or *Sala delle Dignità* where the walls are hung with two beautiful tapestries depicting *The Elements*, by Beauvais weavers (ca. 1695). The next hall is the *Sala degli Staffieri* or *Sala delle Virtù*, or hall of virtues, which are represented in the frieze and painting by Charles Dauphin at the center of the highly ornate ceiling. The walls are hung with Gobelin tapestries portraying the life of *Don Quixote* (1746–47). Then comes the *Sala dei Paggi* or *Sala delle Vittorie*, with paintings and decorations from the 19th c. The next room, the ornate *Sala del Trono** (throne room) has gilt decorations from various periods and an *Allegory of Peace* (1662) by Jan Miel on the ceiling, and a beautiful marquetry floor (Gabriele Capello, 1843). The *Sala delle Udienze* and *Sala del Consiglio* have 16th-c. ceilings, while the furnishings and decorations are by Pelagio Palagi, and were commissioned by Charles Albert. The **Gabi-**

Piazza Castello (from left): San Lorenzo, Palazzo Reale and Palazzo Madama

185

its altarpiece by Defendente Ferrari and Charles Albert's *prie-dieux*, with precious inlay work by Luigi Prinotto (1732) and Pietro Piffetti, one reaches the *Sala della Colazione*, with 17th-c. fresco and frieze and a fine inlaid *fire screen* by Giuseppe Maria Bonzanigo, from which the octagonal alcove opens. The **Galleria del Daniel*** with which Carlo Emanuele Lanfranchi completed, under the auspices of Vittorio Amedeo II, the eastern wing, takes its name from Daniel Seyter, who painted the vaults with the *Apotheosis of Vittorio Amedeo II* (1688–92). Next come the queen's apartment: the *bedroom*, the ceiling painted by Seyter, the *workroom*, the *dressing room* with two pieces of furniture by Piffetti (1731–33), the *prie-dieux*, the *Sala delle Cameriste*, the *Machine Room* (where the queen's private manually-driven elevator arrived) and the queen's private chapel, decorated by Benedetto Alfieri (1739). From the *Gabinetto delle Miniature*, named after the collection of miniatures of the House of Savoy (18th/19th c.), one comes to the *Sala da Pranzo*, or dining room, with tapestries woven in Turin, and then the *Sala del Caffè* decorated by Lanfranchi (1685–90). Part of Charles Albert's collection of Japanese and Chinese vases (1750–1850) is in the sumptuous **Camera dell'Alcova***, with its 17th-c. gilt decorations. The *Sala del Trono della Regina,* or throne room of the queen, follows, with marble oval inlays (1739) and on the ceiling the *Triumph of the Graces* (17th c.), and the *Sala da Ballo**, or ballroom, with its white marble columns, designed by Palagi after joining two salons, who also did the *Olympus* on the ceiling.

On the second floor are other apartments belonging to the dukes of Savoy and Aosta, with decorations and furnishings from the 18th and 19th c. (open on special occasions). On the ground floor, the *apartment of Madama Felicita*, sister of Vittorio Amedeo III, who lived there from 1788 on, has been opened.

Giardini Reali (I, A4-5), or royal gardens. Access to these gardens is through the arcaded courtyard; they were designed by André Le Nôtre (1697–98) and are enclosed by the fortifications, with the grassy rampart and the bastion of San Maurizio; full of statues in the flower beds. The *fountain* with the mythological group at its center is by Bernardo Falconi and Giuseppe Maria Carlone (1688).

San Lorenzo* (I, A4). This church in the northwest corner of Piazza Castello, just

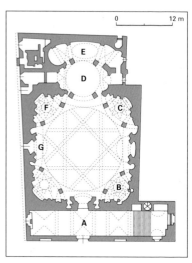

Plan of the church of S. Lorenzo

before Palazzo Reale, has a simple facade (1811–13) which blends in with the nearby buildings. It was built in 1634 to fulfill the vow made by Emmanuel Philibert on the eve of the Battle of San Quintino (10 August 1557). However, it was thanks to Guarino Guarini, the Theatine father and architect, who arrived in Turin in 1666, that the church was finally consecrated in 1680. Across the *Oratorio dell'Addolorata* (1846; plan above, A), built on the site of the ancient church of Santa Maria del Presepe, is the *entrance* to the church, its convex octagonal plan, crowned by a ingenious dome and lantern of interwoven arches. The complex Baroque interior is rich with sculptures, paintings, stucco work, colored marble, and gilding. Guarini also designed the altars. The first altar to the right (B) carries a *Crucifixion* by Andrea Pozzo (1678–79) and the third (C) has a beautiful *altar frontal*. The presbytery is on an elliptical plan, with a small hexagonal dome. Guarini's crowning masterpiece is the *high altar* (1680–84) with its bas-relief showing the *Vow of Emmanuel Philibert before the Battle of San Quintino* by Carlo Antonio Tantardini. In the choir (E) there is an altarpiece with *Saint Lawrence* by Marcantonio Franceschini between the cornice by Ignazio Perucca (1775) and the *stalls* with inlaid panels (Carlo Maria Ugliengo, 1730). The third altar on the left (F) has an altar frontal by Pierre Dufour; the second (G) carries a marble group of the *Annunciation* by Giuseppe Maria and Giovanni Domenico Carlone (1670–80). The beautifully carved *pulpit* is by Stefano Maria Clemente (1752), and the organ with its ornate *cantoria* (organ loft) by Carlo Amedeo Botto.

Palazzo Chiablese (I, A4). The side of this building makes up the left side of Piazzetta Reale (entrance at Piazza San Giovanni 2), and is directly connected to Palazzo Reale. Built in the 17th c., the palazzo was modified and decorated by Benedetto Alfieri (1740). The second son of Charles Emmanuel III, Benedetto Maurizio, Duke of Chiablese, and other members of the Royal Family resided here. It now houses the Soprintendenza Archeologica and the Soprintendenza dei Beni Ambientali e Architettonici (arts and archaeological departments). It was formerly occupied by the **National Museum of Cinema** which closed was transferred to the Mole Antonelliana in 1995; the museum collections include equipment (ceramics, paintings, prints, pantoscopes, and a *magic lantern* from the 18th c.); 14,000 posters, including one of the Cinématographe Lumière (1896); a large collection of stills and films (about 2,500 in all), and a sound library.

Cathedral* (I, A4. *Open 7:30–12, 3–7*). The cathedral is dedicated to Saint John the Baptist, the patron saint of Turin, and is the only example of Renaissance art in the city. Erected in 1491–98 upon commission by Cardinal Domenico della Rovere, the cathedral was designed by the Tuscan architect Meo del Caprina. The classic Renaissance *facade* is in white marble, the upper central order of rounded two-light windows crowned with a tympanum, and three *portals** decorated with reliefs by Meo del Caprina and other Tuscans; the wooden doors are the work of Carlo Maria Ugliengo (1712). Rising beyond the facade is the octagonal dome of the cathedral, and that of the chapel of the Holy Shroud (Sacra Sindone). The church's *interior* is on a Latin-cross plan with a nave and two aisles. In a niche behind the facade is the **Tomb of Anne de Crequi*** (A, plan at the side) by a French sculptor (mid-16th c.), comprising a kneeling figure accompanied by five weeping mourners; on the left (B) are some *tombstones* and a painting by Antonio Parentani depicting *Angels and Patron Saints of Turin* (1602). In the first chapel on the right (C) is a statue in terracotta, the *Madonna Grande* (1460–70); in the second chapel on the right (D), the Cappella di San Crispino e San Crispiniano, is the *polyptych of the Compagnia dei Calzolai** by Giovanni Martino Spanzotti and Defendente Ferrari (1498–1504) and on the walls the eighteen

histories of the titular saints, which also figure in the folding panels of the polyptych. In the third chapel on the right (E) is an altar frontal by Bartolomeo Caravoglia (1655); and in the sixth chapel (F) are frescoes of *The Miracles and Martyrdom of the Sts. Cosmas and Damian,* by Giovanni Andrea Casella (1660). In the south transept (G) is the 15th-c. chapel, or *Cappella del Crocifisso*, with an altar by Ignazio and Filippo Collino (1787), adorned by the *Crucifix* by Francesco Borello and wooden *statues* by Stefano Maria Clemente; the marble statues of St. Christine and St. Theresa by Pierre Legros (1715) were transferred from the church of Santa Cristina (see itinerary 2). Through a 19th-c. portal we come to the *sacristy* (H), where there are some paintings from the Piedmontese school of the 15th c. (*Baptism of Christ* by Spanzotti and Ferrari, 1508–11). In the presbytery (I), there are choir *stalls* carved by Giuseppe Stroppiana (1742–44). In the north transept (L) is the *royal tribune* sculpted by Ignazio Perucca (1775). There are paintings by Caravoglia in the fourth (N) and fifth (M) chapels in the north aisle and in the second (O) is an altar frontal by Charles Dauphin, *Mystical Communion of St. Honoratus.*

Behind two tall portals (14–15 m) at either side of the presbytery a flight of steps in black marble (P) climbs to the **Chapel of the**

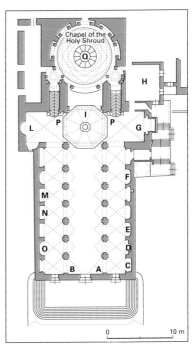

Plan of the cathedral

Holy Shroud*, the ingenious work of Guarino Guarini, begun in 1668 and finished in 1694 after his death. The circular chapel, badly damaged by fire in April 1997, and therefore temporarily closed, is lined with precious black marble and culminates in an extraordinary luminous **dome***. One of the most significant works of Italian Baroque, the dome is composed of six tiers of segmental arches; each one is pierced, admitting a flood of light. The white *funeral monuments*, erected by Charles Albert in 1842 to the memory of his ancestors, stand out against the black marble. At the center of

Guarini's dome on the Chapel of the Holy Shroud

the chapel is the altar (Q) by Antonio Bertola (1694), in which stands a silver casket containing the *Holy Shroud*. The holy relic is held to be the shroud in which the body of Christ was wrapped after His deposition from the Cross; it came to be property of the House of Savoy, and was kept at Chambéry until the duchy was transferred to Turin.

On the left of the cathedral stands the detached *campanile of Sant'Andrea* (1468–70), designed by Filippo Juvarra (1720–23).

Teatro Romano (III, A4), or Roman theater. Along the Via XX Settembre, past the new wing of Palazzo Reale (begun in 1899), we come to the archaeological zone of Turin. On the right, beyond the gate, are the remains of the *Roman Theater*, begun

in the late Augustan or Tiberian period and enlarged to a diameter of approximately 120 meters. Still visible are the outer ring of the colonnaded gallery, and some of the tiered seating of the *cavea*, and part of the *orchestra*.

Porta Palatina* (I, A4). This city gate, one of the best-conserved of its kind, was part of the *Roman walls* enclosing the city, and was built in the 1st c. A.D. It is built of brick and has two towers with sixteen sides which are linked by a bridge (*interturrium*) on two orders of windows, the upper rectangular and the lower arched. There are four barrel-vault passages at the bottom, two for carts and two for pedestrians. On the inside, we can see remains of the courtyard with its Roman paving.

Museo di Antichità (I, A5. *Open Tues to Sun, 9–19; Sunday and public holidays 2–7; closed Mon*), or museum of antiquities. The museum is newly located at Corso Regina Margherita 105, in the old *orangerie* of Palazzo Reale, and has a large collection of archaeological exhibits from prehistoric, late Roman, and Barbarian periods. The original nucleus of the collection dates from the reign of Emmanuel Philibert. Later additions were made and the collection was moved to the gallery linking Palazzo Reale with Palazzo Madama. In 1723 Victor Amadeus II had all the archaeological exhibits from the various Savoy residences gathered up and transferred, together with the Drovetti Egyptian collection acquired in 1823, to the Palazzo dell'Accademia delle Scienze. The collection was further augmented with finds from excavations in Piedmont; the museum was transferred to its present site and reopened in 1989. On the ground floor is the *Sala della Scultura* containing Greek and Roman bas-reliefs (*Kairos; throne** from Luni) and statues, among which were some accomplished Roman replicas of famous works by Polyclitus, Praxiteles, and others (the Phidian *Amazon*; the *Emperor's Torso* in porphyry). The *Sala delle Sculture di Susa* has a series of Greek and Roman portraits (*Head of Caesar*), small sculptures, the polychrome mosaic with *Orpheus and the Wild Animals* (3rd c.), found near Cagliari, Sardinia, three large loricate (cuirassed) statues from Susa (1st c.), and casts of the frieze on arch at ancient Segusio (Susa). On the first floor exhibits include Greek and Italiot ceramics (*psykter* by Euthymides), the *Etruscan collection* (vases, bronzes, bucchero ware, canopic jars, cinerary urns), *prehistoric* bronzes and fibulae, the *Cypriot collection* (ceramics, statues in limestone and decorated terracotta). One hall in the museum is dedicated to archaeological finds in Piedmont from the Paleolithic period onward. Worthy of note: the *horde* found in 1928 at Marengo (*Bust of Lucius Verus*, A.D. 161–169), objects in bronze from the ancient settlement of Industria (*tripod*), a marble acrolith from Alba with *female deities* and funerary objects.

San Domenico* (I, A4). Going west back up Corso Regina Margherita we come to *Piazza della Repubblica* (Gaetano Lombardi, 1819), the largest square in Turin, which is joined to *Piazza Porta Palazzo*. The latter, together with *Via Milano* was designed by Filippo Juvarra. At the intersection with Via San Domenico is the church of San Domenico; the only Gothic building in Turin. It was erected in the first half of the 14th c. and practically rebuilt in 1776. At the beginning of the 19th c. work was carried out by Riccardo Brayda and Alfredo D'Andrade on the facades, especially the one in terracotta with tracery, rose windows, and buttresses with pinnacles. The interior has a basilican plan, comprising a nave and two aisles with rib vaults; the *Chapel of the Rosary* opens out at the end of the right aisle. There is a beautiful painting by Guercino, the *Madonna of the Rosary and Sts. Dominick and Catherine of Siena* (1637), framed by carved panels by Stefano Maria Clemente. On the left of the main altar (Benedetto Feroggio, 1777) is the *Chapel of the Madonna delle Grazie*, with precious **frescoes*** (1350–60) by the so-called Maestro di San Domenico: in the lunettes *Annunciation, Majestas Domini, Virgin Mary Enthroned with Child and St. Thomas, presenting three of the faithful*, in the middle the *Apostles*; the venerated *panel-painting* of the Virgin by a Piedmontese artist of the beginning of the 16th c. On the fourth altar on the left is a fresco of *Charity of St. Anthony Pierozzi*, by Giovanni Martino Spanzotti (1521–28); at the third altar on the left is a late 15th-c. fresco by the Maestro di Sant'Anna (*Blessed Amadeus IX of Savoy*). In the large *Sala Cateriniana*, next to the sacristy and decorated with lunettes of *scenes from the Old Testament* (18th c.), is the *banner* of Andrea Provana at the Battle of Lepanto (1571). In the corridor, previously a cloister, are frescoes and the 15th-c. tomb stones.

The Cottolengo complex, and Maria Santissima Ausiliatrice (II, B3). On returning to Corso Regina Margherita we come to the *Piccola Casa della Divina Provvidenza*, the so-called Cottolengo. It is a vast complex of hospitals, schools and homes for the poor and the sick (run by voluntary staff), founded by Giuseppe Benedetto Cottolengo (1786–1842, canonized 1934) and established on this site in 1832. Further on stands the Salesian institute, founded by Giovanni Bosco (1815–88, canonized 1934) for the teaching of poor children and orphans. The church of *Maria Santissima Ausiliatrice* where the remains of the saint are kept, was designed by Antonio Spezia (1865–68), and later underwent certain modifications. Crowning the huge dome is a statue of the *Virgin Mary* (Camillo Boggio, 1867). The interior has a single nave, and the painting over the altar is by Tommaso Lorenzone (1868).

Santuario della Consolata* (II, C3). On the way back to the center of town we cross the small Piazza della Consolata, with its church of the Consolata. Worship of Maria Consolatrice (Our Lady of Consolation) began in the 12th c. when the original church dedicated to Saint Andrew was built; the church was later enlarged, to plans by Guarino Guarini. A presbytery designed by Juvarra was added in 1729, as were side chapels by Carlo Ceppi, in 1899–1904. Across the neoclassical portico (1860; A, plan p. 190), with the Romanesque campanile of Sant'Andrea (B; 11th c.) to one side, is the entrance to the *hall of Sant'Andrea*, an oval shaped vestibule with frescoed ceilings by Mattia Bortoloni (*Triumph of Our Lady of the Assumption*). Steps on the right lead down to the ancient *chapel of the Madonna delle Grazie* (D), decorated with marble and stucco; the first chapel on the left (E) contains three paintings by Vittorio Amedeo Rapous (ca. 1760). Under the arch is the *Santuario della Consolata*, comprising a hexagonal shrine by Guarini, a high frescoed dome by G. B. Alberoni and G. B. Crosato, to designs by Bibbiena; an oval presbytery by Juvarra; four elliptical chapels and two smaller ones. On the elaborate high altar (F) by Juvarra (1714) note

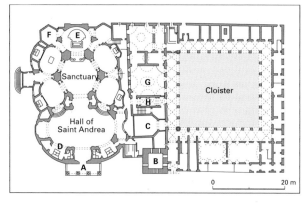

Plan of the Sanctuary of the Consolata

the 15th-c. icon of the Virgin Mary Hodigitria, derived from the Roman icon of Santa Maria del Popolo, and much venerated by the people of Turin. In the choir stalls left (G) of the presbytery are statues of **Queen Maria Theresa and Queen Maria Adelaide in prayer**, by Vincenzo Vela (1861). In the main sacristy (H) are some remarkable carved cabinets (1730–36); in the gallery (I) are thousands of antique and modern votive offerings.

Church of the Carmine (II, C3). Via della Consolata leads to *Piazza Savoia*, dominated by an *obelisk* in commemoration of the Siccardi Laws (1850); along Via del Carmine stands the church of the Carmine, designed by Filippo Juvarra (1732–36), with a facade by Carlo Patarelli (1872). Restored after heavy bomb damage in World War II, the light and airy *interior* with its single barrel-vaulted nave, and three galleried chapels on each side, is worthy of note. Note also the large painting, *Madonna del Carmine and the Blessed Amadeus of Savoy* (1755–60), adorning the apse, by Claudio Francesco Beaumount. In the third chapel on the right is the *Our Lady of the Immaculate Conception with the Prophet Elijah*, by Corrado Giaquinto.

The **Quartieri Militari** (Military Quarters) at the crossroads of Via del Carmine with the Corso Valdocco, were designed by Juvarra (1716–30), along the axis of the third urban expansion project.

Palazzo Falletti di Barolo (I, A3. *Open Mon & Wed 10–12 and 3–5; Fri 10–12; closed Tues, Thurs, Sat & Sun*). Some beautiful aristocratic residences were built in this area, among them *Palazzo Martini di Cigala* (Via della Consolata 3), *Palazzo Paesana di*

Saluzzo (Via della Consolata 1/b) and *Palazzo Falletti di Barolo*; the latter was enlarged in 1692. The Italian patriot Silvio Pellico was a guest in Palazzo Falletti when he returned from the Spielberg prison in 1830. There are inlaid 17th-c. ceilings and decorations and furnishings designed by Benedetto Alfieri in 1743.

Via Garibaldi (I, A3-4). The long pedestrian avenue that begins in the Piazza Castello follows the line of the Roman *decumanus*. It was the main link between Turin and the valley of ancient Segusio (Susa) and thence Gaul, and was called the "Dora Grossa," because a stream – which was used as a sewer – ran along the center of the road. The road was straightened in 1736, and the facades of the buildings aligned along its course.

Santi Martiri* (I, A3). At Via Garibaldi 23, this church is dedicated to the patron saints of the city, Saints Solutor, Adventor, and Octavius. It was built in 1577 by the Jesuits to designs by Pellegrino Tibaldi. The *interior* is richly decorated with marble, bronze, and stucco, and has a single nave, the vault of which was frescoed by Luigi Vacca (1844). The first chapel on the right has a painting by Federico Zuccari, *St. Paul* (1607). The second has a bronze statue by Giuseppe Riva, *St. Francis Saverio*. Behind the high altar designed by Filippo Juvarra is an oval panel painted by Gregorio Guglielmi, the *Virgin Mary and the Titular Saints* (1765–66). The second chapel on the left has an altar dedicated to Saint Ignatius of Loyola by Andrea Pozzo (1678), with an altar frontal by Sebastiano Taricco. The first chapel on the left contains the statue of the *Virgin Mary* by Tommaso Carlone (1663). The *sacristy* is noteworthy, with a frescoed vault by

Michele Antonio Milocco; the wooden carvings are particularly fine.

Cappella della Pia Congregazione dei Banchieri e Mercanti* (I, A3). To the right of the church of the Santissimi Martiri, through the *house of the Jesuits*, we enter this church with its series of domical vaults, and then into the chapel (1692). The fresco on the vault, *Paradise, Prophets, Sibyls and Biblical Scenes*, is by Legnanino. The wood carvings of the *Doctors of the Church* are by Carlo Giuseppe Plura. On the walls over the choir stalls are eleven paintings glorifying the Epiphany, after Andrea Pozzo and his school, Legnanino, Nicolò Carlone, Sebastiano Taricco, and Luigi Vannier. In the sacristy is an altarpiece by Moncalvo, a throne by Michele Brassié (1792), and a universal *mechanical calendar** (1835).

Palazzo di Città (I, A3-4). After turning into the Via Milano we come to the 18th-c. Piazza Palazzo di Città, previously known as Piazza delle Erbe. At the center stands a monument to *Conte Verde, Amadeus VI of Savoy* by Pelagio Palagi (1853). This building was erected in place of the old town hall by Francesco Lanfranchi (1659–65) and was successively modified and enlarged by Benedetto Alfieri, Francesco Valeriano Dellala di Beinasco, Luigi Barberis and Filippo Castelli. Some of the rooms on the second floor still have 17th-c. decorations.

Corpus Domini (I, A4). The nearby church at Via Palazzo di Città 20 was built in 1603 to designs by the architect Ascanio Vitozzi, in memory of the miracle of the Holy Sacrament (a consecrated host that was stolen, and then elevated itself to heaven, 1453). There are four statues by Bernardo Falconi on the marble facade. The red-and-black marble was laid according with a design by Benedetto Alfieri. The main altar (1663) has a painting by Bartolomeo Caravoglia (1667), the *Miracle of the Eucharist*. The confessionals and the carved choir-stalls (18th c.) are remarkable. The church of the *Spirito Santo* is adjoining; the entrance is in the Via Porta Palatina. It was built by G. B. Feroggio (1765) and houses the chapel of the Confraternity of the Spirito Santo (Holy Ghost).

Santissima Trinità (I, A4). The Confraternity of the Santissima Trinità (Holy Trinity), commissioned this church from Ascanio Vitozzi (1598–1606) – who is also buried here. It stands in Via Garibaldi and has a neoclassical facade by Angelo Marchini, 1830. The interior of the church has a central plan with decorations by Filippo Juvarra. The dome was frescoed by Francesco Gonin and Luigi Vacca (1844–47). On the right altar is a painting by Ignazio Nepote. *Santa Maria del Popolo* (1590), a painting by Giovanni Caracca hangs near the left altar. The main altar is by Francesco Aprile, after designs by Michelangelo Garove (1699–1703).

1.2 The 19th-century boulevards and the museums

The itinerary of this section (map, pp. 192–193) is a fairly complex one that takes us from Piazza Castello, winding through the 19th-c. streets that grew up in the area of the demolished Cittadella, and along the wide tree-lined boulevards. A stop at the Galleria d'Arte Moderna is a must. The tour continues from Piazza Carlo Felice to the elegant Via Roma, the main road in the first urban expansion of the 17th c., and then continues on to two of the most elegant squares in Turin: Piazza San Carlo and Piazza Carignano. The latter is made up of three jewels of Baroque architecture: the church of San Filippo, the Palazzo dell'Accademia delle Scienze, and Palazzo Carignano, all of which are the work of the architect and mathematical genius, Guarino Guarini. The most prestigious museums in Turin, the Galleria Sabauda and the Museo Egizio, are lodged in the Palazzo dell'Accademia delle Scienze; while the Museum of the Italian Risorgimento is in Palazzo Carignano.

Via Pietro Micca (I, A-B3-4). This diagonal street, with buildings of many styles, begins at Piazza Castello and was created in 1855 to plans by Carlo Ceppi, who also built the new facade (1897) of the 16th-c. Franciscan church of *San Tommaso*. The road comes out into the elongated *Piazza Solferino,* overlooked by the *Teatro Alfieri* (Barnaba Panizza, 1857). At the center is the *Fontana Angelica delle Quattro Stagioni* by Giovanni Riva, 1930 and the *Equestrian monument to Ferdinand, Duke of Genoa* by Alfonso Balzico, 1877.

Via Cernaia (I, A2-3/B3). This road begins at the Piazza Solferino (opened in 1858) and widening on the right at the Lamarmora gardens, with the *Monument to Alessandro Lamarmora* (Giuseppe Cassano and Giuseppe Dini, 1867). Behind the massive Enel building, in Via Santa Maria, is the church of **Santa Maria di Piazza**, rebuilt in 1751–52 by Bernardo Vittone, with an 18th-

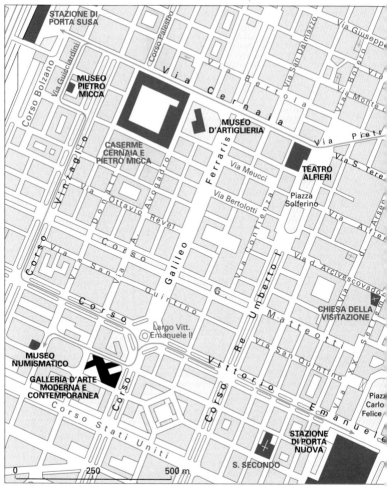

c. facade. The *interior** has a curious elliptical plan. The *Assumption of the Virgin Mary* by Pietro Francesco Guala can be seen at the main altar; also note the *Sacra Famiglia* by Mattia Franceschini (1745–54), belonging since the 17th c. to the University of the Mastri Minusieri, in the left chapel.

Cittadella and the Museo Nazionale di Artiglieria (I, A2. *Open for temporary exhibitions and for groups on request*). We go back to Via Cernaia, the main street in the new quarter which grew up around the bastions of the Cittadella, built by Emmanuel Philibert in 1564 to plans by Francesco Paciotto, and demolished in 1856–57. All that remains of the pentagonal fortress which survived so many attacks, especially the memorable one of 1706, is the *stronghold*, restored by Riccardo Brayda at the end of the 19th c. It houses the **Museo Nazionale di Artiglieria**, or national museum of artillery, founded by

Charles Emmanuel III in 1731 and transferred here from the Arsenal in 1893. The important collection illustrates the development of artillery and firearms, and includes trophies, models, flags, uniforms, and equipment from the Italian army. The rooms on the ground floor feature weapons from various eras. Machines for making gunpowder can be seen on the mezzanine. The main staircase, with various weapons and shields on display, leads up to the upper floor, with artillery equipment and swords and daggers. On the upper floors and in the rotunda, note the prehistoric and primitive weapons.

Museo Pietro Micca e dell'Assedio di Torino del 1706 (I, A2. *Open Tues–Sun 9–7; closed Mon, Dec 25 & 31, Jan 1, Easter Monday & May 1*). If we continue along the Via Cernaia, past the Corso Vinzaglio, we come to Via Guicciardini; at no. 7 is the museum

created in the late 19th c. in Turin. Where they cross, the roads open out; here one can see the monument (39 m) to Victor Emmanuel II, first king of Italy (Pietro Costa, 1899).

Galleria Civica d'Arte Moderna e Contemporanea* (I, C2. *Open 9–7; closed Mon, Dec 25 & 31, Jan 1, Easter Monday & May 1*). This art gallery is in Corso Galileo (entrance at Via Magenta 31). Together with Florence, Turin was one of the first cities to open a civic gallery of modern art. The museum's original nucleus was formed by the collection at the Civic Museum, which opened in 1863, and included early works of art that were later taken to the museum in Palazzo Madama. In 1895 the modern works were transferred to the pavilion of the Fourth National Art Exhibition, held in 1880. This pavilion was destroyed in World War II; the present premises of the museum were designed by Carlo Boschetti and Goffredo Bassi, and inaugurated in 1959. Improvements and enlargements were made to the gallery over the period 1981–93. The collection was greatly enlarged by acquisitions, almost a thousand, made by the Guido and Ettore De Fornaris Foundation, established in 1982. The gallery has about 5,000 paintings, 400 sculptures, and a large collection of drawings and engravings from the 19th c. onward, as well as photographs and photographic plates. The emphasis is on Italian art, especially Piedmontese, but international avant-garde art movements and works from abroad are included in the collection. The tour starts on the second floor with the 19th c. collections. In Rooms 1–2 we see Piedmontese art from the Ancien Régime to the French period (Giuseppe Mazzola, Luigi Baldassarre Reviglio, Giuseppe Pietro Bagetti). Rooms 3–4 are devoted to the Restoration and Romanticism, with aristocratic and royal clients (Antonio Canova, *Sappho**), the work of Massimo d'Azeglio, G. B. De Gubernatis and the collection of Pietro Baldassarre Ferrero (Francesco Hayez, *Portrait of Carolina Zucchi**). In Rooms 5–8 are works from the Risorgimento period in Turin; Carlo Bossoli, Enrico Gamba, Vincenzo Vela. Realism in Piedmont (Rooms 9-10) is illustrated by the works of the Rivara School (Alfredo D'Andrade, Carlo Pittara), as well as Vittorio Avondo and others. Room 11 shows the collection of Antonio Fontanesi's work (*Sleep**, 1860; **April***, *The Clouds**, 1880) bequeathed to the gallery by Giovanni Camerana. Room 12 is dedicated to figurative art 1860–1900; Rooms 13–14 to landscapes

dedicated to the heroic soldier, Pietro Micca. Opened in 1961, this collection includes trophies, prints, paintings, cannon balls, costumes, and models which show the dynamics of the siege of Turin in 1706 (May 13–September 7) by the French and Spanish army, headed by the Duke of La Feuillade. The interesting thing about this museum is that part of the visit leads through a network of underground tunnels that extend for kilometers at a depth of 5–6 meters. It was in one of these tunnels that Pietro Micca lost his life by blowing up a gunpowder storeroom, in an attempt to thwart the besieging French army.

Corso Vittorio Emanuele II and Corso Galileo Ferraris. If we turn back along the Corso Vinzaglio and take the Corso Vittorio Emanuele II we come to the Corso Galileo Ferraris. These are two good examples of the broad tree-lined boulevards from the late 19th c., and the "1890 Turin Impressionists," including Marco Calderini and Enrico Reycend. The paintings of Lorenzo Delleani hang in Room 15 (*Butchered Ox** 1881; *The Jetty** 1883) and other works (A. Fontanesi, *November** G. Pellizza, *Two Shepherds in the Meadows of Mongini*, 1901) from the Ettore De Fornaris collection. Room 16 contains examples of Lombard art and sculpture (Filippo Carcano, *Dance Lesson**; Tranquillo Cremona, *Ivy**). The work of the Pointillists is on exhibit in room 17 (A. Morbelli, *Christmas at the Pio Albergo Trivulzio**, 1909; G. Pellizza

Bowl*, *Man with Barrels**, *Woman and Armor**). Works by Arturo Martini are shown in Room 32 (**Maternity***, *Sitting Boy**). Room 33 is dedicated to the Venice Biennale Exhibition, the Rome Quadriennale and the "Novecento" (Carlo Carrà, **Huts on the Sea***, 1927; Alberto Savinio, *Self-Portrait in the Form of an Owl**); Room 34 is devoted to work by Filippo De Pisis (*Rue de Clichy**, **Still Life with Shrimps and Seashells***, *Flowers with a baroque Mirror**) and Giorgio Morandi (*Town*); room 35 is devoted to Rome and the "School of the Via Cavour"; Room 36 is devoted to the de-

Mirror of life, *Pelizza da Volpedo (Galleria d'Arte Moderna)*

da Volpedo, **The Mirror of Life*** and two panels of the triptych *Love in Life*; Medardo Rosso; *Enfant au sein**). Rooms 18–20 are assigned to works from southern Italy, Tuscany, and the Veneto (Antonio Mancini, *After the Duel**, 1872; Vincenzo Gemito, *Bust of a Boy**; Giovanni Fattori, *Red Cheeks**). Works from outside of Italy are hung in Room 21 (Gustave Courbet, *La prison près du lac**; Pierre-Auguste Renoir, *Portrait of His Son Pierre*, 1885).

The tour continues on the second floor with the 19th-c. collection. Rooms 22–27 feature Turinese art from the end of the 19th c. to the 1920s, with work by Giacomo Grosso and Leonardo Bistolfi (*The Cross**). In room 28 are works by Italians from 1900 to 1920 (Umberto Boccioni, *Portrait of a Woman** 1903; Giacomo Balla, **Portrait of Clelia Ghedina Marani***; Giorgio De Chirico, *Still Life with Salami**, 1919) and the famous avant-garde movements (Rooms 29–30): U. Boccioni, *Giants and Pygmies**; Otto Dix, *Fritz Muller, Sailor from Pieschen**, 1919; Amedeo Modigliani, **The Red Girl***; Max Ernst, *Sketch for Manifesto** and *Un peu malade le cheval**, 1920; Paul Klee, *Disturbed**, 1934; Giacomo Balla, **Iridescent Interpenetrations***, 1912–13. Paintings and terracotta works by Felice Casorati are exhibited in Room 31 (**Girl with a

velopments of Futurism (Fortunato Depero, *Plowing**, 1926; Enrico Prampolini, *Interview with Matter**, 1930); Room 37 is devoted to Italian abstract art in the 1930s (Osvaldo Licini, *Bird 2*; Lucio Fontana, *Sculpture*; Fausto Melotti, *Abstract Composition**); and Room 38 is devoted to works by the group "Corrente." Rooms 39–41 show art in Turin between the two world wars, with particularly significant paintings by the "Six": Carlo Levi, Enrico Paulucci, Jessie Boswell, Gigi Chessa, Francesco Menzio and Nicola Galante. Works bequeathed by Alberto Rossi are exhibited in Rooms 42–43 (F. De Pisis, G. Morandi, A. Tosi, O. Rosai) while Room 44 is devoted to postwar figurative art (Giorgio Morandi, **Still Lifes***; Giacomo Manzù, **Little Girl on a Chair***, 1948, *Cardinal**; Marino Marini, *The Miracle**). Rooms 45–47 contain Italian art from the 1950s, and Rooms 48–49 contain non-Italian postwar works f(Marc Chagall, *Dans mon pays**, 1943; Pablo Picasso, **Still life with melon***, 1948; Mark Tobey, *Verso i bianchi*). Rooms 50–52 contain art from Turin around 1950. Rooms 53–57 contain the *Museo Sperimentale di Arte Contemporanea* founded by Eugenio Battisti (Lucio Fontana, *Waiting**, 1961; Piero Manzoni, *White*, 1961), while Room 58 contains examples of Arte Povera (Michelangelo

Pistoletto, *Man and Woman on the Balcony**, 1964). Artistic events from the years 1950–70 and contemporary works are documented in Rooms 59–60: Alberto Burri, *White**, 1952; Lucio Fontana, Spatial **Concept***; Piero Manzoni, *Colorless**; Andy Warhol, *Orange car crash**; Emilio Vedova, *Absurd Berlin Diary**; Mario Merz, *In the Road**; Michelangelo Pistoletto, *Halo of Mirrors**.

Museo Civico di Numismatica, Etnografia, Arti Orientali (I, C1. *Open 9–7; closed Mon, Dec 25 & 31, Jan 1, Easter Mon, May 1*). Opened in 1989, these collections are housed near the gallery, at Via Bricherasio 8. The *numismatic collection* has some 100,000 coins, including ancient, medieval and Savoyard coinage, medals and seals. It comprises three main collections: from the Museum of Ancient Art, from the House of Savoy (previously in the Palazzo Reale), and from the Civic Museum. The ethnographic collection is on the first floor and includes exhibits catalogued by type and origin: Africa, the Americas, and Oceania. The *Oriental art collection* (third floor) includes works from the Middle East, the Himalayas, Burma, and China, including the contents of a *tomb* from the T'ang dynasty.

Piazza Carlo Felice (I, C3). Corso Vittorio Emanuele II leads toward the River Po and opens into a large square (17,000 sq. m) built in 1824–55 to designs by Gaetano Lombardi, Giuseppe Frizzi, and Carlo Promis. At the center is a garden with rare plants, a *fountain* (1859) and a marble *Monument to Edmondo de Amicis* (Edoardo Rubino, 1923). The square has arcades on three sides, while the large building of the station itself is on the fourth side.

Stazione di Porta Nuova (Centrale) (I, C-D3). This station was built in 1860–68 on the site of the Porta Nuova, part of the fortifications built by Charles Emmanuel I and demolished when Turin was occupied by the French; it replaced the old railway "imbarcadero" for trains to Genoa, and has been extensively restructured; the unusual facade is by Alessandro Mazzucchetti and Carlo Ceppi.

Via Roma (I, B4/C3). This road emerges into Piazza Carlo Felice, connecting it with Piazza San Carlo, and further on with Piazza Castello. It was from the latter that the first scheme of urban expansion began (1620), under Charles Emmanuel I. The main road

was the "contrada nuova," the present-day Via Roma.

The second stretch of the road from Piazza San Carlo to Piazza Carlo Felice was built to plans drawn up by Marcello Piacentini (1933–37); the small Piazza CLN (Comitato di Liberazione Nazionale, a World War II resistance movement) was built at the same time. It contains fountains decorated with statues depicting the Po and Dora rivers behind the apses of the churches of San Carlo and Santa Cristina. The first stretch of Via Roma (between Piazza San Carlo and Piazza Castello) was rebuilt in Baroque style in 1931–33.

In Via Teofilo Rossi, a short street between Piazza CLN and Via Lagrange, is the austere facade of **Palazzo Bricherasio** (III, B4), built in the first half of the 17th c. with later additions. Regular exhibitions of modern and contemporary art are held in its rooms by the Fondazione Palazzo Bricherasio; the fittings and decorations are from the 17th and 18th c.

Piazza San Carlo* (I, B4). Without doubt the most beautiful square in Turin, Piazza San Carlo was formerly a barracks square and a market, but has preserved the harmonious 17th-c. style created by the architect Carlo di Castellamonte (1642–50). In the center is an **Equestrian Monument to Emmanuel Philibert***, who is portrayed by Carlo Marocchetti (1838) as he sheaves his sword after the battle of San Quintino in 1557. It is one of the finest statues of the first half of the 19th c. The shorter side of the square on the southwest features the (almost) twin facades of the churches of Santa Cristina and San Carlo. Numerous noble houses were built in this square, among which is the *Palazzo Solaro del Borgo*, formerly Palazzo Isnardi di Caraglio (at no. 183), which has been home to the Accademia Filarmonica since 1839; the academy was joined by the Circolo del Whist cards club in 1947. It was partially rebuilt in the 18th c. by Benedetto Alfieri and later by Giovanni Borra. The palace rooms are magnificently decorated in 18th-c. style. The concert hall was designed by Giuseppe Maria Talucchi (1839–40). The traditional cafés, *San Carlo* at no. 156 (opened in 1842); the *Torino* at no. 204; and the *Pasticceria Fratelli Stratta* at no. 161, still with its original fittings of 1836, are well worth seeing.

Santa Cristina (I, B4). Christine of France, widow of Victor Emmanuel I, entitled "Madama Reale," ordered the construction of this church (which began in 1639), to plans by Carlo di Castellamonte. The gently

Piazza San Carlo, with the church of San Carlo in the background

concave facade in marble and granite is the work of Filippo Juvarra (1715–18). The four statues are by Carlo Antonio Tantardini and Giuseppe Nicola Casana. The church has a single nave, which was decorated later. At the side of the main altar is a rectangular chapel with a painting by Antonio Triva, *Rest on the Flight into Egypt.*

San Carlo (I, B4).This church, built in 1619, was dedicated to Saint Charles Borromeo by Charles Emmanuel I. The later facade (1834) bears a tympanum decorated with a marble bas-relief of *Emanuele Filiberto Taking Communion from St. Charles* (Stefano Butti). The bell tower was built in 1779. The interior with a single nave is decorated with marble and gilt, and was enlarged in 1863 (Carlo Ceppi). The first chapel on the right of the Addolorata (Our Lady of Sorrows) is the work of Tommaso Carlone, as is the chapel facing it, dedicated to Saint Joseph (ca. 1656). Over the main altar designed by Bernardino Quadri (1653) is a painting of *St. Charles Borromeo Venerating the Holy Shroud* by Casella. The walls of the presbytery are hung with paintings after Giovanni Paolo Recchi, depicting *Scenes from the Life of St. Charles.*

Santa Teresa (I, B3-4). The church is dedicated to Saint Teresa of Avila. It was designed by Andrea Costaguta in 1642. The facade (1764) comprises a double order of Corinthian columns. The interior is built on a Latin cross plan and has eight side chapels, richly decorated with marble and stucco (1878). The first chapel on the right, the Cappella di Sant'Erasmo, contains the *Tomb of Christine of France, Madama Reale*, wife of Victor Amadeus I, who died in 1663. The *Pietà* in the second chapel on the right

is by Ignazio Nepote. In the right transept is the beautiful *Chapel of the Holy Family* by Filippo Juvarra, with statues by Tantardini and a *Holy Family** by Sebastiano Conca (1730–32). The main altar (1679–83) was partly dismantled in 1844. In the apse is the **Ecstasy of Saint Teresa*** after Moncalvo. The frescoes in the dome were done by Luigi Vacca (*Glory of St. Teresa*, 1820) and those on the vaults of the apse by Rodolfo Morgari. In the chapel of San Giuseppe, in the right arm of the transept, commissioned by royal command from Juvarra (1733), is one of the most beautiful altars in Turin, with statues by Simone Martinez (*St. Joseph, Faith, Charity*); the wall hangings and the fresco on the vaults are by Corrado Giaquinto and the two inlaid doors are by Pietro Piffetti (1745). In the second chapel on the left is a gilded wooden statue of *Madonna with Child* (1726) and a painting by Bartolomeo Caravoglia, *St. Teresa of Avila.*

On the right of the church is the entrance to the *Teatro Gianduja* (Via Santa Teresa 5) where the Lupi company holds its puppet shows. The company came to Turin at the beginning of the 19th c. and adopted the Turin tradition of the popular mask, or character, Gianduja, a symbol of the city. The **Museo della Marionetta**, or puppet museum, is housed in rooms next to the theater (*open for puppet shows*) and contains scenery, puppets, costumes, scripts, and *painted backdrops** from the Lupi collection. There is also a collection of puppets from all over the world.

Palazzo dell'Accademia delle Scienze (I, B4. *Library opening hours: Mon–Fri 8:30–1 & 3–5:30; closed Sat & Sun*). Retracing our steps and into Via Maria Vittoria, along the left side of the building, we come to the entrance at Via Accademia delle Scienze 6. The austere brick construction – begun in

1679 by Michelangelo Garove to a design by Guarino Guarini – was destined to house the Jesuit Collegio dei Nobili. The order was suppressed in 1773 and in 1783 Victor Amadeus II assigned the left wing of the building to the Accademia delle Scienze, or science academy, founded in 1757 by the mathematician Giuseppe Luigi Lagrange and the chemist Giuseppe Angelo Saluzzo. The meeting room was decorated by Giovanni Galliari (1768–87). The prestigious institution, which has had such members as Ugo Foscolo and Alessandro Manzoni, has a wonderful library (over 300,000 volumes), which is open to the public. Carlo Felice commissioned Giuseppe Talucchi to complete the right wing of the building, with the grand staircase, with the idea of making it a museum. In 1824 the Egyptian Museum was transferred there, followed in 1832 by the Museum of Ancient Art, moved in 1981 to the old "orangeries" of Palazzo Reale (see itinerary 1); and in 1865 the Regia Pinacoteca, now called the Galleria Sabauda.

Museo Egizio** (*Open Tues–Sat 9–7; Sun 9–2; closed Mon*). The Egyptian museum is considered to be one of the finest collections of Egyptian art in the world, on a par with those in Cairo and London. The exhibits include both art works and everyday materials and tools. In the 18th c. the House of Savoy possessed a collection of Egyptian antiquities, to which were later added other relics and statues brought back from Egypt by Vitaliano Donati, who had been sent there by Charles Emmanuel III. In 1824 Charles Felix bought the collection of Bernardino Drovetti (Consul General for France in Egypt) and created the first Egyptian museum in the world in its present location. Important acquisitions were made under the directorships of Ernesto Schiaparelli and Giulio Farina, who conducted the expeditions carried out respectively from 1903 to 1920 and 1930 to 1937.

The tour begins on the ground floor in the two *statuary* rooms, where we find two *sphinxes* with the face of *Amenhotep III*, a *statue of a goddess** with coronet, a colossal statues of *Amenhotep II*, **Ramses II*** in black diorite, *Set II*, *Princess Redi**, a group with king *Tutankhamen and the god Amen-ka**, a statue of *Thutmose III** and

Ramses II (Museo Egizio)

large stone sarcophagi. The **Rock Temple of Ellessya*** (ca. 1450 B.C.) – donated to the museum in return for the contribution made by Italian archaeologists in the rescue digs at Nubia to save the monuments threatened by the completion of the Aswan dam – is in the next room. In the basement room of the Schiaparelli wing are the finds from the excavations at Ghebelein (fragments of a *linen cloth**, 3500 B.C.; **Tomb of King Ini***), Assiut (*wooden statuettes**) and Qua el-Kebir (*Sarcophagus of Ibu**).

On the second floor in Room 1 are funeral stones and stelai. In Room 2 all the funerary customs are displayed: mummies, sarcophagi (fragment of *lid** in inlaid wood), canopic vases, statuettes, amulets, and the funerary papyrus, the *Book of the Dead*. Room 3 contains items from the Predynastic to the Coptic periods. Three smaller rooms open off the corridor. In the first is the *tomb of the unknown man** (2400 B.C.) found intact at Ghebelein; in the second is the *funerary chapel of the painter Meie** (1300 B.C.); in the third room is a reconstruction of the **Tomb of Khaiè***, director of the works at the Necropolis of Thebes and his wife Meriè (1400 B.C.) discovered at Dair-el-Medina with the grave goods, food, and cooking utensils etc. intact. In Room 4 is the famous **Mensa Isiaca** (bronze altar slab with silver inlay, copied in the first c. A.D.), and various weaving instruments. In Room 5 are some of the many papyri belonging to the museum, among which the **Royal Papyrus***, the *Papyrus of the palace conspiracy**, a *papyrus map**, the *satirical papyrus* * and the *fragment of pottery portraying the figure of a dancing woman**. Room 6 is dedicated to the arts and trades; Room 7 to religion, with mummies and sacred animals; Room 8 to painting, with mural paintings taken from the Tomb of Iti at Ghebelein.

Galleria Sabauda** (*Open Tues–Sun 9–2; Sun: 2nd floor guided tour only 9:30, 10:30, 11:30, 12:30; closed Mon*). In 1832 Charles Albert decided to exhibit 364 paintings from the Palazzo Reale and other royal residences of the House of Savoy. The Reale Galleria (Royal Gallery) was donated to the Italian nation in 1860 and transferred in 1865 to its present location. The original nucleus of the collection grew through donations, especially of Piedmontese artists, and with acquisitions made to compensate for lack of exhibits of other Italian artists. The gallery was reorganized at the end of the 19th c. and underwent a more extensive overhaul from 1952 to 1959. Current work on the gallery has completed the rearrangement of the sections of Flemish and Dutch painters and the dynastic collections of Emmanuel Philibert and Charles Felix.

A tour of the gallery begins with the Italian painters. The first rooms contain works by Tuscan artists: Fra Angelico, *Virgin and Child**; Antonio and Piero Pollaiuolo, *The Archangel Raphael and Tobiolo**; Lorenzo di Credi, *Virgin and Child*; Franciabigio, *Annunciation**; Filippino Lippi, *The Three Archangels and Tobiolo**. Next come the rooms dedicated to the Mannerists (Bronzino, *Portrait of a Lady*; Daniele da Volterra, *Beheading of St. John the Baptist**; the next rooms contain the Lombard school (Bergognone, *St. Ambrose Preaching**, *Consecration of St. Augustine**) and the school of the Veneto (Giovanni Bellini, *Virgin and Child*; Gerolamo Savoldo, *Adoration of the Shepherds**). In the Flemish section there are two masterpieces: Jan van Eyck, **Stigmata of St. Francis****, and Hans Memling, **Passion of Christ***. The collection of Prince Eugene of Savoy-Soissons and the collections of Flemish and Dutch paintings come next, some of the most important in Italy. Prince Eugene's paintings, previously at the Belvedere in Vienna, were bought by Charles Emmanuel III in 1741. The paintings of the Italian school include *St. John the Baptist* and *Lucretia* by Guido Reni. Of note among the Flemish and Dutch painters are: Paulus Potter *The Four Bulls*; Gerard Dou, *At the Window*, 1662; Frans van Mieris the Elder, *The Hurdy-Gurdy' Player* and *Self-Portrait*, 1659; Anthonie Sallaert, *Procession of the Demoiselles du Sablon at Brussels*, and scenes by David Teniers the Younger, various works by Jan Bruegel, landscapes by Jan Griffier, still life paintings by Jan Davidsz de Heem, Cornelis de Heem, and Abraham Mignon. Among the acquisitions of Charles Emmanuel III: Pieter Saenredam, *Interior of St. Odulph's at Assendelft*; Salomon Koninck, *Portrait of a Rabbi*. Paintings from the Regia Pinacoteca include *Portrait of an Old Man* by Rembrandt van Rijn. In the gallery the ten *Battles* by Jan Hutchenburg show the military expeditions of Prince Eugene, who is depicted in the equestrian portrait by Jacob van Schuppen.

The Piedmontese paintings include a *Virgin and Child* by Barnaba da Modena, a precious **triptych*** by Jacques Iverny and, representing the 14th and 15th c., paintings by Giovanni Martino Spanzotti (*Virgin and Child with Saints**), Defendente Ferrari, Giuseppe Giovenone the Elder, Gerolamo Giovenone, Macrino d'Alba, Pietro Grammorseo (*Baptism of Christ*, 1523). 16th-c.

Stigmata of St. Francis, Jan van Eyck (Galleria Sabauda)

Piedmontese artists include Gaudenzio Ferrari (**Crucifixion***) and Bernardino Lanino (*Virgin and Child with Saints*, 1534).

On the floor above are three sections dedicated to the Savoy collections. The first concerns those from Emmanuel Philibert to Charles Felix I (1550–1630). First comes the dynastic iconography (Giacomo Vighi, known as the Argenta) and the first part of the Savoy collection: Rogier Van der Weyden, panels from triptych *Visitation** and *Faithful in Adoration*; Andrea Mantegna, *Virgin and Child with the Young St. John and St. Catherine of Alexandria**. The masters of the Veneto school follow (Francesco Bassano; Veronese, **Supper in the House of Simon***, 1556), painters after the international fashion (Guercino, *The Prodigal Son**; Orazio Gentileschi, *Annunciation**), the Lombard artists, the school of Caravaggio, and the Flemish old masters (Antonie van Dyck; Pieter Paul Rubens, **Deianira Tempted by the Fury*** and *Hercules in the Gardens of the Hesperides**).

The second section includes the collections of Victor Amadeus I and Victor Amadeus II (1630–1730). After the dynastic iconography, we see the artistic tastes of Prince Cardinal Maurizio of Savoy (Francesco Albani), the works of Francesco Cairo, the portrait painter at the European courts (Van Dyck, *Prince Tommaso di Savoia Carignano**, 1634; *The Children of*

Charles of England*, 1635), religious paintings by Guercino, the additions to the duchy's collection (Pierre Mignard), the collections of the "Madame Reali" and Victor Amadeus II (Gaspard van Wittel, **The Colosseum and the Roman Forum***, 1711; Sebastiano Ricci, *Susanna Before Daniel*, 1724; Francesco Solimena, *Heliodorus Expelled from the Temple**, 1723).

The third section is dedicated to the collections of Charles Emmanuel III and Charles Felix (1730–1831) and includes decoration and scene-painting (Claudio Francesco Beaumont, **Triumph of Peace**, 1748) the acquisitions made by the Duchy (Bernardo Bellotto, *View of Turin from the Side of the Royal Gardens** and *View of the Old Bridge Over the River Po at Turin**, 1745; landscapes by Giuseppe Pietro Bagetti and Jules-César-Dénis van Loo) and works from the neoclassical period to the Italian Restoration.

In a separate section is the private collection of a lawyer from Turin, Riccardo Gualino, donated to the gallery in 1928 (closed to the public). It includes various works among which are *Virgin and Child with Saints** by Taddeo di Bartolo, **Mars and Venus*** by Veronese.

San Filippo Neri (I, B4). The church is at the crossroads of Via Accademia delle Scienze with Via Maria Vittoria and was begun in 1675 by Antonio Bettino and rebuilt, after the collapse of the dome, by Filippo Juvarra (1715–30); Giuseppe Maria Talucchi (1835) designed the facade with a tetrastyle (four-column) Corinthian portico surmounted by a tympanum. The *interior**, the largest in Turin, has a single rectangular nave with a majestic barrel vault, elliptical windows, and stuccowork. 17th- and 18th-c. paintings and decorations adorn the altars and the sacristy.

Next to the church is the **Oratorio di San Filippo**, designed by Juvarra (1723) and finished by Ignazio Agliaudo di Tavigliano. It presents a single nave with frescoed vault and walls decorated with stucco work, and with paintings by Mattia Franceschini and Giovanni Conca; *Our Lady of the Immaculate Conception and St. Philip Neri*, at the altar is by Sebastiano Conca.

Palazzo Carpano (I, B4). Formerly Palazzo Asinari di San Marzano, this building was started by Michelangelo Garove in 1684–86 (Via Maria Vittoria 4) and continued by Benedetto Alfieri and Francesco Martinez in the 18th c.; the atrium is delightfully theatrical, with its spiral columns set against a fine architectural backdrop by Camillo Boggio (1883).

Piazza Carignano (I, B4). Returning along Via Accademia delle Scienze we come out into this beautiful square. *Teatro Carignano*, rebuilt in 1787 after fires had destroyed its two predecessors, overlooks the square. It was built by G. B. Feroggio and restored in the 19th c. when Francesco Gonin frescoed the ceiling. He also frescoed the famous *Ristorante del Cambio*, previously a post house, frequented by such historical figures as Camillo Benso di Cavour. However, the square is essentially Guarinian, and is overlooked by the Palazzo dell'Accademia delle Scienze, with the magnificent Palazzo Carignano – to which the square owes its existence – occupying a dominant position.

Palazzo Carignano* (I, B4). This is a strikingly unusual Baroque construction, and was built in 1679–84 by Guarino Guarini, commissioned by Prince Emamnuel Philibert, "the Mute," son of Tommaso of Carignano. The brick facade has alternating concave and convex sections, and the elliptical central section also extends into the internal courtyard. Inside, two curved staircases lead up from the hall to the *piano nobile* where, in 1848, the ballroom was transformed to house the Subalpine Parliament. The building was doubled in size on the courtyard side with the creation of the 19th-c. wing by Giuseppe Bollati to designs by Gaetano Ferri (1864–71). Its somewhat heavy facade looks onto the *Piazza Carlo Alberto* behind. This square has a *bronze equestrian statue of Charles Albert* (Carlo Marocchetti, 1861), and on the opposite side the neoclassical facade of the old stables of the Prince of Carignano has merged with the modern Biblioteca Nazionale (National Library, 1959–73). Palazzo Carignano, where Charles Albert and Victor Emmanuel II were born, was the seat of the first Subalpine Parliament and later of the first Italian Parliament, until the capital was transferred to Florence in 1865. The Museo Nazionale del Risorgimento Italiano, the Deputazione Subalpina di Storia Patria (an institute of national history), and the Sovraintendenza per i Beni Artistici e Storici del Piemonte (Piedmontese commission for heritage and fine arts) are all housed here. The latter is planning to open the ground floors, which have 17th- and 18th-c. decorations, including extensive frescoes and stuccowork; artists include Stefano Maria and Tommaso Legnani.

The elegant brick facade of Guarini's Palazzo Garignano

Museo Nazionale del Risorgimento Italiano* (*Open Tues–Sun 9–7; closed Mon, Dec 25 & 31, Jan 1, Easter Mon, May 1*), or national museum of the Italian Risorgimento. This collection was begun in 1878 and transferred to its present site in 1935. It occupies 27 rooms on the *piano nobile* of Palazzo Carignano. Paintings, statues, books, documents, prints, photographs, trophies, arms, flags, and uniforms illustrate the process of unification from the battle of 1706 to World War II. The *belongings of Silvio Pellico* are exhibited in Room 7; which features a reconstruction of his cell at the Spielberg prison, with the original door. The room in which Charles Albert died in 1849 during his exile in Oporto has been reconstructed – with the original furniture – in Room 13.

In the elliptical **Hall of the Subalpine Parliament***, which housed the Chamber of Deputies of the Kingdom of Sardinia from 1848 to 1860, the Italian cockades mark the parliamentary seats of Garibaldi, Gioberti, D'Azeglio, Balbo, and Cavour. The 108 watercolors by Carlo Bossoli of scenes from the *Second War of Independence** are worth seeing in Rooms 20–21. In the Hall of the Italian Parliament (Room 26), finished in 1871 after the capital was transferred to Florence, and therefore never used, are 172 flags of the workers' movement. The tour concludes with the *Galleria della Resistenza* (Room 27), where documents regarding the anti-Fascist movement are exhibited.

1.3 Urban expansion toward the River Po

This itinerary (map on facing page) follows the expansion of Turin towards the banks of the River Po. Via Po is the backbone of this second phase of urban expansion, planned in 1673. Near the start is the Mole Antonelliana, the symbol *par excellence* of the city. We proceed along Via Accademia Albertina, which emerges in Piazza Carlina, and then we stop off first at the Albertina itself, famous throughout the world; and also at the nearby science museum; followed by the so-called Borgo Nuovo, created in 1825 in the area between Porta Nuova and the River Po. The large Piazza Vittorio Veneto links the old city with the Borgo Po, which developed around the church of the Gran Madre di Dio. We now approach the Villa della Regina and the Monte dei Cappuccini, with the church of Santa Maria del Monte and the Museo Nazionale della Montagna.

The Parco del Valentino – along the left bank of the Po – is the largest green expanse in the city, and is home to the Castello del Valentino, the Borgo Medioevale, and Palazzo Torino Esposizioni. Two important exhibition venues stand in the area called "Italia '61," and the automobile museum is also nearby. The tour ends with the Fiat factories – Lingotto and Mirafiori – milestones of Turin's industrial development.

Via Po* (III, B4-C5). This street served as the backbone of the second phase of urban expansion, planned by Amedeo di Castellamonte in 1673. Starting from Piazza Castello, the road leads toward the River Po and emerges in the 19th-c. Piazza Vittorio Veneto (see elsewhere). With unbroken elegance the beautiful arcaded buildings continue, linked by terraces on the north side, and interrupted only by the Baroque churches of *San Francesco da Paola* (no. 16) and the *Santissima Annunziata* (no. 45).

Palazzo dell'Università (I, B5). The university building stands at Via Po 17, but its entrance is at Via Verdi 6 (formerly Via della Zecca). The University in Turin was founded in 1404 and has been present in Turin on a continuous basis since 1436. The present building was constructed in 1713–20 to designs by Michelangelo Garove. The Palazzo has a striking courtyard on two orders of arcades containing numerous statues and busts. In the main hall are four paintings by Sebastiano Ricci, Sebastiano Conca, and Francesco Trevisani from the chapel of Sant'Uberto in Venaria Reale (see itinerary 5).

Mole Antonelliana* (I, B5; Via Montebello 20). This boldly conceived construction has long been the city's prime symbol, and was begun in 1862 by Alessandro Antonelli as a synagogue. After a period of inactivity, work on the site recommenced in 1878 with the addition of the spire. The tower, then owned by the Town Council, became the tallest building in Europe, rising to a height of 167.5 meters. The uppermost section blew off in a gale in 1953 and the spire was rebuilt with a reinforced metal framework; the structure below was also reinforced. An elevator (at present out of order) takes us up to the small chapel at the base of the spire. From this point there is a wonderful *panorama** of the city and the surrounding countryside and mountains. The tower often hosts temporary exhibitions, and there is a project (1996) to transfer the Museum of Cinema here.

Accademia Albertina (I, B5). The famous Albertina academy was founded in 1678 by King Charles Albert. Since 1837 it has housed the **Pinacoteca***, or picture gallery, on the first floor (*temporarily closed for restoration, for information tel. 889020*). The collection includes paintings, sculptures and the valuable collection of 60 **cartoons*** by Gaudenzio Ferrari and his school, which

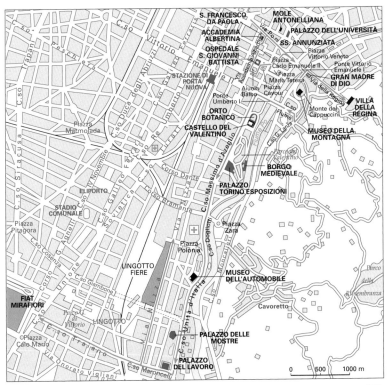

were donated by Charles Albert in 1832. They form the core of a graphics collection unrivaled anywhere in the world. In the first room are works in *terracotta* by Ignazio and Filippo Collino; *landscapes* by Giuseppe Pietro Bagetti; and paintings by Christian Wehrlin, Francesco Antonio Mayerle, and Daniel Seyter. In the second room, of note are: *Tasso at the Court of Ferrara** by Mattia Preti; three *views of Venice* by Michele Marieschi; and two *landscapes* by Francesco Zuccarelli. In the third room *The Ascent to Calvary* by Luca Cambiaso, *Cain and Abel* by Giulio Cesare Procaccini, a *Sacra Famiglia*, by Bartolomeo Cavarozzi. Room 4 contains two *still-life paintings* by Nicasius Bernaerts, and two *landscapes* after Jans Frans Bloemen, called "Orizzonte." Room 5 contains the most valuable works: two paintings of the **Fathers of the Church*** by Filippo Lippi, *Carità* by Francesco Salviati, *Last Judgment** (1554), and a *Deposition* by Maarten van Heemskerck. Room 6 has two paintings by Giovanni Martino Spanzotti, *Adoration of the Child** by Defendente Ferrari, and two *paintings* by Giampietrino, while Rooms 7 and 8 contain the cartoons mentioned above.

Piazza "Carlina"

(I, B-C5). Via Accademia Albertina emerges in Piazza Carlo Emanuele II, and is known locally as "Piazza Carlina." It was planned in 1673–74 by Amedeo di Castellamonte, but its original octagonal form was later altered to a square; it was made the official site of the wine market. At the center is a monument to Count Camillo Benso di Cavour (Giovanni Duprè, 1872); various noble palaces overlook the square. At no. 13 stands the *Palazzo Roero di Guarene*, with a facade designed by Filippo Juvarra (1730); at no. 15 is the *Albergo di Virtù*; at no. 4 the *Collegio delle Province*, by Bernardo Antonio Vittone (1737). On the south side of the square is the church of *Santa Croce*, designed by Juvarra (1718–30), which has a campanile influenced by the Oriental style (G. B. Borra), and a late-19th-c. facade.

Ospedale Maggiore di San Giovanni Battista

(I, C5). We go back into Via Accademia Albertina and come to the hospital with its facade on Via Giolitti. The imposing brick construction was built to designs by Amedeo di Castellamonte in 1680. It is being restored to house the *Museo Regionale delle Scienze Naturali*, or regional museum of natural science. The museum was founded in 1978 and includes collections from university museums with zoological, botanical,

mineral, geological, and petrographic exhibits. There are also entomological and paleontological collections of vertebrates and invertebrates. The library is also well stocked. At present the building is only open for temporary exhibitions.

The **Aiuola Balbo** (I, C4-5), a garden behind the San Giovanni hospital, has statues of *Eusebio Bava* (Giovanni Albertoni, 1857) and of *Cesare Balbo* and a *Monument to Daniele Manin* (Vincenzo Vela, 1856 and 1861). Overlooking the garden is the apse of the church of *San Massimo*, built in 1844–53 by Carlo Sada, to designs by Giuseppe Leoni.

Piazza Cavour is a short distance away and was built in 1835 on the site of old fortifications. There are small tree-covered mounds in the gardens. On the north side of the square is the *church of San Michele Arcangelo*, designed by Pietro Bonvicini (1784–88), where the Byzantine Catholic rite is practiced.

Piazza Maria Teresa

(I, C5). Together with the Balbo gardens, this square comprised the Ripari park (1834), that is, the green area of the so-called Borgo Nuovo envisioned by the 1825 master plan along the Via Mazzini, the Via dei Mille, and the Via della Rocca. Elegant palaces surround the square, including the *Casa Ponzio Vaglia* (Via Giolitti 46) by Alessandro Antonelli (1836), former home of Queen Maria Theresa, the widow of Charles Albert.

Piazza Vittorio Veneto

(I, C5-6). If we continue along Via della Rocca we come out in the large square (ca. 35,000 sq. m) designed

The church of the Gran Madre di Dio

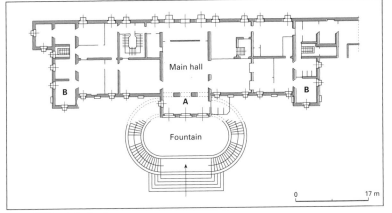

Plan of Villa della Regina

by Giuseppe Frizzi. This square served the purpose of linking the Baroque city with the new urban developments on the sloping opposite bank of the River Po. The exedra arcades at the end of Via Po continue round the entire square, forming a dramatic setting facing the opposite hillside. On the slopes down to the river Carlo Bernardo Mosca built the *murazzi* (1830), a riverside terrace set with deep niches for boat workshops, now occupied by shops and bistros, where one can hire a boat for a **trip on the River Po**.

We cross over the river on the **Ponte Vittorio Emanuele I**, a bridge in stone and brick, built by Charles Mallet to plans by Claude-Yves-Joseph La Ramée Pertinchamp in 1810–14, at Napoleon's behest. In front of us is the church of Gran Madre di Dio, the heart of Borgo Po.

Gran Madre di Dio (I, C6). A broad flight of steps, flanked by the statues of *Religion* (right) and *Faith* (left), leads up to the hexastyle pronaos of this neoclassical church built by Ferdinando Bonsignore in 1827–31 to celebrate the return from exile of Victor Emmanuel I (20 May 1814). Inside the circular church stand (from right) the statues of *St. Maurice,* the *Blessed Margherita di Savoia,* the *Blessed Amedeo di Savoia,* and *St. John the Baptist.* At the main altar is a *Virgin and Child,* by Andrea Galassi; over the altar on the right is a *Crucifix,* and over the left altar, *Sacred Heart of Jesus,* both by Edoardo Rubino. To the left of the steps is the entrance to the *Ossario dei Caduti,* a monument to those who fell in World War I.

Villa della Regina* (II, C4). From Piazza Gran Madre we take the road to the Villa della Regina. Cardinal Maurizio di Savoia, brother of Victor Amadeus I, commissioned Ascanio Vitozzi in 1615 to transform the existing building. Later work by other architects such as Juvarra rendered the house spectacular; particular care went into the scenic parkland, which was landscaped on various levels. The palace became the residence of Anna Maria d'Orléans, wife of Victor Amadeus II, hence its name (Queen's Villa). In 1868 it was donated by Victor Emmanuel II to the Figlie dei Militari (soldiers' daughters). Damaged by bombing in 1942 and abandoned, it is now closed for restoration. A double flight of curved stairs with a central fountain leads to the porticoed entrance (A, plan p. 41): two lateral pavilions (B) frame the facade, crowned at the center with a balustrade and statues. Inside are frescoes and paintings by G. B. Crosato, Daniel Seyter, and Corrado Giaquinto in the *grand salon*; grotesques by Filippo Minei, and paintings by the brothers Domenico and Giuseppe Valeriani in the adjacent rooms. The *Chinese rooms* in lacquered and gilded wood are exquisite examples of the fashion at the time. In the park stands the *Padiglione dei Solinghi* (Solinghi pavilion), a pagoda-like building in which the Accademia dei Solinghi, an intellectual society founded by Cardinal Maurizio, held its meetings.

Monte dei Cappuccini (I, D6). At the top of Corso Giovanni Lanza we reach the church of *Santa Maria del Monte* (elev. 284 m), built in 1584 to plans by Ascanio Vitozzi, and consecrated in 1656. The church has a central plan with an octagonal 19th-c. drum. Over the left altar is the *Martyrdom of St. Maurice,* by Moncalvo; over the main altar (Carlo and Amedeo di Castellamonte, 1634–37) once stood a statue of the *Virgin and Child,* stolen in 1980. In the niches are

203

wooden statues by Carlo Giuseppe Plura (ca. 1732). In the choir is a *Crucifix,* by Bartolomeo Botto and nine *paintings,* among which the *Annunciation,* a 17th-c. copy of the fresco in the Santissima Annunziata in Florence.

The **Museo Nazionale della Montagna "Duca degli Abruzzi"** * (*Open Tues–Fri 8:30–7:15; Sat–Mon 9–12:30, 2:45–7:15*). This museum of the mountains is housed in a convent and is one of the most important of its kind in the world. It was opened by the Italian Alpine Club (CAI), founded in Turin in 1863, and occupies 23 rooms for the permanent exhibition and 12 for temporary exhibitions. The *ground floor* is dedicated to the natural environment of the mountains and, more specifically, the Alps, with various anthropological aspects: fauna, herbariums, costumes, furniture, household goods, sculptures, and even a sled from the 18th c. The history of alpinism is illustrated on the *second floor*: badges, flags, CAI trophies, records and mementos from the expeditions of Duke Luigi of Abruzzi (1873–1942), models and relief maps, and mountaineering equipment. From the *third floor* there is a superb view of the Alps from the panoramic tower, or *Vedetta alpina*, installed in 1874.

Ponte Umberto I (I, D5). Coming down from the Monte dei Cappuccini we reach Corso Fiume, along the same axis as Corso Vittorio Emanuele II, and cross the triple-arched bridge, built in 1903–07 to designs by Vincenzo Micheli and Enrico Ristori, with allegorical statues in bronze (Luigi Contratti and Cesare Reduzzi). After the bridge, on the left, is a monumental arch, the *Arco Monumentale all'Artigliere* (Pietro Canonica, 1930), serving as a backdrop to Corso Cairoli and the northern entrance to the Parco del Valentino.

Parco del Valentino * (I, D4-F4). The park was landscaped in the middle of the 19th c. according to plans by Pierre Barillet-Deschamp, and was one of the first Italian city parks. It is Turin's main greenspace and extends from the bridge, or Ponte Umberto I to the Ponte Isabella (550,000 sq. m). The avenues in the park are reserved mainly for bicycles and pedestrians. The main entrances are from Corso Massimo d'Azeglio. Inside the park stand the Castello del Valentino, the Botanical Gardens, the Medieval Village, and the Turin Expo Center. There is a cycle track along the bank of the River Po and trips along the river leave from the imbarcadero.

Castello del Valentino * (I, E4. *Open 9–7; closed Mon*). Building on the castle started in the 16th c. It was enlarged and transformed under Christine of France, wife of Vittorio Amedeo I, by Carlo and Amedeo di Castellamonte (1620–60). The "Madama Reale" Christine admired the French style of architecture, as noted in the choice of sloping roofs on the castle. The villa was originally a typical riverside mansion built facing the water, but was later transformed when the prospect on the city side was enlarged with a large forecourt closed on three sides. During the 19th c. work was done on the two lateral wings perpendicular to the facade, when arcades and two four-sided towers. Abandoned after the death of Christine, the building was subsequently used as a school of veterinary medicine during the French occupation; as a military barracks in 1824; for a school of applied engineering (1859); later it housed the department of architecture of the science university (Politecnico). The building is now being fully restored. The rooms on the first floor have beautiful 17th-c. decorations in stucco and gilt. The central halls and the rooms to the right, making up the *Appartamento di Moncalieri*, were the first to be decorated (1633–38, 1642), by Isidoro Bianchi and his sons Pompeo and Francesco. In the *central salon*, the pro-French *dynastic scenes* of the Duchies of Savoy rendered homage to the "Madama Reale" (king's widow). The *Green Room* has a painted ceiling: the *Rape of Europa and Apotheosis of the Bull* and other *mythological scenes.* Various rooms follow: the *Room of the Roses* and the *Zodiac Room* with stuccowork featuring the *signs of the zodiac and the constellations*: the room dedicated to *the Valentino* or the *birth of flowers,* with *Flora,* the *Muses* and the *Centaur Chiron in Flight, to whom Apollo entrusts the Castello del Valentino* in the central ceiling panel; the small *Room of Flowers,* the *Lily Room,* with rich stuccowork and a frieze with cupids bearing lilies. To the left of the main salon is the *Appartamento di Torino,* decorated with white stuccowork by Alessandro Casella (1646–49), and frescoes by Giovanni Paolo and Giovanni Antonio Recchi (1662). Various rooms follow: *The War Room,* featuring scenes of *armies and artilleries* in the frieze; the *Room of Audience and Negotiation;* the *Room of Magnificences;* the room with frescoed *views of* urin and landscapes on the frieze; the oom of the Hunt, with *Diana the Huntress* nd *Nymphs* in the central ceiling panel; e *Room of the Labors of Hercules*; and the oom of Feasts.

otanical Gardens (*visits may be booked, tel.* 599884*)* occupy an area of 27,000 sq. m to the ft of the castle. Victor Amadeus II created the rdens in 1729; they feature numerous rare ecies and extensive greenhouses, herbariums ne million plants), and a library, which has aluable 18th-c. *botanical panels.*

orgo Medioevale (I, F4. O*pen 8–8*). Built on e banks of the Po, this is quite a tourist at-raction in the Parco del Valentino. This edieval village was created for the Na-onal Exposition in 1884 by Alfredo D'An-rade, leader of a group of artists, histori-ns, and literati. The Borgo is a reproduc-on of various types of medieval villages und in Piedmont and the Valle d'Aosta. he activities of the artisans help to recre-te a medieval atmosphere. The northern ntrance to the village is via a drawbridge rough the gates of the tower, or *Torre di glianico*; to the left is the *Pilgrims' Hostel*, front of which is a *fountain* and a *bakery*. long the main street in the village are two ouses like those found in *Bussoleno*, the ate into Rivoli, a *house from Alba*, and a ouse from Cuorgnè. The *church* resembles ose from Verzuolo and Ciriè. The street ontinues with *houses from Avigliana* and hieri, the *courtyard from Avigliana*, over-oked by *houses from Borgofranco d'Ivrea* nd *Malgrà*, a *tower from Avigliana*, and ouses from Avigliana and Pinerolo. After the o houses from Mondovì, there is an open pace where the *Issogne fountain* was placed

in 1927. Then come the tavern, or *Osteria di San Giorgio* (1927) and the *house from Oze-gna*, which extends down to the River Po. Along the arcaded road leading up to the castle and drawbridge are various medieval war machines. The entrance is a repro-duction of the entrance of the castle of Fé-nis; from the atrium we go into the court-yard with a guard house from the castle of Verrès; from here we may enter the pantry, kitchen, and the dining room. On the upper floors is a baronial hall with paintings of the heroes and heroines and the fountain of youth from the castle of Manta, a bridal suite, and a chapel.

Palazzo Torino Esposizioni (I, F4). From the Borgo Medioevale we proceed up the slope to a fountain, the **Fontana dei Mesi**, by Car-lo Ceppi for the National Exposition in 1889. The entrance to the complex, which ex-tends over 100,000 sq. m, is from Corso Massimo d'Azeglio 15. It was built between 1938 and 1950 to house exhibitions and commercial fairs. The *central salon* (open when there are exhibitions) is the most ar-chitecturally significant pavilion and was de-signed by Pier Luigi Nervi (1948–50). In the square before it is an **Equestrian Monu-ment to Prince Amadeus*** by Davide Ca-landra (1902).

Museo Nazionale dell'Automobile "Carlo Biscaretti di Ruffia"* (II, E3. *Open Tues–Sun 10–6:30; closed Mon*). Following Corso Mas-simo d'Azeglio and Corso Polonia we pass the new hospital buildings and arrive in Corso Unità d'Italia (no. 40). The national automobile museum was built specifically by Amedeo Albertini in 1960 to house the

ld cars lined up in the Automobile Museum

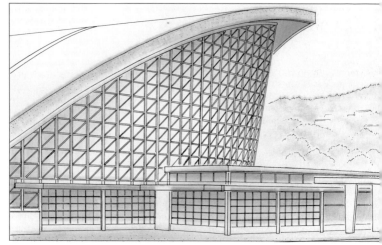

The Palazzo delle Mostre, with its sail-like roof

collections illustrating the history of the automobile from its beginnings to the present day. On the ground floor the evolution of the tire is shown; on the second floor there is a chronological exhibition of cars and carriages and the sports car section is on the third floor. The history of the car is shown with models with steam and wind propulsion and the first Italian cars produced. Of note are the *steam Bordino** built in Turin in 1854, a *steam tricycle* by Enrico Pecori (1891), the **Bernardi automobile*** (1896), the **1901 Fiat***, and the legendary **Itala***, which won the Peking to Paris rally in 1907 (16,000 km in 44 days). The famous *Lancia Lambda** (1923), the *coupé de ville Isotta Fraschini 8A** (1929), and the *Cistalia 202* (1948). Foreign car production is represented by a **Ford Model T*** (1916) and a *Rolls-Royce "Silver Ghost"** (1914).

Palazzo delle Mostre (II, E2). If we follow Corso Unità d'Italia we come to the complex of buildings known as "Italia '61," which was built for the celebrations of the centennial of the Unification of Italy. The most impressive of these are Palazzo delle Mostre and Palazzo del Lavoro. The first pavilion (Via Ventimiglia 145) is called the "Palazzo a Vela" because its hexagonal dome has only three points of anchorage, and resembles a sail ("vela"). Made of glass and reinforced concrete, it was designed by Annibale and Giorgio Rigotti.

Palazzo del Lavoro (II, E2; Via Ventimigli 201). Designed in 1959 by Pier Luigi and Antonio Nervi, it covers an area of 22,500 sq. m with a single square ceiling supported b sixteen metal umbrellas on pillars of rein forced concrete, more than 20 m high. A the moment it houses the International La bor Exchange and temporary exhibitions

Lingotto (II, E2). The Fiat Lingotto factor designed by Giacomo Matté Trucc (1914–16) extends for more than 273,00 sq. m along Via Nizza. It was planned t function with a vertical organization c the production line and is a remarkable ex ample of industrial architecture. The mai section of the factory has five floors wit spiral ramps (1926) and has a test track o the roof (1 km long and 24 m wide).
The project to convert the factory, whic closed in 1983, into a multifunctional exh bition center, was the work of the architec Renzo Piano. The first parts of the conve sion to be opened include the *auditoriur* (1994) with avant-garde acoustics. The spa cious exhibit halls hold important event such as the Motor Show and the Book Fai

Fiat Mirafiori (II, E1). We now procee along Corso Traiano to the Fiat factory de signed by Vittorio Bonadé Bottino and bui in 1935–38; it was later enlarged. There i one work floor and a test track on th ground floor. The factory covers 3 millio sq. m and is one of the largest in the worl

2 The environs of Turin

The countryside around Turin is typically prealpine, that is, made up of gentle hills and plains of rural land, with scattered evidence of pre-industrial activity.
This chapter outlines the chief historical and artistic features of the area, together with the fine parks lying within a short distance of the city. The ring of castles and country estates built by the Savoy court around the city is known as the "crown of delights," and was once reached along fine tree-lined avenues, traces of which are still visible here and there.

2.1 The Hills and the Plains around Turin

This itinerary (about 69 km), winds along the so-called "mountain" of Turin, dotted with villas and vineyards (map below). We stop at the basilica of Superga and then continue to the top of the Maddalena hills visiting the towns of Pino Torinese, Chieri, and Pecetto Torinese. After Moncalieri, famous for its royal castle, we return to the plain through Santena, Carmagnola, and Carignano, with its late medieval and Baroque monuments and then to Piòbesi Torinese. We reach the magnificent Palazzo di Stupinigi, a hunting lodge designed by Juvarra, which now houses the Museo di Arte e Ammobiliamento (museum of art and furniture).

Basilica di Superga* (III, B5. *Open 8:30–12*

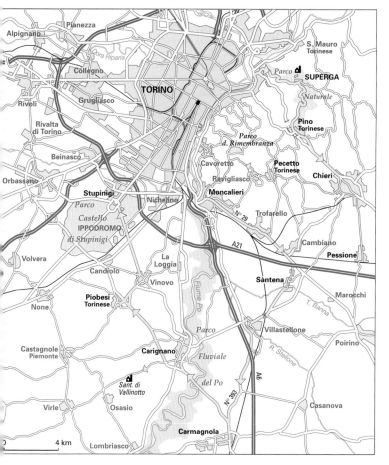

The Superga basilica, Juvarra's masterpiece

& 3–6). Corso Casale leads along the river from the church of the Gran Madre di Dio to Piazza Gustavo Modena. The *Superga rack-railway* which replaced the 1935 funicular, takes us up to the church. The basilica is otherwise reached from the road that runs round the *Parco Naturale della Collina di Superga*. The piazza in front of the church (elev. 669 m) affords a superb *panorama** of Turin and environs. The church was erected by Victor Amadeus II to fulfill a thanksgiving vow for the deliverance of Turin in the battle of 1706 against the French, and is dedicated to the Nativity of the Virgin Mary. It is considered the masterpiece of Filippo Juvarra, who designed the basilica (1717–31). Built in a commanding position on the hill, the church is an eclectic composition of classical elements. The centrally planned church rises in a dome almost as big as itself, on a tall drum with symmetrical campaniles either side that appear to rise from the convent wings, which help to balance the grandiose portico at the front. The circular interior has two main chapels and four side chapels. In the first chapel on the right (A) is a painting by Sebastiano Ricci, *St. Maurice*; in the second (B) the *Nativity of the Virgin Mary*, by Agostino Cornacchini; in the third (C) *the Blessed Margherita di Savoia*, by Claudio Francesco Beaumont (1731). At the main altar (D) is a *marble frieze* by Bernardino Cametti, depicting the fierce battle that raged through Turin in 1706; to the right is the sacristy (E), to the left is the Cappella delle Grazie or Cappella del Voto (F), with a *Statue of the Virgin Mary*. In the third chapel on the left (G) is *St.*

Charles, by Beaumont, in the second (H) *Annunciation* by Cametti, in the first (I) *St. Louis of France*, by Ricci. On the left of the entrance (L) to the basilica we go down to the crypt with the *tombs of the Kings* (open 9:30–12 & 3–6), from Victor Amadeus II (died 1732) to Charles Albert (died 1849), and of other princes of Savoy, buried here from 1731 onward. A gallery leads to the main chapel (1773–78) in the form of a cross, decorated with marble and gilded stuccowork; the *statues of Faith, Charity,* and *Hope* and the *Genius of the Arts* are by Ignazio and Filippo Collino (1778), the *Pietà* at the altar is by Cornacchini. At the center is Charles Albert's tomb, in the side chapels are tombs of Victor Amadeus II, designed by Francesco Martinez, and the tomb of Charles Emmanuel III, and lastly and a painting by Collino (1788) depicting the *Battle of Guastalla*. Behind the basilica a plaque marks the site

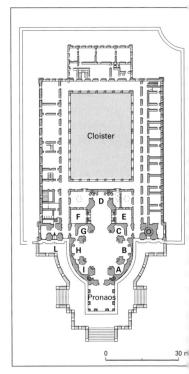

Plan of the Superga basilica

of the plane crash on 4 May 1949, in which 31 people lost their lives, including the entire Turin soccer team.

Pino Torinese

We reach to this small town (elev. 495 m; pop. 8,741) which has grown considerably in recent years, by taking the road to Superga and turning left into the *Superga-Pino panoramic road,* which runs through thick woods. Before reaching the center, a road on the right leads up to the Observatory (*visits may be booked, tel. 4619000*), built in 1912 by Giovanni Boccardi to replace the previous observatory built by Giovanni Plana on the roof of Palazzo Madama (see itinerary 1).

Chieri

This was an ancient Roman settlement and is now an important agricultural and industrial town (elev. 283 m; pop. 31,904). In the 11th c. Chieri was part of the fief ruled by Landolfo, Bishop of Turin. Allied with the republic of Asti in 1155, the town was destroyed by Frederick I Barbarossa. In 1347 it was ruled by the Acaia dynasts, and in 1418 by the House of Savoy. It prospered as a weaving center, especially for the production of fustian. Artistic production and architectural development also flourished.

Piazza Cavour. We reach this square from Via Vittorio Emanuele II. Two *churches* overlook it: *Sant'Antonio Abate*, a Rococo building by Giuseppe Giacinto Bays (1767), and the church of *Santi Bernardino e Rocco*, by Bernardino Quadri. The facade (1792) was designed by Mario Ludovico Quarini, and the beautiful dome by Bernardo Antonio Vittone (1740–44).

Cathedral*. We come to the cathedral, dedicated to Santa Maria della Scala, from Via Balbo. It is one of the most interesting 15th-c. buildings in Piedmont. It was built between 1403 and 1436 on the site of a church erected by Bishop Landolfo. It was restored by Edoardo Arborio Mella in 1875–80. The terracotta facade is enriched with a particularly tall pointed-arch stone porch, characteristic of Piedmontese Gothic, which frames a lunette containing a statue of the *Madonna*. The original was stolen, and was replaced with a copy. On the right is the campanile (1329–1492) and the baptistery, perhaps belonging to the original Romanesque church and later modified. The interior has a nave and two aisles with pointed groin vaults. In the second chapel on the right is the *Incredulity of St. Thomas* by Giovanni Crosio, in the third chapel, *Nativ-*

ity by the same painter. The octagonal 13th-c. baptistery is frescoed with fifteen scenes of the *Passion of Christ*, by the Chierese artist Guglielmo Fantini (ca. 1430). On the left is a *polyptych* from the beginning of the 16th c., and on the right a statue of the *Virgin Mary*, of French influence, as is seen on the facade. In the fourth chapel on the right is the *Virgin and Child with Saints,* by Moncalvo, in the sixth chapel are recently restored frescoes; in the seventh chapel is a painting by Crosio. In the south transept is a beautiful marble icon* after Matteo Sanmicheli. On the walls of the *Cappella del Corpus Domini* are *paintings* by Sebastiano Taricco, Bartolomeo Caravoglia, and Alessandro Mari. At the base of the campanile is the entrance to the *Cappella dei Gallieri** with frescoed *Scenes from the Life of St. John the Baptist* (1414–18). The precious reliquaries and gold work, especially Flemish, are all that remains of the treasure of the cathedral, stolen in 1973. The crypt, which dates back to the church built by Bishop Landolfo, has various tombs, among which those of Cesare Balbo and G. B. Lorenzo Bogino. On the main altar is a 15th-c. wooden *Crucifix* and in the apse are the beautiful carved 15th-c. **choir stalls*** with a lectern by Pietro Botto (1660). In the *Chapel of the Crucifix*, on the left of the main altar, are paintings by G. B. Sacchetti and Caravoglia and on the altar is *Jesus Crucified, with the Virgin and Mary Magdalene* by Charles-Claude Dauphin. After the sacristy, in the sixth chapel on the left is the *Virgin with Sts. Julian and Basilissa* by G. B. Carlone in a carved frame. The fourth chapel was built by Bernardo Antonio Vittone (1757–59), as a votive offering in gratitude for salvation from the plague of 1630.

A little further on at the corner with Via Principe Amedeo is **Palazzo Tana** (15th c.), previously the home of one of the richest families in Chieri.

Via Vittorio Emanuele II. In this street and nearby streets are the ruins of late medieval houses and noble palaces. We continue to the *Triumphal Arch*, erected in 1580 in honor of Duke Emmanuel Philibert and designed by Pellegrino Tibaldi. The arch was modified in 1761 by Bernardo Antonio Vittone. Passing under the arch, on the left is the church of *San Filippo Neri*, with a facade (1759) by Mario Ludovico Quarini. At no. 71 stands Palazzo Solaro, built from the 13th to 15th c. for an important banking family. Further on we come to the Gothic church of *San Domenico*, which was altered in the 17th c. and then restored to its original appearance in 1871. The facade has a fine Gothic portal crowned with a three-light window. On the left is the campanile (1381) with spire. Inside are works by Moncalvo: the *Madonna del Rosario* in the third chapel on the right, frescoes of the *Life of St. Dominick*, and two paintings in the choir.

Five kilometers from Chieri toward *Pessione*, the home of Martini & Rossi, is the interesting "**Museo Martini di Storia dell'Enologia**" (*open 9–12, 2–5*). Exhibits illustrating the history of winemaking include: Etruscan oinochoe, Corinthian jars, amphorae, flasks, bucchero ware, pre-Christian pateras (shallow dishes), Roman glass, 14th-c. ceramic jugs, and wine presses.

Pecetto Torinese

We now go back to Chieri and follow the road to Pecetto (elev. 407 m; pop. 3,500), driving through cherry orchards; in spring these are a mass of blossom. Previously tied to Chieri, Pecetto passed to Turin in 1542. On the right of the main street, in a commanding position is the church of **Santa Maria della Neve**, rebuilt by Bernardo Antonio Vittone in 1730–39, with a campanile and watch tower (1106). The nave has a barrel vault and an altarpiece by Vittorio Amedeo Rapous. Next to the cemetery is the church of *San Sebastiano* in Lombard Romanesque style, with a simple facade. The inside is frescoed with *Life of St. Sebastian and Other Saints* by various Lombard and Piedmontese artists (15th–16th c.). Of note is the *Nativity* (1508) by Jacopino Longo.

Parco della Rimembranza

We leave Pecetto and pass through Revigliasco. The park (*open 9–10*) extends for almost 420,000 sq. m on the *Colle della Maddalena* (elev. 715 m) and marks the highest point on the Turin hills. It was opened in 1925 and is dedicated to the soldiers who lost their lives in World War I. The Arboretum Taurinese, part of the park, has 15,000 specimens of plants. From the broad open square – with the *Faro della Vittoria* by Edoardo Rubino (1927) – one has a breathtaking panorama* of the Alps and the plans of Piedmont.

Moncalieri

The town of Moncalieri (elev. 219 m; pop. 59,626) is spread over two levels, with the modern town on the plain and the old part winding up the hill. It was originally a Roman settlement and in the 13th c. when nearby Testona lost its supremacy, Moncalieri began to assert itself as a defensive outpost. In 1619 it was given the status of a town by Charles Emmanuel I.

Piazza Vittorio Emanuele II. To reach the square we go through the **Porta Navile**, also called "Arch of Victor Emmanuel" which was erected in 1560 and later restored. The square is the heart of the city and many houses and arcaded palaces face onto it. To the right is the church of *San Francesco,* rebuilt in 1788 by Filippo Castelli, and further along is the church of Santa Maria della Scala.

Santa Maria della Scala*. Begun in 1230, the church was finished in 1330 in the Lombard Gothic style. The portal is from the late 17th c., the rose window and the balustrade

The castle at Moncalieri, once a Savoia residence

at the entrance were added in 1857. The interior has a naves and two aisles with groin vaults. Restoration work has been done on the apse and the sacristy. On the back wall is a beautiful carved *organ loft* (1709); at the main altar is a *Virgin and Child with Saints* by Moncalvo. In the presbytery are four paintings of the *Story of the Virgin Mary* by Michele Antonio Milocco (1754), an altarpiece with *Our Lady of the Assumption* by Claudio Francesco Beaumont and Giovanni Domenico Molinari (1768) and the beautiful carved *choir stalls** (Giuseppe Riva, 1749). In the left transept is a statue of *Princess Maria Clothilde at Prayer* by Pietro Canonica (1914), and, in the first chapel on the left, a **Pietà*** in polychrome terracotta from the 15th c.

Castello Reale* Go back up along the Via Principessa Clotilde and you will come to the Piazza Baden Baden, where you will see the imposing castle with a pavilion at each of its four corners (*closed*).

In 1619 Carlo di Castellamonte began the fortress's conversion, which was continued by Andrea Costaguta (1646) and Amedeo di Castellamonte (1664–83). Subsequent work undertaken on the castle, including the furnishings and fittings, was done by Filippo Juvarra (1731), Benedetto Alfieri (1752–56), G. B. Piacenza, and Carlo Randoni (1789–90); further work was carried out later in the 19th c.

Santena

From Moncalieri we pass through Trofarello and arrive in this agricultural and industrial town (elev. 237 m; pop. 10,357), well-known in Italy for its asparagus. In Piazza Visconti Venosta is the entrance to *Villa Cavour*, where the statesman Count Camillo Benso di Cavour stayed. The villa was built in 1708–12 and is surrounded by a beautiful park with English landscaping. Certain rooms have preserved their 18th- and 19th-c. decorations. Of note is the *Chinese drawing room*. In the *cappella funeraria*, or funerary chapel, under the apse is the tomb of Cavour, to whom the museum next door is dedicated (*Museo Cavouriano*, closed for restoration). The museum has portraits, trophies, prints, statues, documents and a room belonging to the great statesman.

Carmagnola

If we continue through Villastellone we reach the town (elev. 240 m; pop. 24,611) which belonged to the Marquisate of Saluzzo in the 13th c., and which still has traces of the medieval and Renaissance periods. Worth seeing is the *Casa Cavassa** in the arcaded Via Valobra, a fine Renaissance building of the 15th c. with the remains of frescoes on the facade. Also of interest is the church of *SS. Pietro e Paolo* in Piazza Verdi, erected in 15th/16th c., with a facade in neo-Gothic.

Carignano

Now a busy agricultural and industrial town (elev. 235 m; pop. 8,581), Carignano has managed to preserve its late medieval character, though there are many examples of baroque architecture. On the main square of Piazza Carlo Alberto is the church of *Santa Maria delle Grazie* or *Sant'Agostino* (1600–67). Its facade is markedly sculptural; the interior has a single nave and a richly decorated choir with stuccoes by Cristoforo Ciseri. On the left wall of the presbytery is the *Tomb of Bianca di Monferrato*, who died in 1519, wife of Charles I of Savoy. We proceed along *Via Vittorio Veneto**, the main street of the medieval town, where one can still see interesting medieval buildings with carvings and paintings and decorations in terracotta. Some of the houses were used as models for the Borgo Medioevale project in the Parco del Valentino (see itinerary 1.3). Of note is the *Casa del Gran Bastardo Renato di Savoia* in Via Borgovecchio, on the corner with Via Bastioni.

Cattedrale. Dedicated to Saint John the Baptist and Saint Remigius, the cathedral dominates Piazza San Giovanni, the heart of the old town. It is one of the most important works of Benedetto Alfieri (1757–64, restored in 1889); the severe sinuous facade is in terracotta, and the rich interior is built on an unusual kidney-shaped plan.

Highly recommended is an excursion (4.5 km in the direction of Virle and Vigone) to the **Cappella della Visitazione al Vallinotto***, a small sanctuary, built by Bernardo Antonio Vittone in 1738, commissioned by the banker Antonio Faccio. It has a mixtilinear hexagonal plan and three superimposed vaults. The frescoes on the dome are by Pietro Francesco Guala.

Piobesi Torinese

In the cemetery of this agricultural center (elev. 233 m; pop. 2,852) stands the Romanesque church of *San Giovanni ai Campi* (10th/11th c.). It has precious frescoes from various periods. Of note are *Virgin and Child, with Angels, Saints, and the Faithful* (1359) in the lunette on the facade; *Christ Pantocrator*, and, below, the *Apostles* (11th c.) in the apse; *Deposition, Martyrdom of St. Bartholomew and St. Catherine* (1411), by Giovanni Beltrami on the wall of the left aisle.

Stupinigi Hunting Lodge*

After *Vinovo*, where we see the castle (16th c.), site of the famous ceramic factory, and the modern hippodrome, we come to Stupinigi, a small town near Nichelino. The straight central avenue running in the direction of Turin is lined with red brick farm buildings, followed by the semicircular stables which mark the entrance to the hunting lodge. In 1729 Victor Amadeus II commissioned Filippo Juvarra to build the house. Subsequently Benedetto Alfieri, Giovanni Tommaso Prunotto, and Ludovico Antonio Bo also contributed. Until 1919 the palace was inhabited by the court of Savoy, where they held sumptuous parties and weddings; together with the farm buildings and stables, the lodge and its grounds were taken over by the state. It was later managed by the monastic orders of San Maurizio and San Lazzaro. It houses the interesting *Museo di*

The Stupinigi Hunting Lodge, set in magnificent gardens and parkland

Arte e Ammobiliamento* (*open 9–11.50, 2–4.20; closed Mon*) which has among its exhibits furniture, paintings, and a wide variety of items gathered from the Savoy residences. Juvarra planned the building on a St. Andrew's cross. The huge elliptical salon is the fulcrum of the construction, whose dome was crowned by a statue of a deer by Francesco Ladatte (1766). Today it has been replaced with a copy. The rooms to the south and the east are still as they were designed by Juvarra. The museum, which spreads through several of the palace's apartments, has a rich collection of furniture from the 18th c. Worthy of note are the pieces by Pietro Piffetti (*pregadio**, or priedieu, in the bedroom of the *Queen's apartment*) and Giuseppe Maria Bonzanigo (*deskcabinet** in white and pale blue lacquer in the *Bonzanigo room*), wall coverings, fabrics and various fittings (a beautiful light fitting in bronze and ceramic in the *Hall of Mirrors* in the *East apartment*, an elegant wall *candelabra** by Bonzanigo in the *East Gallery*),

statues, door panels, painted doors. Of the many frescoed ceilings and walls, note: the **scenes of a deer hunt*** by Vittorio Amedeo Cignaroli (1772–78) in the *Sala degli Scudieri* in the *King's Apartment* and the fresco of the *Sacrifice of Iphigenia* * by G. B. Crosato (1733) on the ceiling of the entrance hall in the *Queen's apartment*. Many other artists contributed to the decorations, among them Rapous, Giovanni Pietro Pozzo, G. B. Alberoni, Gaetano Perego, Christian Wehrlin, and Charles-André Van Loo.

The central salon is particularly spectacular, with frescoes (*Triumph of Diana*) by Giuseppe and Domenico Valeriani, *36 fans*, executed in 1734 to designs by Juvarra and a large light fitting in bronze and crystal from 1773. At the end of the tour we come to the *Galleria dei Cimeli Napoleonici* (*carriage* used in Napoleon's journey to Milan for the coronation). The gardens, landscaped in 1740, are part of the complex, as is the *parco protetto*, or reserve, created in 1992, and covering an area of 1,700 hectares.

2.2 The Road to France, Venaria and La Mandria

From Piazza Statuto, the itinerary of 35 km (map on facing page) starts in Corso Francia and on to Rivoli (15.5 km.), with the castle which houses the Museo di Arte contemporanea. Passing through Alpignano and Pianezza we come to another of the Savoy residences, which made up the "crown of delights" of the city of Turin, the castle of Venaria Reale, with the nearby park, known as "La Mandria."

Piazza Statuto (II, B-C2). Construction of the square started in 1864; it links Via Garibaldi (see itinerary 1), the main axis of the urban development to the west of the city, with Corso Francia, the long straight road leading to Rivoli, and ultimately to France. In the central garden is a monument (Luigi Belli, 1879) commemorating the work on the *Fréjus Tunnel*, the first of the great train tunnels through the Alps.

Corso Francia (II, C1-2). Along the first stretch of this wide avenue are interesting houses in the *Art Nouveau* style by Pietro Fenoglio. At no. 8 stands the *Villino Raby* (1901), at the corner with Via Principi d'Acaja is *Casa La Fleur* (1902), the house with tower; at no. 32 is *Casa Macciotta* (1904); on the other side at no. 23 is the *Palazzo della Vittoria* by Gottardo Gussoni (1920). Other Art Nouveau buildings can be seen in Via Piffetti at nos. 12, 10, 7, 5/b, 5, and 3; in Via Cibrario at nos. 39, 15, and 9 and on the opposite side at nos. 56, 58, 62, and 65. We go back into Corso Francia, past Piazza Rivoli, and on our right reach the *Villa Sartirana* or *Tesoriera*, built in 1715 by Giacomo Maggi for Aimone Ferrero di Borgaro, treasurer of Victor Amadeus II; the villa was later enlarged, and in 1970 it was bought by the city council, which opened the vast gardens to the public and housed the *Music Library* in the villa.

Rivoli

Continuing along Corso Francia we reach Rivoli, an important town in the Turin hinterland (elev. 390 m; pop. 53,259), which conserves many reminders of the Middle Ages. From Piazza Martiri della Libertà walking up Via Fratelli Piol we reach the terracotta facade of the so-called **Casa del Conte Verde** (14th/15th c.) and further on, at Piazza Matteotti 2, the old *Palazzo Comunale*.

Castle*. The climb up to Piazza Castello is rewarded by a superb *panorama** of the entire plain around Turin and the hills of Monferrato. Over the years, the old 11th-c. fort was gradually transformed by the Savoy into a sumptuous country residence. Re-

modeling work was begun by Francesco Paciotto (1562), who was succeded by Ascanio Vittozzi, and then Carlo and Amedeo di Castellamonte until 1670. Further enlargements were carried out on the castle in 1703–13 by Michelangelo Garove. Filippo Juvarra also drew up ambitious plans for the castle, but they were left unfinished; and Carlo Randoni designed new decorations and fittings throughout. During the French period the castle was left untended, and consequently fell into disrepair; it became the property of the council in 1883. A new restoration scheme was started in 1979 (Andrea Bruno), and now the building houses the *Museo d'Arte Contemporanea* (*open Tues–Fri 10–5; Sat & Sun 10–7; closed Mon*), inaugurated in 1984. The museum exhibits the latest artistic tendencies, with particular attention to figurative and expressive media including cinema, photography and theater. Contemporary art, including many experimental exhibits, are now installed in the rooms, which have retained their 16th- and 17th-c. decorations.

Pianezza

The itinerary now takes us through *Alpignano* and up to the industrial town (elev. 325 m; pop. 11,372) that was originally founded in Roman times on the banks of the River Dora Riparia. Via Parrocchia leads us into the square with the church of **SS. Pietro e Paolo**, built in 1727–29 to designs by Filippo Juvarra; the facade dates from 1881. After a tour of the gardens of *Villa Lascaris* we enter the old city, where stands the church of *San Pietro*, a fine example of Romanesque style; the lunette over the left portal shows *Christ Emerging from the Tomb,* by Aimone Duce. Inside the church

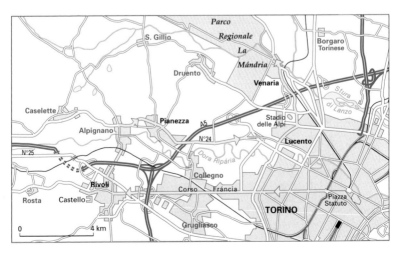

are frescoes executed from the 15th to 17th c.; of note are those in the presbytery, *Stories of St. Peter, the Evangelists, and the Apostles,* by Giacomo Jaquerio and his school. On the way out of the town we pass by the *Cappella di San Sebastiano* (15th c.) in Piazza Primo Maggio.

Venaria Reale

An important industrial and agricultural center (elev. 325 m; pop. 31,639), which took its name from a game reserve belonging to Charles Emmanuel II. Via Mensa crosses the town, which was planned in the 17th c. together with the castle. In Piazza dell'Annunziata stands the church of **Santa Maria** on the right, modified in 1753–75 by Benedetto Alfieri.

Castello*. In 1658 Charles Emmanuel II commissioned Amedeo di Castellamonte to design a hunting lodge. In time, the *Royal Palace of Diana* became one of the most admired Savoy residences, noted especially for its beautiful gardens, which regrettably no longer exist. The castle was damaged in 1693 by General Catinat's French troops; an extension was built on the south side by Michelangelo Garove in 1699–1713.

(see itinerary 1.1). There were ten other paintings of *equestrian portraits,* but only two remain. In some rooms (*Gabinetti delle Cacce, Stanza dei Cervi Famosi, Sala dei Templi Dedicati a Diana*) the frescoes (1660–71) by Giovanni Paolo and Giovanni Antonio Recchi and Giacomo and Giovanni Andrea Casella, are still well preserved and framed in elaborate stuccowork by craftsmen from Lugano. The rooms in the *pavilion* designed by Garove were decorated in white stucco by Pietro Somasso. From here we enter the beautiful *Galleria di Diana** by Juvarra, who took over from Garove. Other remarkable creations by Juvarra are the church of *Sant'Uberto,* built on a central plan; the *Grande Scuderia*; and the *Citroneria.* Alfieri designed the *tower,* the *Galleria,* the *Piccole Scuderie,* and the *riding school.*

The "Mandria" Regional Park*. From the castle Via Amedeo di Savoia leads us to the entrance to the park (*open Apr–Sept 8–8; Oct–Nov 8–6; Nov–Feb 8–5*), which was established and opened to the public in 1978; it covers an overall area of some 6,500 hectares, including both private and regional property. Victor Amadeus II used this land to graze horses from Venaria

The Mandria Regional Park, a favourite haunt for walking or cycling

Filippo Juvarra (1716–28) and Benedetto Alfieri (1739–52, 1765) further enlarged the building to the southeast, creating a complex of formidable size, sadly destined to abandonment and decay. Renovation work, which started in 1961, is still underway to restore the building for future use. (*Open Tues, Thurs, Sat & Sun 9–11:30, 2:30–6*). We now go past the *clock tower* and enter the *courtyard of honor.* Looking onto the courtyard is the grand *Salone di Diana,* the main hall of the Castellamonte's palace. The ceilings are partially frescoed by Jan Miel (1663), who also painted the ten canvases of *Hunting Scenes,* now in Palazzo Madama

Reale. The *Palazzina Reale* was built in 1702–09, and was later enlarged by both Juvarra and Alfieri. Victor Emmanuel II turned the park into a game reserve and the villa into a country residence (1863–68). There is a plan to open the royal apartments frescoed by Francesco Gonin to the public. Walking or riding (bicycles may be hired) through the park, one can see the hunting pavilion called the *Bizzarria,* the *Cascina Rubianetta,* and the Romanesque church of *San Giuliano.* The park is one of the few remaining examples of the woods that once covered the plains of the River Po, full of deer and wild boar.

2.3 Two residences of the House of Savoy

A little further away from the city, though still rightly part of the "crown" of Savoy residences of great historical, artistic and environmental interest, are the castles of Racconigi and Agliè.

Racconigi lies south of Turin (40 km on the SS 20 after Carignano and Carmagnola), and Agliè to the north, in the Canavese hills (36 km on the SS 460 to Rivarolo Canavese, then right for 5.7 km).

Racconigi

An agricultural and industrial town (elev. 260 m, pop. 9,979) on the right bank of the River Maira, with a well-preserved historic city center of attractive arcaded streets.

Castello Reale (Royal Castle). Its origins date back to the end of the 12th c., under the Marquises of Saluzzo. After it became the property of the Savoy, the building was extensively renovated by Prince Emmanuel Philibert of Carignano, who commissioned Guarino Guarini to transform the castle into a royal palace. Guarini actually only completed the prospect overlooking the park, and the large central salon in the internal courtyard, which was roofed in 1719 by Francesco Gallo. In 1755 work began again, this time under G. B. Borra, who designed the brick south facade, preceded by the steps and small portico, and the two neoclassical sections at the sides. The two pavilions at the corners of the facade are by Ernesto Melano, commissioned by Charles Albert to further extend the building. Both Guarini and Borra modified the interior; in the 19th c. extensive architectural and decorative work was done under Pelagio Palagi, the Bolognese architect.

The sumptuous salons of particular interest (*second floor open Tues–Sun 9–1 & 2–5; closed Mon*) include the *Grande Salone* with its statues, stuccoes, and gilt decorations; the *Salone di Diana*, with marble fireplaces and reliefs from the 18th c.; the *Appartamento Cinese*, with valuable oriental wall coverings. There are numerous paintings in the building by artists such as Charles-Claude Dauphin, Jan Miel, Claudio Francesco Beaumont, Louis-Michel Van Loo, and Vittorio Amedeo Cignaroli. Sculptures include those by Francesco Ladatte,

G. B. Bernero, Giuseppe Gaggini. There are also valuable fittings and furnishings. Behind the palace is a magnificent park (*open Tues–Sat, by appointment only*), which was landscaped in the 17th c. by Morello and Giovenale Boetto, and then enlarged in 1670 to a plan by the Parisian André Le Nôtre; further alterations were made in the 18th c.. Charles Albert had the gardens reworked in the Romantic style, with irregularly shaped ponds and lakes, plants of different varieties and remarkable vistas. Certain areas were utilized for experiments in farming and a model farmhouse called "La Margherita" was built in neo-Gothic style in 1834. The park was enlarged again later and now extends over approximately 170 hectares.

Agliè

This little medieval town (elev. 315 m, pop. 2,647) developed on the site of a previous Roman settlement called *Alladium*. The town passed to the Savoy in 1391. On the slope going up is the Baroque church of Santa Marta, built in 1760, with a pleasantly undulating facade. The parish church of San Massimo was erected by Ignazio Birago di Borgaro in 1775. The **Castello Ducale** (*open Thurs–Sun 9–12 & 2–6; closed Mon–Wed*) was formerly a stronghold built around a 12th-c. court. Work to transform the building into a palace was begun in 1642 under Filippo di Agliè; work continued until 1657, and has been attributed to Amedeo di Castellamonte. The residence was renovated and refurnished during the second half of the 18th c. at the behest of the Duke of Chiablese, by Birago di Borgaro. The town was also renovated during this period. The castle was used most, however, at the beginning of the 19th c. by King Charles Felix, who retired here regularly. Between 1821 and 1831 the furnishings and fittings were replaced and in 1839–40 the park was landscaped in the English style, including the addition of an 18th-c. fountain by the Collino brothers featuring the *River Dora Flowing into the River Po*. Inside, the building's three hundred rooms are all conserved with their antique furnishings and paintings. Of note is the ballroom with stucco work and frescoes showing the *Splendors of King Arduin*, by Giovanni Paolo Recchi (17th c.).

Travel information:
Hotels, restaurants, places of interest

Town by town, the list includes hotels, restaurants, campsites and recommended resorts (as well as a list of hostels and agritourism), indicating each place's star rating, which follows the official classification established under Italian law (1983). The traditional TCI classification is by fork symbols, assigned on the basis of price, comfort, service, and also atmosphere. The following are indications of price: ¶ up to 45,000 lire; ¶¶ 46,000–65,000 lire; ¶¶¶ 65,000–85,000 lire; ¶¶¶¶ 86,000–105,000 lire; ¶¶¶¶ over 106,000 lire.
As of 18th December 1998 the code must also be dialled for local calls, indicated in the following list next to the symbol ☎. For those calling Italy from abroad, the local code (including the 0) must be dialled after the international code for Italy, followed by the subscriber's number. The information has been carefully checked before going to print. We would, however, advise readers to confirm certain data which is susceptible to change, before departure. All observations and suggestions are gratefully accepted.

Turin   ✉ 10100 ☎ 011

Page 162

[i] *APT*, Piazza C.L.N. 222/226, tel. 635901.
APT, Atrium of the Porta Nuova railroad station, tel. 531327.
Vetrina for Turin, Piazza S. Carlo 161, tel. 4424740 (free phone, 1670/15475).
InformaCittà, Via Palazzo di Città 24/b, tel. 4222888, 4222121, 4222244.

Hotels, restaurants, campsites and holiday villages

*** G.H. Sitea. Via Carlo Alberto 35, tel. 5170171, fax 548090. 117 rooms. Access for disabled. Air conditioning, elevator; garden (I, C4, **f**).

*** Jolly Hotel Ambasciatori. Corso Vittorio Emanuele II 104, tel. 5752, fax 544978. 199 rooms. Access for disabled. Elevator; garage (I, B1, **e**).

*** Jolly Hotel Ligure. Piazza Carlo Felice 85, tel. 55641, fax 535438. 169 rooms. Access for disabled. Air conditioning, elevator; garage (I, C3, **m**).

*** Jolly Hotel Principi di Piemonte. Via Gobetti 15, tel. 5629693, fax 5620270. 107 rooms. Air conditioning, elevator; garage (I, C4, **a**).

*** Starhotel Majestic. Corso Vittorio Emanuele II 54, tel. 539153, fax 534963. 152 rooms. Air conditioning, elevator; garage (I, C3, **g**).

*** Turin Palace Hotel. Via Sacchi 8, tel. 5625511, fax 5612187. 123 rooms. Access for disabled. Air conditioning, elevator; garage (I, C3, **c**).

*** Villa Sassi. Strada Traforo del Pino 47, tel. 8980556, fax 8980095. 17 rooms. Access for disabled. Air conditioning, elevator; parking, garden (II, B5, **bf**).

*** Alexandra. Lungodora Napoli 14, tel. 858327, fax 2483805. 56 rooms. No restaurant. Air conditioning, elevator; garage (II, B3, **be**).

*** Amadeus e Teatro. Via Principe Amedeo 41 bis, tel. 8174951, fax 8174953. 26 rooms. No restaurant. Air conditioning, elevator; garage (I, B5, **z**).

*** Boston. Via Massena 70, tel. 500359, fax 599358. 50 rooms. No restaurant. Air conditioning, elevator; garage, garden (I, E2, **v**).

*** Crimea. Via Mentana 3, tel. 6604700, fax 6604912. 49 rooms. No restaurant. Elevator; garage (I, E6, **t**).

*** Des Artistes. Via Principe Amedeo 21, tel. 8124416, fax 8124466. 22 rooms. No restaurant. Elevator; garage (I, B5, **o**).

*** Genio. Corso Vittorio Emanuele II 47, tel. 6505771, fax 6508264. 90 rooms. No restaurant. Air conditioning, elevator (I, C3, **s**).

*** Genova e Stazione. Via Sacchi 14/B, tel. 5629400, fax 5629896. 57 rooms. No restaurant. Access for disabled. Air conditioning, elevator; garage (I, C-D3, **p**).

*** Giotto. Via Giotto 27, tel. 6637172, fax 6637173. 45 rooms. No restaurant. Air conditioning, elevator; parking, garage (II, D3, **r**).

*** Gran Mogol. Via Guarini 2, tel. 5612120, fax 5623160. 45 rooms. No restaurant. Air conditioning, elevator; garage (I, C4, **b**).

*** Piemontese. Via Berthollet 21, tel. 6698101, fax 6690571. 35 rooms. No restaurant. Air conditioning, elevator; garage (I, D4, **x**).

*** Plaza. Via Petitti 18, tel. 6632424, fax 678351. 65 rooms. No restaurant. Access for disabled. Air conditioning, elevator; garage (II, D2-3, **k**).

★★★ **President.** Via Cecchi 67, tel. 859555, fax 2480465. 72 rooms. No restaurant. Air conditioning, elevator; parking, garage (II, B3, **bi**).

★★★ **Universo.** Corso Peschiera 166, tel. 3852943, fax 3859761. 35 rooms. Access for disabled. Elevator; garage (II, C2, **bl**).

🍴🍴🍴 **Carignano.** Via Carlo Alberto 35, tel. 5170171, fax 548090. Closed Sat evening and Sun, August. Air conditioning. Traditional and Piedmontese cuisine (I, C4, **f**).

🍴🍴🍴 **Del Cambio.** Piazza Carignano 2, tel. 546690, fax 535282. Closed Sun, New Year-Epiphany and August. Air conditioning.Traditional and Piedmontese cuisine (I, B4, **ra**).

🍴🍴🍴 **Neuv Caval d' Brôns.** Via S. Carlo 151, tel. 5627483, fax 543610. Closed Sun, part of August. Air conditioning. Piedmontese and classical Italian cuisine (I, B4, **br**).

🍴🍴🍴 **Vecchia Lanterna.** Corso Re Umberto 21, tel. 537047, fax 530391. Closed Sat lunch and Sun, part of August. Air conditioning. Traditional cuisine – fish (I, C2-3, **rj**).

🍴🍴🍴 **Villa Sassi-El Toulà.** Strada Traforo del Pino 47, tel. 8980556, fax 8980095. Closed Sun, August. Parking, garden. Traditional cuisine (II, B5, **bf**).

🍴🍴🍴 **Villa Somis.** Strada Val Pattonera 138, tel. 6614626, fax 6613086. Closed Mon, and midday weekdays from October to May, part of August. Parking, garden. Avant-garde cuisine (II, E3, **sh**).

🍴🍴🍴 **Balbo.** Via A. Doria 11, tel. 8125566, fax 8151042. Closed Mon, part of July and August. Air conditioning. Piedmontese cuisine (I, C4, **rl**).

🍴🍴🍴 **Due Lampioni.** Via Carlo Alberto 45, tel. 8179380, fax 887260. Closed Sun, part of August. Air conditioning. Innovative Piedmontese cuisine (I, C4, **rm**).

🍴🍴🍴 **Gatto Nero.** Corso F. Turati 14, tel. 590414, fax 590477. Closed Sun, August. Air conditioning. Traditional cuisine and sea food (I, E2, **rb**).

🍴🍴🍴 **La Prima Smarrita.** Corso Unione Sovietica 244, tel. 3179657, fax 3179191. Closed Monday, part of August. Air conditioning, garden. Avant-garde cuisine(II, D-E2, **si**).

🍴🍴🍴 **Tiffany.** Piazza Solferino 16, tel. 535948. Closed Sat lunch and Sun, part of August. Air conditioning. Traditional cuisine – fish (I, B3, **re**).

🍴🍴 **Al Bue Rosso.** Corso Casale 10, tel. 8191393. Closed Mon and Sat lunch, part of August. Air conditioning. Traditional cuisine (I, C6, **rg**).

🍴🍴 **Ghibellin Fuggiasco.** Via Leoni 16/F corner via Tunisi, tel. 3196115. Closed Sun evening, Mon, part of Jan and in August. Air conditioning. Traditional cuisine – fish (II, D2, **sq**).

🍴🍴 **Mina.** Via Ellero 36 bis, tel. 6963608. Closed Mon(and Sun evening mid June-mid Sept), August. Air conditioning. Piedmontese cuisine — special mushrooms and truffles (II, D2, **sw**).

🍴🍴 **Porta Rossa.** Via Passalacqua 3/B, tel. 530816. Closed Sat lunch and Sun, August. Air conditioning. Traditional cuisine – fish (II, C2, **bx**).

🍴🍴 **San Giorgio.** Viale E. Millo 6, tel. 6692131, fax 6508100. Closed Tue and Wed lunch, August and part of Jan. Traditional and Piedmontese cuisine (I, F4, **bt**).

🍴 **Spada Reale.** Via Principe Amedeo 53, tel. 8171363. Closed Sun, part of August. Avant-garde cuisine. (I, C5, **ri**).

Youth Hostels

🛏 **Ostello della gioventù.** Via Alby 1, tel. 6602939.

Cafés and pastry shops

Al Bicerin. Piazza della Consolata 5, tel. 4369325. Since 1763, famous for its "bicerin" (a combination of coffee, chocolate, and cream).

Baratti & Milano. Piazza Castello 29, tel. 5613060. Since 1875 it has never lost its drawing-room elegance.

Fiorio. Via Po 8, tel. 8170612-8173225. Opened in 1780, was an artists haunt; nowadays popular with ice-cream lovers.

Mulassano. Piazza Castello 15, tel. 547990. Small but full of history and period decor.

Peyrano. Corso Moncalieri 47, tel. 6505074. Famous for its chocolates.

Platti. Corso Vittorio Emanuele II 72, tel. 535759. Art Nouveau decor; once frequented by the writer Cesare Pavese.

San Carlo. Piazza S. Carlo 156, tel. 5625317. Founded in 1822; haunt of intellectuals from the Risorgimento.

Stratta. Piazza S. Carlo 161, tel. 547920. Famous for its candies.

Turin. Piazza S. Carlo 204, tel. 545118. Opened in 1903. Members of the House of Savoy sat in front of its marble fireplaces.

Museums and places of cultural interest

Accademia delle Scienze. Via Maria Vittoria 3, tel. 5620047/1877.

Archivio di Stato – Sezioni Riunite. Via Santa Chiara 40, tel. 5211521.

Archivio di Stato. Viale Luzio 48, tel. 540382, 5624431/4610.

Archivio Storico della Città. Via Corte d'Appello 1, tel. 4222693.

Auditorium RAI. Piazza Rossaro (Via Rossini 15), tel. 8104653, 8104961.

Auditorium Lingotto. Via Nizza 294, tel. 6644111.

Basilica di Superga. Strada della Basilica di Superga 73, tel. 8980083. *Open: 8:30–12, 3–6.*

Biblioteca dell'Accademia delle Scienze. Via Maria Vittoria 3, tel. 5620047, 5621877. Closed Sat and Sun. *Open: 8:30–1, 3–5:30.*

Biblioteca Civica Centrale. Via della Cittadella 5, tel. 4423912.

Biblioteca d'Arte dei Musei Civici. Via Magenta 31, tel. 5629911.

Biblioteca Musicale "Andrea Della Corte". Corso Francia 192, Villa Tesoriera, tel. 746072.

Biblioteca Nazionale. Piazza Carlo Alberto, tel. 8173509.

Biblioteca Reale. Piazza Castello 191, tel. 545305, 543855. Closed Sun. *Open: every day 9–1:30; Mon and Wed open until 5:45.*

Borgo and Rocca Medioevale. Parco del Valentino, tel. 6699372. Borgo: *open Summer: 9–8; winter 9–7.* Rocca: closed Mon. *Open: 9–7.*

Cappella della Pia Congregazione dei Banchieri e Mercanti. Via Garibaldi 25, tel. 5627226.

Castello del Valentino. Viale Mattioli, tel. 6699372. Closed Mondays. *Open: 9–7.*

Conservatorio di Musica Giuseppe Verdi. Via Mazzini 11, tel. 888470, 8121268.

Duomo. Piazza S. Giovanni, tel. 4361540. *Open: Mon–Sat 7:30–12, 3–7.*

Fondazione Palazzo Bricherasio. Via Lagrange 20, tel. 5171660, 5629604. Closed Monday mornings. *Open: Tues–Sun 9–7; Mon 2–7.*

Galleria Civica d'Arte Moderna e Contemporanea. Via Magenta 31, tel. 5629911. Closed Mon, Dec 25 & 31, Jan 1, Easter Mon and May 1. *Open: 9–7.*

Galleria Sabauda. Via Accademia delle Scienze 6, tel. 547440. Closed Mon. *Open: Tues, Wed, Fri, and Sat 9–2; Thurs 9–7; Sun 9am–11pm.*

Mole Antonelliana. Via Montebello 20, tel. 8170496. Closed for renovation.

Museo Armeria Reale. Piazza Castello 191, tel. 543889. Closed Sun, Dec 25 & 31, Jan 1, Easter Mon and May 1. *Open: Mon, Wed, Fri, and Sat 9–2; Tues–Thurs 1:30–7.*

Museo Civico di Numismatica, Etnografia e Arti Orientali. Via Bricherasio 8, tel. 541557, 541608. Closed Mon, Dec 25 & 31, Jan 1, Easter Mon and May 1. *Open: 9–7.*

Museo Civico di Arte Antica and Palazzo Madama. Piazza Castello, tel. 543823. Closed for restoration.

Museo Nazionale dell'Automobile "Carlo Biscaretti di Ruffia." Corso Unità d'Italia 40, tel. 677666. Closed Mon. *Open: 10–6:30.*

Museo della Marionetta. Via S. Teresa 5, tel. 530238. *Open: Tues–Fri 9–1; Sat and Sun 2–6; public hols for shows.*

Museo di Antichità. Corso Regina Margherita 105, tel. 4363082, 5212251. Closed Mon. *Open: Tues–Sun 9–7.*

Museo Egizio. Via Accademia delle Scienze 6, tel. 5612677, 5617776. Closed Mon. *Open: Tues-Sat 9am-10pm; Sun and public hols 9am–8pm.*

Museo Storico Nazionale di Artiglieria. Mastio della Cittadella, Corso Galileo Ferraris, tel. 5629223. Closed Fri afternoons, Sat, Sun. *Open: Mon–Thurs 9–4; Fri 9–1.*

Museo Nazionale del Risorgimento Italiano. Via Accademia delle Scienze 5, tel. 5623719, 5621147. Closed Mon, Dec 25 & 31, Jan 1, Easter Mon and May 1. *Open: Tues–Sat 9-7.*

Museo Nazionale della Montagna "Duca degli Abruzzi". Monte dei Cappuccini, Via G. Garden 39, tel. 6604104. *Open: Tues–Fri 8:30–7:15; Sat–Mon 9–12:30, 2:45–7:15.*

Museo Civico Pietro Micca e dell'Assedio di Torino del 1706. Via Guicciardini 7/A, tel. 546317. Closed Mon, Dec 25 & 31, Jan 1, Easter Mon and May 1. *Open: 9-7.*

Museo Regionale di Scienze naturali. Via Giolitti 36, tel. 4323080. Closed Tues. *Open: Wed–Mon 9–7; Thurs 9am–11pm.*

Museo della Sindone. Via S. Domenico 28, tel. 4365832. *Open: Mon–Thurs 3–6. Also on request for groups.*

Palazzo Falletti di Barolo. Via delle Orfane 7, tel. 4360311. Closed Tues, Thurs, Sat and Sun. *Open: Mon–Wed 10–12, 3–5; Fri 10–12.*

Palazzo Reale. Piazzetta Reale, tel. 4361557, 4361455. Closed Mon. *Guided tours only, 9, 9:40, 10:20, 11, 11:40, 12, 1.*

Teatro Alfieri. Piazza Solferino 4, tel. 5623800.

Teatro Carignano. Piazza Carignano 6, tel. 547048, 537998.

Teatro Nuovo. Corso Massimo d'Azeglio 17, tel. 655552.

Teatro Regio. Piazza Castello 215, tel. 88151.

Tombe di House Savoia. Strada della Basilica di Superga 106, tel. 8980083. *Open: 9:30–12, 3–6.*

Unione Musicale. Piazza Castello 29, tel. 544523, 5175188.

Sanctuaries and churches

Cathedral and the Cappella della Sindone. Piazza San Giovanni, tel. 4361540.

Carmine. Via del Carmine 3, tel. 4369525.

Chapel of the Pia Congregazione dei Banchieri e Mercanti. Via Garibaldi 25, tel. 5627226.

Corpus Domini. Piazza Corpus Domini, tel. 4366025.

Consolata. Piazza Consolata, tel. 4363235.

Gran Madre di Dio. Piazza Gran Madre di Dio, tel. 8193572.

Maria Ausiliatrice. Piazza Maria Ausiliatrice 9, tel. 5211913.

San Carlo. Piazza San Carlo, tel. 5620922.

Santa Cristina. Piazza San Carlo, tel. 539281.

San Domenico. Via San Domenico corner Via Milano, tel. 4362237.

San Filippo Neri. Via Maria Vittoria 5, tel. 538456.

San Lorenzo. Piazza Castello, tel. 4361527.

Santissimi Martiri. Via Garibaldi 25, tel. 5622581.

Santa Teresa di Gesù. Via Santa Teresa 5, tel. 538278.

Superga. Strada Basilica di Superga 73, tel. 8980083.

Tombe di Casa Savoia. Strada della Basilica di Superga 106, tel. 8980083.

Parks and gardens

Colle della Maddalena. Parco della Rimembranza.

Giardini Reali. Inner courtyard of Palazzo Reale.

Parco del Valentino. Left bank of the River Po.

Parco di Villa Genero. Strada Comunale Santa Margherita.

Parco Europa. Town of Cavoretto.

Parco Colletta.

Parco Pellerina.

Parco Vallere. Corso Unità d'Italia.

Shows and Entertainment

Arte Antica (biennial in Feb). Via Nizza, Lingotto Fiere.

Artissima. September, tel. 4337054.

Da Sodoma a Hollywood. April, tel. 534888.

Experimenta (from May to Oct.). Villa Gualino, Viale Settimio Severo 65, tel. 4324388.

Festival del Cinema Sportivo. October, tel. 534275.

Festival Internazionale Cinema Giovani. November, tel. 5623309.

Giorni d'Estate. July/September, tel. 4424736.

Gran Balôn (second Sunday of month). Porta Palazzo, tel. 4369741. Antique and flea market.

Maratona di Torino (April). Tel. 6631231. An international event starting from Avigla-

na and ending in the center of Turin.
Nuove Tecnologie (technology fair; June). Torino Esposizioni.
Salone dell'Automobile (car show; alternate years in spring). Lingotto, tel. 4337054.
Salone del Libro (book fair; May). Lingotto.
Salone della Musica. October, tel. 4337054.
Settembre Musica. Tel. 4424703.
Torino Danza (June/July). Teatro Regio, tel. 8815383. International dance festival.

Sport

Aero Club Turin. Strada Berlia 500, tel. 720734.
Canoes and rafting. C/o ES.PA. Sport, Corso Matteotti 10, tel. 4363159, 0330/471819.
Circolo Golf Stupinigi. Corso Unione Sovietica 502bis, tel. 3472640.
Palazzo del Ghiaccio (ice skating). Via Petrarca 39, tel. 6569.
Società Canottieri Caprera. Corso Moncalieri 22, tel. 6603816.
Stadio delle Alpi. Strada Comunale di Altessano 131, tel. 4550122.
Tiro a Segno Nazionale. Via Reiss Romoli 64, tel. 2201696.

Shops, crafts and fine art

Antica Erboristeria della Consolata. Piazza della Consolata 5, tel. 4366710. Herbs and infusions in a beautiful old-fashioned apothecary.
Antix. Via Urbano Rattazzi 5, tel. 5625264. Models and toys from yesteryear.
Armando Muratori. Piazza Vittorio Veneto 12, tel. 882076. Artistic glass objects.
Armando Vocaturi. Via Bava 8, tel. 882239. Masterpieces in wrought-iron.
Bolaffi. Via Cavour 17, tel. 5625556. The Mecca of Italian stamp collectors.
Bourlot. Piazza S. Carlo 183, tel. 537405. A legend for Turinese book lovers.
Colenghi. Piazza Solferino 3, tel. 5622550. All kinds of candles, made by one of the oldest firms in Italy(1795)
Corno. Corso Re Umberto 72, tel. 504529. Succulent veal from Fassone.
Emerson. Via Battisti 1, tel. 5621960. Clothes for men and women.
Farmacia Algostino & Demichelis. Piazza Vittorio Veneto 10, tel. 8178007. Empire-style pharmacy; the only place you'll find snail syrup for coughs.
Farmacia Bosio. Via Garibaldi 26, tel. 4369636. Alpine violet cough syrup and rhubarb tincture for the digestion.
Farmacia Masino. Via Maria Vittoria 3, tel. 542067. One of the oldest court pharmacies (1667) with 18th-c. fittings and Ligurian majolica jars.
Galleria Principe Eugenio. Via Cavour 17, tel. 5624209. Twenty-four antique shops under one roof; don't miss it.
Il Cartiglio. Via Po 32, tel. 8179005. Antique geography books and atlases.
La Bottega del Natale. Via Barbaroux 20, tel. 531764. It's Christmas all year round; specialized in nativity cribs and Christmas decorations.
Lenci. Via S. Marino 56 bis, tel. 323960, 3241241. Special felt dolls are made here; more collectors' items than children's toys.

Libreria Antiquaria Piemontese. Via Monte di Pietà 13, tel. 535472. Books, prints, and posters.
Mastro Corradin. Borgo Medievale, tel. 6699170. Armor and lampshades all in wrought-iron work.
Moda del Guanto. Via S. Teresa 19, tel. 540536. Gloves only, all kinds for every type of hand.
Musy, Padre e Figli. Via Po 1, tel. 8125582. One of the oldest jewelers in the world (1707). Shop sign and wall hanging in red velvets in 1815.
Peyrot. Piazza Savoia 8, tel. 4369654. Antique Piedmontese books.
Pregliasco. Via Accademia Albertina 3bis, tel. 8177114. In the antiques district, old manuscripts, books, and prints.
Regia Farmacia. Via XX Sept 87, tel. 4360740. "Balm of Jerusalem," a seventeenth-century prescription; the shop is even older.
Soave. Via Po 48, tel. 8178957. Science books from the sixteenth century onward.

Day-trips and excursions

Grande Traversata delle Alpi. (G.T.A.): Center of Alpine documentation, tel. 3856406 (Sig. Furio Chiaretta).
Navigazione sul Po (boat trips on the River Po). Imbarco Murazzi, tel. 888010. From June to Sept from Mon to Sat 3–10:45, Sun 10:30–10:45; from Oct. to May public hols 10:30–10:45.
Tranvia Sassi-Superga. Piazza G. Modena, tel. 8980211. Time: every hour 9–8.
Turismo Equestre. (A.N.T.E.): National Association of Equestrian Tourism, tel. 547455.

National Parks and Protected Areas

Centro di Documentazione e Ricerca sulle Aree Protette. Information: at Moncalieri, Cascina Vallere, Corso Trieste 98, tel. 642831.
Fascia Fluviale del Po, Tratto Torinese (River Po, information). Information: a Moncalieri, Cascina Vallere, Corso Trieste 98, tel. 642831.

Agliè   ☒ 10011   ☎ 0124

Page 215

ⓘ   *APT*, at Ivrea, Corso Vercelli 1, tel. 0125/618131.

Museums and places of cultural interest

Castello Ducale. Piazza Castello 2, tel. 330102. Closed from Mon to Wed. *Open: Thurs–Sun 9–12, 2–6. Guided tours only.*

Moncalieri   ☒ 10024   ☎ 011

Page 210

ⓘ   *APT*, at Turin, Corso Ferrucci 122/128, tel. 3352440.

Hotels, restaurants, campsites and holiday villages

***   **Poker.** A Borgo San Pietro, Via Leopardi 12, tel. 6068382, fax 6068382. 27 rooms, of which 24 with bath or shower. No restaurant. Elevator; garage.

Castello Reale. Strada del Castello, tel. 4361332. Closed.

Racconigi ✉ 12035 ☎ 0172

Page 215

ℹ️ *Tourist office,* c/o Municipal council, Piazza Carlo Alberto 1, tel. 84562.

Hotels, restaurants, campsites and holiday villages

★★★ **Carlo Alberto.** Via Umberto I, 40, tel. 84885, fax 84889. 20 rooms. Elevator; parking.

Museums and places of cultural interest
Castello Reale dei Savoia. Piazza Carlo Alberto 1, tel. 84005. Closed Mon. *Open: Piano nobile (from Tues to Sun) 9–1, 2–5. Guided tours only.*
Parco del Castello Reale. *Open: Tues to Sat, reservations only.*

Rivoli ✉ 10098 ☎ 011

Page 213

ℹ️ *APT,* at Turin, Corso Ferrucci 122/128, tel. 3352440.

Hotels, restaurants, campsites and holiday villages

🍴 **Nazionale.** Corso Francia 4, tel. 9580275. Closed Sat and Sun evening, August. Airconditioning. Cuising from Emilia and Veneto, fish and mushroom specialities.

Museums and places of cultural interest
Museo d'Arte Contemporanea, Castello di Rivoli. Piazza del Castello, tel. 9581547, 9587256. Closed

Monday. *Open: from Tues. to Fri 10–5; Sa and Sun 10–7; first and third Thurs of each month 10–10.*

Stupinigi ✉ 10040 ☎ 011

Page 211

ℹ️ *APT,* at Turin, Corso Ferrucci 122/128, tel 3352440.

Hotels, restaurants, campsites and holiday villages

🍴 **Le Cascine.** Strada for Orbassano, tel 9002581. Closed Mon, Jan to mid Feb and August. Parking, garden. Traditional cuisine - fish.

Museums and places of cultural interest
Palazzina di Caccia. Museo di Arte e Ammobiliamento. Piazza Principe Amedeo 7, tel 3581220. Closed Mon. *Open: 9–11:50, 2–4:20.*

Venaria Reale ✉ 10078 ☎ 011

Page 214

ℹ️ *APT,* at Turin, Corso Ferrucci 122/128, tel 3352440.

Museums and places of cultural interest
Castello. Piazza Repubblica 4, tel. 5623530. *Open. Tues, Thur, Sat.*

Natural Parks and Protected Areas
Parco Regionale "La Mandria." Information Viale Carlo Emanuele 256, tel. 4593993, 4593636 *Open: from April to Sept 8–8; from Oct to Nov 8–6, from Nov to Feb 8–5.*

Index of Places and Things

Milan (city)

A
Alzaia Naviglio Grande, 90
Alzaia Naviglio Pavese, 90
Aquarium, 106
Archivio di Stato, 81
Archivio Storico Civico, 103
Archivio Storico Diocesano, 49
Arch of Peace, 106
Arena, 106
Arengario, 40

B
Baggio, 114
Bar Giamaica, 70
Biblioteca Ambrosiana, 53
Biblioteca Braidense, 71
Biblioteca Trivulziana, 103
Bicocca degli Arcimboldi, 117
Borgo Pirelli, 117
Botanical Gardens, 71
Broletto Nuovo, 53

C
Ca' Bruta, 77
Ca' Granda, 49
Canonica di S. Francesco di Paola, 74
Cappella Portinari, 91
Cappella Trivulzio, 50
Carrobbio, 55
Casa Agostoni, 106
Casa Apostolo, 106
Casa Borletti, 106
Casa Donzelli, 106
Casa Falck, 106
Casa Feltrinelli, 78
Casa Galimberti, 78
Casa Laugier, 97
Casa della Meridiana, 86
Casa degli Omenoni, 47
Casa dei Panigarola, 53
Casa Rasini, 78
Casa di Riposo per Musicisti, 100
Casa Rustici, 108
Casa Silvestri, 81
Cascina Pozzobonelli, 115
Cascina Torretta, 117
Castello Sforzesco, 102
Centro Culturale dei Gesuiti di San Fedele, 47
Centro Nazionale di studi Manzoniani, 46
Certosa di Garegnano, 108
Churches and basilicas
- Annunciazione, 50
- Cathedral (Duomo), 36
- Sant'Agostino, 95
- Sant'Alessandro, 51

Churches and basilicas
- Sant'Ambrogio, 95
- Sant'Angelo, 77
- Sant'Apollinare, 114
- San Babila, 47
- Santi Barnaba e Paolo, 85
- San Bernardino alle Ossa, 49
- San Calimero, 86
- San Carlo al Corso, 48
- San Carlo al Lazzaretto, 118
- San Celso, 88
- San Cristoforo sul Naviglio, 90
- Sant'Eustorgio, 91
- San Fedele, 46
- San Francesco di Paola, 74
- San Giorgio al Palazzo, 55
- San Giuseppe, 72
- San Gottardo al Corso, 89
- San Gottardo in Corte, 41
- San Lorenzo Maggiore, 92
- San Marco, 70
- Santa Maria Annunciata, 117
- Santa Maria Bianca della Misericordia, 119
- Santa Maria del Carmine, 68
- Santa Maria della Passione, 83
- Santa Maria delle Grazie, 98
- Santa Maria delle Grazie al Naviglio, 90
- Santa Maria Incoronata, 69
- Santa Maria della Pace, 85
- Santa Maria alla Porta, 100
- Santa Maria Podone, 54
- Santa Maria presso San Celso, 88
- Santa Maria presso San Satiro, 55
- Santa Maria della Sanità, 82
- Santa Maria Segreta, 106
- San Maurizio al Monastero Maggiore, 100
- San Michele ai Nuovi Sepolcri, 84
- San Nazaro Maggiore, 50
- San Paolo Converso, 88
- San Pietro in Gessate, 84
- San Sebastiano, 55
- San Simpliciano, 69
- San Sisto, 55
- Santo Stefano Maggiore, 49
- San Vittore al Corpo, 96
Cimitero Monumentale, 69
Cineteca Italiana, 76
Circolo della Stampa, 81
Città degli Studi, 119
Clinica Columbus, 108

Colonna del Verziere, 82
Colonne di San Lorenzo, 92
Complesso residenziale Monte Amiata, 109
Conca fallata, 90
Conservatory, 84
Convent of Sant'Angelo, 77
Convent of San Simpliciano (ex), 69
Corso Buenos Aires, 118
Corso Garibaldi, 69
Corso Italia, 87
Corso Magenta, 97
Corso Matteotti, 47
Corso Monforte, 83
Corso di Porta Romana, 51
Corso di Porta Ticinese, 90
Corso di Porta Vittoria, 84
Corso San Gottardo, 89
Corso Sempione, 108
Corso Venezia, 78
Corso Vittorio Emanuele II, 48
Cusago, 114

D
Darsena, 89
Diaframma Gallery, 72
Duomo, 36

F
Fiera di Milano, 108
Fondazione Corrente, 77
Fondazione Feltrinelli, 73
Fondazione "Antonio Mazzotta", 102
Fondazione Mudima, 119
Fontana Metafisica, 105
Foro Buonaparte, 101

G
Galleria d'Arte Moderna, 80
Galleria d'Arte P. Daverio, 75
Galleria del Corso, 48
Galleria del Credito Valtellinese, 98
Galleria Il Diaframma, 72
Galleria Lorenzelli Arte, 119
Galleria G. Marconi, 119
Galleria del Sagrato, 35
Galleria C. Sozzani, 69
Galleria della Triennale, 105
Galleria "Vittorio Emanuele II," 42
Gardens, see Parks
Grattacielo Pirelli, 115

H
Hippodrome, 114
Hotel Diana, 78
Hotel Four Seasons, 76

221

I

Idroscalo, 120
Ippodromo, 114

L

Largo Cairoli, 101
Largo Croce Rossa, 75
Largo Donegani, 77
Largo Marinai d'Italia, 120
Last Supper, 99
Loggia degli Osii, 52

M

Magazzini Bonomi (ex), 48
Messaggerie Musicali, 48
Monastero Maggiore, 99
Monte Stella, 109
Monuments and Statues
- a C. Beccaria, 49
- al Carabiniere, 42
- a Cavour, 76
- alle Cinque Giornate, 84
- a G. Garibaldi, 101
- al generale Missori, 51
- a S. Pertini, 75
- a O. da Tresseno, 53
- a Vittorio Emanuele II, 35
Museums and Art Galleries
- Ambrosiana, 53
- Archeologico, 99
- d'Arte Contemporanea, 40
- d'Arte Moderna, 80
- Bagatti Valsecchi, 75
- Brera, 70
- del Castello Sforzesco, 103
- del Cinema, 76
- del Duomo, 41
- Francesco Messina, 55
- del Giocattolo e del
  Bambino, 90
- La Scala, 46
- Manzoniano, 47
- di Milano, 76
- Navale Didattico, 97
- Navale "Ugo Mursia," 76
- Pinacoteca di Brera, 70
- Poldi Pezzoli, 74
- del Risorgimento, 75
- di Sant'Ambrogio, 96
- di Sant'Eustorgio, 91
- di Santa Maria della
  Passione, 83
- della Scienza e della
  Tecnica, 96
- di Storia Contemporanea,
  76
- di Storia Naturale, 78

N

Naviglio Grande, 90
Naviglio Pavese, 90
Niguarda, 117

O

Opera house (La Scala), 43
Orto Botanico, 71
Ospedale Maggiore, 117

Ospedale San Carlo
  Borromeo, 114
Observatory, 71

P

PAC (Padiglione d'Arte
  Contemporanea), 81
Palazzina Liberty, 120
Palazzo Acerbi, 51
Palazzo Anguissola, 73
Palazzo Annoni, 51
Palazzo Archinto, 84
Palazzo dell'Arcivescovile,
  49
Palazzo dell'Arte, 105
Palazzo delle Assicurazioni
  Generali, 53
Palazzo Belgioioso, 47
Palazzo Berri-Meregalli, 79
Palazzo Borromeo, 54
Palazzo Borromeo d'Adda,
  74
Palazzo Bovara, 79
Palazzo Brentani, 73
Palazzo di Brera, 70
Palazzo della Camera
  Confederale del Lavoro,
  84
Palazzo della Camera di
  Commercio, Industria e
  Artigianato, 100
Palazzo del Capitano di
  Giustizia, 49
Palazzo Carmagnola, 101
Palazzo Carminati, 35
Palazzo Castiglioni, 79
Palazzo della Chase
  Manhattan Bank, 47
Palazzo Citterio, 72
Palazzo Clerici, 68
Palazzo Cusani, 72
Palazzo Dugnani, 76
Palazzo Durini, 82
Palazzo Isimbardi, 83
Palazzo Fidia, 79
Palazzo Gallarati Scotti, 74
Palazzo dei Giornali, 76
Palazzo dei Giureconsulti,
  52
Palazzo di Giustizia, 84
Palazzo Litta, 99
Palazzo Litta Cusini, 48
Palazzo Marino, 46
Palazzo Melzi di Cusano,
  75
Palazzo Mezzanotte, 54
Palazzo (ex) Montecatini, 77
Palazzo della Montedison,
  106
Palazzo Morando Attendolo
  Bolognini, 76
Palazzo Moriggia, 75
Palazzo della Permanente,
  77
Palazzo della Prefettura, 83
Palazzo della Ragione, 53
Palazzo della RAI, 108
Palazzo Reale, 40

Palazzo della Riunione
  Adriatica di Sicurtà, 88
Palazzo Rocca Saporiti, 79
Palazzo delle Scuole
  Palatine, 52
Palazzo del Senato, 81
Palazzo Serbelloni, 81
Palazzo Sormani-Andreani,
  84
Palazzo Spinola, 48
Palazzo dello Sport, 114
Palazzo già delle Stelline,
  97
Palazzo della Telecom Italia,
  115
Palazzo del Toro, 47
Palazzo del Touring Club
  Italiano, 87
Palazzo Trivulzio, 51
Parks and Gardens
- Giardini Pubblici, 78
- Parco delle Basiliche, 91
- Parco Sempione, 105
- Villa Reale, 80
Piazza degli Affari, 54
Piazza Beccaria, 49
Piazza Belgioioso, 47
Piazza Cavour, 76
Piazza Cinque Giornate, 84
Piazza Cordusio, 53
Piazza Diaz, 42
Piazza del Duomo, 35
Piazza Fontana, 49
Piazza Liberty, 48
Piazza Meda, 47
Piazza Medaglie d'Oro, 85
Piazza Mercanti, 52
Piazza Missori, 51
Piazza della Repubblica, 77
Piazza Sant'Alessandro, 51
Piazza Sant'Ambrogio, 95
Piazza San Babila, 47
Piazza Sant'Erasmo, 75
Piazza San Fedele, 46
Piazza Santo Stefano, 49
Piazza della Scala, 43
Piazza della Vetra, 92
Piazzale Cadorna, 106
Piazzale Loreto, 118
Piazzale XXIV Maggio, 89
Piccolo Teatro della Città di
  Milano, 101
Pinacoteca Ambrosiana, 53
Pinacoteca di Brera, 70
Planetarium, 78
Politecnico di Milano, 119
Porta Garibaldi, 69
Porta Nuova, 76
Porta Romana, 85
Porta Ticinese, 89
Porta Ticinese medievale,
  93
Porta Venezia, 78
Porta Vigentina, 86
Porta Vittoria, 84
Porta Volta, 69
Pusterla di Sant'Ambrogio,
  96

Q

Quarto Cagnino, 114
QT8, 109

R

Ripa di Porta Ticinese, 90
Rogoredo, 121
Rotonda della Besana, 84

S

Sant'Agostino, 95
Sant'Alessandro, 51
Sant'Ambrogio, 95
Sant'Angelo, 77
Sant'Apollinare, 114
San Babila, 47
Santi Barnaba e Paolo, 85
San Bernardino alle Ossa, 49
San Calimero, 86
San Carlo al Corso, 48
San Carlo al Lazzaretto, 118
San Celso, 88
San Cristoforo sul Naviglio, 90
Sant'Eustorgio, 91
San Fedele, 46
San Francesco di Paola, 74
San Giorgio al Palazzo, 55
San Giuseppe, 72
San Gottardo al Corso, 89
San Gottardo in Corte, 41
San Lorenzo Maggiore, 92
San Marco, 70
Santa Maria Annunciata, 117
Santa Maria Bianca della Misericordia, 119
Santa Maria del Carmine, 68
Santa Maria della Passione, 83
Santa Maria delle Grazie, 98
Santa Maria delle Grazie al Naviglio, 90
Santa Maria Incoronata, 69
Santa Maria della Pace, 85
Santa Maria Podone, 54
Santa Maria alla Porta, 100
Santa Maria presso S. Celso, 88
Santa Maria presso S. Satiro, 55
Santa Maria della Sanità, 82
Santa Maria Segreta, 106
San Maurizio al Monastero Maggiore, 100
San Michele ai Nuovi Sepolcri, 84
San Nazaro Maggiore, 50
San Paolo Converso, 88
San Pietro in Gessate, 84
San Sebastiano, 55
San Simpliciano, 69
San Simpliciano (convento, ex), 69
San Sisto, 55
Santo Stefano Maggiore, 49
San Vittore al Corpo, 96
San Siro, 114
Scala, La (opera house), 43

Scuole Palatine, 52
Seminario Arcivescovile, 81
Sforza Castle, 102
Società storica lombarda, 47
Società Umanitaria, 85
Spanish Walls, 85
Stadio, 114
Statues, see "Monuments"
Stazione Centrale, 115
Stazione Ferrovie Nord Milano, 106
Stazione di Porta Garibaldi, 116
Stazione di Porta Genova, 90

T

Teatro dell'Arte, 105
Teatro Carcano, 85
Teatro Dal Verme, 106
Teatro Gerolamo, 49
Teatro (ex) Fossati, 69
Teatro Manzoni, 74
Teatro Nuovo, 47
Teatro Franco Parenti, 86
Teatro di Porta Romana, 85
Teatro alla Scala, 43
Teatro Studio, 69
Tecnomasio Italiano Brown Boveri, 121
Torre del Parco, 105
Torre Velasca, 51
Triennale di Milano, 105
Trottatoio, 114

U

Universities
- Cattolica del Sacro Cuore, 96
- Bocconi, 88
- degli Studi, 50

V

Verziere, 82
Via Ascanio Sforza, 90
Via Bergognone, 90
Via Borgonuovo, 75
Via Broletto, 75
Via Buonarroti, 108
Via Cappuccio, 55
Via Cerva, 82
Via Cesare Correnti, 93
Via Circo, 55
Via Conca del Naviglio, 90
Via Dante, 101
Via Domodossola, 108
Via Durini, 82
Via dei Giardini, 75
Via M. Gioia, 115
Via Laghetto, 49
Via Lanzone, 95
Via Larga, 49
Via Magolfa, 90
Via Manzoni, 73
Via Marina, 80
Via Mazzini, 51
Via Meravigli, 100
Via Mercanti, 52

Via Monte Napoleone, 75
Via Morigi, 55
Via San Calimero, 86
Via San Marco, 70
Via San Vittore, 96
Via Torino, 55
Via Turati, 77
Via Verdi, 72
Via Vigevano, 90
Via XX Settembre, 106
Viale Ca' Granda, 117
Viale Certosa, 108
Viale della Liberazione, 116
Viale F. Testi, 117
Viale Zara, 116
Vicolo Lavandai, 90
Villa Dellora, 114
Villa Figini, 117
Villa Litta Modignani, 108
Villa Mirabello, 116
Villa Reale, 79
Villa Simonetta, 108
Villaggio dei Giornalisti, 116

Milan (environs)

A

Abbey of Chiaravalle, 122
Abbey of Mirasole, 123
Abbey of Morimondo, 144
Abbey of Viboldone, 123
Abbiategrasso, 144
Agliate, 136
Arcore, 134
Arese, 139
Arsago Seprio, 143
Assunta (cascina, Paderno d'Adda), 135
Azzurro Park (Segrate), 120

B

Bardena (cascina, Cassinetta di Lugagnano), 144
Basiglio, 122
Bollate, 139
Bresso, 138
Brivio, 130
Buccinasco, 145
Busto Arsizio, 142

C

Canale della Muzza, 128
Canale Villoresi, 141
Capriate San Gervasio, 129
Carate Brianza, 136
Casa Sironi Marelli (Robecco sul Naviglio), 144
Cascina Assunta (Paderno d'Adda), 135
Cascina Bardena (Cassinetta di Lugagnano), 144
Cassano d'Adda, 128
Cassinetta di Lugagnano, 144
Castellanza, 142

Castles and forts
- Abbiategrasso, 144
- Borromeo (Peschiera Borromeo), 120
- Borromeo d'Adda (Cassano d'Adda), 128
- Brivio, 130
- Cusago, 114
- Sforzesco (Milan), 102
- Trezzo sull'Adda, 128
- Turbigo, 143
- Visconteo (Somma Lombardo), 143
Cernusco sul Naviglio, 127
Charterhouse of Garegnano (Milan), 108
Charterhouse of Pavia, 124
Cesano Maderno, 138
Chiaravalle Abbey, 122
Chiaravalle Milanese, 121

Churches and Basilicas
- San Bernardo (Morimondo), 145
- San Colombano (Vaprio d'Adda), 128
- San Giorgio (Cuggiono), 143
- San Lorenzo (Monluè), 120
- San Maria alla Noce (Inverigo), 136
- San Pietro (Gallarate),142
- San Rocco (Seregno), 136
- San Vito (Somma Lombardo), 143
Cormano, 138
Cornate d'Adda, 129
Corsico, 145
Cremnago, 136
Crespi d'Adda, 129
Cuggiono, 143
Cusago, 114
Cusano Milanino, 138

D
Desio, 137

G
Gaggiano, 145
Gallarate, 142
Garegnano Charterhouse (Milan), 108
Giussano, 136
Gorgonzola, 127
Groane Park, 139

H
Hydroelectric Power Stations
- Cassano d'Adda, 128
- Porto d'Adda, 130
- Resega, 130
- Robbiate, 130
- Trezzo sull'Adda, 128

I
Imbersago, 130
Inverigo, 136
Inzago, 128

L
Legnano, 141
Lentate sul Seveso, 139
Lissone, 137

M
Magenta, 143
Meda, 138
Merate, 135
Mezzana Superiore, 143
Milano Due (Segrate), 120
Milano Tre (Basiglio), 122
Minitalia (Capriate San Gervasio), 129
Mirasole Abbey, 123
Monasterolo, 128
Monluè, 120
Montevecchia, 135
Montevecchia Park, 135

Monza, 131
Autodromo (racetrack), 133
Cathedral, 132
Monument to M. Bianchi, 133
Museo Serpero, 132
Park, 133
Santa Maria, 133
San Pietro Martire, 133
Villa Reale, 133

Morimondo Abbey, 144
Museo d'Arte Moderna della Fondazione Pagani (Castellanza), 142
Museo d'Arte Sacra (Gallarate), 142
Museo della Società Gallaratese di Studi Patrii (Gallarate), 142
Museo Storico (Arese), 139
Museo della Tecnica e del Lavoro (Gallarate), 142
Muzza canal, 128

N
Naviglio Grande, 143
Naviglio di Paderno, 130
Nerviano, 141

O
Obelisk-Ossuary (Magenta), 143
Opera, 121
Oreno, 134
Osnago, 134

P
Paderno d'Adda, 135
Paderno Dugnano, 138
Parabiago, 141
Parks
- Azzurro (Segrate), 120
- di Monza, 133
- Naturale regionale delle Groane, 139
- Naturale regionale di

Parks
di Montevecchia e della valle del Curone, 135
- del Ticino, 143
Pavia Charterhouse, 124
Peschiera Borromeo, 120
Pontesesto 121
Porto d'Adda, 129

R
Resega, 130
Rho, 140
Robbiate, 130
Robecco sul Naviglio, 143
Rocchetta, 130
Rodano, 120
Romanò Brianza-Villa Romanò, 136
Rozzano, 121

S
San Giuliano Milanese, 121
Santuario della Beata Vergine del Carmelo (Montevecchia), 135
Santuario della Madonna dei Miracoli (Rho), 141
Santuario della Madonna dei Miracoli (Saronno), 139
Santuario della Madonna della Ghianza (Mezzana Superiore), 143
Santuario di Santa Maria di Piazza (Busto Arsizio), 142
- di Santa Valeria (Seregno), 137
Saronno, 139
Segrate, 120
Semenza hydroelectric power plant (Robbiate), 130
Seregno, 137
Seveso, 138
Somma Lombardo, 143

T
Taccani hydroelectric power plant (Trezzo sull'Adda), 128
Ticino Park, 143
Tornavento, 143
Trenzanesio, 120
Trezzano sul Naviglio, 145
Trezzo sull'Adda, 128
Turbigo, 143

V
Vaprio d'Adda, 128
Villa d'Adda (Arcore), 134
Villa Alari Visconti (Cernusco sul Naviglio), 127
Villa Antona Traversi (Meda), 138
Villa Arconati (Bollate), 139
Villa Arese Lucini (Osnago), 134
Villa Arrigoni (Robecco sul

Naviglio), 144
Villa Belgioioso (Merate), 135
Villa Borromeo (Oreno), 134
Villa Borromeo, già d'Adda (Cassano d'Adda), 128
Villa Castelbarco Albani (Monasterolo), 128
Villa Clari Monzini (Cassinetta di Lugagnano), 144
Villa Cornaggia Medici (Rho), 141
Villa Crivelli (Inverigo), 136
Villa Crivelli (Magenta), 143
Villa Cusani Confalonieri (Carate Brianza), 136
Villa Cusani, poi Traversi (Desio), 137
Villa Dellora (Milan), 114
Villa Dugnani (Robecco sul Naviglio), 144
Villa Eusebio (Cassinetta di Lugagnano), 144
Villa Facheris (Inzago), 128
Villa Figini (Milan), 117
Villa Gallarati Mezzanotte (Romanò Brianza-Villa Romanò), 136
Villa Gandini (Robecco sul Naviglio), 143
Villa Gnecchi (Inzago), 128
Villa Gromo di Ternengo (Robecco sul Naviglio), 144
Villa Krentzlin (Cassinetta di Lugagnano), 144
Villa Lampugnani (Nerviano), 141
Villa Litta (Rodano), 120
Villa Litta Modignani (Milan), 108
Villa Mirabello (Milan), 116
Villa Mörlin Visconti (Cassinetta di Lugagnano), 144
Villa Nai (Cassinetta di Lugagnano), 144
Villa Reale (Milan), 79
Villa Reale (Monza), 133
Villa Scotti (Robecco sul Naviglio), 144
Villa Simonetta (Milan), 108
Villa Sola Busca (Gorgonzola), 128
Villa Terzaghi (Robecco sul Naviglio), 144
Villa Trivulzio (Cassinetta di Lugagnano), 144
Villa Visconti Maineri (Cassinetta di Lugagnano), 144
Villa Vittadini (Arcore), 134
Villaggio Operaio (Crespi d'Adda), 129
Villoresi canal, 141
Vimercate, 134

Turin (city)

A
Accademia Albertina, 201
Accademia delle Scienze (Palazzo dell'), 196
Aiuola Balbo, 202
Albergo di Virtù, 202
Alfiere dell'Esercito sardo (monument), 176
Alfieri (theater), 191
Antonelliana, Mole, 201
Archivio di Stato, 184
Arco Monumentale all'Artigliere, 203
Armeria Reale, 184
Arte Moderna e Contemporanea (gallery), 193

B
Balbo, Cesare (monument), 202
Barolo, Falletti di (Palazzo), 190
Basilica of Superga, 207
Bava, Eusebio (monument), 202
Biblioteca Reale (Royal Library), 184
Borgo e Rocca Medioevale, 205
Botanical Gardens, 205
Bricherasio (Palazzo), 195
Bridge Umberto I, 203
Bridge Vittorio Emanuele I, 203

C
Caffè S. Carlo, 195
Caffè Torino, 195
Cambio Restaurant, 199
Cappella della Pia Congregazione dei Banchieri e Mercanti, 191
Cappella della Sacra Sindone (Holy Shroud), 187
Cappuccini (Monte dei), 203
Carignano (Palazzo), 199
Carignano (theater), 199
Carlo Alberto (monument), 199
Carmine (church), 190
Carpano (Palazzo), 199
Casa La Fleur, 213
Casa Macciotta, 213
Casa Palazzo della Vittoria, 213
Casa Ponzio Vaglia, 202
Casa Villino Raby, 213
Castello del Valentino, 203
Cathedral, 187
Cavalieri d'Italia (monument), 176
Cavour, Count of (monument), 202

Chapel of the Holy Shroud, 187
Chiablese (Palazzo), 187
Church Basilica of Superga, 207
– Cappella della Pia Congregazione dei Banchieri e Mercanti, 191
Churches
– Carmine, 190
– Cathedral, 187
– Chapel of the Holy Shroud, 187
– Consolata Sanctuary, 189
– Corpus Domini, 191
– Gran Madre di Dio, 203
– Maria SS. Ausiliatrice, 189
– S. Carlo, 196
– S. Cristina, 195
– S. Croce, 202
– S. Domenico, 189
– S. Filippo Neri, 199
– S. Filippo Oratory, 199
– S. Francesco da Paola, 201
– S. Lorenzo, 186
– S. Maria del Monte, 203
– S. Maria di Piazza, 191
– S. Massimo, 202
– S. Michele Arcangelo, 202
– S. Teresa, 196
– S. Tommaso, 191
– SS. Annunziata, 201
– SS. Martiri, 190
– SS. Trinità, 191
– dello Spirito Santo, 191
Cittadella, 192
Colle della Maddalena, 210
Collegio delle Province, 202
Collina di Superga (Parco), 208
Consolata (santuario della), 189
Conte Verde Amedeo VI di Savoia (monument), 191
Corpus Domini (church), 191
Corso Francia, 213
Corso Galileo Ferraris, 193
Corso Vittorio Emanuele II, 193
Cottolengo see Piccola Casa della Divina Provvidenza

D
De Amicis, Edmondo (monument), 195
Duomo (Cathedral), 187

F
Falletti di Barolo (Palazzo), 190
Faro della Vittoria, 210
Ferdinando duca di Genova (monument), 191
Fiat Lingotto, (factory), 206
Fiat Mirafiori, (factory), 206
Fondazione Palazzo Bricherasio, 195

Fontana Angelica delle Quattro Stagioni, 191
Fontana dei Mesi, 205
Fréjus, tunnel (monument), 212

G

Galleria d'Arte Moderna e Contemporanea, 193
Galleria Sabauda, 197
Gianduja (theater), 196
Giardini Reali, 186
Gran Madre di Dio (church), 203

I

"Italia '61" buildings, 206

L

La Fleur (Casa), 213
Lamarmora, Alessandro (monument), 191
Lavoro (Palazzo del), 206
Lingotto (Fiat factory), 206

M

Macciotta (Casa), 213
Madama (Palazzo), 176
Maddalena (hill), 210
Manin, Daniele (monument), 202
Maria SS. Ausiliatrice (church), 189
Martini di Cigala (Palazzo), 190
Mole Antonelliana, 201
Monte dei Cappuccini, 203
Monuments
– Alfiere dell'Esercito sardo, 176
– Arco all'Artigliere, 203
– C. Balbo, 202
– E. Bava, 202
– Cavour, 202
– Charles Albert, 199
– Cavalieri d'Italia, 176
– Conte Verde Amadeus VI of Savoy, 191
– Edmondo de Amicis, 195
– Emmanuel Philibert, 195
– Emmanuel Philibert Duke of Aosta, 176
– Faro della Vittoria, 210
– Ferdinando Duca di Genova, 191
– Fréjus Tunnel, 212
– A. Lamarmora, 191
– D. Manin, 202
– Siccardi Laws Obelisk, 190
– Prince Amadeus, 205
– Victor Emmanuel II, 193
Mostre (Palazzo delle), 206
Murazzi, 203
Museums
– Antichità, 188
– Armeria Reale, 184
– Arte antica, 177
– Artiglieria, 192

Museums
– Automobile "Carlo Biscaretti di Ruffia," 205
– Biblioteca Reale, 184
– Cinema, 187
– Egizio, 197
– Galleria d'Arte Moderna e Contemporanea, 193
– Galleria Sabauda, 197
– della Marionetta, 196
– della Montagna "Duca degli Abruzzi," 204
– Numismatica, Etnografia, Arti Orientali, 195
– Pietro Micca e dell'Assedio di Torino del 1706, 192
– Pinacoteca dell'Accademia Albertina, 201
– del Risorgimento Italiano, 200
– di Scienze Naturali, 202
– della Sindone, 218
Musical Library, 213

N

National Library, 199

O

Obelisk in memory of the Siccardi Laws, 190
Oratorio di S. Filippo, 199
Ospedale di S. Giovanni Battista, 202

P

Paesana di Saluzzo (Palazzo), 190
Palazzo dell'Accademia delle Scienze, 196
Palazzo Albergo di Virtù, 202
Palazzo Barolo, Falletti di, 190
Palazzo Bricherasio, 195
Palazzo Carignano, 199
Palazzo Carpano, 199
Palazzo Chiablese, 187
Palazzo di Città, 191
Palazzo Collegio delle Provincie, 202
Palazzo Falletti di Barolo, 190
Palazzo del Lavoro, 206
Palazzo Madama, 176
Palazzo Martini di Cigala, 190
Palazzo delle Mostre, 206
Palazzo Paesana di Saluzzo, 190
Palazzo Reale, 185
Palazzo Roero di Guarene, 202
Palazzo Solaro del Borgo, 195
Palazzo Torino Esposizioni, 205

Palazzo dell'Università, 201
Palazzo della Vittoria, 213
Parco della Collina di Superga, 208
Parco della Rimembranza, 210
Parco del Valentino, 203
Pasticceria Fratelli Stratta, 195
Pia Congregazione dei Banchieri e Mercanti (chapel), 191
Piazza Carignano, 199
Piazza Carlina, 202
Piazza Carlo Alberto, 199
Piazza Carlo Emanuele II, 202
Piazza Carlo Felice, 195
Piazza Castello, 175
Piazza Cavour, 202
Piazza Maria Teresa, 202
Piazza Porta Palazzo, 189
Piazza della Repubblica, 189
Piazza S. Carlo, 195
Piazza Savoia, 190
Piazza Solferino, 191
Piazza Statuto, 212
Piazza Vittorio Veneto, 202
Piazzetta Reale, 184
Piccola Casa della Divina Provvidenza, 189
Pinacoteca dell'Accademia Albertina, 201
Po River day trips, 203
Ponzio Vaglia (Casa), 202
Porta Nuova (station), 195
Porta Palatina, 188
Porta Palazzo (Piazza), 189
Prince Amadeus (monument), 205

Q

Quartieri Militari, 190

R

Raby (villino), 213
Reale (Palazzo), 185
Regina (Villa della), 203
Regio (theater), 184
Rimembranza (Parco della), 210
Ristorante del Cambio, 199
Roero di Guarene (Palazzo), 202
Roman theater, 188

S

Sabauda (Gallery), 197
Sacra Sindone (chapel), 187
S. Carlo (café), 195
S. Carlo (church), 196
S. Cristina (church), 195
S. Croce (church), 202
S. Domenico (church), 189
S. Filippo (oratory), 199
S. Filippo Neri (church), 199
S. Francesco da Paola (church), 201

S. Giovanni Battista
   (hospital), 202
S. Lorenzo (church), 186
S. Maria del Monte
   (church), 203
S. Maria di Piazza (church),
   191
S. Massimo (church), 202
S. Michele Arcangelo
   (church), 202
S. Teresa (church), 196
S. Tommaso (church), 191
SS. Annunziata (church), 201
SS. Martiri (church), 190
SS. Trinità (church), 191
Santuario della Consolata,
   189
Sartirana (Villa Tesoriera),
   213
Segreterie di Stato, 184
Solaro del Borgo (Palazzo),
   195
Spirito Santo (church), 191
Station Porta Nuova, 195
Stratta, Fratelli (pastry
   shop), 195
Superga (basilica), 207

T

Teatro Alfieri, 191
Teatro Carignano, 199
Teatro Gianduja, 196
Teatro Regio, 184
Tesoriera (Villa Sartirana),
   213
Torino (café), 195
Torino Esposizioni
   (Palazzo), 205
Trip on the Po, 203

U

Università (Palazzo dell'),
   201

V

Valentino (Castello del), 203
Valentino, (Parco del), 203
Vela (Palazzo a), 206
Via Cernaia, 191
Via Garibaldi, 190
Via Milano, 189
Via Pietro Micca, 191
Via Po, 201
Via Roma, 195
Villa della Regina, 203
Villa Tesoriera (or
   Sartirana), 213
Villino Raby, 213
Vittoria (Palazzo della),
   213
Victor Emmanuel II
   (monument), 193

Turin (environs)

A

Agliè, 215

C

Cappella della Visitazione al
   Vallinotto (Carignano),
   211
Carignano, 211
Carmagnola, 211
Chieri, 209

L

La Mandria, Parco
   (Venaria), 214

M

Moncalieri, 210
Museo "Martini" di Storia
   dell'Enologia (Pessione),
   210
Museo di Arte e
   Ammobiliamento
   (Stupinigi), 212

O

Observatory (Pino
   Torinese), 209

P

Palazzina di Caccia
   (Stupinigi), 211
Parco La Mandria (Venaria),
   214
Pecetto Torinese, 210
Pessione, 210
Pianezza, 213
Pino Torinese, 209
Piobesi Torinese, 211

R

Racconigi, 215
Rivoli, 213

S

Santena, 211
Stupinigi (Hunting Lodge),
   211

V

Venaria Reale, 214
Vinovo, 211
Visitazione al Vallinotto,
   Cappella della
   (Carignano), 211